PLAYLAND

John Gregory Dunne was born in Hartford, Connecticut, and attended Princeton University. He is the author of twelve books, including *Vegas*, *True Confessions*, *Dutch Shea, Jr.* and *The Studio*. He is a regular contributor to the *New York Review of Books* and the *New Yorker*.

John Gregory Dunne

PLAYLAND

Granta Books
London

Granta Publications, 2/3 Hanover Yard, London N1 8BE

First published in the USA by Random House 1994
First published in Great Britain by Granta Books 1995
This edition published by Granta Books 1998

A CIP catalogue record for this book is
available from the British Library.

1 3 5 7 9 10 8 6 4 2

Printed and bound in Great Britain
by Mackays of Chatham PLC

This book is for some people I know
Who have the gift of friendship

It is for Shelley Wanger and David Mortimer
And for their daughter Lily Lanier Harriman Mortimer

It is for Leslie Abramson and Tim Rutten
Their daughter Laine and their son Aidan

It is for David Rieff

And it is for Alice Mayhew
A friend for all seasons, especially the bad

With witness I speak this. But where I say
Hours I mean years, mean life. And my lament
Is cries countless, cries like dead letters sent
To dearest him that lives alas! away.

—Gerard Manley Hopkins

PART ONE

SETTING THE SCENE I

FIRST THINGS FIRST:
   She was born Melba Mae Toolate (or maybe not, but certainly, or so I think, close enough, although Myrna Marie Toolate still has a core of adherents, the way Los Angeles with a hard *g* also has its core vote) in San Bernardino, California, April 28, 1928. That is, if she was not born in Yuma, Arizona, on the same date a year earlier (in other words, April 28, 1927), or then again in Shoshone, California, October 29, 1929, but that was the day the stock market crashed, and a few years later, after Melba Mae Toolate became Baby Blue Tyler, Hollywood's number-one cinemoppet and biggest box office star, studio publicists, always looking for an item, would claim that her birth was America's only bright spot that day, which did not exactly lend the date, as Blue Tyler's birthday, verisimilitude.

   Her father died shortly before her birth, or shortly thereafter, or perhaps he was in prison in Ohio when she was born, or then again maybe it was in Pennsylvania, Nebraska or Montana. The prison stories surfaced only after her disgrace; Blue Tyler was a woman, a child really, to whom disgrace attached itself with a certain regularity, but the disgrace here in question was her appearance before the House Committee on Un-American Activities, when she was either nineteen, twenty or twenty-one years old. The prison reports came up again after her disappearance from what *Collier's* magazine called "the baleful glare of the public eye," in any event when those same studio publicists who had been so quick to claim, for Jimmy Fidler's deadline, that Blue Tyler was born the day the market went belly-up were no longer available to keep the legend, such as it was (and even more so such as it became), free from taint.

Anyway. Melba's father (if indeed he was). Among other names, he was known as Herman Toolate or Herbert Tulahti ("Too-late" and "Too-lah-tee" being the two conflicting pronunciations of the name she abandoned when she became, or was reborn as, Blue Tyler), or (this from those French cinéastes who kept Blue Tyler's torch from being extinguished in those decades when she was, as it were, in the desert) Henri Tulaté. Mr. Toolate (or if you will Mr. Tulahti or M. Tulaté) was in some accounts a pharmacist, in others a would-be trombonist or a failed Tin Pan Alley songwriter (sample unpublished song titles: "Mimi from Miami" and "Yolanda from Yuma," the latter giving an uncertain advantage to those who favored Arizona as Melba Mae's birthplace, and the added possibility that Yolanda was in fact her real name, a father's hymn to his daughter), even a ballroom dancer who had murdered his partner during a dance marathon in 1931 (this scenario, in a French monograph on Blue Tyler's career, stolen without apology from Horace McCoy's *They Shoot Horses, Don't They?*).

The former Melba Mae Toolate's musical talent, such as it was, was said to come from this man cast as her father (in his trombonist, songwriter, or marathon dancer incarnations), unless it came via her mother (Irma in most cases, although Erna, Ursula, and heaven knows how many other Christian names were also candidates), a God-fearing (in later revisionist versions, as theological fashions changed and theories about the death of God were abroad in the land, God-hating) woman who taught piano, or the harp, or (this from a piece in *Film*

Comment entitled "The Geometry of Dance in the Classic Hollywood Musicals") mathematics. Irma (or Erna or Ursula) Toolate's emergence as the more dominant influence on Melba Mae was a feminist theory that came into currency after the brief reappearance of Blue Tyler as a middle-aged woman in Hamtramck, Michigan, when for a moment she became, to her surprise (although I cannot say amusement, because when one spends an entire professional life cosseted by the apparatus of a motion picture studio, one does not easily learn to be amused at one's own expense), a heroine of the women's movement, a victim, in that liturgy, of the system and the male oppressors who would extinguish any spark of female spirit or independence.

You begin to see the difficulty.

SETTING THE SCENE II

C HUCKIE O'HARA DIED yesterday. The obituary in the *Times* said he was seventy-seven, but I knew he was older than that, to the very end vain about his age in that poofter way of his, eighty-two or eighty-three more likely, because when he lost his leg on Peleliu he had already received an Oscar nomination, for directing *Lily of the Valley*. Most of the obits carried the picture, the famous photograph, of Chuckie testifying before the Un-American Activities Committee, the day he took off his wooden leg when the chairman asked if he was now or ever had been a Communist. It was quite a sight on those grainy old Movietone newsreels I tracked down and ran when I was trying to find out anything at all about Blue Tyler, who as it happened was the star of *Lily of the Valley*, her performance earning her a third Academy nomination, all before she was twelve.

In the stock footage, Chuckie began pulling up his pant leg just as he started to answer the chairman's question. Every eye in the hearing room was on him as he unbuckled that old-fashioned prosthetic device with all the straps, laid it on the witness table, and then said, clear as a bell, "Yes, Mr. Chairman, I was a Communist," not taking the First, as the Ten had done, and not the Fifth either, and he listed the dates, from October 1938 to July 1941, and, no, he would respectfully decline to name names, all the time massaging that raw stump of the leg he lost on Orange Beach. It was a real director's touch, a perfect piece of business. Chuckie always knew exactly how to stage a scene, and he knew that no one at the hearing was listening to what he had to say, they were just looking at that stump, all pulpy and white with red crosshatching where the stitches had been. "Darling," he told me when I asked him about that day in front of the Committee, "it was divine." Sydney Allen stole the hearing scene and used it in one of his pictures when it was safe to do safe pictures about the blacklist. The *Times* tried to get a quote from Sydney for Chuckie's obit, but Mr. Allen's spokesman said that Mr. Allen was in the cutting room and was not available for comment. Sydney never disappoints, as always a thoroughbred shit-heel.

In a movie, Chuckie's performance would have taken the steam out of the hearings, which naturally it did in Sydney Allen's piece of crap, but in real life, of course, it didn't. Only time accomplished that. Still the scene had good value. Chuckie was certainly a Red, he admitted that, but I doubt if it had anything to do with politics. Blue told me it was because he was really stuck on Reilly Holt, the writer at Paramount, and a high-muckety-muck in the Party, and from things Chuckie told me later I suspect she was getting close to the truth. In his defense, it should also be said that no one on that Committee had ever hit a beach, let alone had a leg blown off on one.

The Marine Corps must have had some idea about Chuckie's politics, it had to be why he was never given a commission, when they were making A.D.s from Poverty Row captains and majors. Chuckie said he preferred being an enlisted man anyway. The farm boys in the barracks were more susceptible to my roguish charms than officers in a BOQ might have been, he said, the roughest of rough trade, my dear, it comes from being so louche with all those sheep on cold winter nights. And the farm boys were more than compensation enough for having to salute Jack Ford and Willie Wyler, even, sweet mother of God, D.Z.

But if the Corps did not think Chuckie was officer material, it did realize that Corporal, later Sergeant, Charlton O'Hara, USMCR, was a pretty country fair director, just the man to shoot invasions, and so they gave him a film crew and put him on the beach with the first wave when the Fifth Marines hit Cape Gloucester the day after Christmas 1943 ("Not the way one would ordinarily choose to spend Boxing Day, dear," he said once), and then again nine months later with the first wave at Peleliu, a pointless and bloody fiasco, again with the Fifth Marines. All the Marine brass really wanted was film of jarheads hitting the beach to show Congress when it was time for the next year's appropriations. To the Corps, Chuckie's politics (and the sexual orientation the brass must have suspected) did not matter as much as the footage he was getting, when the chances were he was going to end up in a body bag anyway, a dead Commie nance, longevity not generally accruing to people who landed often enough with the first wave. Meaning Chuckie was probably lucky to lose only his right leg from the knee down on D-Plus-Two at Peleliu, Orange Beach, from an unexploded mortar round buried in the sand that he accidentally kicked while he was moving his crew around the beach looking for a better angle. Force of habit, the old Cosmopolitan Pictures training, directors at Cosmo always overcovered so that any mistakes could be fixed in the editing room.

Chuckie was blacklisted after he testified, no studio would hire him, no independent would back his projects. He could have gone to England but he hated the cold and he hated the dark wet English winters. Anyway the blacklist was not an economic hardship for Chuckie, as it was for so many others in the same boat, because he was rich, his family owned most of the highway billboards in the state of California. Not old money, darling, he told me, but money, and pots of it. He left his tiny perfect house in the Hollywood Hills and moved up to his family's place in the Carmel Highlands, where he was in no danger of being constantly reminded of the Industry from which he had been banished. The old O'Hara house on the Carmel bluffs looked as if it had grown out of the rock formations that fell into the Pacific hundreds of feet below, and there on the sea he spent his period of exile with his trick of the moment and with his dotty old mother, Vera O'Hara, who even when I met Chuckie several decades later was always asking him when he was going to get married. That was when I was taping his memories of Blue Tyler, and he was at the same time pumping me about her. During the hours and days we spent together, I kept trying to imagine his life in those years when he was a professional nonperson. All over the Carmel house there were photographs of Chuckie from that period, all in silver Tiffany frames; as much as any of the actors he directed, Chuckie loved having his picture taken, and in fact favored catamites who were photographers, although he never photographed them in turn. In the comfort of this Elba, he seemed to want for nothing, the man of principle as the man of leisure.

So I can understand the surprise of those who had canonized him when one day Chuckie flew to Washington on his own, and in executive session with the Committee's investigators purged himself. Because of his earlier appearance—a public relations disaster the Committee did not wish to repeat—he was treated with kid gloves, and his testimony never made public. There was only an announcement that he had appeared voluntarily and that his testimony would be most helpful in allowing the Committee to prepare its final report. That was it. Chuckie never said who he had named—less than I could have, more than I should have, was all he would tell me—and he went back to work as untroubled by his decision as he was by most of the events in his life. Why did you do it? I asked. Not very complicated, he answered. What it boiled down to was that he missed working. He missed the costume tests and the looping and the mixing sessions and the big mugs of coffee the script girl would hand him during the shoot and the crossword puzzles he would work with his thick black Mont Blanc pen while the D.P. was lighting the next scene. I could never feature myself as this queen hero of the revolution, he said during one of our tapings, it was in the most revolting taste.

For a while after his recantation he worked steadily if without particular distinction, accepted again in the commissaries and the private studio dining rooms, at the same time denounced as a pariah and stool pigeon by those of his peers who had been so quick to acclaim him a hero on that earlier occasion before the Committee when he had removed his prosthetic leg. The younger historians of this period, ideologically correct, dismiss him as absent character and kidney, but they were never able to appreciate the social weave of Hollywood, what it was like to live and work there, to understand that the priority was always making pictures, the black sheep accepted back in the fold always a reliable story line. After a time, he more or less slipped into professional oblivion, doing an occasional *Hallmark Hall of Fame* special, but never segment television, Chuckie was too much a snob for that, he had after all directed Crawford and Davis and Kate and Claudette and Blue Tyler.

Ah, yes. Blue Tyler. Or Melba Mae Toolate, as she had become once again when I sought her out in Hamtramck, Michigan, her real name the perfect disguise. Chuckie knew so many of Blue's early secrets, as I knew so many of her later ones, although she was such an elaborate fantast (a fastidious construct, liar being more to the point) that no one could ever really pin down the truth, such as it was, about her. Melba Mae covered her tracks.

—◄○►—

Chuckie's stories were wonderful. Not always believable, but wonderful. He tended to look at life as if he was setting up a shot, his hands joined at the thumbs, framing what he wanted the camera to see. A story was only meant to advance the action, and sooner than I should have I found myself going along with him, adding some set decoration of my own. You get in the mood. See the possibilities. Did it really matter if what happened did not actually happen that way? Who was to know? Everything is subjective. We were just advancing the action.

Story-conferencing the truth. A shading here, a shading there, in the interest, always we would tell ourselves, of clarification. Facts are unforgiving, so fuck facts, make the scenes work.

Anyway, Chuckie's stories, as such they were. About Blue, of course. And her passion for Jacob King. People in Hollywood have always had this romantic idea about gangsters, and Jacob, with his slick hair and perfect teeth and his dark brooding looks and his volcanic furies, satisfied every fantasy. Even his sexual appendage was given demonic proportions, the *schlong* on him, the *schwanss,* the *schmekelah,* Chuckie said, and he a student of such instruments, with a student's capacity for priapic exaggeration, a foot and a half, I saw it in the shower at Hillcrest. The venue explained Chuckie's lapse into Yiddish, the anti-Semitism that came so easily to him no reason not to play gin at the Industry's top Jewish country club, to take a little steam and case a few cocks in the locker room. This blissful reverie of an aged pederast allowed me to contemplate how many psychic miles Jacob King had traveled from the Red Hook section of Brooklyn, where he was born, to the shower room at Hillcrest, where Chuckie could swoon over his swinging dick. And Jacob the only man in that shower of whom it could be claimed that he had made his bones at the age of twelve. Or was it ten? Or had he just been brought along as a decoy, on that hit when he was ten, because his youth made the professional cannons doing the dirty less suspicious-looking?

Jacob King admitted nothing.

And denied nothing.

Twenty or thirty times he had whacked someone out.

Or so people said.

Did I know, Chuckie said, that Jake once killed somebody by wrapping his face in duct tape so he couldn't breathe? A murder meant to make a statement.

Or so the story was.

Chuckie saw the duct-tape caper as a high-angle crane shot, with a slow pan down, then a 120-frame hold on the mummified victim before the cut.

When Jacob King was killed, his left eye was blown out of its socket and landed on the unfinished portrait he was having painted of himself. Like a piece of snot, Chuckie said about the eyeball. Jacob was wearing jodhpurs in the portrait and laced boots and a beige silk shirt and a polka-dot ascot. Yet another indication of the mileage from Red Hook he had put on his psychic pedometer.

Or perhaps he was only traveling in place. On a treadmill with a fancier wardrobe.

It was said that Blue bought the portrait after Jacob King was killed. In any event, it disappeared.

Chuckie said that Jacob always carried a silver Tiffany locket in which he kept two of Blue's pubic hairs. Why just two? I said. Why not one? Or one short-and-curly for every time he fucked her? They couldn't have taken up all that much room. It wasn't like it was a load of hay.

These were the sorts of questions I always asked. Chuckie would never answer, but would just go off on another tangent about someone else. About Blue's lawyer, Lilo Kusack, and Lilo's girlfriend, Rita Lewis. About J. F. French. The Mogul. Founder of Cosmopolitan Pictures. J. F. French claimed to have personally discovered Blue Tyler when she was only four years old. Arthur French figured in Chuckie's reminiscences, too. Arthur was J.F.'s son and Blue's designated fiancé when she was under contract to Cosmopolitan. Chuckie saw the whole story as a movie, when his mind stopped wandering. It will be my comeback picture, he said. And then he would say, Doesn't it bother you the way these vile children directors say *film?* We made *pictures.* Adding after a moment, "I sound like some faggot female impersonator doing Norma Desmond."

I was surprised at how many people turned out for Chuckie's funeral. All the oldtimers who were still around, and for whom a funeral was an outing, many of them with canes and walkers and private nurses. In the end he was one of them, whatever his transgressions; membership in the closed society of the motion picture industry is almost never revoked for moral failings.

Of course Chuckie had scripted the service, down to the music cues. He wanted a bugler to blow the Marine Corps hymn at his graveside, slow tempo, "From the halls of Montezuma, To the shores of Tripoli," and then a segue into taps. Even from beyond the grave the *fageleh* son of a bitch was manipulating me, and I cried, as I knew I was meant to. And through the tears I remembered the day the story began.

The day Lizzie died.

JACK

PERSONALITY PARADE

Want the facts? Opinion? Truth? Write Walter Scott, Box 9277, Beverly Hills, California, or phone (213) 555-2121. Full name will be used unless otherwise requested. Volume of mail makes personal replies impossible.

Q. *I'm interested in former child star Baby Blue Tyler, who I think I went to grade school with in Fontana, California, way back when. I heard she has fallen on bad times. Is it true that she is a homeless bag lady in the Midwest with a criminal record?—Altula Bell, Shoshone, California.*

A. Blue Tyler, born Myrna Marie Toolate (pronounced Too-lah-tee) in San Bernardino, California, April 28, 1928, was Hollywood's top child star and number-one box office draw from 1936 to 1938, and thereafter was in the top ten until she left Hollywood in 1951 after being identified as a Communist by the House Un-American Activities Committee. Her many hits included *Little Sister Susan, Carioca Carnival,* and *Lily of the Valley.* While in her teens, Tyler had a relationship with famous hoodlum Jacob King (born Jacob Kinovsky), who in 1948 was rubbed out at his palatial Las Vegas hotel, King's Playland, reputedly by Mob cohorts angered by the mobster's flamboyant style. After Hollywood, Tyler made movies in Italy, then was briefly a nightclub singer in New York before she vanished from the public eye. In 1979 an item in the *National Enquirer* reported that Tyler had been arrested in Ypsilanti, Michigan, on drug charges. Bond was allegedly posted by an unnamed secret admirer, after which, according to the *Enquirer,* she promptly jumped bail. Her whereabouts are currently unknown, although there are unconfirmed reports that she died a few years ago in Kalamazoo, Michigan, where she is said to be buried in an unmarked grave in a potter's field.

Q. *I have heard that billionaire tycoon Hugh Broderick disinherited his son, screenwriter John Broderick. Is this true? What happened to John Broderick after his brother, Father Augustine Broderick, and John's former wife, Leah Kaye, were murdered together in San Francisco?—V.V.B., McAllen, Texas.*

A. John ("Jack") Broderick is a Hollywood scriptwriter (the remake of *Mildred Pierce* is his best-known credit, and his most recent the box office dud *Metro Vice II).* Broderick's first wife, left-leaning lawyer Leah Kaye Broderick, and his brother, liberal cleric and presidential adviser Father Augustine ("Bro") Broderick, were assassinated in San Francisco in 1984 by former Vietnam vet and disappointed local political candidate Richard ("Richie") Kane. (Contrary to rumor at the time, there was never any evidence of a relationship between Kaye and Father Broderick.) Kane was convicted and sentenced to a mental institution in Napa, California, where he committed suicide (by hanging) in 1987. Broderick's father, billionaire Hugh Broderick, died that same year of complications from a stroke. His fortune was left to a number of foundations and trusts. Although not named in the will, John Broderick was well compensated by his father during his lifetime. He lives with his third wife (and his father's onetime nurse), the former Elizabeth Innocent, and is currently working on a number of film projects.

I

"YOU SEE WHERE we made *Parade* this morning?" All I got was the back of Lizzie's head. "You, me, and Blue Tyler." I tried again. "Wasn't that her picture you were watching the other night on the tube? The one you said was a piece of shit?" But preferable, it seemed, to talking to me. That night, and apparently this one, too. *"Carioca Carnival."*

Lizzie kept staring out the window of the Porsche, as if she were trying to memorize all the houses on this particular stretch of Sunset. A mental map of enemy territory to report to her confederates in the feminist maquis. That she was always identified as my father's former nurse never bothered her; indeed she took it as a point of pride, because it seemed to embarrass the people, mainly professional friends—correction, acquaintances —of mine, with whom she most often came into contact, and who preferred not to be reminded that they, like her, had come from circumstances more modest than those to which they had become accustomed. She hated Los Angeles—correction again, Hollywood, third correction, the movie business—hated the way women in The Industry (she equally hated the way she claimed I used those two words, with an upper-case *T*, and an upper-case *I*, as if The Industry was some kind of superior life-giving force; I thought I was only being ironic) were relegated to the categories of wife or fuck. Or development slut. Her term. Meaning those women—*girls* was a word one used in front of Lizzie at one's peril—with looks (the overweight need not apply, nor those with moles or the faintest palest shadow of downy mustache), drive, and no discernible talent, to whom the studios would sometimes give a housekeeping fund for an office and a secretary and some development money to work with would-be and never-will-be screenwriters whose primary virtue was that they were not in the Guild, and thus not eligible for minimums and benefits. Occasionally a screenplay might actually be written, perhaps even put into production, by which time the developer had been removed from the project (via a clause in the boilerplate of the contract she had never bothered to read, and would not have understood if she had) and was setting up still another office paid for by still another studio, all the while realizing but never quite admitting (in her quaint Spanish-style apartment off Laurel Canyon with the high-tech sound system and the frig filled with cranberry juice for her chronic cystitis, and in the garage the BMW 315 whose payments she could not quite manage) that the reason she was being sponsored by her economic and, in Hollywood terms, social betters was that occasionally she be available to service someone more important on The Industry food chain, with an itch and no one to scratch it.

"Hello," I said after a moment. It was Lizzie who had told me that cranberry juice was a cure for cystitis. Nurse info. And further nurse info (dubious though I thought it was) that cunnilingus exacerbated it. This imparted after a drinks party in one of those Laurel Canyon apartments when she asked if I had ever gone down on the hostess when I was seeing her between marriages. I pleaded the Fifth, my psyche being insufficiently robust to sustain the weight of being a cystitis exacerbator on top of my many other derelictions. The party and the ambient noise about start dates and back-end money and negative pickups and most-favored-nation clauses had so bored her that she had gravitated to the kitchen on the pretense of getting some ice and while there had taken a stock inventory of the refrigerator. "Anyone home?"

Still no response.

"Here's something I bet you didn't know." Pedantry, oddly enough, was one way I could always get her attention. "When the Germans occupied France during the war—"

"What war?" Lizzie said, turning slowly away from the window. What I called pedantic she called patronizing. Lizzie always claimed that when I did not wish to communicate, as at that particular moment I most certainly did not, I would fill the silences with bits of arcane information—that Anne Boleyn had six fingers on one hand, or that William Howard Taft weighed 352 pounds. Once she bought me a book called *Little-Known Facts,* and on the flyleaf she had written "Here are a few things I bet you don't know." In fact I hadn't known it was illegal to hunt camels in Arizona, or that it never rained in the town of Calama in Chile's Atacama Desert, or that in the year 1221, in the Persian city of Nishapur, Genghis Khan killed 1,778,000 people in one hour, or that in France, in 1740, a cow was found guilty of sorcery and hanged.

"World War Two," I said. "Anyway, the Germans liked the guillotine so much, they often used it to execute people rather than hanging them or shooting them. But they added a little wrinkle of their own."

I waited for Lizzie to respond. Of course this was not what she wanted to talk about, but what she wanted to talk about I was not about to talk about, and I was playing for time.

"You see, when the French topped somebody, a certain delicacy prevailed, and they let the accused kneel face down. But the Germans, the Nazis, they turned the poor bastard around so that he was looking straight up at the blade, and then they taped his eyelids open so he couldn't shut his eyes. The last thing he saw was that mother coming down." Lizzie was staring out the window again. "Fuckers played rough."

"We have to call Lois tomorrow, and Miranda, too, and get

the taillight on my Volvo fixed, and I suppose the hoses, too, I mean, you should get them all replaced when one gives out," Lizzie said finally as we pulled over the rise on Sunset, just east of Anita, and then the Fiat Spider hit us.

Lois and Miranda were the lawyers she wanted to represent her in the divorce.

Which is what I hadn't wanted to talk about.

◄◦►

I am he. Him is me.

◄◦►

They told him in the emergency room that Lizzie had been killed instantly, as had the boy in the Spider. The boy had lost control coming around the curve, a three-sixty into his lane, going too fast, of course, at least eighty, according to the LAPD accident report filed with the Motor Vee and introduced as evidence during depositions. The boy's father said there would be no problem with the insurance, but then the lawyers for the boy's father got involved, and the lawyers tried to make it look as if he was at fault for driving on Sunset at ten o'clock on a Sunday evening, under the speed limit and in the lane he should have been driving in, after dinner at Spago, a window table, just he and Lizzie, Lizzie staring out at the billboard for the latest Martin Magnin Production, *Metro Vice II,* he trying to keep his third marriage from breaking up, three divorces showed a certain instability. The lawyers for the boy's father tried to make a case out of his two J&Bs and the two Beck's beers at dinner, but only 0.044 on the Breathalyser when the LAPD finally got around to administering the test after the accident, well under the limit for DWI. His alcoholic intake came out in the depositions, every drink recorded on the dinner check the lawyers for the boy's father subpoenaed from Spago (including Lizzie's one glass of the house white wine), as had the boy's misadventures with speed, and his semester at Betty Ford for substance abuse, records his own lawyers had subpoenaed in turn. His lawyers also subpoenaed the autopsy report, and the report's toxicological tests showed a residue of cocaine in the boy's system.

Don't get rough with us, his lawyers told the lawyers for the boy's father. You're not getting a penny. What his lawyers meant was a penny of the Broderick money, there was enough Broderick money to keep the boy's family in court for as long as the Broderick lawyers could file motions, until the boy's father declared bankruptcy or caved in, Bleak House on the Pacific littoral.

We could live with no fault, the boy's insurance company said.

A funny concept, considering. No fault.

◄○►

If I was a former first lady, Lizzie had once said, I'm not sure I'd want my name memorialized on a drunk tank.

◄○►

He had not counted on having to identify Lizzie. When he got home from the morgue after making the ID, he wrote it down exactly as he remembered the way it happened. Waste not, want not. Grist for the mill. It was a way to distance himself from it.

To see the bizarre side.

As it were.

Naturally he added a little filigreeing. Layering and subtext. Some pacing. For the flow.

This is what he wrote:

Have you ever identified a body in a morgue?

I hadn't, but I thought I knew how to do it. First I would be asked to go down to the morgue in order to identify the deceased, as I was her closest, and in this case her only, relative. Lois and Miranda would have gone, in fact asked to go, but I did not think it entirely appropriate for the lawyers who were handling her divorce petition to make the ID, especially as Lois and Miranda had already asked about my alcoholic consumption earlier that evening at Spago. So I went downtown myself—it's always downtown where the morgue is located, and for that matter the police station, too, otherwise cops would not always be saying in the kind of movie I write,

"Let's go downtown." It was the first time in all the years I had been going downtown in the interests of research that I had no trouble finding a place to park, but then I rarely go downtown at five in the morning. The morgue is located across the street from a Dunkin' Donuts franchise, and through the window in the thin dawn light I could see several people at the counter dunking donuts in their coffee, as they were meant to do in a franchise of that name, it occurred to me. What struck me was that all the customers were wearing yellow jumpsuits with blue lettering on the back that said, in block letters, MEDICAL EXAMINER, and I kept turning over in my mind what it must be like to be a counterman in that particular Dunkin' Donuts, serving guys in yellow jumpsuits who had been picking up stiffs all night long.

One of whom must have been Lizzie.

Scraped off the windshield of the Porsche at Sunset and Anita.

Then brought downtown.

Finally I went inside the morgue (the people who work there call it the Medical Examiner's Office, but I prefer morgue, it has more nuance) and gave my name at the desk, and after a while a plainclothes cop appeared and he talked to me quietly, without ever actually meeting my eye, about "the victim," her age and her weight and her height and her eye and hair color and then out of the blue he asked me if I had ever been on the cops. That was the phrase he used—"on the cops." I love the way cops talk. It has such a particularity about it. I said, no, I had never been on the cops, why, and he said that he was a great fan of *Code 7*. That was a picture I had written, from a novel I had also written. The first line of the novel read, "You treat people right and they treat you right, then you can retire in very nice shape—the golden rule of the police department." A *roman policier* with existential overtones, I always say defensively. Civilians don't ever get cops down right, the cop said, and you did. The compliment seemed to embarrass him, as it did me, and he fiddled with a ballpoint pen until another cop arrived, and then he said, Follow me.

I expected to walk into a room with all sorts of cabinets and cupboards and then the first cop would say it's cold, and the second cop would say we won't be in here long, just long enough to make a proper ID, and then we would get to the right cabinet and a morgue attendant who wore a white coat with a lot of pens in the pocket would open up the cabinet door and slide out the deceased, who would be lying under a sheet. One of the cops would pull down the sheet and the other would practically be leaning on me to catch me in case my knees began to buckle. The first cop would say don't worry if you faint, a lot of people do, and I would look at the body and think it's a funny color, that must be how you look when you're dead. Then I would nod at the cops and the morgue guy would pull the sheet over her face and slide the tray back into the cabinet. All quite traumatic. A good scene. I had seen it in God knows how many movies, some of which I had written myself.

Except it was Lizzie I had to identify, not some stiff in a screenplay.

And it's not done that way at all.

It's done on television. Closed circuit. When the cop said follow me, I followed him into a small room, a cubicle with glass walls, like the kind office clerks have who don't rate windows. Hanging off the wall in one corner was a television set, like the kind you see in a hospital room. There were a couple of chairs and a small couch, I guess in case the whole family wanted to come in and make the ID. The cop said are you okay, and I nodded, and he punched some letters on a computer keyboard and all of a sudden, there on the screen, there she was, Lizzie herself, an overhead shot, on a gurney, under a sheet, face all black and blue, eyes closed, mouth open because her jaw was broken when she went through the windshield, hair all wild, I'll be goddamned, it *was* Lizzie, as beat to shit as she was, I could still recognize her. In a way it was kind of great, brave new world, and I said to the cop, material always being hard to come by, is this how you do it now, and he said yes, it keeps the survivors from getting all emotional and trying to throw themselves on Uncle Bob or Aunt Sue, he couldn't count the times family members knocked the victim onto the floor before this new system was installed, it would be kind of humorous if it wasn't so serious, this way you just press the remote and the deceased disappears from the screen.

Then he pressed the remote and Lizzie disappeared from the screen.

It was the last time I saw her.

That's exactly how it happened.
More or less.

-◦-

I thought, What if Lizzie had died of a lingering illness and not in an automobile accident? A lingering death gives both the victim and the survivors time to prepare, to put on a serious courageous face, to define grace under pressure. So long, it goes without saying, as death was not postponed for such an inordinate period of time that friends and family got bored with the idea and began finding excuses not to visit the patient with their offerings of succor and praise. And after a while left for the weekend without giving a number where they could be reached in the event of the inevitable. Time enough to read about it on the obituary page, society's scorecard, and mull the reasons why the deceased appeared below the fold, or without a photograph.

A reasonable time frame, then. Something out of a movie. People dying in movies did not have catheters inserted into their urethras. Nor did they have dementia. And no drooling and no incontinence and no shit on the sheets, those crosses of the terminal illness. Six weeks. A strain, but not too much. Time to remember Lizzie's virtues and gloss over her faults. Which of course were so few they did not bear mentioning, except to elucidate that she was not perfect, but then who was? How is she, Jack? I hope when I go, he would answer, that I show as much . . . and his voice would trail off. Jack is really bearing up well, people would say.

What kind of six-week terminal illness then? Lizzie's last mammogram showed her breasts to be fibrocystic, but the only mass was a benign cyst that the oncologist aspirated in his office. But what if the lump had not been benign. Breast cancer, detected late. A CAT scan and a spinal tap. A small locus of the renegade cells had taken residence in the meninges. No. The liver. The liver does not regenerate. An operation was out of the question, the oncologist would have said. Let him be a cancer bureaucrat, and be affected with the professional coldness of the breed. Just vamping now. Lizzie would ask to see him, a half hour of his time to let him explain all the options she had available, and to let her put into words all the fears that were rattling around in her imagination.

"I have sixty patients," he would say to her coldly. "I am a very busy man, and if you think I have a half hour to discuss your case alone with you, I suggest you get another doctor."

No. No doctor would ever say that. On the other hand, a deathbed speech was always good value.

"Dr. Korn," Lizzie would say (a perfect name, Korn, Bernard Korn, M.D., P.C., file that), "we are discussing cancer, and with it the possibility of my death." Of course this was not the way Lizzie talked, even at the end, when we were only speaking monosyllabically. Her style ran in the direction of, You know, it's been ten days since we fucked. Not accusingly. A statement of fact.

Back to the plot line.

"I have always been terrified of cancer," Lizzie would say, "because I have always been terrified of death. I believe in certainties and death is the great unknown. I hate unknowns. To you I am a patient, an abstraction. A humanoid, not a human being. One does not have a half hour to discuss fear and death with a humanoid. The humanoid should get another doctor. So be it. You are hereby dismissed as my doctor." Could she have ever talked in that way? No. But it plays. "I do not wish you ill. I only hope that when you are forced to confront your own death that you will be frightened, as frightened as I am now, and that you are alone. That is perhaps sentimental of me. I do not care. Please leave."

◄◦►

It needs work, Jack thought, but it has possibilities. Cut from, "You are hereby dismissed as my doctor" to "Please, leave."

Oh, Christ, Lizzie, it would have been a better way to go.

◄◦►

"You ever think of therapy, kid?" Marty Magnin asked. Marty was a movie producer with whom I had worked off and on for over twenty years. He called me kid and he called me pal, and in a way I guess we were pals. Or what passed for pals in Hollywood. Lizzie never could stand him.

"No, Marty, why?" I said.

◄◦►

If it had to be an accident, this one might have been better:

When I walked into the TWA terminal, the notation next to Lizzie's flight number on the Arrivals monitor said, "See Agent." I turned around and left the building immediately, not knowing exactly why I had to see the agent, but knowing I would find out on the car radio soon enough. I had seen the scene too often on television—the minicam holding on "See Agent," then the cut to the special room the airline had set aside for the people who had come to the airport to pick up those loved ones who would never arrive. The grief managers would move in, and strangers would hug each other, and promise to keep in touch, and the airline would try to get us to sign release forms. I even knew how much the figure was— $75,000, and an agreement not to sue.

◄◦►

The accident was in February. In March I began to write letters to public figures:

Hon. Clifton Mayo
United States Senate
Washington, D.C. 20510

Dear Senator Mayo,

On Saturday last, I saw you and a young woman in a mink coat who I would hope was your wife, although she did not look like your wife's photographs, checking into the Beverly Wilshire Hotel. Later that same evening, I happened by coincidence to be dining at Michael's Restaurant in Santa Monica and saw you sign the check for a party of eight. There were by my count four bottles of Cristal Roederer champagne consumed at your table. According to the sommelier, the Cristal Roederer was of the 1979 vintage and is listed at $125.00 per bottle. As I am not aware of any Senate business that was being conducted in Los Angeles that weekend, and as you are an elected representative of the people of Utah, I would like to think that you were not staying at the most expensive hotel in Beverly Hills on the public tit, nor that you charged the taxpayers of America for a $1,400 private dinner with French champagne when the domestic wine industry is currently in such difficult straits.

I look forward to your prompt reply.

John Broderick

◄o►

"He's not really a shrink," Marty Magnin said. "He's what they call a psychological counselor."
"Who?"
"Say again?"
"Who calls him a psychological counselor?"
"Everybody. Morty Wishengrad swears by him."
"Morty Wishengrad's an agent. You're taking testimonials from agents now?"
"I'm just saying you got to get over this Lizzie thing."

"What Lizzie thing is that, Marty?"

"Jack, she's dead."

"I know. I saw her on the monitor."

"Jack, you need help."

"I'm moving, Marty. Picking up stakes. Leaving Cheyenne."

"You live in Brentwood, for Christ's sake."

"Marty, did you know that every Emily Dickinson poem can be sung to the tune of 'The Yellow Rose of Texas'?"

II

I FOUND A NINE-MONTH SUBLET on Seventh Avenue and Fifty-eighth Street. A landmark building, the real estate woman said. "A City Home for People with Country Houses" was its advertising slogan when it opened its doors in 1909, the smallest apartment having seventeen rooms. The real estate woman had that nervous conversational tic that did not allow for dead air. Woody Allen used the exterior in *Hannah and Her Sisters*, it's one of his favorite buildings in New York, that's high praise, no one knows New York like Woody, you must know him, you're a screenwriter, it's such a small world, isn't it, Mark Hampton decorated it, he doesn't do many apartments on the West Side, I love chocolate cut velvet, don't you? No, not really, but the apartment had good space, four and a half rooms, two baths, twelve-foot ceilings, original moldings, and I didn't have the heart to look at any of the other buildings on her list, or, more to the point, the will to listen to any more of her irrelevancies.

"So how are you, kid?" Marty Magnin said. Every other Monday I was on his list of calls. Marty kept in touch with me as he kept in touch with his broker and his bookie. His telephone had twelve buttons and speed dial. I was not on speed dial. "Getting much?"

"Enough." Meaning none at all.

"You working?"

"On a novel." Why not? "How's this for a first line?" I could always come up with a first line. The second line was always a pain in the ass, but first lines—ready, aim, fire: " 'It was the kind of hotel that looked like you could bang the waitress in the coffee shop, which I did.' "

"Film noir."

"That's what I had in mind." God, I loved dealing with Marty Magnin. You put out bait, he would always bite.

"Good area. You need a couple of vedettes, only one of them a gross player, and you keep production costs down."

"Exactly."

"Listen, I'm interested. Fax me the story line, I'll tell you if there's a picture there. But keep it down to a page, you wouldn't believe the amount of reading I have to do every weekend."

STEEPLES

He called her Steeples because, he said, that was what her nipples reminded him of when they made love. Through the years, he would send her postcards of church steeples, e.g., Cologne Cathedral or a New England church spire, with no message and no signature. It was how they kept in touch.

◄○►

"What the fuck is this?" Marty Magnin said.

"You told me to fax you what I had."

"That's it? What about the chick in the coffee shop the guy boffs."

"This is just a possible back story I'm playing around with."

"To tell you the truth, Jack, I don't think there's a picture in it."

CHOCOLATE

I went to bed exhausted one night. The chambermaid had put two little chocolate mints with gold foil wrapping on my pillow. In the middle of the night, I had to pee. When I staggered back to bed, there was a huge spot of dried blood on the bed, right under where my stomach would have been. I panicked, felt around my body for a stab wound. There was nothing there. Finally I found the lamp on the bedside table and turned it on. The spot was not dried blood after all. One of the chocolate mints had slipped under my body, and during the night, my body heat had melted it.

—◁◦▷—

"Jack, no more faxes, okay? The fruitcake letters made more sense than this shit."

"It's incident, Marty, part of the weave. I'm just giving you a taste."

"Listen, kid, my taste buds tell me you keep on like this you're going to end up in the bin."

I began to sing. " 'She dwelleth in the Ground—Where Daffodils—abide—' "

"You're singing songs now?"

"Emily Dickinson. Remember I said you could sing all her poems to 'The Yellow Rose of Texas.' "

"Leonard Fox, Jack. He's the one to call. The best shrink in New York. Sydney Allen swears by him."

"I'll make a note of it, Marty."

"You getting it regular?"

"Regular."

"That's swell. Lizzie would've wanted you to get laid."

"I know that, Marty."

"Great, Jack. Really great. I come to town next time, we'll schmooze."

"I look forward to it, Marty."

III

THEN A MONDAY six weeks later.

I knew she was going to get her purse snatched. Knew it with an absolute certainty the moment I first set eyes on her on West Fifty-eighth Street. I had just bought some sheets at Bergdorf's. Some people wait for the white sales—Lizzie always did—others get their sheets at Abraham & Straus or the discount houses on Delancey, but I said fuck it, so it cost $331 for two sets of plain white New York king-sized sheets and twelve pillow slips, Bergdorf's was only a block away, and my time, when I was working, was valuable. It was even possible to say, and I was happy to do so in the discourses with myself that had become my primary mode of conversation (even on the street, where I was no longer embarrassed when other pedestrians gave me that strange sideways look they give to people they catch talking to themselves in public), that with the time factor, I was saving money; I had also learned from the saleslady at Bergdorf's that New York king-sized beds were shorter and wider than Los Angeles kings, which were longer and narrower, and information, even as trivial as this, was power, although this was a proposition, as it pertained to bed linen, that I was not prepared to argue too strenuously while talking to myself on my daily constitutional.

It was the first time I had ever bought sheets, and I had not realized how heavy they were, like a load of bricks, so heavy that as I walked up Fifty-eighth Street toward my apartment I had to keep switching the shopping bag from hand to hand. I was switching hands when I noticed the young woman. Nice legs, sensible pointy tits, and I would wager the barbered rectangular trim that had become, now that I was back, however hesitantly, in circulation, my new benchmark for measuring erogenous indulgence. The uniform tailored blue suit and the uniform white silk blouse with two gold buttons at the neck and the uniform black Mädler briefcase and the oversized Bottega Veneta bag swinging from a shoulder strap. Mistress, she thought, of all she surveyed, and no one knew how wrong she was more than the slender young black with the dreadlocks and the bombed-out Stevie Wonder look trailing just a few paces behind her, the one who also knew, as did I, that if she had an ounce of brains she would be walking on West Fifty-seventh Street or on Central Park South and not on Fifty-eighth between Sixth and Seventh, a street that looks like a tunnel, even at high noon on a sunny day in July, which this was not.

Smash and grab. He had that bag off her shoulder and was heading east on Fifty-eighth like a DB high-stepping toward the end zone with an interception. Neon Deion. This was where I made my mistake. I decided to be a hero. No, not decided, it's not something you decide, any more than the grunt who throws himself on a hand grenade to save Lou and Tiny and Leroy and Geraldo and the other joes in his platoon decides to be a hero. It is something done by instinct, and if I had time to think it over rationally I would have said no way, Jose, fuck you, Lou and Tiny and Leroy and Geraldo. It just happened that I was switching the Bergdorf bag full of sheets from left hand to right as he passed, and without thinking I hauled off and hit him in the face with it. You get hit with $331 worth of sheets and pillow slips, it tends to get your attention. In this case, the bag of sheets upended him, ass over tea kettle. His head bounced off the sidewalk, like someone was dribbling it, and then he just lay still. Of course he dropped the young woman's bag. She didn't even have time to scream, and now this spade is stretched out cold and her bag is sitting there on the sidewalk, and what does she do? She picks up the bag, puts it over her shoulder, and continues on her way as if nothing has happened.

Wait a minute, I said, call the police, I'll watch this guy. And she said, not breaking stride, I don't want to get involved, fuck him, and I said, He could be dead, and she said, That's your problem, and I said, Jesus, lady, and she said, flipping me the bird, Up yours, and with that she heads for Sixth Avenue under a full head of steam and disappears around the corner, gripping that bag of hers like grim death, and if she had done that in the first place, the dumb bitch, none of this fucking nightmare would have happened. I was just left standing there, no victim, no bag, and this spade Stevie Wonder clone is lying on the sidewalk with blood coming out of his ears. I didn't have Lizzie's nurse info, but I knew that blood pouring out of the ears was not a good sign. Then from out of nowhere this yuppie Rambo in a three-piece suit blindsided me with a cross-body block, and he says, I saw you hit that black man, and someone else said, Racist, and a third person said, Murderer, and a fourth said, Call the police, and the long and the short of it was that I wound up at the precinct house on West Fifty-fourth Street, where I was interrogated, picked out of a lineup by three eyewitnesses, informed of my rights, fingerprinted, photographed, and finally after twelve hours booked for assault with intent to kill.

It was like a bad dream. The arresting officer hung a number around my neck when they took my mug shots, full face, left and right profiles, and in every angle I looked furtive, cornered, in need of a shave, my asshole screwed tight as if I was already anticipating the buggery awaiting me when I was transported by bus to the Riker's Island lockup. Even today I find myself waking up in the middle of the night reciting the number—NYPD-

45-23-9387. The reason for the bust and the charge sheet was that when the purse snatcher—John Doe in the initial paperwork, later identified as one Shaamel Boudreau, no known address, but with a yellow sheet showing twenty-three arrests and six felony convictions—hit his head against the sidewalk, his brain was so rotted with crack and smack and booze and by assorted traumas he had picked up at Attica and other resorts maintained by the New York State Department of Corrections that the knock on the noggin took care of him. Bought him the farm.

—◦—

"So, John, you have a history of violence?"

"Look, I just want to call a lawyer."

"Why? You haven't been charged with anything yet. We're just having a fucking chat here, trying to find out what happened, why you busted Mr. Doe, what'd he do to you got you so pissed off."

"Don't I get my rights read to me?"

"Hey, you must've seen too many movies, you want your rights read to you, that's what Robert Redford does in the movies, 'You have the right to remain silent,' and all that shit."

"I write them." A big mistake. Wrong place to list your credits.

"Hey, Leo, this guy writes movies for Robert Redford."

Leo was the bad cop in the good-cop/bad-cop tandem, although his partner Al was no day at the beach. Leo said, "I suppose you think knowing Robert Redford is going to get you a free fucking ride, cowboy."

I tried to parse how Robert Redford had got into this conversation and then thought there was nothing to be gained by saying that actually I did know him, we talked about doing a picture once, and nothing came of it. Just nod and keep cool. Easier said than done.

Leo again: "So what've you got against niggers, you like to beat them up on the street so much?"

"Look, can we take this from the top again?"

"Is that what they say in your movies, take it from the top? That's cute, right, Al?"

"Cute as shit."

"You ever done this sort of thing before?"

"I mean, there's nothing wrong with not liking niggers, John, a lot of guys don't." Al, the good cop. "For that matter, a lot of cops." An exegesis of police racial attitudes was an aspect of the good-cop role that I had never considered. "So you say you don't like niggers, there's guys in the department will say, 'Welcome to the club,' you know what I mean?"

"No, I don't know what you mean. Look, all I am telling you is there was this woman—"

"He's taking it from the top again, Al."

"Like Robert Redford. He a good guy?"

"She was coming down Fifty-eighth Street—"

"You got to give us a name, John . . ."

"I don't know her name. She was carrying a Bottega Veneta bag."

"Say again."

"An expensive leather handbag." I knotted my fingers to indicate the meshing pattern. I must have been mad. "The leather is all meshed."

"What the fuck is this Bodega Venta, you ever heard of it, Al?" To me: "You jerking my chain or something, cowboy?"

"It's a store. Bottega Veneta. On Madison Avenue. They sell leather bags. She was carrying one. This guy grabs it."

"The John Doe."

"I don't know his name. She just took her bag and left."

"What bag?"

"The bag the guy grabbed."

"That must be the bodega bag, Leo."

"Bottega Veneta—"

"How do you spell that, cowboy?"

"B-O-T-T-E-G-A V-E-N-E-T-A."

"He knows how to spell, Al. Even in spic."

"He's a writer is why, Leo. You got to be a good speller to be a writer, right, cowboy?"

"You find this woman—"

Al said, "What woman?"

Leo said, "What bag?"

"The one he took—"

"We didn't find any bag."

"She took it. She grabbed it back, and took off."

"I thought you said he took it," Al said.

"Got to keep your stories straight, cowboy," Leo said.

"There were people in the street, somebody must've seen what happened."

Leo said, "Well, they're not busting down the door of the precinct, cowboy, so I wouldn't count on that. Anyway, you see this coon—"

"Leo . . ."

"Sorry, I forget you're so sensitive, Al." To me: "So anyway, you see this colored guy with the curls."

Al on cue: "Those fucking curls can really get to you—"

"And you just boil over, you hit him with the sheets, it happens, right, Al?"

"All the time."

"Look, if you can just find this woman—"

"What woman? You're the only one who's seen her. What does she look like then?"

Great tits, nice ass, and put your money on a bush with a bikini cut. No. Hold that. I did not need an additional charge of sexual deviation added to my rap sheet. "Young."

"Hey."

"Hair. Short. I mean, above the shoulder. Brown, I think."

"That really narrows it down. I thought writers were supposed to have powers of description, didn't you, Leo."

I was losing control. "I'm telling you, he took her fucking bag."

"What bag?"

◄○►

BILLIONAIRE BRODERICK HEIR IN RACIALLY MOTIVATED MURDER INVESTIGATION was one of the more muted headlines, in the *Times*, page one, below the fold. The rest of the press was in what it likes to call, in retrospect, when it examines its collective conscience and absolves itself of its excesses, a feeding frenzy, with me the sacrificial offering. I was a Broderick and I carried all the overweight baggage of my family's history and wealth and arrogance and entitlement. Beginning with my father the billionaire. After his stroke, which kept his natural litigiousness in check, and even more so after his death, Hugh Broderick was the stuff of cheap headlines, the spotlight focusing on how he had made his money, and who he had fucked (the real object of interest, you can be sure), practically everyone (and here the inventiveness soared, a sonata of sexual fantasy) from Eleanor Roosevelt to Mother Theresa, Mme. Nehru to Mrs. Thatcher, from Blue Tyler to Marilyn Monroe (the ground somewhat firmer here), even my first wife, Leah Kaye, although this was more in the form of sly innuendo than outright allegation, as my own disposition for litigation had not been tested. Leah, the radical lawyer shot and killed in San Francisco with my brother, Bro, the Benedictine priest and adviser to presidents. A saga of license, tragedy, and meaningless death, with all the opportunities it offered for prurience and sentimental vulgarity. I had thought that with Lizzie's death the narrative had played itself out. I had not counted on Shaamel Boudreau. The story was made for tabloid ironies. The Broderick fortune and the homeless indigent felled by $331 worth of Bergdorf-Goodman sheets and pillow slips. Silk sheets, the *Post* insisted, naturally. For a few days I was on the evening news once again, of course with an insert of my mug shots, along with the number NYPD-45-23-9387.

Of course it finally got straightened out.

‑‹o›‑

"Nice of that chick to show up," Marty Magnin said.

"Finally," I said. Charges had been quickly dropped, and for a moment the former murder suspect became an urban hero. Citizen action against street crime. "After I thought I was going to spend the rest of my life in Attica."

"She just got scared. She's not a bad kid."

"Oh?"

"We schmoozed, her and me. After she came forward. She did the right thing, Jack. She did right by you. You know, she's a broker. A securities analyst at Drexel. Motion picture stocks. We had lunch. I gave her a few tips. Who's in, who's out. Touted Sydney Allen's new picture. A blockbuster, Jack, and I've got his next under his old deal."

By his smirk I knew he wanted me to ask if he had fucked her, screwing everything available and then talking about it was a tropistic instinct with him, but I really didn't care if he had. "You weren't going to call, were you? Until I got my name in the paper."

"I had a lot of appointments, Jack. I had to make time. And I made it, right? That's what friends do."

"I'm honored you could fit me in, Marty." We were making our way up Fifty-seventh Street toward the Russian Tea Room. The skies were leaden and threatened snow. A cab slowed and the driver shouted at me through the open window, "How to go, killer," and then flashed the V sign before speeding off.

"Jesus," I winced.

"Go with it, Jack. You're a hero. Answer me this. How many times does a writer get to be a hero?"

"The man is dead, Marty."

In Marty Magnin's mind an irrelevancy. Perhaps he was right. Maybe I was making too much of a meal out of it. How much of a pose was this ostentatious show of regret? Was it only because I thought this was the way I was supposed to feel? Guilt is a luxury of the entitled.

"What kind of name is Shaamel anyway?" Marty Magnin asked.

"I never got a chance to ask."

"They got funny names, these people. The Rams have got two guys in the defense secondary, Tyreese Snipes and Safrican Smith. You think they knew him?"

I pretended not to hear.

"He could have been named after his parents. They do that. Shana and Mel, say. That gives you Shaamel, right?"

"Give it a rest, would you?"

"Salou. Salou Magnin."

"What?"

"Sadie and Lou. My parents. If they'd named me like the *schwartzes* do, I'd be Salou Magnin. You like that? I like it."

We entered the Tea Room and took a booth across from Sydney Allen and Sam Cohn. Marty went over and kissed them on both cheeks and then I heard him try out Salou Magnin on them and the agents in the adjoining booths. Much laughter. Two of the agents whistled at me and made the pumping gesture tennis players make after winning a big point at Wimbledon. I wondered if Sydney Allen would incorporate my sheets adventure into the picture he was working on with Marty Magnin. If not there, I knew he would use it at some future time in some other project. Sydney was a born *gonif*.

"Sydney's sending over a bottle of Dom Perignon," Marty said when he slipped back into the booth.

"And charging it to the budget of whose picture?"

"You're very touchy, you know?"

The waiter brought the champagne and handed me a note. " 'You've made our town a safer place. Thanks. Sydney A.' " As opposed to Sydney P. I swirled the amber liquid around in the champagne tulip and then raised the glass in the direction of Sydney A. "*Ciao, bene*," Sydney Allen mouthed from across the room.

"What kind of name is Sydney Allen anyway?" I suddenly said to Marty Magnin.

"What does that mean?"

"I've got to get out of here, Marty."

"You going to be sick?"

"No. I mean out of here. Out of town. I'm sick of cabdrivers blowing their horns at me in the street and asshole directors sending me bottles of Dom Perignon on someone else's fucking tab. I got asked for my fucking autograph yesterday in the park. And a fucking Japanese tour group wanted to take my fucking picture. Jesus. The guy with the name you think is so fucking funny is dead."

"Calm down, Jack." Marty Magnin was smiling at the room and talking like a ventriloquist trying to throw his voice. "People are looking."

"Let them look."

Marty suddenly rose. "Sydney, *ciao*. See you on the Coast." Beads of sweat appeared on Marty's brow as he sat down. It was as if I were a bomb he was afraid would go off at any minute. "Listen, Jack, you want to get out of town?" He snapped his fingers as if a lightbulb had just gone off in his brain. "I've got a great idea. Detroit."

"Detroit? Detroit's not the out of town I had in mind, Marty. Australia. Tuscany. Antarctica. Not fucking Detroit. I've never been to Detroit, I don't know anybody in Detroit, what am I supposed to do in Detroit?"

"You remember that idea we kicked around once? The cop and the basketball player. A *schwartze*, his knees are fucked up, he can't play anymore, he and the cop become a team, the cop's not crazy about darkies, the *schwartze*'s into black power, you can see the conflict already. I mean, he's seven feet two, this guy, this *schwartze*, who's going to fuck with him? I see Kareem, maybe, he's got some film I can look at. I already got a title registered. *Murder One*."

A title I had given him, but to Marty that was only a technicality. "So?"

"There's this cop I know in Detroit . . ."

"How?"

"Say again."

"How do you know a cop in Detroit?"

"We were doing publicity on *Cave Man*. The cop assigned to us had a million stories. A homicide cop . . ."

An alarm bell. "What's a homicide cop doing babysitting a movie press junket anyway?"

"Temporary desk job. They took away his gun for shooting some spade . . ." Marty glanced quickly at me. "That going to be a problem? It was all cleared up. Investigation board. The whole shmeer. A good shoot. A hell of a good shoot, they said. A great shoot."

"You make it sound like a picture, like a fucking production schedule."

Marty was in overdrive. "Two weeks in Detroit, you drive around with him, you soak up a little atmosphere, you're good at that, Jack, the best, you come back, we go to the Kahala, we work out a story . . ."

"An awful lot of *we* in this, Marty. It's me who'll be doing all the work."

Marty Magnin smiled and without answering directly picked up his champagne flute. He knew I had agreed. "Detroit," he said, "the Paris of the Midwest . . ."

IV

MAURY AHEARNE ON TAPE (Tape 3, 12:14:27 to 13:21:09):

"There's this guy, Elephant, he's the worst. Five hundred fucking pounds he weighs. He whacked a guy once just by sitting on his face, suffocated the bastard, he can't even breathe and he's got Elephant dropping farts down his windpipe. Another guy, a hype, he's got a bulletproof vest he stole someplace, and he says to Elephant he'll trade it for some crack. Elephant, he says the vest won't stop shit, the crackhead says no, it'll stop the best you got. So Elephant says we'll try it out, and he takes the crackhead down into the cellar, tells him to stand against the wall with the vest on, then he shoots him with this big fucking cannon, with a solid brass round, can penetrate thirty layers of Kevlar. Nearly drove the fucker through the wall. Carried the vest into the wound channel, halfway through his fucking body, the shock waves even ruptured some blood vessels in his brain. Elephant, he was happy as shit, he saved himself the crack he promised this deadbeat, and now he knows for sure his hardware will take down a cop in a vest, research and development, I think, is what he called it, R&D, like he was working out at GM . . ."

◄o►

"So how's it going?'

"So far so good."

"You getting good stuff?"

"Great."

"The cat got your tongue or something? Give me a taste."

"I really haven't listened to the tapes, Marty."

"There's nothing you can remember?"

"A few things."

"Like what, for Christ's sake? I got to pay long-distance rates to get the runaround?"

"Well, let's see." I had been exposed to so much of man's inhumanity to man, directly and indirectly, in the two weeks I had been in Detroit that I had begun to think of the aberrant as the norm. "There's a rapist loose around town, the cops call Fido. That's because he—"

". . . fucks them up the ass, right?"

"Right."

"Doggie style, right?"

"Right."

"So they can't see him, the chicks, right?"

"Right." Marty was not usually that swift. I suspected that Maury Ahearne had already told him the same story that time he was babysitting Marty's publicity junket. Showing him the goods, so to speak, there's more where this came from. Maury Ahearne's stories, as polished and smooth as old stones, were a kind of black-market currency, selling at less than the official rate. He was like a sidewalk vendor looking for a mark, and in Marty and me I think he saw the main chance.

"I like that. Tough to shoot, but a good dialogue scene. A bunch of the guys bullshitting around the precinct . . ." He made a noise into the telephone, something like *ba-ba-ba-BOOM,* I am sure miming at his end of the line the pelvic thrust he imagined the detective (or his actor surrogate) performing in the squad room. "Anything else?"

"Nothing else I can really think of," I said. Not for Marty, not over the telephone, make him wait. "Offhand."

"Say again."

"Nothing else I can really think of. Offhand."

"That's it? Two weeks in Detroit living in the lap of luxury, and that is it, that is all?"

"That's funny."

"I wanted funny, Jack, I could hire Letterman, he's funnier, save myself some expense money."

"No, I mean you're thinking living in downtown Detroit is the lap of luxury. That is really funny. Hilarious." When he did not immediately reply, I said, "Marty, what exactly is your deal with Maury Ahearne?"

"What do you mean what's my deal with him? He's a pal. I slipped him a couple of Jacksons that time I was in Detroit, he said anytime I needed anything, just give him a call, he'd help me out. You trying to tell me I'm out two cees?"

I loved Marty when he tried to be street hip. He was incapable of ever getting the dialogue right. "Forty bucks," I said. "That explains it then."

"You have a hearing problem? I said two hundred."

"That'd be two Franklins, Marty."

As expected bluff and bluster. "What the fuck are you talking about? You back to writing those nut letters again? They have any shrinks in Detroit? Maybe you can find some Polack. They got a lot of them there, I hear."

His heart was not really in it. I laid out for him exactly what Maury Ahearne had said. It was simplicity itself.

◄○►

"So, Jack, how much you getting paid for this movie?" Maury Ahearne stared at me over the cup of lukewarm coffee he held in his strangely soft hands. His fingers were manicured, I noticed for the first time. Cuticles trimmed, moons perfectly shaped. I suddenly remembered an article of faith from my childhood: Someone with no moons on the fingernails had Negro blood. Was it the nuns at St. Peter Klaber's parochial school in San Francisco who had spun this old wives' tale? Or my mother?

More likely my mother. Gertrude Mary Mahoney Broderick, living saint though she was (and indeed so eulogized at her funeral), would occasionally reveal an antipathy to those she invariably referred to as "people of color." The prissy choice of words betrayed perhaps more than she intended, and in a spasm of penance she was always adopting some "little pickaninny" (again her words) with large eyes and a famine-distended stomach she had seen staring from the back pages of the Catholic magazines she subscribed to and read from cover to cover, *America* and *Maryknoll* and *Commonweal*. Every month she would dutifully write to little Joseph in Senegal or tiny Moise in Ghana, occasionally receiving in reply a letter from the nuns who took care of them, Joseph had died of diphtheria or Moise of dysentery, and please keep your contributions coming, dear Mrs. Broderick, our work is never ended, and your reward will come in the kingdom of heaven.

"I don't have a deal yet, Maury." We were sitting in a window booth at the coffee shop across from St. Cyprian's Roman Catholic church. Through the peeling red letters on the window—CAFÉ CYPRIAN, named after the church, I supposed—I watched the small knots of blue-uniformed policemen on the far side of the church slowly disperse. A cop funeral. With all the trimmings that accrued to the rank of the deceased, a decorated captain. An honor guard and the mayor and the chief of police in attendance, the cardinal on the altar. A death not in the line of duty, but a stroke at age fifty-one. In his prime, the monsignor delivering the homily had said. In the saddle, Maury Ahearne had corrected. On top of his girlfriend. Human fallibility seemed to comfort Maury Ahearne. It was an attitude we shared. Maury, with his soft hands wrapped around his coffee cup, his blue patrolman's uniform unbuttoned and peeled back so that the badge and the brass buttons did not show. The uniform appeared to make him uneasy, embarrassed. Worn only at department funerals and at parades he could not escape. I hate the fucking bag, he said, a rare confidence, the bag his blue uniform I figured out after a moment. You know why I never took the sergeant's exam? Because I'm back on patrol wearing the bag if I make it. Department regs. Promotion puts you back in uniform. Out on the fucking streets. Or in a black-and-white with a fucking siren. With some jiveass kid, wants to run upstairs and go break down doors, gets himself decorated and me iced. Fuck that shit.

Maury Ahearne was persistent. "What do you usually get?"

"Never enough."

"Stop jerking me around."

I concentrated on the manicure, the soft hands, hands that had delivered abuse to miscreants who expected to be abused. "I'm not jerking you around, Maury. It varies."

"You know how I find out how much you get?" he said reasonably. I did not reply. This was the kind of cop SOP I was there to learn. You had to hang out to get it. Be available. "I call a pal in the LAPD. I met him once, I had to go out to L.A., pick up a guy, bring him back here for trial. A real sweetheart, this guy. He ties his girlfriend to a chair and throws her out the window. Fourth floor in the back. You know with that thing in her mouth that she sticks up her cunt so she don't get knocked up, you know what I mean . . ."

He snapped his fingers. My cue. "Diaphragm."

"That's it." As always I was struck by Maury Ahearne's ability to find a deviant footnote for every situation. It was as if the stories lent weight to his place in the world. "So she wouldn't scream, I guess. Then he heads for L.A., this guy. LAPD picks him up, holds him till I get there. Which is how I meet my pal. A dumb fuck in Robbery-Homicide, but I got to think he can handle something like this. He knows people who know people in the picture business. He asks around, finds somebody he can squeeze. Everybody can be squeezed one way or the other, you get right down to it. I tell my pal to ask around, maybe squeeze somebody, get me a quote on your last price." A large smile. "I think I get the quote on what your last price is. L.A., Detroit, it's all the same, the way cops operate."

I did not doubt it for a second.

◄O►

"Marty, he wants half."

"Half of what?"

"Half of my fee."

"I can hang with that, Jack."

◄O►

"I tell you how Jimmy Jesus gets it?" Maury Ahearne asked the next afternoon. I was riding shotgun in a beat-up police department Chevy Nova, tape recorder at the ready. Hollywood screenwriter picking up gritty gutter wisdom.

"I don't think so." Don't interrupt, no detours, don't ask how Jimmy Jesus got his name.

"He's having a sitdown with the spades. Ribs, collard greens, the works. Fixing things. This is my side of the street, this is yours. I sell here, you sell there. He picks himself up a slab of ribs, Jimmy, and the dumb fuck chokes on it. Face turns blue. One of the spades gives him the Heimlich hold. I don't know where the fuck he learned it. I thought they were too dumb. Anyway this big spade, Milk Shake I think his name is, he puts his arm around Jimmy's chest, and when he starts to heave, he feels the wire Jimmy's wearing under his shirt. He's looking at fifteen in Jackson, Jimmy, a narcotics beef, so he's working undercover for some federal strike force, he wants to get into witness protection. The spades let him choke. An accident. Nothing on the fucking tape, it turns out except Jimmy dying."

I was struck once again by the element of theatricality in Maury Ahearne's performance, the sense that the 9-mm Beretta in his shoulder holster and the handcuffs hanging from the back of his heavy leather belt were the ultimate social equalizers that made him more than my match. There was about him a tendency to show off, a willingness, perhaps even a need, to push. I was only a tourist in Maury Ahearne's world, a visitor with a limited visa, while he was in harm's way, as contemptuous of my civilian airs and screen credits and brush with the world of fame and money as Al and Leo had been in New York.

"You talk to the Jewboy?"

I had to remember to tell that to Marty Magnin. "He said to say hello, give you his best."

"Don't smart-mouth me. You're deadweight, you know that? I'm supposed to carry you around. Fuck you." His voice began to rise, his face turned a choleric red, and I suspected that were I a felon I would at any second be on the receiving end of those soft manicured hands. "You could get me killed. For a hand-shake and a couple of cees stuffed in my pocket like I'm some kind of fucking headwaiter."

With that Maury Ahearne picked up my tape recorder and threw it out the car window. I looked back and saw it bouncing on the street, three hundred dollars' worth of Sony recharge-able, and in the gathering dusk I could see a pack of black children suddenly appear and begin fighting over it, as if they were predators feeding at a carcass too small to provide for all of them. Then Maury Ahearne stopped the Nova, reached over and opened the door on my side, and said, "Out."

I got out. He drove off. The children abandoned the fight over the tape recorder and surrounded me, demanding money, not really children on closer look, but fifteen-year-olds in high-tops and turned-around baseball caps and hooded sweatshirts, hardened by schoolyard basketball and petty street crime, as big if not bigger than I. I gave them everything I had. It did not seem the place to argue, nor to hope that Maury Ahearne was just circling the block and, like the cavalry, would soon return. In retrospect it seemed that there was a kind of justice in this humiliation, the revenge of Shaamel Boudreau from beyond the grave. But of course that idea derived from my propensity for seeing all sides of every question, my ability to dispense benefit of the doubt as if it was a sacrament. They had my money and had rejected my digital Casio watch as cheap honky shit. Then they simply melted into the early evening, leaving only the ech-oes of their slurs on my color and my manhood and my wristwear. On the skyline I saw a skyscraper and headed for it, the point on a one-man patrol.

Which was how I happened to be having dinner alone that

night on the seventy-third floor of the Renaissance Plaza. With a panoramic view of downtown Detroit. Where the bills from my wallet were helping prime the ghetto economy. Not quite listening to the tube, remote in hand, changing channels as often as I blinked my eyes. Click. *Gilligan's Island*. Gilligan would have kept his money and given them the watch. Click. *M*A*S*H*. Alan Alda would have reasoned with them. Had them get in touch with their feelings. Turned them into caring feminists. I hate fucking Alan Alda. Click. *Geraldo*. Geraldo would have had them onstage, we didn't do the dude, what's the big fucking deal, man. Click.

I contemplated the room-service cart. The iceberg lettuce salad was wilted, the Salisbury steak congealed in its gravy, the coffee cold, the creamer turned. The minibar would have to provide dinner. Macadamia nuts and house-brand vodka, no ice, the ice machine was not working. Why should it? Nothing else at the hotel seemed to work. Options. It was too late to get a plane back to New York. Anyway I would have to take at least a shot at mending fences with Maury Ahearne. Personally I hoped he had suffered a myocardial infarction, but in the event he hadn't, Marty Magnin had said he would go to five large. He had actually said "five large." As always trying to master the lingo. Until then I had a free night on my hands.

To Maury's tapes. Anything to make the time pass. "You got a wife?" I had asked. Getting personal. Dangerous territory. Because as usual I had avoided sharing confidences about myself, volunteering only my name, credits, and, reluctantly, my current widower marital status. I have discovered that my family's history and the millions or the billions I am alleged to have as sole surviving Broderick heir tend to inhibit free discourse.

"Two exes. And a cunt daughter doesn't speak to me since I threw her mother out." That terrible laugh. "She thinks I'm all broke up about not seeing her. Fat chance."

I pressed the Stop button and rewound the tape. It occurred to me that shock value had a law of diminishing returns, and I suspected that between Maury Ahearne and me that law was just about ready to kick in.

I picked up the complimentary copy of the *Free Press* that had come with breakfast. Still folded to the obituary page. The obituaries were a new fascination since birthday number fifty. Five-oh, and the sense of days dwindling down, September, November. Most mornings I turned to the obituaries right after a cursory glance at the headlines. The obits were a relief. A first look to check the ages of the recently deceased. Fifty to sixty. Those hurt. Too close to home. Then cause of death. AIDS now, too often. Some people still hiding it: "39 . . . respiratory illness . . . survived by his mother." More and more were to the point, like deaths in combat: "43, from complications caused by AIDS, his companion, Randy Smith, said." Sometimes "long-term companion." Now giving way to "lover." "His lover, Dwight, said." Cancer was a relief. Lung, liver, prostate, brain tumor. An automobile accident seemed a positive fucking blessing. Although maybe Lizzie wouldn't think so. Screenwriter's Wife. Elizabeth Innocent Broderick, 39. Erase that tape. Can't think about it. That was what put me in Detroit in the first place. Forget accidents. Natural causes. The cardiac cases were the ones I really hated. Congestive heart failure, 52. Cardiac arrest, 50. Coronary artery disease, 57. Over sixty was a good time to check out. Closer to sixty-five, actually. Over seventy was even better. "In his sleep. Had not been ill. Two sets of tennis that afternoon." And maybe a great fuck afterward. Even a lousy fuck. Jerking off, if that's all that's available. "Quietly, in his sleep." That's the one I would like to reserve.

Happier stuff. There was something else, something I remembered from that morning's quick read. Ah, yes. The page listing all that week's singles' get-togethers in the metropolitan Detroit area. Tonight looked busy. *"If She Fixes My Breakfast, Do I Have to Buy Her Dinner?"* (Discovery Singles, Haskell Unitarian Church, Admission $3.) Uh. Stay away from the Unitarians. *"Everything You Need to Know About Love Bugs—Sexually Transmitted Diseases."* (Jewish Singles Connection, Newport Jewish Community Center, $4.) Jesus Christ. Under the circumstances perhaps not the most appropriate response. *"After Hello . . ."* Another Unitarian get-together. Question:

Why so many Unitarian singles? Answer: Because they're Unitarians. *"I Don't Want the Hassle and I Don't Want to Be Alone."* (Roundtable Singles, $5.) All hassle and a lonely night, bet the mortgage on it. *"Sexaholics and Sexual Selfishness."* (Elizabeth Seabury-Walsh Singles Forum, Chatham Neighborhood Nondenominational Church, $7.) A beat-up session on male chauvinist pigs. *"Race & the Supreme Court—Constitutional Issues."* (ACLU Singles Chapter, $6.) Chat, chat, chat, chat. No, no, no, no. *"The Death Penalty—Is It the Solution?"* (Socially Responsible Singles, Beachwood YWCA, $4.)

Socially responsible singles. A type I knew. For whom I had a rap as polished as one of Maury Ahearne's stories. An anodyne for a very difficult day, a chance to salve a wounded sense of self-esteem.

V

I AWOKE AND FELT her side of the bed. She was not there. The digital clock on the bedside table said 3:47. I fumbled for the control switches and lowered the brightness level. The green fluorescent numbers always gave me a headache. A migraine warning. I wondered where she was, glad for the moment it gave me to remember her name. Frances. Francine. Fernanda. Fern, short for Fernanda. That rang a bell. Sort of. Her side of the bed was still warm. Meaning she had not been gone for long. Fern. Am I sure about Fern? The Socially Responsible Single. Divorced mother of two.

"Did you know," I had said at the mixer after the lecture earlier that evening at the Beachwood YWCA, "that before they strap a man into the electric chair they make him . . ."

"What?" The questioner was the woman whose name I now could not remember.

"I'm not sure this is a proper subject . . . what I mean to say is . . ." I searched for the precise phrasing. "It's . . . it's gross."

"The death penalty is gross. The state's taking a life is gross. As you put it."

"Of course."

"Then what do they make the victim do?"

No backing up now. Maury Ahearne was my source. His father had been a prison guard on the death row detail at Jackson State Penitentiary when Michigan still had the death penalty. "They make him . . . cram cotton up his anus." There. It was out.

"That's barbaric."

I speared a wedge of stale Gouda with a toothpick and with my thumb eased it on top of a Ritz cracker. No wine at the Y. Only a nondenominational punch. "And then they make him wear a rubber diaper."

"I guess I don't have to ask why." She was the one who had asked most of the questions during the Q-and-A session after the public defender from the Death Watch Association had made his presentation. On the racial configuration of juries in death penalty cases. On homicide rates in states that had banned the death penalty versus those in states that exercised it. On the proportion of death penalty convictions in cases involving white against white, white against black, black against black, black against white. I concentrated on the questions. Or to be more specific the questioner. On the way she absentmindedly scratched her ribs when she talked, right hand left rib, left hand right rib, the action outlining her breast against the silk blouse she was wearing, some shade of tan or beige, the half acorn of her nipple pressed against the fabric until she stopped scratching. I focused on the way the woman's glasses slipped down her nose when she talked, and on the way her eyes seemed to lock into some further plane as her thoughts took shape. It was disconcerting to be the object of that gaze. "How do you know this, Mr. . . . ?"

I was not wearing a paper name tag. Nor was she, I noticed. "Broderick. It's research. For a project I'm working on."

"On the death penalty?" I wondered if her commitment to the abolition of capital punishment would outlast this session of social responsibility.

"On the law enforcement community." A tiptoe along the fault line of truth.

"I thought there was only one attitude in that community."

She had begun to scratch again. I could not concentrate on what she was saying as she scratched, even though I fastened my eyes on her face and not the swell and the acorn under the silk. Time to act. After all, how much different was a Socially Responsible Singles meeting from an ad in a magazine Personals column. She could have hung the Personal around her neck: "Classy, sensual DWF seeks gentle, intelligent, sensitive, thoughtful, imaginative, physically fit SWM (40–50) to share the joy of commitment." Scratch commitment and I more or less qualified. Sudden thought about Personals: Why didn't any SWM or DWM or SJM ever write, "So horny I'd fuck the crack of dawn." I would like to see the response on that one. Especially from the Socially Responsible Single. "Would you like to get a real drink?" I said suddenly. No. No hard stuff. She was not the type. "A glass of Zinfandel." Oh, God, I thought I was beyond using wine chat. "Chardonnay." Christ. "I'm parched."

"I'll get my coat."

She drove a silver four-door sedan, with a dashboard so full of climate- and audio-control buttons that it was as if you were not driving a car but commanding a spacecraft, like the *Challenger* that blew up over Canaveral, with the schoolteacher from New Hampshire, and the black and the Japanese-American astronauts, and the Jewish girl from Ohio, and the three crew-cut Protestants who made up the rest of the crew, so gender- and demographically balanced, it occurred to me as I sat next to this woman, that perhaps the *Challenger* had to blow up, it had enough constituencies to satisfy the needs of the gods. This was the kind of extraneous idea I contemplate more and more as I get older and find myself about to couple with someone with whom I do not wish to share a commitment, that terrible word from the Personals, topped only by *relationship*. Irrelevant thoughts passing as conversation. Noise. An aural blockade.

So: She drove a Cressida. Maybe that was why the automobile industry was in the crapper, even people in Detroit were buying Japanese. The women I had known in California had not driven

Cressidas, nor any Toyota cars, for that matter, the Toyota was an extra car for the maid. The women I had known in California, the women Lizzie did not try to conceal her dislike for, drove BMWs in the 300 line, the bigger BMWs in the 700 class were a husband's car. No Cressidas. Reason enough to leave L.A. right there.

There was a baby seat in the back, facing the rear as it was supposed to, the baby seat another surprise, a child not an element I had factored in when I winnowed through the list of singles' mixers in the *Free Press*, and some pink and yellow hair bows suggesting that the child who used the baby seat was a girl. She was talking now, something about Humacao, on the Atlantic coast of Puerto Rico, had I ever been there, the swimming was dangerous on the Atlantic, then something about a Club Med somewhere, then something about Cozumel, resorts, she was a travel agent, that explained the resort chat, she was a part owner of a travel agency in one of the lesser Pointes. A less Grosse Pointe. Joke. Pointless-thought division. Not a particularly felicitous time to be in the travel business, I had volunteered, looking out the car window and wondering exactly where we were, and she had said why, and I said that from my limited exposure to the city, Detroit seemed to be in the grip of hard times, a fucking disaster area, I wanted to say, the South Bronx looks like Humacao compared with this, and she had said, I get by, things will get better, I have to believe that. A depressive, I thought. Just what I need. One to match me.

But a direct one at least. With no bullshit about what we were going to do when we reached our destination. We had already made a pit stop, at an all night minimall. The drugstore had decals of all the credit card companies in the window, as well as the health care prescription programs, PCS and RECAP, and underneath the decals two signs, one that said THIS STORE UNDER THE PROTECTION OF JESUS CHRIST, and right below another that said CONDOMS AVAILABLE AT CHECKOUT COUNTER. Which was where she was headed, even as I was wondering if Jesus Christ had staked out a position on safe sex. "Lubricated or unlubri-

cated?" she said, and I realized she was talking to me, my
choice, and all I could do was give a ponderously rakish nod as
the black woman behind the cash register impassively moni-
tored my response, the black woman wearing dreadlocks that
reminded me, a sharp unexpected pain, of the late Shaamel
Boudreau, and then I followed up the nod with a silly little
comme ci, comme ça smile, even in this liberated age the first
time a woman had ever asked me a question like that, why not
ask if I want extra ribbing, too, although I suppose that's her
call, not mine.

◄○►

Now she got back into bed. For a moment I panicked. I was not
all that sure about Fern. Maybe it was Fawn. Shit, maybe even
Caroline or Beth.

"Fern was crying."

There. That was it. Fern was the daughter, the Mensa child
with an IQ of 179, with a bullet. Terence was Fern's baby
brother. Fern and Terence. Fern wouldn't go to bed, the babysitter had said. A pain in the ass is what the babysitter, with all
her heavy sighs, had meant about Fern. The babysitter was seventeen, overweight, a blimp with zits like BBs (except kids
don't have BB guns anymore, they buy the real thing, a semiau-
tomatic with extra clips), three Milky Way wrappers and an
empty bag of nacho-flavored corn chips on the coffee table, and
she looked me up and down, a knowing goddamn look, like she
was wondering if I could still get it up, figuring that was what I
was there for. Fern's mother said she would clean up, would I
give the sitter a ride home in the Cressida. The sitter sat close,
hip to hip, as if she was my date, and when I stopped in front of
her apartment complex she just waited there, and finally she
said, You can feel me up if you want. Going to the slam for
criminal trespass of a minor was not on my agenda, thank you
very much. I kept my hands firmly on the steering wheel until
she flounced out of the car. She fucks everybody, you know, the
babysitter said. Her parting shot. Jesus God, what a day, what a
night, how do I get out of this? No way. I had to bring the

fucking Cressida back. And now, please, what in the name of Christ is the name of this woman lying next to me who had the genes to produce a Mensa child and whose fat babysitter says she fucks everybody. Maybe that's how she learned to do it so great. With all that experience.

I had an erection. If we began to get it on again maybe I could remember her name. A hard-on to jog the memory. A new physiological concept. Something for the medical journals. The Broderick Effect. Try the Beth area. Liz. Betsy.

Lily.

A sigh of relief. Lily. Lily what. Lily White. That was it. Lily White.

Her fingers moved down my stomach. Like a centipede. She touched me. Then she licked my cock, and quickly put it in her mouth, as if to see if it was a good fit. "Thumping and beating and hard as a rock," she said when she just as quickly removed it, every syllable equally stressed. "We used to say that in the girl's locker room at Mount St. Mary's. None of us knew what it meant."

She had learned.

"Lily. Jesus. Lily. Jesus. Jesus. Mama." Wait a minute. I didn't say Mama.

"Mama."

Oh, shit. Fern. Lily scrambled up as I tried to pull the sheet over me. The sheet stuck up in the air.

"Why is the man making so much noise?"

"It's all right, Fern." She was surreptitiously removing a hair from her tongue. Things to dislike about sex. God. We had talked about that earlier, after the first time. What do you dislike most about sex, she had said, after I had fucked her backside front, her choice, her tits hanging down like triangular bugger grips. The question an indication of the quirkiness of her mind. Most people want to know what you like best, what kinkiness, what equipment, what multiple of participants, what obscure position, what melding of what member or aid to what orifice or protuberance, primary or secondary. Dislike? What is there to

dislike? Lots, she said. The bad breath in the morning. Agreed.
The curly strand of pubic hair on the tongue. Absolutely. The
dab of shit on the rubber. Definitely. The acrid smell of
postcoital micturition. Ah, yes. She was a tenured professor of
fucking's downside. Your turn, she had said. All the above, I
said. No, no, something just yours. Ah. Okay. Taking off my
clothes, I said finally. No one looks good taking off his clothes.
It was too humiliating to elucidate, but she insisted. Well. Does
your stomach fall out over the elastic band of your shorts? A
concern at my suck-it-up-suck-it-in age. Is there a small embarrassing streak on your underwear? Sit down to take off your
shoes and socks, stand up to take off pants and underwear.
Leave your pants on the floor or hang them over a chair. One
way a slob, the other a priss. Rip off your shirt the way they do
it in the movies and you can't put it on again afterward. There is
no rakish way to undress.

Why is that fucking child staring at me?

"Were you hurting the man, Mama, when you were biting
him?"

Something else to dislike about sex. A precocious child catching you in the act.

"No, Fern." Lily could not seem to find her robe. Nor her
slippers. Her shoes were under a chair. She put them on, using
Fern's shoulder for support. I tried not to laugh. A naked
woman with black high-heel Charles Jourdan pumps. "See,
Fern, he's laughing. I didn't hurt him. How's Terence?"

"Terence never wakes up. When he sleeps, his peepee sometimes sticks up like the man's."

I thought, Terence's peepee probably had more resonance
than mine right now.

"Let's go back to bed." She took her daughter by the hand, a
naked woman in black pumps. "School day tomorrow."

She came back a few moments later, carrying a terrycloth
bathrobe. She—why do I have such trouble calling her Lily?—
said she must have left it in Fern's room earlier. Now she re-
arranged the robe on the foot of the bed, then got in under the

sheets. Her hand found me again. No answer. She said, "I guess we can forget about that."

"I'm sorry."

"Listen. A seven-year-old who strolls in wondering why Mommy is biting the man's peepee is not one of the greatest turn-ons in the world." She ran her hands through her hair. "You think she'll be telling that to some shrink when she's the same age as I am now, and wondering why she's so fucked up?"

I made a noise in my throat signifying yes, no, or maybe.

"You don't even like to think of your mother going down on someone. My mother's sixty-two now. I can't imagine her giving head to some guy, carries a return ticket in his pocket."

"Oh." Guilty as charged. Sexual harassment, one-night-stand subsection.

"I looked at it. It's on the desk. Next to your money clip and your Hertz rental agreement and a dollar ninety-seven in coins." Bed talk. It seemed nonjudgmental. But rarely, of course, does postcoital tristesse not find fault. "You're a divorced woman with two small children, thirty-three years old, no alimony, chancey child support, you notice things about men. Like a return ticket. If I ever write my autobiography, I think I'll call it *Open Return*."

"Mmmmmmmmm." Or no comment.

"I've been divorced three years in July, and I haven't had a single relationship with a man since." Why do women feel this compulsion to talk to me? This human sponge soaking up confidences I would prefer not to hear. "The perils of living in Detroit. Oh, I get laid. Getting laid is never the problem. Not for a socially responsible single." Lizzie used to say I was not giving. If this was giving I would prefer not to give. "I've slept with thirty-one men since my divorce. Once each. I mean, one weekend, one Super Bowl week, one night. I think every one of them had an open-return ticket. In the travel business, you tend to meet people with return tickets."

I wondered how many of those weekends she had spent at Humacao or Cozumel or that Club Med somewhere.

"They never call the next time they come back through town. Adultery on the road." I thought she was careering toward commitment, and her inability to attract it, perhaps even to give it. In my experience, conversations about commitment usually ended with tears, or recriminations, usually both. "Do you think I'm a slut?"

"Of course not." A discussion I would rather not have in a terrace condominium in a suburb of Detroit whose name I could not remember. As I had not remembered the name of the condo's owner. I should have bailed out when I was asked my preference in condoms. Unlubricated was what she had bought, it turned out, lubricity not being her problem. And she had bought a dozen. Either she was expecting me to stay a long time, or her motto was *Semper Paratus*. Was I number thirty-one or thirty-two? And how could she remember so exactly? Did she keep a dossier on all of us? And know the cities we returned to?

"I don't think so either. Although I think I'd have a hard time proving it if I ever got involved in a custody fight. Which I won't. Harry has the kids every Christmas and for three weeks every summer. He and Patty've gone skiing the last two Christmases, and left them with me, and he's never kept them the full three weeks in the summer."

I thought, I am on information overload. Whatever happened to name, rank, serial number. Harry and Patty. Two new players. The ex-husband and new wife. Or maybe live-in?

Lily felt me again. That was more like it. Or should have been. No luck. Suddenly she sat up, leaned over, and kissed me on the forehead. Her voice was insistent. "Would you please go? Just call a cab and go. Go. Please go."

◄◦►

It was not until later that I thought putting on your clothes in such a situation is at least as humiliating as taking them off.

But:

Had Lily White not told me to go, please go, I would not have been in that taxi, at nearly five o'clock in the morning, sitting behind a hopelessly lost Chaldean driver, a stranger in a strange land, a stranger to its customs and its language and especially to the geography of the city where he was plying his trade, illegally so, of course, without a green card and using the hack license of his wife's cousin, violating in the process God knows how many ordinances in the transportation codes of metropolitan Detroit and Wayne County (the storyteller always accumulating stories and coincidences to explicate and preserve the moment); then, to repeat, I would not have been in that taxi out near Hamtramck, the cab heading in a direction exactly opposite that in which I wanted to be going, when at nearly five o'clock in the morning it hit a dog, a mangy mongrel dog that belonged to Melba Mae Toolate.

"You murdering asshole" were the first words Blue Tyler ever spoke to me.

BLUE

"... one of the most mysterious and potent figures
in the history of cinema ... she was that rare performer,
and certainly the only child, to penetrate to the heart
of screen acting ... a wanton presence provoked
by the idea of being seen."

—Barton Turnbull, *Sight & Sound*

I

"MEETING CUTE" was the way Chuckie O'Hara described the way I met Blue Tyler. That most basic and most enduring (some might even say endearing) of Hollywood clichés. Meet cute, you save time and eliminate dialogue. Example: A man and a woman meet at a pajama counter. He only wants the bottom, she only wants the top. They share the pair, complications ensue, and when they finally make it to bed a hundred and twenty script pages later, the soundtrack plays "But if, baby, I'm the bottom, you're the top," slow fade to black.

It was Chuckie's contention that Blue had always known in some inchoate way, because she was a creature of the movies and because the films she made at Cosmopolitan Pictures, by edict of J. F. French, always had happy endings, that one day someone would rediscover her, and the more unlikely the locale the more dramatic, the more cinematic, that rediscovery would be. It was not a conscious move that had brought her to Detroit and the wrong side of the tracks, but with her innate story sense, that ability she never lost, even when she was at her most down-and-out, to project what was best for her character, Detroit and her menagerie of house pets and the multiple husbands, many of whose names she claimed not to remember, and the endocarditis and the emphysema—all the factors real and fancied—provided the perfect contrast to the life that late she had led, the star that once she had been.

Like most actors and actresses, Blue Tyler preferred anecdote to fact and mistook, as if by act of will, one for the other. Anecdotes are nothing but factoids of questionable provenance, burnished to a high gloss and purged of subtext in the interest of keeping the narrative flowing, for best effect usually set against gilded venues (or mean streets for contrary effect) and populated with the famous and the familiar as background atmosphere, as if the famous names and the gilded venues and mean streets certified authenticity. Whether biographical or autobiographical, all anecdote is essentially self-aggrandizing, allowing the anecdotalist to bask in his or her own created (or someone else's reflected) glory, and to demonstrate whatever it is in the anecdotalist's interest to demonstrate, either for his or her own good, or for someone else's ill fortune (an equally winning hand under certain propitious conditions). As these anecdotes are usually provided by professional storytellers, the not-altogether-unbecoming result is that the stories show folk tell about themselves have the shorthand sense of being scenes from a screenplay, with dialogue, set decoration, and camera movements. In such circumstances, truth is an acceptable casualty, the narrative all.

Fame once experienced is a narcotic. In the theater of her dreams Melba Mae Toolate was still the famous Blue Tyler, and like so many famous people, she accepted the kindness of strangers as natural acts of fealty, no more than what she was due. At Cosmopolitan's Little Red Schoolhouse (so called because studio art directors had built it on a soundstage and dressed it to resemble a prairie school, which it often was, in Cosmo's low-budget program Westerns), it had been drilled into her that the toughest audience of all was that soundstage dress circle of hardened grips, gaffers, best boys, makeup men, and wardrobe mistresses, those who even in her adversity she still regarded as "the little people." As I was a writer, and therefore in her hierarchical scale a little person, I could never be immunized against her magic; in her mind her wish must always be my command. If she was to be rediscovered, if that was what the fates had ordained, then the denouement must be playable in a Blue Tyler vehicle. Little Sister Susan and Lily of the Valley transmogrified by the ravages of time into Apple Annie, a comeback vehicle she might consider if the billing and the money were right, and if the shitbirds in charge did not try to bring her to heel, harness her spirit, as they had always tried to do when she was on top. (Fuck them, she would say, suddenly, venomously, eyes aflame, like sulphur matches, the old memories like fishhooks caught in her gills, and fuck them again!) Admittedly a risky bet, a long shot, but if it worked, what a payoff.

I I

MAURY AHEARNE'S watch commander said he was in court
testifying. I found him in the cafeteria during a recess. He
did not seem surprised to see me. Nor curious about what
might have happened after he threw me out of his car the previ-
ous day. To me a century before. "Say hello to Jerome Highsmith," he said, waving in the general direction of a huge black
man standing in front of the cafeteria's bank of vending machines.

Jerome Highsmith kicked a candy machine with the toe of a
steel-plated industrial work shoe. It teetered until I thought it
was going to topple over on him before rocking back into place.
A second kick, and a third. Still no coins in the coin return, no
candy bar in the tray. Jerome Highsmith stepped back, taking
the measure of the machine, then removed his moth-eaten
brown sweater. Deliberately he wrapped it over his right hand
and made a fist, clenching and unclenching it. Suddenly
glass shattered as Jerome Highsmith smashed his covered fist
through the vending machine's display window. I started as if a
gun had gone off. Jerome Highsmith stared belligerently at me,
daring me to object, then reached through the shards of glass
and removed a Reese's Peanut Butter Cup. He stripped away

the foil, licking his fingers for any chocolate that might have stuck to them, then pushed the whole bar into his mouth, closing his eyes as he chewed, a dreamy look on his face.

"I would have thought that was against the law."

Maury Ahearne scratched a scab on his scalp and examined the residue in his fingernails. "So make a citizen's arrest." More scratching, more scab. "I bust him, then he doesn't testify when we go back inside. He doesn't testify, there's no case, and this guy Emmett that's on trial walks. It's a question of who you want on the bricks. Emmett or Jerome." He smiled. One of those smiles designed to show how ignorant I was in the ways of his world. "Doesn't mean a shit to me. Jerome took out a guy for a pack of cigarettes once, he's such a solid citizen. Emmett's up because he did a door-to-door vacuum cleaner salesman. The reason he did him is he's got this new gun, a Glock he stole from some white guy shoots at a target range, you know, with the earmuffs so the noise don't hurt his ears." In his world guns were supposed to make noise, and the noise was supposed to scare people, and people who wore earmuffs not to hear the noise were pussy hairs. "He wanted to see if it worked, Emmett." Another smile. "It did." The inevitability of the result seemed to satisfy him. "So Emmett stole his wallet and nine Hoovers while he was at it. A Cuban guy, the salesman. Ignorant fuck, thinking he was going to sell a vacuum cleaner to those people, you ever look at the shitholes they live in? But 'Cuban' means 'white' to the D.A. Killing white, can't have that, he says. Waste of time. He's going to walk, Emmett, Jerome or no Jerome." It was like listening to an oral historian of urban carnage and anthropology. "Twelve jurors, two alternates, and ten of the fourteen are wearing shades, cool as shit. Judge loses his car keys yesterday, he was pissing and moaning about it to the court reporter, and one of the jurors raises his hand and says, 'Your Holiness,' I swear to Christ, that's what he says, 'Your Holiness,' and then he proceeds to tell His Holiness how to hot-wire his fucking car. So I ran a check on him. What he does is work in a chop shop. Naturally. And draw unemployment. Naturally." The detective detecting. "Forget the judge's car, this guy could hot-wire an F-16. Then break it down and sell the spare parts to Saddam whatever the fuck that A-rab's last name is. Bet the fucking house Emmett's going to walk."

I looked around the cafeteria. On the walls were shadowy outlines of oversized graffiti cocks and cunts that custodial scrubbing had not quite succeeded in erasing.

"So." Another Maury Ahearne smile. "You survived."

No thanks to you, I thought. Perhaps he had been standing by the day before after all, ready to move in if the situation did get out of hand. I was not going to give him the satisfaction of asking. He would have answered that my murder was not worth the paperwork or the overtime. I had also bought a new tape recorder. Two, in fact. A spare in case Maury Ahearne destroyed another one. "I need some information."

He showed no interest.

"I was coming back to the hotel last night . . ."

"From where . . ."

"Someplace out near Grosse Pointe."

"What were you doing out there?"

"Getting laid." I was learning. It was exactly the kind of answer I knew would satisfy him. "Anyway. I was in a cab, the driver got lost, the cab hit a dog, the lady that owned the dog, some kind of bag lady, she got all twisted out of shape, and the long and the short of it is she gave a cop some lip and got herself a citation."

"So."

"I'd like to know something about her. Help her out if I can. In some way." It sounded fraudulent even to me, as I knew it must to him, suspicion being the coin of his realm.

"You're yanking my chain."

I was suddenly very sick of Maury Ahearne. "Yes, I am." Why not admit it? It had the virtue of honesty, a virtue that had not exactly informed our relationship. "I'm curious about her. If that's not good enough for you, go fuck yourself."

It was a tone he was used to, one he would work with. "So

what's in it for me?" He held up five fingers. I held up two. "Two now, three later," he said. It seemed safer not to bargain. Five hundred for everything he could get on Melba Mae Toolate. A name I had not even known until it appeared in Walter Scott's *Personality Parade* along with mine the day Lizzie was killed.

Maury Ahearne could not resist the last word. "You're still jerking me around. That's okay. When I find out why, and I will, we'll play some more."

—◇—

Maury Ahearne had the information by the next afternoon. Melba Mae Toolate lived in the Autumn Breeze RV camp near Hamtramck, Slot 123, Forsythia Lane. She had been married eleven times, according to the records kept by the domestic relations court, she had been arrested seven times for disturbing the peace, usually for fighting with her neighbors in various RV camps over the number of dogs and cats, sometimes twenty or more, she let live in her trailer of the moment. The courts finally made her give all her animals save one to the pound. At various times she had used the names Mae Tyler and Melba Blue. In 1979 there had been a drug bust in Ypsilanti, but the charges were reduced to disorderly conduct and were subsequently dropped, without a hearing, for insufficient evidence. She was currently unemployed, and there was no record of recent employment, nor any record of taxes of any kind having been withheld.

"That's the funny part," Maury Ahearne said.

"Why?"

"She's not on welfare. No public assistance of any kind. I checked all the way to Lansing."

"Which means?"

"Well, it's not exactly pig heaven she's living in out there, but she's not on the streets either. She seems to survive without a tin cup."

I considered his silence. "So someone must be kicking in something."

The awful smile. "Unless she's got one of those trust funds rich people like you got."

I vertically creased three one-hundred-dollar bills and handed them to him. "Thanks, Maury."

"I'll be in touch."

On that I should have made book.

I I I

IMAGINE IT:

The Autumn Breeze trailer park and recreational-vehicle encampment, with its RVs and house trailers neatly lined up like a military armored column, tanks and APCs on parade, each mobile home with corrugated aluminum awnings, some with metal window boxes filled with plastic flowers that had long since lost whatever color they might once have had. The streets in the trailer park had been carefully laid out into lanes, and every lane was named after a flower, Camellia Lane, Poinsettia Lane, Forsythia Lane. Every RV and trailer had its own slot, with a sidewalk and a mailbox and a tiny patch of sad brown lawn that could be crossed in a stride and a half.

Slot 123 Forsythia Lane then: The trailer was pale blue and an even paler bleached yellow. The name on the mailbox was "Occupant," an attempt at humor that antedated the current tenant, although she said she was perfectly comfortable with the designation, an assertion one could hardly doubt, as she had by choice (as well as by circumstance) been one of the world's missing for over thirty years. She claimed not to know the names of her neighbors, and could identify them only by their physical ailments, the randy old fart with the prostate cancer in Slot 122, I give him a semi, she said, and the old prune with Alzheimer's in 124, and there was one in 210 over on Poinsettia that died in her sleep, and no one knew she'd gone until the smell got so bad, the mailman complained, what happened was her cat had chewed up her nose and sucked out her eyeballs, can't blame the kitty, nothing else to eat. She said her neighbors called her Mrs. Toolate, pronouncing it Too-Late, which suits me fine.

When the item about Blue Tyler had appeared in Walter Scott's *Personality Parade*, Melba Mae Toolate said, she was living in Pontiac then, and she had said no, she was not the one, she was Melba, not Myrna Marie, like Walter said, and she was alive and here to tell about it, not like that Myrna Marie, dead and buried in Kalamazoo, anyway she was only a Toolate by marriage, but she had always heard tell that her husband's second cousin once or twice removed had once been in show business, *Your Show of Shows* she thought was the program the second cousin by marriage had been on, then she had a mastectomy and retired, she had heard, singers with one boob not being much in demand, what with the strapless gowns they all wear, and their titties all pushed up, that was all she knew about it, and anyway that branch of the family pronounced it fancy, Too-lah-tee, la-di-da. The explanation seemed to satisfy, but she moved from that RV camp near Pontiac a week or so later, so she could be closer to her daughter, she said at the time, a daughter she had never before mentioned, come to think of it, and moved to Hamtramck.

There was foil crimped in the windows of the trailer, a precaution against the summer heat, and a skirt of heavy fabric wrapped around the undercarriage, insulation against the winter cold, and there was a fake wrought-iron fence leading to the two rickety metal steps outside the front door, and on the top step there was a worn hemp doormat on which could be made out the word WELCOME.

—◇—

Well, hell, yes, she said, I know who you are, you were in Walter Scott's *Personality Parade* the same day I was, and if that's not a pisser, I don't know what is, we're in the same newspaper column and then, what is it now, six, seven months later, you hit my dog, then you turn up the next day at Number 123 Forsythia Lane, Ms. Toolate, you say, get that, *Ms.*, in Hamtramck, Michigan, you don't say *Ms.*, asshole, then the fancy-Dan Toolah-tee, my name is Jack Broderick, shit, honey, you are big rich, richer than Mr. French and Arthur put together, of course I know who Jack Broderick is, Bro Broderick's brother, Hugh Broderick's son, I think I might've even fucked your dad one time, or it could've been one of those Rockefellers, maybe it was Bill Paley or Jock Whitney, whoever it was he painted his pecker with gentian violet, because he was afraid of the clap, or was that my driver on *Freedom Belle*, anyway, I would have gone to Mr. French and complained if some writer came up with a coincidence like that, you and me meeting the way we did when we were both in Walter Scott's *Personality Parade,* and Mr. French would have said, Arthur, that was his son Arthur, Arthur was my fiancé in those days, Arthur, go get Lamar Trotti or Nunnally Johnson or Reilly Holt or one of them to smooth out the story line, Reilly Holt was Chuckie O'Hara's boyfriend, I bet you didn't know that, he was a big-time Commie, but you got to admit it needs work, the way we met, and there's one thing I was always good at, that was structure, you can ask Arthur, he'll tell you, I was the best on the lot, and it's cold out there, isn't it, come on in here and take a load off your feet, do I have a story to tell you, and one more thing, now that I think of it, maybe I do like that coincidence, it has a certain je ne sais quoi, and I bet you never thought you'd hear any of that French shit in some RV camp in Hamtramck, Michigan, the reason is I took French at the studio school and I always had a French governess all those years I was at Cosmo, the number-one box office star in the country, that was Mr. French's idea, Mr. French's French idea, that's cute, it's a fairy tale is what it is, the way we met, and fairy tales was what the Industry was all about in my time, before you got all this *Raging Bull* shit, with the dirty words, they only make pictures about fat people today, and Italians, and whatever happened to tall actors, Randy Scott was tall, Cary, too, and Clark, but every one of them around today is a Singer midget, Richard Dreyfuss, Dustin What's-his-face, Pacino, none of them any taller than an agent, that Dustin's got a face like a dirt road, you ask me, and you out there in 124, stop listening, she's loony, and what's-his-face in 122, he wants to get in my pants, and I want to tell you, if he ever knew whose pants he wanted to get into, he would cream in those polyester jeans he wears, he probably beat off in the balcony when he saw me in *Little Sister Susan,* and you know something, I didn't know this at the time, because the publicity department handled all my mail, I never saw it except when President Roosevelt wrote me, or someone like that Chiang Kai whatever his last name was, the Chinaman, but some of my fan mail had come in it, Arthur told me that. *Jism,* can you believe it?

◄◦►

God, she was on.

A motor driven by an energy that had been bottled up, capped like an oil fire, for decades. Did you ever bang your finger in a car door? The blood wells up under the nail, the pain is excruciating, throbbing, then the doctor drills a hole in the nail, the pressure is relieved, it's like coming, you feel so good, the blood spurts like a geyser.

She was that geyser.

Old Faithful.

Or Old Unfaithful.

As the case may be.

◄◦►

Imagine again, this time the interior of that recreational vehicle in Slot 123, Forsythia Lane, Hamtramck, Michigan 48212:

One large space cut into three sections by two accordion room dividers. A king-sized bed, covered with an Indian blanket, so completely filled the rear third of the trailer that there was no room to maneuver on either side of it without risking a

barked shin. Next to the bedroom a small bathroom with a
shower, a chemical toilet, and in the medicine cabinet, along
with the over-the-counter pills and the Medicare prescriptions
for calcium deficiency and for bloat (yes, I looked, of course I
looked), an unopened package of twelve ribbed Trojan-Enz
condoms. The living space was in the center section. An ancient
Sylvania television set, vintage 1950, with a circular screen. An
artifact, it turned out. *Un objet trouvé,* she said in her best
French-governess French, but where it was found she did not
offer. Two VCRs, Mitsubishis with twin digital autotracking,
and a 30-inch Panasonic color TV set with wraparound sound,
cable ready, 156 channels. A couch with bad springs from
Goodwill. Four wooden kitchen chairs, none of which matched.
A portable Royal typewriter with the question mark and the
dollar sign missing. Oilcloth curtains, once pink, now faded by
the sun. Worn and patched diamond-pattern linoleum floors.

The final section contained the kitchen, with its Mr. Coffee
coffeemaker, a six-slice toaster, a gelato maker, a Cuisinart, a
microwave oven, a two-burner stove, and a Sub-Zero freezer
crammed full of packaged food, junk food, but that's another
story, it'll have to wait, in due time, don't worry, it explains the
top-of-the-line appliances, those two VCRs, the giant TV, the
Cuisinart, and the gelato machine as well. Empty half-pint bottles of supermarket-brand vodka were lined up along the base-
boards like so many ducks in a shooting gallery. The glasses had
all once been jam or peanut butter jars. Stuck to the freezer with
a miniature magnetized naked woman was a mimeoed list of
weekly events at St. Anton the Magyar Roman Catholic Church
in Hamtramck—a get-together for new converts, prayer sessions
for divorced parishioners, a meeting of the Shut-in Committee,
Mrs. M. M. Toolate, chairperson. There was a two-shelf book-
case, its only volumes movie star biographies—Marilyn Monroe
and Carole Landis and Lana Turner and Joan Crawford and
Hedy Lamarr and Elizabeth Taylor and Marlene Dietrich. No
men, two suicides, and a million and a half fucks and blow jobs.
Her description of her library, not mine. On top of the book-

case a quilted tea cozy, and under the cozy not a teapot but the pint-sized special Oscar given her in 1939 by the Motion Picture Academy of Arts and Sciences for being the Industry's top box office draw three years running, all before she was ten years old.

And everything neat as a pin.

Baby, she said, I just fell off the planet earth.

IV

WHO WAS SHE?
What was she?
That, I think, the more difficult question.
Genius. Whore. Individualist. Iconoclast. Liar. Free spirit.
Bag lady. Madwoman. Spoiled. Willful. Pathological. Self-indul-
gent. Self-destructive. An eternal child. A fantast willing to sacrifice everything—fame, career, and fortune—to satisfy her need
to flout convention. A case of severely arrested development
whose first priority was always the maintenance of her own in-
terests. A moral force more honest and uncompromising than
her contemporaries. Everyone living or dead seemed to have an
opinion about Blue Tyler, whether they knew her or not. Even
Maury Ahearne, who claimed not to care about her, weighed in
with "crazy cunt."
So.
Take your pick.
All the above would be my choice. Including the verdict of
Maury Ahearne.

—◦—

Her filmography, which I diligently gathered over time via computer modem from newspaper morgues (*The New York Times*
and the *Los Angeles Times*, in particular, although the tabloids

and the penny press in both cities, most of them no longer publishing, contributed their own particularly raffish take, too); from an assiduous search-and-save of Winchell and Hedda and Louella and Kilgallen and Jimmy Fidler and Jack O'Brian, all gone to their eternal reward now (skewed views, but dramatically interesting, adding primary colors, the softer tones in the historical palette not coming naturally to gossip columnists); from interviews with those who it turned out knew her less well than they claimed, and with others (more interesting) unwilling (in some instances with good reason) to share easily their considerable fund of memories; from delving into the archives of mainstream motion picture libraries and the dusty files of college film societies as well—all these many sources yielded few clues, and the ones they did yield were conflicting, contradictory, and in some cases shamelessly fabricated, the irony being (as I was to learn) that the fabrications did not do justice to the real story; or the real story as I (another fabricator: an added spin) began to imagine it, with inductive leaps (mine) and addenda (these much later) from long-forgotten rap sheets and criminal-investigation files still open after nearly fifty years because the capital crimes reported therein remain unsolved. Meaning murder, P.C. 187 in the California penal code, on which the statute of limitations never runs out.

Ah, yes. Murder is part of the mix. Something I had not anticipated. My mistake.

◄○►

Caveats:

I admit a certain impatience with Hollywood and all its orthodoxies. I hear that film is truth at twenty-four frames a second, Godard's formulation, and I want to grab an AK-47 and spray the room. Try it this way: truth at sixty words a minute. I like writing movies. I am good at it, quick and always in demand. Movies provide me a good living that I don't actually need, with more laughs than in most businesses; the heartbreaks, such as they are, are generally carnal. I don't get all twisted out of shape by the law of nature (Hollywood division) that says a director who gets paid twice as much as I do is therefore twice as smart as I am. I like the Marty Magnin types I work for, and am willing to entertain the idea that I like them in part because they give me something to which I can feel superior. I have no particular enthusiasm for the masters who used to be called directors and are now called filmmakers, Hitchcock, for example, and Ford, and only occasionally do I warm to Chaplin. Nor am I won over by the argument that black-and-white is the real cinema (that shit word; they shot in black-and-white because color was clumsy and expensive and washed out, it was certainly not for any artistic reason) and that movies (a far better word) took a turn for the worse when sound came in. I do not haunt the rerun houses to see Garbo in *Queen Christina*, I have never gone to the Cinémathèque Française in Paris to see *Pandora's Box* at four in the morning (have never gone to the Cinémathèque at all, in fact), and I have no position on the importance of Gregg Toland's lighting to the films of William Wyler, or William Cameron Menzies's sets on the success of *Gone With the Wind*.

All this is by way of saying, however defensively, that the cult of Blue Tyler was one of which I was only vaguely aware, and I paid no more attention to it, and to the cinéastes who worshiped at its altar, than I did to the cult of Jerry Lewis that the French in all their perversity have perpetuated. For me, Blue Tyler was only an occasional presence lingering on my TV screen for a second or so in those many predawn hours when I scrolled through the channels with my remote, searching for a sedative movie to relieve my chronic insomnia, something talky without too much movement or fancy cutting that might delay sleep. If asked before I met her, before (God help me) I studied her pictures in an editing room (I can tell you now that in her famous—sweet Jesus Christ, even I am succumbing to the fatuous vocabulary of the cinéaste—Haitian fire dance with Shelley Flynn and Chocolate Walker Franklin in *Carioca Carnival*, there were 177 separate setups), if asked, I repeat, what she looked like, I would have been hard put to give an answer.

Shirley Temple I could describe: moon face, a ringlet of curls, the pouty lower lip when she cried, the nauseating smile she directed at Bill "Bojangles" Robinson as she tapped, tapped, tapped. Margaret O'Brien: the eyes. Natalie Wood: harder, because one remembers her better as a grown-up in pictures in which the screenplay actually called for her to get poked, little Marjorie Morgenstern with a bagel in the oven.

Of Blue Tyler, all I remembered, the first thing anyone remembered, was the voice, the voice that even when she was six and eight and ten and a stranger to the indulgence she later never tried to resist was a voice that carried the hint of too many cigarettes and too much booze and too many late nights and too many dark erotic liaisons. A vaginal voice. Husky, inviting, a midget Dietrich, a dwarf Tallulah. "Butch Blue," Bob Hope called her the first time she appeared on his radio show when she was five, and Butch Blue she remained through all her subsequent appearances on the show, Butch Blue Tyler playing the Jimmy Cagney and Humphrey Bogart parts in Hope's parodies of their movies, once on a holiday broadcast even singing bass to Bing Crosby's baritone in a "White Christmas" duet. Hers was an aberrant attraction, I realize now, a pedophile's nocturnal emission. She was Eve not just before the apple, but before puberty, a siren at six, the child who would come to no good, erotic catnip to those who would despoil her: to all of us.

◄○►

Consider now the photographs. The hundreds I saw of the thousands that I suppose were taken—studio candids mostly—on the set, in the schoolroom, at leisure, a documentation of a child growing up that was so total and so false, evoking not so much truth as the generic truth of the celebrity machine. Publicity was the oil of the star system, the way by which an ordinary little girl could be lent, even in her ablutions, even feeding the Labrador puppy it turned out she never actually had (called Chocolate in the caption, after Chocolate Walker Franklin), a quality of transcendence that touched even the ordinary with the shimmer of possibilities, of what might be. There were entire (and in many cases entirely manufactured) social and political histories in these photographs and in the press releases scotch-taped to the back of each one. By demonological scrutiny one could discern shifting alliances, hidden agendas, secret vanities, new hierarchies. Take for example Melba Mae Toolate at age four, with Shelley Flynn and Chocolate Walker Franklin, democracy in action the subtext of that simple time. And in this less simple time a different subtext: the realization that those blacks who crossed over in show business during the 1930s all seemed to have names like Chocolate or Bojangles or Butterfly, subservient names, nigger names, to put an uglier (and truer) handle on it, that defined their relationship to the whites with whom they performed, and who, at least in the publicity handouts, named their house pets after them. Melba Mae in that photograph (stamped on the back PROPERTY OF COSMOPOLITAN PICTURES), selected at an open dance call on Cosmo's Stage 17 by J. F. French himself, according to the text on the back of the photo, mogul of moguls, founder of Cosmopolitan, 1934's Humanitarian of the Year (again according to the caption), Entertainment Industry Division, National Conference of Christians and Jews. It was J. F. French, the release said, who came up with the name Blue Tyler, after his wife's favorite color (his wife, or to be more accurate, his then-current wife, the former silent screen vamp Chloe Quarles), and after the tenth president of the United States, John Tyler, with whom J. F. French said he felt a special bond as they shared the same August 4 birthday (although later, when I checked, I discovered that John Tyler's birthday was actually March 29). Blue Tyler. Or Baby Blue Tyler, as many tried to call her. A name she hated. Fuck you, she would say to fan magazine reporters who called her Baby Blue. Fuck you in the eyeball. She was then six.

A Little-Known Fact: Did you know that John Tyler had fifteen children? I asked Melba Mae Toolate.

Stupid fuck, she had answered. And then: Who's John Tyler?

◄◦►

PROPERTY OF COSMOPOLITAN PICTURES: a perfect description, because that is exactly what Blue Tyler was. Her mother in effect was pensioned off by the studio, given a position in something called Special Projects that kept her, as a press release said, "on the go," although where she was on the go to was never specified. If she appeared in the photographs at all, it was only as a shadowy figure in the background, sometimes identified, more often not, and easily cropped out. On official studio occasions, Chloe Quarles assumed the maternal role, or the senior character actress in whatever picture Blue was then starring in. Her upbringing was entrusted to governesses hired by and loyal to Cosmopolitan Pictures. Did your mother live with you? I asked. More than once. A series of questions over the days we were together. She answered or she did not answer, depending on her mood. Sometimes she was evasive, sometimes truculent, sometimes she offered a story to some other point, with the answer I was seeking buried deep within it, often an untruth. The questions, the answers, the evasions, the lies became in time a seamless piece. And so again, a second, a ninth, a forty-fourth time: Did your mother live with you? Of course. Another time, another answer: She lived in the guest house. Question: Where did Chloe Quarles fit in? (A leading question, of course, from intonations I had picked up.) Answer: She was a dyke, Mr. French did not like her around me too much. (Confirming the intonations.) I had the sense of a household out of the 1939 New York World's Fair, run by machines and service personnel. There was a maid, Esmeralda, a would-be actress and cousin of Chocolate Walker Franklin (democracy in action again), and Madame. Who was Madame? All the governesses, it seemed, were called Madame. For fear of kidnappers, her house was never photographed; the rooms that appeared in magazine layouts were always dressed sets on a soundstage. Sometimes the Pacific was the featured backdrop, sometimes the Santa Monica Mountains, sometimes a ranch in the San Fernando Valley, the exteriors blue-screen process shots superimposed on the windows, the magic of motion pictures. Her mother's absence from these photo spreads was covered by the assertion that Irma Tyler (her contract with the studio stipulated that she too abandon the name Toolate) did not wish to "capitalize" on her daughter's fame, that being the mother of such a loving and talented child was reward enough. Question: What happened to Irma Tyler? And again: What ever happened to your mother? Blue was vague. Answer: She cut out.

When?

I was fifteen, I think.

Did you ever see her again?

She died.

How?

In a car crash.

Who told you she died?

I don't know.

Who?

I can't remember.

Who?

Mr. French. The publicity department.

◦

In fact, her mother was not her mother at all.

Or might not have been.

Or in all likelihood wasn't.

Or so Blue claimed. Indirectly. Her voice on a tape. The tapes she said she made when she decided it was time to do her autobiography. ("To do" is the operative infinitive in this kind of enterprise, never "to write.") The autobiography is an inclination that all has-been movie stars have. Another grab at the brass ring. Youth recaptured and old scores settled on talk shows and in newspaper Style sections.

Arthur French gave me the tape and let me dupe it. The son of J. F. French. Son as in the son also rises. Old Hollywood joke. The man Hedda Hopper had said Blue was "dating." The man Louella Parsons said was her "intended." A "woosome twosome," Winchell said. "The Son and the Star," the fan magazines said. "Setting the date," Jimmy Fidler said. Arthur and I went back a long time. By the time Arthur gave me the tape, I had already talked to him about Blue several times at his ranch in Arizona, trips undertaken when I had more knowledge than I cared to impart but needed him to fill in some of the blanks, although I knew how difficult a task debriefing him would be. He had not mentioned the tape during those visits. He mentioned it only later, when I was talking to him at Willingham, his father's preposterously named and preposterously huge estate on lower Angelo Drive in Beverly Hills. The tape, he said, had turned up in his mail one day. No note. No identification. No return address. Just the voice on the tape. That unmistakable voice.

This is what was on the tape, beginning to end:

"That was the night Jack Rabbitt called me a son of a bitch. I told him I couldn't be a son of a bitch because I was a daughter. Smart talk like that. If he wanted to call me a name, then call me a daughter of a bitch. And I want to tell you one thing and not two things. I was the daughter of a bitch. The lady who gave birth to me was fifteen when I was born. I say 'the lady who gave birth to me' because I never saw her. She dropped me like an animal does, then she sold me to Irma for a bus ticket out of town. Irma said the bus ticket was to Chicago, but I think she was just trying to get me off the scent in case I ever wanted to go look for the lady who gave birth to me. Fat chance is what I said to that idea. Irma was my mother, if you call being a mother raising you. That's what Irma did. Irma was a waitress out there in that pisshole in the desert, and I guess with tips and all she could scare up the cost of a bus ticket to Chicago. Or Cleveland or Milwaukee or Atlanta or wherever it was that lady who gave birth to me took off to. She wanted a kid, Irma, without having to fuck to get it.

"Now to Jack Rabbitt. Of course Rabbitt wasn't his real name. I'm not even sure that Jack was. He just said he was Jack, and that whole summer he wouldn't tell me his last name, so I just called him Jack Rabbitt, with two *t*'s, like it was a real name, and not just a carrot eater.

"That Jack, he was a pistol. At least I didn't marry him. Or I don't think I did."

It just appeared, this tape? I asked Arthur French. We were walking through the orchid house at Willingham. J. F. French had been dead for years, but Arthur still maintained Willingham despite the rarity of his trips to Los Angeles from Arizona, where he had lived for as long as I had known him. It was a mansion built at a time when mansions were mansions, with a nine-hole golf course and ponds that had been dug and aerated, with swans swimming in them, and entire English gardens imported from the Wiltshire countryside to bake and wither in the subtropical sun, only to be replaced again the next season. Arthur kept a skeleton staff of housekeepers and gardeners on duty, down from the nearly two dozen servants his father had terrorized when he was alive, and when Arthur showed up, always on short notice, there were fresh flowers in all the vases and phalaenopsis plants in the master bedroom and the linen was starched and the crystal and the china and the silver sparkled. There was no reason for Arthur to keep the place. He could have sold it or given it to a school and saved the prodigious upkeep and the equally prodigious taxes, but I think he just liked the pointless extravagance of it, and the way this pointless extravagance seemed to irritate people.

It was a pattern, Arthur French said. Through the years. She was always sending me things.

What sort of things?

Things. Newspaper clippings. Walker Franklin's obituary. Chloe's retrospective at the Biarritz Film Festival. Shelley Flynn getting married again. Things like that.

And you always knew they were from her? Even with no return address?

Of course. Who else would be interested in clippings about people nobody else knew. Or remembered. Or cared about. She knew I'd remember.

(He was equivocating. You had to wait Arthur out. Approach him from a different direction. Come back at a later time. And at a time after that, and after that time, too. Wait until he was ready to tell you, until he knew what he was going to find out in return. And as he was keeping things from me, I of course was keeping things from him. Darker things. Things Melba Mae Toolate had intimated in Hamtramck, other things she had said straight out, perhaps true, perhaps not, perhaps true only in part. The problem was how to find out what to believe and what not to believe. Arthur knew I was equivocating, as I knew he was. Our discourse was like poker. Lose one hand, play the next. The trick was not to show your hole card. Arthur enjoyed the game more than I did, but then for Arthur, life was a game for which he seemed to have the only copy of the rulebook.)

Who is Jack Rabbitt? I said.

He shrugged. Never heard of him.

Never?

Maybe he was somebody she fucked. That wasn't all that unusual with her. She didn't even know his name. That wasn't unusual either.

Is it true, the tape?

After a fashion. It jibes with things we knew.

Like what?

Irma wasn't her mother, we knew that.

How?

The studio was not without resources, Jack. (With that high irony Arthur often affected. Meaning, or at least implying, that the studio owned, or, more precisely, rented, if not the police department then individual officers in it, who, with at least the tacit approval of superiors who would share in the payoff, could bring the intimidating powers of their organization to bear.) There was no birth certificate. One day Irma didn't have a child, the next day she did. We found that out. We couldn't send her packing. So J.F. just put her under contract. In return for which she had to answer certain questions about where Blue came from. And agree to certain stipulations.

How did Irma really die?

An auto accident.

Really?

She drove off a cliff. In the hills up behind San Diego.

Was it really an accident?

We didn't *kill* her, Jack, if that's what you're *getting* at. (This was Arthur in his ironic mode, when certain words and certain phrases in every sentence appeared to be italicized.) The studio might try to cover up a murder, but we never *ordered* one. We did have *certain* standards.

Then it wasn't an accident?

It was made to appear that way.

The studio not being without resources.

If you have resources, you use them. That's why they're called resources.

Thank you, Arthur. For explaining that to me. Anyway. The hills behind San Diego . . .

The mother of a child star is not supposed to commit suicide. It looks bad. Especially when the child star has a picture ready for release.

Why did she do it?

I suppose her contract was not going to be renewed. Her usefulness was more or less at an end. Or maybe she had just had it. It happens. Anyway, finding a surrogate guardian was never any problem.

Because Cosmopolitan Pictures was her real mother and father?

Sarcasm doesn't become you, Jack. But yes, the studio was her family. I bet Blue would agree with that even today.

Who was Toolate?

Irma's ex-husband, as near as we could figure. Long gone by the time Melba Mae appeared on the scene.

Gone where?

I'm sure I don't know.

In prison?

A possibility.

Did he ever show up?

(Carefully): Over the years a number of people showed up claiming to have some kinship with Blue. The legal department handled all the claims.

You're a cool customer, Arthur.

Yes.

--◆--

Blue usually claimed that she had lost the tapes. Or then again that she was keeping them in a safe place. Mad money, she would say. My little annuity.

A nice way to say extortion money.

That she still thought there were people around that she might be able to blackmail is evidence, I suppose, of how far off life's radar screen she had wandered.

V

HER EVERY PUBLIC MOVE was recorded on camera (and many of her private ones, too, as a star of her magnitude was always expected to be on public display, a condition written into the boilerplate of her contract). Here a photo of Baby Blue Tyler at age six being taught by a studio stunt coordinator how to climb trees at Cosmopolitan's ranch in the San Fernando Valley. There a photo of Blue at age ten receiving from Clark Gable that special Oscar at the 1939 Academy Awards. Another of Blue giving Eleanor Roosevelt a contribution to the March of Dimes on behalf of the Motion Picture Producers Association. Blue with Bronx Bomber Joe DiMaggio and Brown Bomber Joe Louis. Blue with the French Fillies, the chorus line that appeared in all of Cosmopolitan's musicals, each Filly personally selected by J. F. French himself (the better the head the Filly candidate gave Mr. French in her job interview, Chuckie O'Hara would tell me later, the better her chances for selection). Blue with Congressman Martin Dies, chairman of the Un-American Activities Committee, and Blue with Secretary of the Interior Harold Ickes. With Harold Arlen and Irving Berlin, "both penning Tyler songfests," according to the caption. Blue being comforted by Norma Shearer outside the Wilshire Boulevard Temple, where she was "the youngest mourner at the funeral of Beloved Industry Legend Irving Thalberg." Blue in January 1942, weeping at the news that Carole Lombard's plane had crashed in Table Rock, Nevada, outside Las Vegas, killing everyone on board. "Blue Misses Fatal Flight," read the caption headline. "Teen Tot had been on bond-selling tour with late star and good friend Carole Lombard. Strep throat canceled homecoming flight, saved life." And Blue, now fourteen, at Cosmo's Little Red Schoolhouse with fellow student Meta Dierdorf, described in the caption as a "non-pro," and "further proof that Cosmo wants its most priceless asset to meet with people from all segments of society, and not just those associated with the Motion Picture Industry." Blue reading *Little Women* with Meta Dierdorf, and at the blackboard with her, solving algebra problems. Blue and Meta Dierdorf serving doughnuts and coffee to soldiers and sailors at Hollywood's Stage Door Canteen. Meta Dierdorf then disappears from Blue Tyler's pictorial and print biography until three weeks before the end of the war:

BLUE'S TRAGEDY
NON-PRO CLASSMATE FOUND STRANGLED IN TUB
NO CLUES

The murder was never solved. According to the newspapers, Meta Dierdorf was an "oil heiress." Her mother had died of puerperal fever after a second child was stillborn, and her father was said to be an "independent oil operator" who had been in Bahrain on a field exploration when his daughter was suffocated in her bathtub by someone who had crammed four inches of what the newspapers said was a Turkish towel down her throat. The day of her murder, Meta Dierdorf had attended, in her capacity as a hostess at the Stage Door Canteen, a publicity luncheon given by Chloe Quarles at Willingham for a contingent of U.S. Marines billeted at the Naval Auxiliary Shore Station in San Pedro. The marines had been assigned as extras to a military musical comedy Cosmopolitan Pictures and J. F. French were preparing called *Ready, Aim, Fire.* The Cosmopolitan publicity department said that J. F. French had not been present at the luncheon, that the event was part of his former wife's continuing and valuable contribution to the war effort, that he had never met any of the lovely young hostesses, and that he had been in script conferences all that day so that his personal production of *Ready, Aim, Fire,* starring Shelley Flynn, Chocolate Walker Franklin, and the French Fillies, would be the great success that everyone at Cosmopolitan knew it would be. It was further added that a percentage of the studio's profits would be given to the Army-Navy Relief Fund, that J. F. French himself and all the studio's employees mourned Miss Dierdorf, and that in her name Cosmopolitan would make a cash donation to the Stage Door Canteen.

The largesse of Cosmopolitan Pictures was forgotten the next day when the *Express* reported that shortly before she was strangled Meta Dierdorf had "engaged in an act of intimacy." It was the kind of delicate construction indulged in by newspapers of the period, one inviting all kinds of prurient speculation, especially in the studio commissaries, with fellatio leading the morning line. According to Chuckie O'Hara, now medically discharged from the Marines and newly back at the studio with his prosthetic leg, the story in the Cosmo executive dining room, via the studio police, was that homicide investigators had discovered several used rubbers in a bedroom wastebasket and that the medical examiner had also found evidence of semen both in the victim's mouth and on the tile floor next to the toilet.

In an effort to protect the image of his number-one star, J. F. French refused to let Blue attend Meta Dierdorf's funeral, at the same time killing a release from Cosmo's publicity department saying that America's number-four box office attraction (and top-ranked actress) was too grief-stricken to make an appearance, and then fired the studio's publicity director for allowing the item to appear in some early editions. Chuckie

O'Hara said that J.F. did not want Blue's name associated in any way with the crime, nor even to have it further reported that she and Meta Dierdorf had gone to school together, let alone that the studio had picked Meta Dierdorf to be Blue's best friend, it being bad enough in his view that Chloe Quarles had invited the little cunt to the luncheon at Willingham. If the mother of a cinemoppet is not supposed to have committed suicide, neither is that cinemoppet supposed to have a best friend naked in a bathtub with come in her mouth and a towel shoved down her throat. It was to change the focus that J. F. French called upon his long friendship with Hugh Cardinal Danaher, ordinary of the Roman Catholic archdiocese of Los Angeles, with whom he was associated in a number of anti-Communist crusades, and arranged for Blue to represent Cosmopolitan Pictures at an armed forces mass at St. Basil's Cathedral the day Meta Dierdorf was buried, a mass celebrated by the cardinal himself. In the next morning's newspapers, there were front-page photographs of Blue and His Eminence on the steps of St. Basil's, she in a white linen dress and a wide-brimmed blue straw hat, carrying a white missal (the missal from the Cosmo property department, Chuckie said, as she had never been baptized in any denomination). But of course *Life* magazine's picture researchers remembered the published studio photographs of Blue with Meta Dierdorf, and after that the publicity department's effort became an exercise in damage control.

Blue Tyler was not questioned officially, although in the presence of her lawyer, Lilo Kusack, she did have an informal conversation with a homicide detective named Spellacy ("Subject was forthcoming but could add nothing pertinent to the investigation") that went unreported in the local press, and that I only discovered years later when I had an opportunity to examine the Dierdorf case file. As I grew to anticipate, and to appreciate, the better I came to know him, Chuckie O'Hara had the raciest footnote to the Dierdorf affair, as he was present at a studio meeting between Lilo Kusack and J. F. French about the matter. (The reason he happened to be in J.F.'s office, Chuckie said, was to go over a list of pictures he might direct now that his discharge was final, and to discuss whether his having only one leg would preclude his doing a certain kind of outdoor film that he did not wish to do anyway, the soundstage being where he was most in his element). Why he was not asked to leave when Lilo was ushered into the office he never bothered to explain (nor in truth did I ask), but whether accurate in every detail or not, his story did have the virtue of verisimilitude (at least insofar as it pertained to my own experience in the Industry, and my knowledge, however secondhand, of the behavior of the principals), and it also indicated the milieu in which Blue had grown up, and whose values she had taken as her own.

"We can't have our little girl friendly with someone who gives blow jobs on the crapper," J. F. French said in the O'Hara version.

"Moe," Lilo Kusack said, "Moe" being the name that only his closest associates were allowed to call J. F. French, "Blue is famous for, uh . . ."

"Never on the crapper," J. F. French shouted. "I swear on my mother's grave, Blue has never sucked anyone off on the crapper."

There was one last headline about the Meta Dierdorf murder, an example of damage control Cosmopolitan Pictures–style, as it applied to Blue Tyler:

BLUE OFFERS REWARD
IN SLAYING OF BEST SCHOOLFRIEND
COSMOPOLITAN PICTURES WILL MATCH OFFER

As it happened, the banner headline across the front page that day was:

B-29 DROPS SUPERBOMB ON JAP CITY IN PEARL HARBOR PAYBACK
NIPS TALK SURRENDER

To J. F. French and Cosmopolitan Pictures, the dawn of the atomic age had the entirely satisfying side effect of driving the murder of Meta Dierdorf and her putative friendship with Blue Tyler out of the newspapers.

◄◌►

With the war over, there were more headlines, better publicity. BLUE INKS RECORD MULTI-PIC PACT MAKING HER HIGHEST-PAID STAR IN COSMO GALAXY, and with the story a photograph of Blue on Soundstage 27 with J. F. French and (in captionese) "Blue's steady flame, Producer Arthur French," as she "prepares for new song-and-dance role in *Red River Rosie,* with former Marine war hero Charlton ('Chuckie') O'Hara, who has megged three Tyler hits for Cosmo, behind the camera." And a photo of Blue standing under the American flag in the ballroom of the Ambassador Hotel delivering the Pledge of Allegiance at 1947's "I Am an American Day" dinner, "where Hollywood pledged to stand four-square against the forces of Communism." A photo of Blue in a box at Santa Anita with "Millionaire Sportsman Jacob King." And at the Grauman's Chinese opening of *Red River Rosie,* again with "Millionaire Sportsman and Man About Town Jacob King." Then the high point: the cover and an eight-page layout in *Life,* the story leading off with a bleed double truck of Blue, almost twenty, sitting at the huge oval teak table in the conference room at the William Morris Agency, surrounded by her retainers—the lawyers and agents and publicists and accountants and managers and financial planners dedicated to her professional care and feeding. BLUE PLOTS CROSSOVER CAREER MOVES, read the headline. And the subheads: FORMER MOPPET SEEKS ADULT ROLES. THE WORLD HER OYSTER.

A tainted oyster, it turned out.

I still have a copy of that conference-room photograph pinned to the bulletin board in my office. It was one of the three I kept, of all the hundreds I looked at, as if in those three photographs I would find the secret of Blue Tyler that for so long eluded me.

◄◌►

It was as if she was not meant to grow up.

"Naughty, naughty, Blue Tyler's hips were hiccuping at the Mocambo with J. F. French's lad Arthur . . . they're that way, they say, but ukiddinme? We hear she's only fit for a king." Winchell, of course, antennae quivering.

Fit for a king.

Specifically Jacob King. Born Yakov Kinovsky, Red Hook (Brooklyn), 1907. Playboy. Man About Town. Millionaire Sportsman. Hotel Investor. Polo. Tennis. Yachtsman. A man who collected headlines. DENIES MOB LINKS . . . ACQUITTED . . . NOT CHARGED . . . NOT UNDER INVESTIGATION . . . PLANS NEVADA HOTEL EMPIRE . . . WILL PRODUCE TYLER WESTERN, OTHER PIX . . . DENIES HOTEL OPENING POSTPONED . . . "JUST FRIENDS," BLUE SAYS . . . "ONLY BUSINESS ASSOCIATES," KING SAYS.

Then:

KING SLAIN
MOBSTER GUNNED DOWN IN NEVADA SHOWPLACE
MANY THEORIES, NO CLUES

VI

THERE HAVE BEEN two indifferent cut-and-paste biographies of Jacob King written over the years, the tone of each reflecting the national infatuation with the underworld and its more marketable citizens. Both books are a collage of the same old clips and the same old police files and booking sheets and court transcripts, the same unsubstantiated accusations, the same slipping memories and inductive leaps and fanciful conjectures. The films about Jacob King, in which his character appeared either pseudonymously or under his own name (or to be more precise the Americanization of his own name), were no less inventive. Usually he was portrayed in one of two conflicting ways, the low-budget version being Jacob as a murdering, sexually impotent hood, impotence that all-purpose motivation in bad movies, cut-rate filmmakers (and upmarket ones as well) never having understood that motivation is a terrible explanation of character. Then there is the big-budget version, with Jacob as tragic romantic hero trying to go straight and grab a legitimate slice of the American dream, but unable, or perhaps unwilling, to cut the umbilical cord tying him to his violent past. Whatever the medium, whatever the perverse alchemy of fact, factoid, and fantasy, Jacob King was always perceived as larger than life, a criminal of many parts.

-<o>-

It is instructive here to examine the criminal passport of Jacob King, preserved in the archives of the New York Police Department, and on microfilm as well at the United States Department of Justice, Federal Bureau of Investigation, Washington, D.C. 20537, the result of a 1949 federal investigation into the circumstances of his death, and of the 1951 Kefauver hearings on the world of organized crime. In the dull abbreviations of police bureaucrats, Jacob King's yellow sheet, as it is more familiarly called, shows the stopovers he made as he traveled the world of crime, absent the romantic filter through which his actions were later viewed. I quote at random:

PD, NY, NY Yakov Kinovsky 6/18/24 PC 1897 #1 Fel assault #2 PL dangerous weapon 9/12/23 Complaint withdrawn and dismissed.

PD, NY, NY Yakov Kinovsky aka Jacob King 7/27/25 poss bookmaking records, usury 12/12/26 Case dism.

Two entries, of interest primarily in that sometime between the ages of sixteen and eighteen Yakov Kinovsky decided that his personality and his success in the criminal calling warranted his Americanizing his name to Jacob King. K-I-N-G. Four letters that would fit neatly into the tabloid headlines he would later court so assiduously. K-I-N-G. Even in his teens Yakov Kinovsky already considered himself the stuff of criminal royalty.

PD, NY, NY Jacob King (Yakov Kinovsky) 11/12/30 aslt 2d degree; poss of loaded revolver 3/18/31 Complaint withdrawn.

PD, NY, NY Jacob King 8/19/31 Aslt WITC Murder 1st, Kidnapping, Extortion 3/2/36 Case dism. (insuff. evidence).

There were a number of other arrests for assault with intent to commit murder in the first degree, and in every instance the result was "Case dism. (insuff. evidence)," Jacob King's reputation over the years inducing a passion for discretion among those in a position to testify against him. Only once did he ever go to trial in a capital case, on the charge of "Mrdr 1st," and the disposition (1/6/47) was "not glty. by jury," a verdict Jacob King owed largely to the fact that while he was in custody at the Tombs, remanded there without bond throughout the investigation and trial (the only time he was ever incarcerated for a sustained period), the state's two leading witnesses were murdered, the first blown apart by a bomb delivered in a Christmas poinsettia, the second shot to death as he was evacuating his bowels in a men's room stall at Sunnyside Arena in Queens during a preliminary four-rounder the night Lulu Constantino won his twenty-ninth consecutive featherweight fight against Lefty Lew Mann in the main event.

As a record of mayhem, Jacob King's rap sheet was not all that more evocative than those of more run-of-the-mill thugs. What made him distinctive was the spur-of-the-moment inventiveness with which his forays into criminal violence were said, if only on the basis of hearsay, to have been conducted. In the case of Jacob King, "aslt w/dang. wpn" could mean severing the victim's fingers from his left hand with a hammer and chisel ("complaint w/drwn, case dism., 6/26/39"), or wrapping another victim in duct tape until he suffocated and died ("case dism., insuff. evidence, 5/25/42"). Such was his fame as time wore on that all the more esoteric crimes of violence throughout the five boroughs began to be ascribed to him, alibis notwithstanding, even when Walter Winchell would vouch that Jacob King was at Hialeah the day Vincente Crociata was thrown off the Williamsburg Bridge, even when Damon Runyon would attest that Jacob King was sitting in the press box at Briggs Stadium in Detroit (Yanks over the Tigers, 6–5, two homers by Hank Greenberg) the day Leo Spain's tongue was cut out in the laundry room of a whorehouse on Fort Washington Avenue in upper Manhattan. It did not matter. In the city rooms and the police shacks, he had become a man to whom stories attached, like lint to a cheap suit, and in the world in which he had chosen to travel, being known as a man of spontaneous violent invention only enhanced his criminal pedigree.

Murder, the skill at which Jacob King was said to be most proficient, has an almost sexual appeal, and sexual undertones ripple through the descriptions of the more heinous of his alleged homicides. Here, in *Jake—A Gangster's Story,* is how the murder of a small-time hoodlum named Pittsburgh Pat Muldoon is described:

Pittsburgh Pat Muldoon never knew what hit him. That's what a gunsel's dum dum does. One shot, and one shot only, is all it takes. Jake's shot hit Pat Muldoon just above and to the right of his left nipple. Moving like a jet fighter, the projectile tore through flesh and lungs and cartilage, destroying tissue and shattering bones and ribs. So close was Jake to Pittsburgh Pat when he fired that flakes of unburned gunpowder were forced through Muldoon's expensive maroon silk jacket, charring the skin and making a tattoo pattern around the edges of the entrance wound.

Pat Muldoon had less than a minute to live. Jake's slug crunched through the sternum, bored through both lobes of the left lung, veered down through the left ventricle of Pittsburgh Pat's ticker, and then tore out his back, fracturing his seventh rib. The path of the bullet created a wound channel, and for a fraction of a second, the walls of the wound channel were stretched like a rubber band, displacing the heart muscles, the valves and chambers, forming a cavity the size of an orange in Pat Muldoon's heart. The heart continued to pump, squirting blood from the bullet holes in the heart wall, filling the pericardium and pouring into the chest cavity itself, at a rate of about five quarts a minute.

There was, however, no pressure to carry blood through the aorta and the network of arteries to Pat Muldoon's brain.

No blood, no oxygen. No oxygen, no working body cells. The veins collapsed. Electricity and neuromuscular activity stopped.

Pittsburgh Pat Muldoon died.

It was Jake King's seventh hit.

Or his ninth. Or his fourteenth. That Jacob King was never charged with the murder of the unfortunate Pittsburgh Pat Muldoon (who was born Hyman Krakower on Staten Island and who had, to the best of anyone's memory, never been to Pittsburgh) and that there were no witnesses to the crime were quibbles easily overridden by city editors with deadlines to meet and headlines to write. There was speculation, and there was an autopsy report whose dry medicalese lent bogus authenticity to the speculation. Even this was not enough. "This is for being a rat and a fink," Jacob King is reported to have said when he shot Pittsburgh Pat Muldoon that dark December night in Brighton Beach, in the borough of Brooklyn, in the city of New York, although Pat Muldoon was not available to testify as to the accuracy of the last words he is supposed to have heard, his corpse having been dropped into New York Harbor lashed to a pinball machine to weigh it down, and punctured with an ice pick to let its air and body gases dissipate, further discouraging flotation, with the result that it did not surface until the spring solstice, and then with its face and all other identifying features having been worn away by its season in the roiling winter waters of Sheepshead Bay. Even his pecker had fallen off, a source of great good humor in the press shack, his shriveled dingdong, it was said, a tasty hors d'oeuvre for a bluefish with delicate taste buds, another footnote in the continuing legend of Jacob King.

❧

Why Pittsburgh Pat Muldoon had been marked for assassination has never been satisfactorily explained, although it has been said (so often that it has assumed the weight of fact) that Jacob King took the contract as a way of cementing his bona fides with the man who later became his mentor and protector (at least while

it suited him), Morris "The Furrier" Lefkowitz, who was indeed a furrier, a student of mink and fox and sable and ermine
and Persian lamb, as well as the lesser pelts, those he called with
some scorn the unimportant furs, the raccoon, the seal, the
beaver, and the coypu. "I am only a simple furrier," Morris
Lefkowitz would invariably say on those occasions when the
authorities asked him to comment on some civic perfidy or municipal outrage with which they thought he might have been
associated or about which he might have the kind of knowledge
that any public-spirited citizen might wish to share, and it is a
fact that in a life of crime that spanned sixty-one years, Morris
Lefkowitz was such a solid citizen that he never spent a single
night in jail.

It is also said that Morris Lefkowitz had no particular quarrel
with Pittsburgh Pat Muldoon, a minor hit man who had practiced his murderous art for him on a number of occasions, his
only crime (in the eyes of Morris Lefkowitz, if not in the eyes of
a dozen federal, state, and municipal law enforcement agencies)
being that Morris Lefkowitz had grown used to him, uncomfortable with him, the way a man with sap still rising in his
system begins to grow uncomfortable with a wife who has begun to snore in her sleep with her mouth open, a wife whose
stomach muscles have grown slack like a rubber band that has
lost its snap. Jacob King was new and brash, contumacious, it is
true, but smart (an adjective that had never been applied to
Pittsburgh Pat Muldoon, example enough his being a Jew who
took an Irish nom de guerre, the harps to Morris Lefkowitz
being the fattest of the world's fatheads), and Morris Lefkowitz
liked the cut of his jib, liked both Jacob King's head for figures
and his capacity for violence, the two rarely, in Morris Lefkowitz's experience, going hand in hand, wondered in fact if Jacob
King should be placed in his organization's line of succession.

This was the kind of thought one began to consider after
fifty-plus years in the criminal trade, a trade where luck such as
that experienced by Morris Lefkowitz did not generally last for
so many decades, and when the prospect of dying in one's bed,

even, in one's decline, of being fed watery Cream of Wheat by relays of nurses with big tits, held a certain appeal. Jacob King's mettle was all that was in question (not his willingness to kill, of course, but only his willingness to kill on someone else's command), and that question he more than answered when he shot, at least in the popular imagination, his unfortunate landsman Hyman Krakower of Staten Island through the left ventricle.

VII

B LUE TYLER was never interrogated under the full glare of tabloid publicity about the murder of Jacob King. The questioning, such as it was, was conducted by two detectives from the Robbery-Homicide division of the Los Angeles Police Department, acting upon instructions of law enforcement authorities in Las Vegas, and took place not in an official setting but in J. F. French's library on Angelo Drive in Beverly Hills, with Lilo Kusack present in his capacity as family friend and legal adviser to all the parties concerned, that is to say, Blue Tyler, J. F. French, and Cosmopolitan Pictures. Under the terms Lilo Kusack had negotiated with the LAPD, the proceeding was informal, and the presence of either a police stenographer or tape-recording equipment was prohibited. The detectives were allowed to take handwritten notes, and later an abstract of these notes was typed up and placed in the case file, where I found it forty-odd years later as I burrowed through the detritus of Blue Tyler's life; the report said that Miss Tyler had been helpful but had no knowledge either of the reason Jacob King might have been killed or of who the perpetrators might have been.

Coincidentally the detective who wrote this report was the

same Lieutenant Thomas Spellacy who had earlier investigated the murder of Meta Dierdorf, and who on that occasion as well had informally interviewed Blue Tyler. During the thirty-minute interview, Lieutenant Spellacy and his partner, a detective named Crotty, were served iced tea, cucumber sandwiches, and sponge cake by J. F. French's household staff, while (according to later newspaper reports) Cosmopolitan Picture's most valuable asset, wearing a simple cotton sundress and no makeup, her hair fastened in the back by a rubber band, sat perfectly composed, answering every question put to her in a calm and controlled manner, and indicating to Detectives Spellacy and Crotty that her relationship with Mr. King was of a professional nature only, that as her occasional escort to motion picture industry events he was never anything but a perfect gentleman, and that it was a shock to her to learn of those aspects of his private and business life that were the source of so much current speculation in the press. Immediately upon the conclusion of the meeting on Angelo Drive, a press release paraphrasing her remarks (which in fact had been prepared prior to the unannounced interview with the police) was given to reporters, who had been summoned to a press conference at the Cosmopolitan studio commissary. Quoting from the release for the benefit of local and network radio newscasters, a studio spokesman said, "Miss Tyler had engaged Mr. King as a production and business-affairs adviser under the terms of her new contract with J. F. French and Cosmopolitan Pictures. Although their association was only of a short duration, Mr. King was a trusted and valued employee."

◄◦►

On the night of Jacob King's funeral, Blue Tyler had hobo steak at Chasen's, the first banquette on the left inside the door, in the company of J. F. French, Arthur French, and Lilo Kusack, and afterward they all went to Ciro's, the object of the evening, of course, that Blue be seen, a star on display in her native habitat, happy and guileless, without a care in the world, certainly not the murder of a trusted and valued employee. The second of the three photographs I have pinned to my bulletin board is the one that went out over the wires that night, of Blue on the Ciro's dance floor with Arthur French. Arthur had a copy of the picture made and gave it to me when I went to Arizona to see him about Blue shortly after I left Detroit. As I said earlier, conversation with him was always a duel. Thrust, parry. Hint and pull back. See how forthcoming he would be. And how evasive. He had lived on a ranch outside Nogales (he claimed contentedly) for almost thirty years, a widower for a second time after two more or less uxorious marriages, dabbling in the movie business but too rich and too bored and too out of touch to be involved in any substantial way. When I was a postulant in the picture business, I had written a treatment for him from an idea he had, a piece of shit about a tycoon who has an Olympic athlete murdered so that the athlete's sturdy heart can be transplanted to replace the tycoon's own diseased organ. With raised eyebrow, Arthur said perhaps we could call it "To an Athlete Dying Young." It was his way of letting me know that he had areas of knowledge of which perhaps I was not aware, and it was at that moment, when he was so obliquely defensive, that I knew I was going to like him. Nothing ever came of the story (I suspect Arthur was no more interested in it than I, the idea just an opportunity for him to bring someone new to Nogales who he thought might amuse him), but every holiday season brought a Christmas card from Arizona, with a sardonic comment about getting the transplant picture on track again. In all our conversations, which only rarely had anything to do with the picture I was supposed to be writing, he never once mentioned Blue Tyler, although he talked about everything and everyone else, usually in the most indiscreet way, with that ironic assumption of entitlement I have always found came so easily to the assimilated second generation of Hollywood's founder class, an elegant compensation, I suppose, for the brutishness of their fathers and for the fires that in the offspring had been banked, or perhaps never lit. It was not until I met Melba Mae Toolate in Hamtramck that I was even aware that Arthur had played so important a part in the Blue Tyler phase of her life. You never asked, he said when I called after Blue disappeared once again, why don't you come on down, I have some new ideas about our transplant epic. It was the invitation of a lonely old man, and it struck me that in his affluence Arthur was as lonely as Melba in her poverty, an idea he of course would have ridiculed as sentimental nonsense.

The night I arrived at his ranch outside Nogales, Arthur gave me the photograph of him dancing with Blue at Ciro's, and told me to examine it. It's all there, he said. If you get it, no explanation is necessary, if you don't, no explanation will suffice. Arthur's method of conversing was always to make one feel like a particularly backward student taking an exam he was expected to fail, and in his late seventies this ability had not deserted him, nor had its capacity to annoy me. So I studied the photograph with a certain amount of irritation. First the dress. Something J.F. (Arthur always referred to his father as "J.F.," never "Moe," Moe the diminutive for Moses, last name Frankel— Moe, Moses, and Frankel all too déclassé for Arthur) had Edith run up, Arthur said. His was always a world of familiar first names, and to ask who Edith might be he would consider a lapse in taste. Edith Head, I assumed (correctly), who had personally designed Blue Tyler's wardrobe in all the pictures she made for Cosmo. A black wool jersey with puff sleeves, its Empire waist gathered below the bosom with a velvet cord. Edith ran it up that day, Arthur said, from scratch, no excuses, forget the cost, J.F.'s orders. It's only a dress, I said. You don't get it, he said. Then two strands of natural pearls around the neck. Black gloves, over which she wore, on her left wrist, a diamond bracelet, and on her right a diamond watch. Dark hair in a bun, and a small hat with a point d'esprit veil. Rather elaborate, I said. Even the underwear was new, he said. Even the girdle. Who would know? I said. That was the point, he said. What point? I said. He did not answer.

Her head was thrown back, her long swan neck smooth as marble, and she was laughing, mouth open, eyes sparkling, her right hand barely touching Arthur French's left shoulder. Arthur was smiling, listening, the ever-attentive escort, the dauphin, I understood now, the perfect first husband. She was nineteen, he thirty-two, and she educated by life in ways Hollywood's laws of primogeniture had not prepared him for. That at least I did intuit. There seemed to be no one else on the Ciro's dance floor. In the background, what appeared to be apparitions were on closer inspection two other diners watching from a ringside table. Arthur identified them: J. F. French and Lilo, both toasting the young couple with champagne flutes.

Sitting shiva, I said.

For a way of life, Arthur said.

There was a sadness about Arthur that made me hesitate to ask him further about Blue, or Melba, as I could only think of her as, and of some of the things she had told me. I thought I would wait for another time, as if time, for Arthur, was an infinite resource.

—◇—

Blue Tyler never made another picture for Cosmopolitan.

She never made another picture in Hollywood.

She went to Europe.

She was forgotten.

She came home.

She vanished.

VIII

Now imagine the voice. The vaginal voice:

That goddamn voice. I don't have an uvula, that's why I sound the way I do. An uvula. Not a vulva. I had one of them, all right. Still do. And I don't mean are you interested. Or then again, maybe I do. All right, all right, take a joke, will you? Lighten up. Uvula. The thing that hangs down in the back of your throat. Like a nipple in heat. I lost mine. A fucked-up tonsillectomy. Studio doctor. Lou Lerner, M.D. Kept his job on the lot because he supplied morphine to all the heavy hitters. Plus he did all the abortions. Two of mine. The first when I was fourteen, and is that a story. Not now. Maybe not ever. Too many skeletons I don't want to rattle in too many closets. Anyway. He crapped up my tonsillectomy. So I couldn't hold pitch or any of that musical bullshit. I just had to invent a sound. Vibrato was what they called it. Sounded okay to me, so I went along with it. I hadn't even had my first period yet, shit, I was only six years old, for Christ's sake, and already I was sounding like some boozed-up diesel dyke with fifty years of bad liquor and cheap cigars.

Got me in a whole lot of trouble, this voice, Melba Mae Toolate said. I didn't even have pussy hair, and still everyone thought I was a dyke. Not my style. I tried once or twice. Hell, I suppose I'd still give it a whirl, the opportunity ever arises, but just to keep warm at night. I like dykes, they're fun. You ever heard of Frenchy Ray? She was in the line at the Latin Quarter that time I was in New York, when was that, after I came back from Italy, I think, I'll get to Italy later, what I remember of it. She named herself after some ballplayer nobody ever heard of, Frenchy. The most beautiful woman in New York. Everyone was fucking her. And giving her cars and apartments and furs and jewels. Men kept women in those days. The thing was, Frenchy fucked more showgirls than all those studs who were fucking her put together. She liked boys when she was sober and girls when she was drunk. Or maybe it was the other way around. I never heard anyone put the knock on her, though, man or woman, so she must've been pretty good in the hay. Not that I ever had any personal experience. She had her eye on me, I was still famous, ha, ha, but I just said, I'm easy, Frenchy, but not that easy, and anyway I lost my curiosity about that a long time ago, it's nice, but not that nice, and she just laughed and said if she had been the first I wouldn't think that way.

She finally went out a window, Frenchy. On West End Avenue. Sat in it for a couple of hours, both legs hanging out over the sill, skirt caught up beneath her ass, you could see her garter belt even, except they airbrushed it out of the pictures. The cops tried to talk her back in, they even called me to talk to her, like I was her fucking hair pie girlfriend, and all the times the cops were talking, they were setting up this suicide net on the street, you know, like they do in the circus for the trapeze artists, in case they fall. Then one of the cops, he makes a grab for her, and she dives, or she falls, who knows what the fuck happened, into the net. But the net was stretched too tight, like a trampoline, and when she hits it, she bounces like a basketball, out of the net onto the sidewalk, and breaks her neck. They don't even run Frenchy's picture in the *Mirror*, they run mine, a still from *Little Sister Susan*, COMMIE CINEMOPPET BLUE TYLER FAILS TO SAVE CHORINE GAL PAL is what the headline says, dyke's best friend is what they really mean, you read between the lines, just the kind of publicity I needed. You think Winchell didn't run with that, the miserable fuck, he's dead, I hear, I hope, cancer of the bowels, I hope, something that really hurt, I hope, made him scream, I hope.

◄◦►

She paused for breath.

◄◦►

Listen, I saw you look in my medicine cabinet, you wonder what I'm doing with a box of rubbers, you nosy bastard. Jesus, sex. Arthur told me once, this was before I left L.A. and went to Italy, that was Arthur's idea, by the way, and I was fucking a lot of people, even for me, and that's saying something. It was the bad time, I was tapped out, and I was getting worried, and he said to me, Arthur, they're only going with you because they want to say they slept with Blue Tyler, if I stayed around any longer I'd end up as a call girl. He had a kind of pig sense, Arthur. You know, I never could get him to say the word fuck, even when we were doing it.

I suppose you really need that tape recorder. It's funny. There's so many things around now that weren't around when I was at Cosmo, and I always had the best when I was at Cosmo, the newest, the latest, every kind of gizmo, but nothing like they have nowadays. Answering machines. Computers. TV sets. Fax machines. VCRs. Tape recorders. I had one once, a tape recorder. What I wanted to do was tape my memoirs. Then I was going to edit them. And get a big fucking best-seller. And go on the TV. With that blonde on *Prime Time*. The one that looks like Mae West. She's my favorite. Diane Something. Sawyer. I liked Mae. She was funny. Took a high colonic every day. That's French for enema. Her big beauty secret. You think Diane takes a high colonic? You think she even remembers me? No one's heard of me anymore. There's this impressionist, Rich Little, he used to do me in his act, I heard it one night on Carson, he wasn't bad. And then I thought what kind of fucking secondhand life in show business is that, doing impressions of people better than you are, and I said fuck that. Do I have the tapes? Yes, they're around someplace, I think. I think I hocked the tape recorder for vodka money. You know the funny thing? I suppose my voice would've got this way even if I had my uvula, because of all the booze.

What happened? Baby, I just fell off the planet earth. I said that, didn't I? I tend to repeat myself. When I was five, I really couldn't read my scripts, so Mr. French had someone read them to me, and I would memorize them that way, repeating them over and over, I always knew the good lines, and "Baby, I fell off the planet earth" is one of them, you ever know Sammy Cahn, is he still around? Give that to Sammy or the Bergmans, they could run with that title, a perfect season, a perfect reason for making whoopee. Drink is what happened. Booze, skag, scumbag men. Flophouses, a nickel a night. Just someplace to collapse. Anyplace. Even jail. Finally a gas station crapper with a spike behind my knee, the only place I could find a vein, I was dead, not dying, D-E-A-D, they put the sheet over my face, I was going to buy the fucking farm in Ypsilanti, Michigan. And then this intern. A young squirt. One of those eastern niggers. Indian. Paki, maybe. One of them, anyway. Keep 'em alive till eight-oh-five. The motto of the emergency room. Squirt didn't want me to check out on his watch, all that extra paperwork he'd have to do, and his not speaking English all that good. That's why he gave me that last jolt with the resuscitator. What I'd like to have, what I would really like to have, is that sheet, the one they pulled over my face when they thought I was dead. That'd be a memento, sell it at Sotheby's, when they auction off my personal effects after I die. Like Judy's shoes. Me Dorothy, you Toto. You think some fag would like that sheet?

◄○►

A sudden squall.

◄○►

Fuck you. I know why you're looking at me that way. I'll cry tomorrow, Lillian Roth. Whatever happened to Baby Jane? You know what I think? You think I'm your meal ticket. You bought yourself a little piece of Hollywood history. You're not the first asshole who found me, thought he could cash in on me. Don't you ever forget that, and fuck you again.

◄○►

I did not take offense. It was the way her brain worked, rerouting itself past burned-out connections. There was still a lot of power in that system. She knew what would hurt. But she had been born with that. A tropistic instinct. The only way to survive.

Handle with care.

Do not rise to the bait.

Wait her out.

◄○►

She took a cigarette from the pack of unfiltered Pall Malls on the Formica table, the pack opened the way women open cigarettes, with the foil and the tax stamp ripped away and all the cigarettes exposed. She tapped the cigarette on her thumbnail, firming up the loose strands of tobacco, and then held it between her fingers and waited for him to light it. He found a wooden safety match on the hot plate in the kitchenette and when he returned to the Formica table he flicked it lit with his thumbnail, a piece of business he had learned on the set of a period cop movie he had once written for Burt Lancaster. The way he lit the match seemed to strike a responsive chord, a softening of the harsh lines around her mouth and the hawser veins in her neck. It was the sort of flourish specific to the pictures she had starred in. She drew deeply on the Pall Mall, but did not inhale. After a moment she let the smoke billow out, then inhaled it back in again, through her nose, finally exhaling through her mouth. A small smile, a lightening of her mood, as if she had done a close-up in one take. With a thumb and a finger she removed a bit of tobacco from her tongue. The whole procedure dated her, he thought. Smokers don't tap filter cigarettes against their fingernails anymore, and rarely French inhale, a good visual but from another time.

◄○►

Perfect, Chuckie O'Hara said when I told him of this first meeting, you have a good eye for a writer. A remark intended as a compliment, and I had been around the business too long to take offense. Like all directors, good and bad, Chuckie fed on the details, in the details, he would say, is the character. His hands framed a shot, moving in close, perhaps in his mind focusing on the bit of tobacco she had lifted from her tongue, or the smoke curling from the face in profile, then with a reverse from the other side.

What did you call her? Blue?

No. If I had to call her by name, I'd call her Mrs. Toolate. Most of the time, though, I didn't call her anything.

But what, Chuckie O'Hara wanted to know, did she look like?

◄○►

She was sixty-three, and she looked every minute of it. It had been forty years since she had left Hollywood, and more than thirty since she abandoned public life and the cosmetic ministrations available to even the most minor of celebrities, the nip, the tuck, the dyes, the clamps. Her face was never really beautiful, just arresting, discomforting in its pre- and post-pubescent availability, and now it was not so much worn by her travails as lived-in, less a face than an open book, dog-eared and much sampled, an encyclopedia of living. She had a racking cough that periodically contorted and reddened her face, her breath coming in short spurts until the attack eased. Her movements were extremely precise, not a motion wasted. Her eyebrows had always been incongruously thick; in her days of fortune, she was too young to have her eyebrows plucked and penciled in the style of the time, and incongruously lush they still were, drawing you, however much against your will, into her gaze. Her hair was dark, shot here and there with gray, and short as it had always been, but long enough to be drawn together with a rubber band into a tiny ponytail, and over her left brow a shock of pure white, like a skunk's back, through which she would constantly thrust the hand not holding the omnipresent Pall Mall.

Only her hands betrayed her years and then some, knotted with veins and mottled by liver spots. Her nose, disturbingly sensual when she was young, was now more generous, and still sensual. Tall and tomboyish as a child, she had sprouted accordingly, and as a young woman she grew only to medium height, neither mannish nor voluptuous. Though the weather had gone chill, she still wore a shapeless summer sundress, and appeared to carry neither undue weight or bloat or distention or the more disfiguring components of age and gender. Sticking from the pocket of the sundress, as if she had forgotten to remove them when the gardening season ended, were a pair of pruning scissors and a dirt-encrusted trowel; over her shoulders she wore a gray cardigan buttoned only at the neck. No stockings, and on her feet an oversized pair of fleecy mules.

Did she shave her legs? Chuckie O'Hara asked.

Yes.

Recently? Like she knew you were coming, and lathered up and maybe cut herself with her little Bic.

No cuts, no nicks. A little stubble.

So heterosexual of you to notice. Did you fuck her?

Oh, for Christ's sake, Chuckie.

That's not an answer.

◄○►

It comes from being alone, flying off the handle like that, she said, crushing the cigarette into an ashtray that said *Detroit Pistons NBA Champions 1989*. I should know better. My motto always was, at least it used to be, it still should be, it's not a bad thing to live by, someone's pissed on you, don't ask questions, go your own way, you got no beef, because you come right down to it, you probably deserved it. You asked for it. Still. You know what I do, I feel like that? I make a new will. It gives me something to do. Putting people in it, scratching the fuckers out, settling scores. I know what you're thinking, what has she got to leave? I've got something, it doesn't look like it, but I do, yes, I do. I don't need much myself. I got one suitcase, that's it. If it gets heavy, I just get rid of stuff. The story of my life. No, fuck that. No self-pity, it's the lowest form of human emotions, I read that once in Miss Manners, I love her column. I made my bed, Christ, I made a lot of them. Or at least I was in a lot of them, but maybe that's not the same thing. I had a lot of husbands, that's for sure, ten, eleven, I lost count. You get right down to it, I'm probably some kind of bigamist, I mean, I'd wake up with some asshole, and he'd say we got married, and I'd say is that right, and I'd head for the bus station without getting a divorce. It's against the law, I think, but shit, if you can't remember getting married, let alone remember the name of the guy you were married to, then what kind of marriage was that? Your eyes, your lips, your pubic hair, are in a class beyond compare, da da da da-de-da, na-nu-na-na, and when I tell them how wonderful you are, they wouldn't believe me, they wouldn't believe me. Now I just have my dog, the one you hit, you bastard, look at that mutt, he's got the mange, and his insides aren't too good. I love that mutt, in dog years he's the same age I am, and if he leaves a little deposit under the bed sometimes, what the hell, he doesn't cheat on me, and he doesn't gab about me, and he doesn't bite me, and I guess that's what passes for love these days.

◄o►

Was she drunk? Chuckie O'Hara said.

Not really.

You mean you couldn't tell?

I mean she wasn't drunk, at least she wasn't drinking then and she didn't seem in any way impaired. But the whole trailer had this peculiar smell of stale booze and sweat and cigarette smoke. It's hard to appreciate how tiny it really was. There was a small portable heater on the floor turned up full blast, which made the whole place terribly hot, there were no windows open, of course, and it trapped this stale stink inside. I suppose I remember it so well because it was so goddamn hot, as hot inside as it was cold outside. Once she got going I just let her ramble, I didn't ask her any questions, I was afraid if I tried to guide her, to ask her anything specific, she would have flashed, and that would have been that. The specifics I would get to in time. At this point all I wanted to do was gain her confidence. And so I just let her jump around. She was putting me on, of course, and I think she knew I knew it.

Darling, of course she didn't, Chuckie O'Hara said. She's an actress, an actress believes everything she says the moment she says it, and if she says something different the next minute, that's the way she is, she believes that, too. What next?

We went shopping.

Shopping . . . it's too wonderful.

She wanted to go shopping, drive in my car, she didn't drive anymore, fill up the trunks from the rebate coupons she'd saved, she had drawers full of them that she'd clipped out of the newspapers, for Joy liquid, Micro Magic Tater Sticks, two dozen Mars bars, junk food . . .

Divine.

I'm not sure I can describe it.

Why?

We order by telephone, people like us, let the housekeeper take care of it, pay the full freight, have it delivered, tip the driver, don't check the bill. We get ripped off, what the hell, it's not worth the aggravation of doing it ourselves.

What a sequence, a tracking shot down the aisles, no cutaways . . .

IX

ITT WAS DOUBLE-COUPON DAY at Farmer Dell's.

She worked the empty aisles as if she was on a search-and-destroy mission, half-humming, half-singing in her no-uvula vibrato the Farmer Dell jingle: Sock it away every day, every way, sock it away at Farmer Dell's. Jack followed behind her, pushing her shopping cart, trying to keep up. She hardly paused, flipping boxes and packages and cans and bottles into the cart without looking back, certain he would be there, for items on the higher shelves beyond her reach using a two-pronged pulley stick she said she had bartered a dozen Duracell size-D alkaline batteries for at a convenience store in Flint. All the while dispensing a running commentary on coupon shopping lore: "Stay away from the freezer section, freezer items spoil, forget freezer discounts." Down aisle one, up aisle three, down aisle five. "Pick a slow time, two in the afternoon, after lunch and before the day shift at the auto plants lets out and the line workers come in to buy their one package of Stouffer's frozen macaroni and cheese, half pint of Hershey's chocolate-flavored milk and two Hostess lemon cupcakes with marshmallow filling." Food for fuel. Not serious enough for her. Not her aim, not her game.

Three bottles of Smucker's Mint-Flavored Apple Jelly, four six-packs of Sunsweet Prune Juice. You can never get enough prune juice. Drano for the lower bowel, that's what it is. Cleans it out. Whoosh. And that Fleet's Ready-to-Use Enema with Comfortip. The best. Need a testimonial, come to me. It might put me back in show business. Spokesperson on the Fleet's commercials. Slips right up there past those troublesome hemorrhoidal tissues. Not many can say that on the tube and make you believe it. You ever hear June Allyson in that commercial for sanitary diapers those old ladies wear who wet their pants? If Juney can do it, I can do it, Juney could never act her way out of a paper bag. Too Miss Priss. Four Heinz Sweet Gherkins, five packages of Oscar Mayer All-Beef Franks, eight to a pack. Six jars of Colman's hot mustard to garnish the franks. Four crocks of Curley's Old-Fashioned Boston Baked Beans. Beans, beans, the musical fruit, the more you eat, the more you toot.

Sock it away every day, every way.

"Never empty the shelves, it's not considerate, these are people on fixed incomes, you've got to let them in on the bargains, they've got to make ends meet too. Unless the offer's going to expire, then you grab everything you can. Can't use it, give it to the shut-ins down to the church." She turned up aisle three, school supplies, paper goods, detergents, the cart already half full, and still ten aisles to go. A half dozen eight-by-eleven spiral notebooks and a package of ballpoint pens. Ziploc quart-size heavy-duty freezer bags. Bounty two-ply towels. S.O.S. steel-wool soap pads. White Rose cellulose sponges. New Hefty thirteen-gallon degradable kitchen garbage bags. "I never used food stamps, don't have to, don't believe in government handouts, that's for deadbeats. There's so much free stuff, you put your mind to it. Just have to plan ahead. Never pay the full price. Never. You have to pay the full price, look for another item. They don't have a special on Scott Tissue, go to Dulcey. A definite difference with Dulcey. Remember that one? A big hit on the jingle hit parade." Her vibrato rose once again, "'There's a definite difference with Dulcey . . .'" Six packages of Reynolds Wrap Quality Aluminum Foil. "Why pay money when you can always get something for next to nothing, you got the time to spend, and baby, time is what I got a lot of. Everyone needs Reynolds Wrap. It's the old barter system. I trade my Reynolds Wrap to my neighbor for Campbell's Pork and Beans. You say what do I need with a dozen cans of Edge Shaving Gel, and I say I'll trade two Edge at three forty-nine a can for some sixty-watt pink bulbs. I love pink bulbs. I always had them in my house on Linden Drive. In Beverly Hills. You know Linden Drive?"

Her reminiscences were so unexpected, like a radio signal that cut in suddenly from another band, loud and clear, always taking him by surprise. "In the flats."

"I lived at six fourteen. Then Mr. French said I had to move north of Sunset, a star of my magnitude shouldn't live in the flats, it reflected badly on Cosmopolitan Pictures, and the studio found me a house up on Tower Road, around the corner from Bing and Dixie Crosby, Dixie was always sloshed. Writers lived in the flats, Mr. French said, and B-picture directors. Not stars. You only lived in the Valley if you had a ranch. People make fun of the studios, but they really looked out for you, they always had your best interests at heart."

Gold, Jack thought. Keep her talking. A stroll down memory lane. But the signal was fading again. There was shopping to be done, bargains to be had. She kept her eye on the sparrow. Maxwell House Colombian Supreme. Fancy Tomato Catsup. Hershey White Chocolate with Almonds. "For the sweet tooth. Never had a zit, always had a sweet tooth. Don't starve. I may eat an awful lot of tuna fish and soup and franks and beans and not enough vegetables, but the weight is good as long as I stay away from too many nachos and the Chee-wees." She was warming to her recital. "You got to learn the ropes. Soak empty bottles for the labels. Keep a pair of scissors handy, cut the coupons off. Clip, scrape, mail, redeem. I just do it for myself, I don't join any of those coupon clubs where you trade your stamps for someone else's. Not me. I'm no entrepreneur, I'm just me."

She opened her tote and removed a fistful of stained and

crumpled and torn coupons. Two for one. Half off. Special. "Coin of the realm," she said as she dropped them back into the tote. Jack noticed again how old and mottled her hands were. "I find them in Dumpsters. Trash bins."

Every day, every way.

"You can't believe the things people throw away." Her voice had the messianic quality of a lay preacher's. "The coupons, the POPs, the little baby faces on the Pampers boxes. Sometimes the mothers throw out the boxes with the dirty Pampers inside, the cunts, so you get poo-poo all over your hands. But so what. Trash means cash, don't you forget that. You never knew that, you've always been rich, I know all about you, I think I fucked your father once, did I tell you that?"

He nodded. It was a question he had never expected to be asked in Hamtramck, Michigan. At Farmer Dell's double-coupon day. Could she really have fucked my father? he thought. This ex-cinemoppet? Oh, yes. Entirely possible. Hugh Broderick didn't miss many comfort stops. Something he would rather not know, in any case. There had to be some secrets. Some gaps in life's knowledge. He wondered what POPs were. That was a gap in his knowledge.

"I'd pay the garbage men to let me look through what they'd picked up. I didn't have much to pay them, but I never fucked them, I'd never fuck for garbage." Sound thinking, he thought. You have to take a stand. He wished she would lower her voice. "You go into Dumpsters, though, you got to be careful. I always wear workman's gloves, you never know what you're going to run up against. Rats, dog shit. I've been bit by rats twice, had to go to the hospital and get a shot. And the ants. They can skin you alive. Those big red army ants, they're like those little fish with the teeth . . ."

"Piranha . . ." He thought, She's like a combat veteran talking about a war I evaded.

"That's the one. Piranha fish. Run in schools. Like these ants. And raccoons. You get in a Dumpster with a raccoon, you got to give him pride of place, you don't want to mess with those 'coons."

Her logic seemed unassailable.

"One time I fell into this big industrial Dumpster, this was in Ypsilanti, it was so slippery with slop on the sides I couldn't hardly get out, and wouldn't that have been an obit, 'Former Child Star Suffocates in Dumpster.' Anyway, the upshot was I invented this stick to spear things. I took a mop handle and hammered some nails in it, bingo, I could spear things, look them over, there comes a time when you don't want to climb into Dumpsters anymore."

As there had been a time when a house in the Beverly Hills flats was socially unsuitable for a star of her magnitude. It was almost too much to assimilate.

"Hi, Melba."

"Herb, what's your best buy today?"

"Just for you, Melba." Herb was wearing a long white grocer's coat and a reddish-brown toupee that sat rakishly askew on top of his head. A plastic name tag identified him as store manager. "There's a can of Arrid Extra Dry for ninety-nine cents on special, Arrid's offering a twenty-five-cent coupon, and the store's doubling that, that's fifty cents, so you get the Arrid for forty-nine cents."

"I'd rather pay nothing, Herb."

"Wouldn't we all, Melba."

"But I guess you got to put something down, you want a good deal."

"That's how it works, Melba." Herb nodded in Jack's direction. "You got yourself a new box boy, I see." A broad wink for Jack's benefit. "I bet you didn't know Melba was an old-time movie star, did you? Silent pictures, that right, Melba? Rudolph Valentino. Clara Bow. Before my time. She's some kind of shopper, though." He spoke as if she was not visible, as if she was just another lonely older customer he had to humor while at the same time making sure that she was not shoplifting. "I'll give her that."

"Your hair's falling off, Herb, better fix it." She did not take offense, seemed in fact to be enjoying the byplay. Even the jocularity about her once having been a movie star. "There's a special on Elmer's Glue, I noticed. That should keep it down in a high wind."

"Say hello to Clark Gable, you see him, Melba. Tell him I loved him in that *Casablanca*."

"That was Bogie." But Herb had cruised off into housewares.

"How does he know you were in the movies?"

"He doesn't, really." She did not stop talking as she popped cans into the cart. Progresso lentil soup. College Inn chicken broth. Chicken of the Sea tuna, two dozen cans. Manischewitz unsalted matzos. "Someone must've heard a rumor I was, and so I always just say yes, it's true, as a matter of fact, never deny it, just give a smile and a wink. Sometimes the best way to lie is to tell the truth." She hadn't lost the Industry shrewdness. " 'Yessir,' I say, 'I was the biggest box office star in Hollywood. The envelope, please. And the winner is . . . Melba Mae Toolate.' On the face of it, it looks ridiculous, right?" A cackle. "I'm going to pass on that Arrid special of Herb's. I don't go in for deodorants much. Carole Lombard always said soap and water, that's the ticket, it's all a girl needs." Suddenly she was pensive. "I was supposed to be on Miss Lombard's plane when it went down. In Nevada. War-bond tour. Nineteen forty-two."

Jack thought the memory was going to make her cry.

"I was fourteen. The good lord Jesus Christ was looking out for me."

That was out of left field. He wondered when Jesus Christ had turned up at Slot 123, Forsythia Lane, Hamtramck. The new man in her life.

She turned up another aisle, the feminine-hygiene shelves. Underwear, sanitary napkins, vaginal sprays, prophylactics. Her mood suddenly lightened. "You know they make a brand of rubbers now that's got a mint taste, I saw that in *Esquire* magazine, I think a taste of mint wouldn't be what I'd be looking for. Vanilla, though, that might not be bad, I love the smell of vanilla, a vanilla dick, I think I'd like that. I always preferred sucking people off to fucking them. Less wear and tear on the plumbing, you don't get knocked up if you're dumb enough to swallow it, and you're in charge." She gave a lewd wink. "It's in your hands, get it?" He got it. Now she was fingering a display of training bras. "My boobs were just beginning to show that year." The year she was meant to be on Carole Lombard's plane, he guessed. "And the parts I was playing, I wasn't supposed to have any. So Mr. French sent a memo down to wardrobe. 'Do something about Miss Tyler's tits.' I used to have a copy. Arthur got it for me. I framed it and hung it in my dressing room. Anyway. All my costumes had to be tailored so my tits wouldn't show. Big collars. And every time I came into a shot, I was carrying a bag of schoolbooks or a bunch of flowers, some shit like that."

Her voice began to rise again. "My tits were always giving me trouble." Her troublesome tits and the advantages of a blow job and not fucking the garbage man. Quite a conversational parlay for Farmer Dell's. "I remember this other time, when I was in Italy, it was that time I couldn't get arrested in Hollywood, so I went to Rome. And this ginney director wanted me to show a little tit. I didn't know they let you do that in pictures, you couldn't even show cleavage when I was at Cosmo, you did, Will Hays got on your ass, and those Catholic fuckers at the Legion of Decency. This was 1951, '52, the wops got away with murder in those days, it wasn't like today when what's-her-name, the blonde with the accent, shows her pussy, and nobody gives a shit. They already said I was a Commie and a whore, so I say to myself no big deal if this dago wants to light my boob. The scene was, I was supposed to be getting laid in the back of a car. And it was a real car, it wasn't a cutaway car like on a stage at Cosmo, it was one of those little ginney cars, there was no way you could get fucked in it, it was so small my legs would've had to go out the window, and garlic breath, this actor, his ass would've been bouncing off the roof. But would he listen to me, this director? No. So I had to hold my right tit up in my hand, let him get a light reading. It was night shooting. Out in the street. Via something. Those Italians. They never heard of a closed set. Half the people in Rome were watching him trying to light my boobs. Then it turns out he didn't think they were big enough, he wanted molds made to make them look bigger. So there I was, twenty-three years old, and some makeup guy was rubbing petroleum jelly all over my tits so he can lay plaster on them for the molds. Right out there in the street. I think I ended up fucking him. I mean, why not? You talk about foreplay, that's right up there, I get hot just thinking about it."

She was like a bag lady talking to herself on the street, non-stop, aggressive, daring him or anyone else to contradict her, all the while throwing cans and boxes and plastic jars so belligerently into the overloaded shopping cart that one or two bounced out onto the floor. Jack picked them up and tried to find a place for them in the cart, at the same time watching her out of the corner of his eye in case she tossed a tube of K-Y Lubricating Jelly at him. No wonder Herb had heard the stories about her being a movie star. Herb, that crazy lady Melba's at it again, over in aisle seven by the strawberry-scented vaginal sprays, she's talking dirty about the movies and how she was in them once, her mouth needs washing out with soap, she says the *f*-word so much, and I don't care how old she is, that is exactly what she needs, can't you do something about her, Herb, she makes my little granddaughter Opal cry, she's only seven, Opal, and already she's asking me what the *f*-word means.

"This cart's full, I'll get you another one."

"No. Just one cart every trip. It's a matter of principle with me."

"I can see that." What can I see, for Christ's sake, he thought. I'm beginning to sound as loony as she is. He aimed a smile in her direction and, holding the overload steady with one hand, pushed the cart toward a checkout line. The cashier was concentrating on her nails, flourishing an emery board, shape, buff, not acknowledging his presence even with a glance.

"No, not that one," Blue hissed. "That's Tiara. She's a real pain in the ass."

He smiled brightly at Tiara, who still did not look up, and with difficulty wheeled the shopping cart toward another line. Blue was talking loudly now, not so much to him as to the store at large. "You got to get the exact item on the coupon or she yells at you. Just yells. These colored girls . . ." He thought, Jesus, will you shut up. ". . . been on food stamps most of their lives, you think they'd learn." Then she disappeared down an outer aisle. "Forgot the Band-Aid special. You start checking out. I'll be right back. Use lane one. That tall colored girl."

The cashier at the new checkout counter stared blankly at him. "This the express lane."

"I beg your pardon?"

"Ten items or less."

"Sorry." It occurred to Jack how little he knew about grocery shopping. It was not something he did. In any case he ate most of his meals out, whatever city he was in. He was sweating. A shopping cart loaded with what seemed to him enough items to provision a medium-sized city was harder to maneuver through the narrow aisles than he would have thought. Like a goddamn tank. And the shit was beginning to give way. The last thing he wanted was for that bottle of A-1 Sauce to smash on the floor. He wondered if it would be his responsibility to clean it up. He looked around. Tiara was the only other cashier on duty. Still working on her nails. I need a tug to dock this fucking thing, he thought, jerking the cart back into her checkout line. "Hi, Tiara."

"How come you know my name?"

"I heard it around."

"That crazy woman tell you my name?"

"Actually she's not so crazy."

"Bitch said I was a pain in the ass."

So she had heard that. Why not? Everyone else in the store had. "I don't think she really meant it." He was unloading items fast onto the conveyor belt. Mild long-lasting Ivory Liquid. Canada Dry Ginger Ale. Tucks's Vaginal Wipes. A half dozen Fleet's enemas. These aren't for me, he wanted to say, the postprandial dump is regular as clockwork. "It's what you call a figure of speech."

"A what?"

Blue was bearing down on the checkout line, holding up her Band-Aid special. "I thought I told you not to use Tiara." She might have been complaining to a director about a grip who was in her sight line. "Use that girl on register one."

"That's the express lane over there. Ten items or less." He was not up to a racial incident at Farmer Dell's. "And as you can plainly see, we have more than ten items." Do I sound as demented as I think? Yes. No contest. Nolo contendere.

"Well, she's supposed to take you if there's nobody else on line. That's the rule. Call Herb."

"Forget it," he said, and kept unloading. Get into the game. "Make those bar codes hum, Tiara. Put the emery board away. This is the checkout Olympics."

For a moment Tiara stared truculently at Blue, then stuck the emery board into her hair, took a can of Chicken of the Sea tuna and deliberately ran its bar code over the magnetic scanner.

"Go for the gold, Tiara."

"Shit, you is as crazy as the crazy lady."

If Blue heard, she gave no indication. She seemed mesmerized by the mounting numbers on the cash register. Turning her tote upside down, she emptied all her coupons and rebates onto the counter. A few fluttered down under the register. Sixty dollars. Eighty. Ninety. A hundred. Jack struggled to keep pace with his unloading. Blue was on her hands and knees picking up the coupons that had fallen. A hundred and ten. Herb suddenly appeared at the register. He had straightened his hairpiece. "You going for the record, Melba?"

"This won't even hit two hundred, Herb." On her feet now. Content to win the race, not set a new Farmer Dell's record. "You been at this as long as I have, you get a feel for how much you've got." She shoved the pile of coupons toward him. "There was this time in Kalamazoo, at Kroger's in the mall, I bagged two hundred ninety-six dollars and thirty-seven cents' worth, one cart like always, got it down to nine dollars and sixteen cents with my coupons. The funny thing was, I had to call a cab, take me back to my trailer, and it cost more to get home than it did the groceries. Eleven dollars. Ten dollars and thirty-five cents for the fare, sixty-five cents for the tip."

"You're some kind of big tipper, Melba, that cabdriver must've been glad he picked you up." The register stopped at one hundred seventy-two dollars and nine cents. Herb smoothed the crumpled coupons and began discounting. Tiara began bagging. "Melba." Herb talking. "How about taking your picture for the Farmer Dell's employee newspaper. Our number-one shopper at location twenty-seven. Might even be, the picture comes out good, we can put you on the TV." An elaborate smile. "You should like that, you being from the movies and all. You and Farmer Dell. Talking about our discounts. Our double-coupon days . . ."

Sock it away at Farmer Dell's.

She looked stricken. "No."

"It'll mean a little money come in your direction. And be a feather in my cap."

Every day.

Every way.

Herb's serious, Jack thought. He wondered how she would react. Go fuck yourself, I bet. But she surprised him. A hauteur he had not seen before. The kind of piss elegance that only a star of her generation could get away with. "I don't do commercials. I don't believe a star should. It detracts from her mystery."

Sock it away at Farmer Dell's.

"You're a pistol, Melba. Isn't she a pistol?"

Jack nodded. "She sure is."

"I wouldn't look a gift horse in the mouth, but that's show business, isn't that what they say?" Herb was making his final calculations. "Melba, that's going to be seventeen dollars and fifty-one cents exactly."

"He will pay."

He. Of course. The old studio training. The star never carried cash. The flack picked up all the bills. Herb, you are seeing star power, and you don't even know it. He paid with a twenty and left the change on the counter for Tiara. Recompense for the crazy lady's calling her a pain in the ass. However accurate the assessment might have been. And conversely, however crazy the crazy lady might be.

Plenty.

—◇—

It had grown cold in the parking lot. Eddies of snow were scudding across the blacktop. There were twelve bags in all. Blue did not help him load them into the trunk of the rental Ford Taurus. She stood apart, preoccupied, withdrawn into that middle-distance space he had so often seen actors occupy when they wished to appear oblivious to the attention focused on them.

"I always liked to shop." It was a pronouncement. He was surprised that she had not used the royal "we." As in We are not amused. As I am not now, he thought.

"When I was at Cosmo, and I'd go to New York to do publicity, I'd always go to Macy's on Sunday mornings. Mr. French would talk to Mr. Macy or whoever it was he talked to, and they'd open the store just for me. I couldn't go during the week, they were afraid I'd be injured by my fans . . ."

It was as if she was being recorded for some oral history program. Archives of Film 101—The Publicity Tour. Jack tried not to move too fast, to do anything that would interrupt the flow.

". . . and so I'd show up at the store with a publicity man from the New York office and take the elevator to the top floor. The antique department. There was just the two of us. And someone from store security. And someone to take the orders. And a vice-president. Sometimes, after I got older, Arthur would come with me, but Arthur didn't really like to shop, all he came to New York for was to see the shows. I always bought him a present, though. A tie. A pipe. Once I got him a toboggan. And had a rose painted on it, like the sled in *Citizen Kane*, because I knew how much Arthur and his father hated that picture, Arthur said it was un-American, but of course he picked that up from his father. Mr. French was such a good friend of

Mr. Hearst's. We'd take his private car up to the ranch for the weekend, they'd just hitch it on to the Starlight, and when we woke up in the morning, we'd be at the ranch siding."

She paused, as if wondering if she should explain that the ranch was San Simeon. No. Back to Macy's, in that strange disembodied voice.

"I'd come down the escalator, floor to floor, picking out exactly what I wanted. It was so much fun. They even let me run up the down escalator. I always bought toilet paper at Macy's. Hundreds and hundreds of rolls. It was extra soft, and didn't scratch your pussy like the kind my household staff always bought in Los Angeles. And I never had to pay. The man from the store would add it up, and the publicity man from the New York office would take the bill, and he'd pay it, I think they just billed it to the publicity budget of whatever picture I was publicizing. I don't think the studio even deducted it from my salary, although I don't know, because everything I made went directly to my business manager. I had a maid and a secretary and a chauffeur the studio paid for. Mr. French fired the chauffeur because he thought I was fucking him. I think I only fucked him once. His name was Rod. Rob. Something like that. It was during the war. I loved the war. The war-bond tours. Visiting the troops. Mr. French wouldn't let me go overseas with Bob and Bing. He thought my plane would crash and I would die, like Miss Lombard and Glenn Miller and that English fairy, what's his name, that played Ashley in *Gone With the Wind*. I could always get cigarettes during the war. From Lilo Kusack, he knew people. I mean cartons. A gross of cartons. Chesterfield. Philip Morris. Mr. French would never let me smoke in public. And silk stockings. In my size. I read someplace that after the war the girls in Germany would fuck somebody for a pair of nylons. That was so cute. I was doing a little marijuana those days with Shelley Flynn, and I promised him some head if he got me a dozen pair. He did, and then so I didn't have to blow him I told him I would tell Mr. French he was giving me Mary Jane."

Suddenly she smiled. A dazzling close-up smile for the cameras that were not there. "So Farmer Dell's might not be Macy's, but I guess you can say I've been shopping all my life."

"Yes, I guess you can," Jack said carefully.

"You know, it was after one of those shopping trips that I met Jacob."

He held his breath. It was the first time she had mentioned his name. Maybe she was not that crazy after all. Just not entirely screwed in tight. She seemed to take for granted that he was intimately familiar with the Tyler hagiography in its entirety, the legend down to its most esoteric footnotes, and of course including the part that Jacob King had played in her life, and she in his. This was the real thing. The scenes with Herb and Tiara were acting.

"I was staying at the Plaza, that corner suite on the top floor overlooking the park, and when I came back there after Macy's, I fucked Arthur, or at least I think I did, Arthur always liked to fuck in the afternoon, so it's natural to think that's what we did, and then we went out to dinner at 21, and then we ended up at the Copa. Jacob was there. He was the best-looking man I had ever seen in my life. He had just been acquitted of something, murder, I think, something like that. Arthur said he'd wrapped some guy who ratted on him all up in duct tape, that shit plumbers use, so he couldn't breathe, he must've been really funny to look at, with all that tape all over him, like a mummy, I guess, but that's just Arthur, he read that in the *Daily Mirror*, I bet, and that was another one anyway. He was celebrating, Jacob, with his lawyer, Jimmy something, and that old man, the furrier, Morris, I think his name was, but of course he had done it, he told me that later."

She must mean the murder, Jack thought.

-◦-

A gust of wind. She shivered and went silent, then stood by the right rear door of his gray Taurus, waiting for him to open it, a residual instinct, the star who took it for granted that a suitor or servitor would always be there to open doors for her, a car available, and a chauffeur or a studio teamster to see that she was comfortable in the back seat, a lap robe available, if necessary, the chauffeur or teamster or suitor or servitor there but to be commanded, and to speak only when spoken to. "Would you drive me home now?" she said. As if home were still on Linden Drive in the Beverly Hills flats, or the larger place on Tower Road north of Sunset, around the corner from Bing and Dixie Crosby, where there were no writers or B-picture directors to taint the neighborhood, or perhaps that corner suite at the Plaza where Arthur French would mount her after her Macy's shopping expedition late on a winter Sunday afternoon, with the reflections of the Christmas lights on Fifth Avenue twinkling in the bedroom mirror when she came, the kind of special effect Cosmopolitan Pictures was famous for.

1947

I

IN THE FULLNESS OF TIME, I have tried to consider why certain gangsters become legend, and why others do not, why Jacob King was a legend and why Pittsburgh Pat Muldoon is remembered, if at all, only because he was, putatively, a legend's victim. Jacob King had style and girls and the national racing wire Morris Lefkowitz had given him (a testing insisted upon by Morris's attorney Jimmy Riordan, who thought Jacob King too headstrong for the demands of the business world), and run it well he did, turning the wire into a multimillion-dollar monopoly whose competitors decided to seek retirement in Florida and Arizona when the suggestion was tendered that their fingers, noses, and tongues might be imperiled if they continued in operation. He called Winchell Walter, and Walter called him Jake, as did bespoke tailors and headwaiters and the chorines he was said to enjoy two or three at a time. If Jacob King had not been photographed as often as Blue Tyler, neither was he a stranger to the pop of flashbulbs and the biography of headlines. In the newspaper morgues there were photographs of him cutting a wedding cake the day of his marriage to the former Lillian Aronow, and leaving the Temple Orach Chaim a year later with his wife and their infant son, Matthew, and a year after that a picture taken by the house photographer at the Latin Quarter of Jacob smoking a cigar, a girl on each arm, neither of whom was the former Lillian Aronow, and then in 1943 a candid of Jacob and Lillian and Matthew and six-week-old Abigail King outside their new house overlooking the harbor in Bay Ridge, with Staten Island in the background and in the background as well the USS *New Jersey* steaming toward the Narrows and the war Jacob King's Brooklyn draft board had declared him physically unfit to fight in because of his flat feet, and perhaps also because of the emoluments that Morris Lefkowitz, through layers of underlings, had the forethought to direct to the draft board's members. There is a Weegee photograph of Jacob King entering a building in the garment district with two men who held their hats in front of their faces while he waved cheerfully to the photographer, and a Weegee photograph of Jacob King in a double-breasted dinner jacket dancing with a WAVE lieutenant junior grade at a war-bond rally at the Statler Hotel, and still another Weegee photograph of Jacob King in a camel's-hair overcoat being fingerprinted at the Thirty-fourth Precinct in upper Manhattan. Then there were the headlines, a sampling of which sketch the outlines of a life lived dangerously: JUDGE IM-PLICATED IN MOB BRIBERY PROBE; DA ACCUSES KING WITNESS OF PERJURY; KING ACCUSED IN MOB SLAYING; KING: "JUST TAKING A LITTLE STEAM"; KING WITNESS KO'D; CHRISTMAS PACKAGE RIPS KING WITNESS.

Legend, however, is more than just headlines and appearance, because Morris "The Furrier" Lefkowitz was also a legend, and he nearly an old man when he became one, a nearly old man with rimless glasses and a suit with a vest and what seemed to be, in the rare photographs of him that appeared in the press, only seven strands of hair taped to his liverish skull, a legend because his fingerprints were not on file with any law enforce-ment agency even after half a century as banker and secretary of state in the country of crime, a legend as well because he could become rapturous about the qualities that would make nutria the fur of the future, the fur for women who had never before owned a fur.

It was this capacity for looking into the future and seeing how it could work, seeing its potential for profit, both licit and illicit, that led Morris Lefkowitz, when the war was over and the victory processions ended, to send Jacob King to Los Angeles as his personal emissary to those who would make the desert of Nevada bloom, to show them how an entente cordiale between East Coast and West Coast and the criminal city states of the large empty in-between could only benefit them all. It was a delicate mission, because the men of the West wanted to keep Nevada for themselves, a mission calling for a certain flair, and flair Jacob King had in abundance. It was also a good time for Jacob King to leave New York for a spell, as the murder trial in which he had been found "not glty." by jury had focused the kind of attention on Morris Lefkowitz that he had spent a lifetime trying to avoid, and with it speculation that he had ordered the bomb in the poinsettia and the hit in the crapper at Sunnyside Arena in Queens the night Lulu Constantino won a split decision over Lefty Lew Mann in the main event.

What Morris Lefkowitz had not factored into the equation was Blue Tyler.

◄○►

On the afternoon of Twelfth Night, 1947, in the Criminal Courts Building at 100 Centre Street in lower Manhattan, a dozen good men and true, some perhaps fearful of their lives, and not entirely without reason, acquitted Jacob King of the murder of one Philly Wexler, a gambler who in the absence of good sense had tried to move in on the vending-machine business that was one of Morris Lefkowitz's lesser enterprises, one to which he paid such scant attention that Philly Wexler apparently thought he could take it over with but a minor rebuke, if indeed any rebuke was in order, as it was Philly Wexler's stated objective to revitalize the vending-machine franchise, to run it on a more cost-effective basis, and by rallying it from the inertia brought about by Morris's inattention, increasing the tribute he claimed he was more than willing to pay into the Lefkowitz coffers. It is unnecessary to say that when this transgression was brought to Morris Lefkowitz's attention, he did not appreciate the favor Philly Wexler maintained he was doing for him. If Morris Lefkowitz encouraged the notion that he was a benign despot, a despot he still was, and not one willing to countenance the grab of even the most insignificant asset of his criminal conglomerate. Though they were at best minor profit centers, and sometimes even liabilities, these were ventures Morris Lefkowitz kept in reserve so that he might bestow them upon deserving subordinates for services rendered, a piece of the action, as it were, albeit a small one.

It was through such foresight that Morris Lefkowitz inspired loyalty, while at the same time discouraging attempts upon his domain, and one must also add his life. If Philly Wexler were allowed to take over the minute principality of the vending-machine business without Morris Lefkowitz's benediction, then the whole Lefkowitz empire in all its many parts would be at risk. Morris Lefkowitz would be seen as old, not in charge, and talk of coups would be in the air; it was the predatory law of that world in which he had staked his claim. Morris Lefkowitz, however, had survived in this world for nearly six decades, had become its elder statesman precisely because he was such a student of all the clauses and subsections in the constitution of crime. Age had not dimmed the clarity of his vision, as some had thought, and perhaps even wished, nor his ability to see and play all the angles, which of course was why, as a statement against institutional anarchy, Philly Wexler was marked, had to be marked, for execution, the ultimate penance.

It was a hit that in the normal course of events Jacob King would not have been nominated to perform, prince royal that he was seen to be, at least by himself, in the kingdom of Lefkowitz, but it was Jacob who had argued that if Philly Wexler's death was intended to be a statement, then the statement, on organizational principles, would best be made by someone in a position of authority rather than by an out-of-town hitter, or worse by an ambitious young shooter who upon its successful conclusion might get ideas above his station. In other words Jacob King himself. There was nothing personal in the decision,

only a belief in order, especially insofar as an assault on that
order might compromise Jacob King's own position in the succession. The fact was that if Jacob King could be said to like
anyone, he liked Philly Wexler. They had gone to school together in Red Hook, at least until the fifth grade, which was the
extent of the education Jacob King thought he needed in order
to persevere in the world. Indeed Philly Wexler's sister Ruth had
been Jacob King's first piece of ass, under a stoop on Luquer
Street, a commercial transaction when he was ten and she thirteen, arranged by Philly, who took half the two dollars and then
fucked Ruth himself free of charge.

Hubris came too easily to Jacob King, and it was hubris that
almost led to his undoing in the murder of Philly Wexler. What
had made him so effective an assassin when he was a boy and on
the make was the planning he would put into each hit. He
always picked an isolated spot on a meaner street in a lesser
borough than Manhattan (never Staten Island, however, because it was an island, and if something went wrong, hard to get
off, and who would want to hole up in Staten Island?), an isolated neighborhood where there would be no witnesses and
where silence was seen as a virtue and people did not rush to
their windows if they heard the sound of gunfire outside. If by
chance some poor unfortunate happened upon the wrong place
at the wrong time, then that poor unfortunate might well become, if he could not be bribed or intimidated, an ancillary
victim himself. There must be, as well, a place to dispose of the
body, and the cemetery of choice, vide Pittsburgh Pat Muldoon, was the harbor that made the city the world's greatest
seaport.

It had been some years, however, since Jacob King had killed
except in anger, and it was as if he thought, in the prime of life,
that his Broadway fame and newspaper glamour exempted him
from exercising the cold-blooded care that had come so naturally to him in his youth. He was Jacob King, and if he chose to
put two slugs in the base of Philly Wexler's skull in front of the
apartment of Philly's girlfriend in Washington Heights at eleven

o'clock of a winter's evening, then that was the way Jacob King would do it. He had not taken the trouble, however, to learn that the apartment on West 180th Street belonged to Ruth Wexler, his first fuck, who Philly at forty was still fucking, his sister the love of his life, and witness number one to his murder. It was also inopportune that Philly Wexler fell in the street under a mailbox onto which the U.S. Postal Service had affixed a card that said, MAIL EARLY FOR DELIVERY BEFORE CHRISTMAS. Here was the kind of irony that of course caught the eye of Weegee, that photographer-poet of urban violence, when he arrived on the scene. Weegee took the photograph—it can be seen in *Weegee's New York,* a book that Blue Tyler showed me in the Hamtramck public library years later, pointing to the picture of Philly Wexler on the sidewalk under the post box, covered by a raincoat, and saying, "Jacob did that guy, I bet you didn't know that"—and after it appeared in the *Daily News,* another witness, in a momentary and ultimately fatal surge of good citizenship, came forward, a cut man who worked in the corner at Sunnyside Arena in Queens. It was he that minions of Morris Lefkowitz murdered when he was taking a dump during the preliminaries the night Lulu Constantino beat Lefty Lew Mann in the main event (KING WITNESS KO'D), as it was to Ruth Wexler that other minions of Morris the Furrier delivered the poinsettia that blew small pieces of her against the walls of her Washington Heights apartment (CHRISTMAS PACKAGE RIPS KING WITNESS). With the untimely (or perhaps timely) departures of his two eyewitnesses, the Manhattan district attorney's case disappeared, and the jury on that sixth day of January, 1947, took only eighty-seven minutes to find Jacob King not guilty of murder in the first degree. The judge told Jacob King he was free to go about his business and congratulated the jury of his peers on a job well and quickly done.

—◇—

"Philly Wexler was my boyhood friend," Jacob King said that afternoon on the steps of the Criminal Court Building in lower Manhattan, "and Ruthie, while she was a disturbed personality when she got older, seeing things she didn't see, Ruthie was one of the world's beautiful people, and I prefer to remember her like she was when we were all kids together on Luquer Street in Red Hook." In the tabloid photographs he was wearing his double-breasted camel's-hair overcoat, and was hatless in the cold. In one arm he held his daughter, Abigail, only three, while his son, Matthew, clung to his other hand, peeking out at the photographers from behind his father's arm, by now a boy of seven in a blue sailor coat adorned with petty officer's stripes, and with a cap on his head. Lillian Aronow King held her son's other hand. She was wearing a seal coat courtesy, I would assume, of Morris Lefkowitz, and in the photographs she had the pinched unhappy face of a woman the years would not treat kindly, broadening her nose, I would have wagered, and further opening the already generous pores of her skin. "I don't know who it was that did Philly and Ruthie," Jacob King continued, his use of "did" a reminder that his was a society in which all the tenses of the verb "to do" promised extinction of life, "but I want Lew Valentine"—the chief of police since 1934, a nice touch—"and Frank Hogan"—the Manhattan district attorney, another nice touch—"to know I don't hold no hard feelings, *any* hard feelings, I mean, they got a job to do, and they should know that anything I can do to help, they got it, and I want to especially thank Mike and Brendan here"—his attorneys, Meyer Feiffer and Brendan Kean, relegated to the background in the photographs, and almost invisible—"for a hell of job, the case never should've been brung, *brought,* they proved that, and now thanks, boys, I been in the Tombs four months, I want a bath, a shave, and I want to go home and tell Lillian how much I love her and the kids, thanks again, and no more questions, and Arthur, okay, for you one more picture," Arthur being Arthur Fellig, the great Weegee himself, in some way Jacob King's court photographer during his New York period.

I do not know if Jacob King fucked Lillian when he got home to Bay Ridge and shaved and bathed and put Matthew and Abigail to bed, but I do know that he ended up the evening at the Copacabana, with Lillian and with Morris Lefkowitz and James Francis Riordan, celebrating his acquittal and planning his future.

◄○►

"Tell me about Jimmy Riordan," I said to Arthur French.

   "He was Morris Lefkowitz's lawyer."

   "I already know that."

   "A genius."

   "You're bullshitting me, Arthur."

   "No. He was a man of vision in his way."

   "And Jacob?"

   "A sharp dresser with fast moves."

◄○►

I try to imagine that night at the Copa as Jacob King and his party took their seats, Joe Romagnola lifting the velvet rope and pocketing the hundred-dollar bill Jimmy Riordan gave him without looking at the denomination, the tip unnecessary because Julie Podel had made it clear to Joe Romagnola that a ringside table would always be available to Jacob King, Jacob King was Morris Lefkowitz's man, and he, Julie Podel, was not in business to antagonize Morris Lefkowitz, antagonize Morris Lefkowitz and the laundry might not get done or the band might not show up or there might even be an accidental fire in the kitchen. There was a buzz in the packed house, the kind that Shelley Flynn got and Frank got and Jimmy Walker used to get, dying but still a sweet memory, an ex-mayor who liked girls and sticking his dick into them, people craning for a look at the city's most recently acquitted celebrity murderer, people with money in their pockets now that the war was a year and a half over and already a fading memory, and onstage Helen O'Connell, spotting Jacob, snapped her fingers at her trio, and then as if it were a planned part of her set segued into "I Like the Likes of You," singing it directly into Jacob King's ear, a rendition full of innuendo and invitation.

   "A very special song for a very special guy, Jacob King, ladies and gentlemen," Helen O'Connell said to her audience when she finished. "Glad to see you back on the town, Jake, we missed you." Back on the town, the words making Jacob King's acquittal that afternoon seem an absolution, Philly Wexler in the revisionist version having deservedly been condemned to death for the sin of incest, a sin against nature, with Jacob King's slate wiped clean, his public appearance a proclamation that he considered himself innocent of the crime attributed to him, and he himself a bulwark against perversion who had been ill used by small and ambitious public men. He stood and aimed a kiss toward the stage. "I like the likes of you, too, Helen," he said, and there was applause at the surrounding tables. A club photographer in mesh stockings and a black skimp snapped his picture, the flashbulb not even making him blink, and then aimed her camera at Morris Lefkowitz, who pretended to blow his nose into a linen napkin so large it covered his entire face. Jimmy Riordan already had a bill in his hand, a twenty, and he stuck it between the twin globes of the photographer's breasts. "Mr. Lefkowitz says no more pictures, sweetheart," Jimmy Riordan said, "get rid of the plate." The photographer said, "Excuse me, of course, Mr. Riordan," then bent and whispered into his ear, the twenty still sticking out between the tits she rested on his shoulder, and after a moment Jimmy Riordan said, "You tell Winchell he wants to congratulate Jake, all he has to do is walk over here."

Morris Lefkowitz turned to Jacob King. "You get your face in the newspapers too often."

"I've got a pretty face, Morris," Jacob King said.

"You get your face in the newspaper nuzzling too many broads not named Lillian."

"You don't think they got newspapers out there in California?" Jacob King said. "You think they don't got broads? You think it's all avocados out there?"

Lillian King toyed with the paper umbrella in her empty glass and pretended not to hear, her whole married life an exercise in not hearing or, if she did hear, forgetting quickly. Helen O'Connell was singing "Love Is Just Around the Corner," and

Lillian King, with no one at the table paying any attention to her, mouthed the lyrics in perfect sync, it being her fantasy, when she fingered herself on those all-too-frequent nights when Jacob did not come home, that one day she would head the bill at the Copa.

A waiter set down a fresh round of drinks, a club soda for Morris Lefkowitz, a Rob Roy for Jimmy Riordan, a White Horse and soda for Jacob King, nothing for Lillian. "I ordered a Scotch sour," Lillian King said.

"You already had a Scotch sour, Lillian," Morris Lefkowitz said. "In fact you had three." He turned to Jacob and without a pause said, "I hope you appreciate this is a ground-floor opportunity I'm handing you in California. A major assignment. I look at the state of Nevada, the silver state, and you know what I see—"

Lillian King interrupted, her voice louder than it should have been, "What am I, a little girl, Morris Lefkowitz counts my drinks now?"

A waiter and a captain were hovering near the table, Joe Romagnola's orders, a perquisite that accrued naturally to Morris Lefkowitz. Jacob King raised his arm and both the captain and the waiter sprang to his side. "A Scotch sour for Mrs. King," he said, and then to Morris Lefkowitz, "You look at Nevada and you see someplace that's not the *schmata* business."

"All gold is what I see," Morris Lefkowitz said. "A gold mine in the goddamn desert." His scalp glistened with sweat, as it often did when he talked about money, and his voice lowered. "Jimmy . . ."

"Morris . . ."

"The name of the place they're going to build out there?"

"La Casa Nevada. They begin pouring the foundations the first of next month."

"La Casa Nevada. A nice name. Italian, Jimmy?"

"Spanish."

"What does it mean, this Spanish?"

"Nevada House, Morris."

"I like La Casa Nevada better," Morris Lefkowitz said. He leaned close to Jacob King. "Expansion, Jacob. We have to go national."

"You going to let the California boys move into New York then, Morris?" Jacob King said. If he was an unlettered man of violent urges, he was also not without irony, a rare combination in a gangster.

Morris Lefkowitz had an old man's laugh, more cough than laugh. His face would redden, and if he did not get his handkerchief to his mouth, he would spray mucus indiscriminately. Now he laughed and sprayed.

"Morris, you hit me with a clam," Lillian King said.

Morris Lefkowitz ignored her. "That's why I love this boy like the son I never had, Jimmy. Always kidding. Jacob, I know you since you were, what . . ."

"Since he was fifteen years of age," Jimmy Riordan said.

". . . fifteen years of age and you come around telling me what you could do for me. I laughed. I admit it. I laughed. Then I saw. Some of what you said you could do"—Morris Lefkowitz shrugged expressively—"you could do." Another shrug, as if to shake away the bodies that were the by-product of Jacob King doing what he could do. He patted Jacob on the cheek. "This little *boychik,* Jimmy . . ."

Jimmy Riordan nodded, all the while playing with a gold pencil. He rarely spoke unless it was necessary. Listening was what he did best, next to remembering, his Irish welterweight's face as always impassive. The criminal bar had never attracted him. Too many elements over which he had no control. Wild cards. He hated wild cards. A jury was the wild card he hated most. He did however vet the attorneys who appeared for members of the Lefkowitz enterprises when they were caught up in criminal proceedings. He favored Jews and Irishmen who had sharpened their courtroom skills in a district attorney's office of any of the five boroughs or for the U.S. attorney in the southern district, men, now private practitioners, who knew their opposite numbers at the prosecutors' table, knew the judges and the political clubs and what markers might be called in at what courthouses, men absent social advantages and with limited educational credentials who had not been recruited by the Wall Street law firms, class resentment being, to Jimmy Riordan, an essential element for success in the makeup of a criminal lawyer. Meyer Feiffer and Brendan Kean, out of the Bronx and Inwood respectively, City College for one, St. John's for the other, each a former Queens chief deputy D.A. specializing in the more difficult homicide cases, both with top conviction rates, had defended Jacob King. If they had qualms about the coincidences attendant to the deaths of Ruth Wexler and the corner man at Sunnyside Arena, they kept their own counsel, the single exception Meyer Feiffer's spontaneous spasm of distaste when he learned of Ruth Wexler's demise. This was a lapse suggesting to Jimmy Riordan, with his compulsive attention to detail and his ability to anticipate the possibility of future problems, such as some later onset of virtue, that Meyer Feiffer's services not be required in any future cases alleging criminality in the Lefkowitz domain. It is needless to say that Meyer Feiffer and Brendan Kean were not included in the party at the Copa. They were hired help, well-paid help, but help nonetheless.

"I'll call some people out there, Jacob," Morris Lefkowitz said. "Lilo Kusack. Rita Lewis. She'll show you around. You remember Rita."

"One of my husband's whores," Lillian King said to no one in particular, just loud enough so that Jacob and Jimmy Riordan and Morris Lefkowitz could hear, but not so loud they had to acknowledge what they had heard. Her Scotch sour arrived and she sucked on an orange slice.

"You think the L.A. guys don't know what they got in Nevada, Morris?" Jacob said, ignoring his wife. "You think they're just waiting for someone to come out from New York so they can cut him in?"

"That's what I'm sending you out there for, Jacob. To convince them." Morris Lefkowitz turned to Lillian King. "Lillian, you should order something to eat, you just eat the fruit in the

Scotch sours you like so much, the orange slices and the mara-schino cherries, you'll starve. The shellfish is good here, they tell me. And the creamed spinach is a treat. Waiter," Morris Lefko-witz said. "A plate of spinach for Mrs. King."

"Who're you, Popeye, Morris?" Lillian King said.

But Morris Lefkowitz had expended all the attention he in-tended to expend on Lillian King. The spinach was his way of telling her to shut up. Morris Lefkowitz did not so much talk as send out signals, and not to pick up his signals was to make the kind of mistake Philly Wexler had made. Lillian King heard the signal and said, "I hate spinach, I'll have a steak instead. Well done. And a shrimp cocktail with the mustard and mayonnaise dressing, and not the red cocktail sauce. And a baked potato with sour cream and chives." She could not resist one last sally. "Is that all right, Morris?"

"That's nice, Lillian," Morris Lefkowitz said. "Jimmy, tell Jacob what we're offering the people in California."

"National management," Jimmy Riordan said. "We'll help them maximize their profit potential." James Francis Riordan, attorney at law, of counsel to Morris Lefkowitz and the Lefko-witz enterprises for twenty years and more, had grown up in Yorkville, on streets where words like *cocksucker* and *mother-fucker* were the currency of communication, and he had once fought Golden Gloves, which accounted for his flattened pug's nose. He thought the ring would be his ticket out of Yorkville, as dancing had been his pal Jim Cagney's ticket out, but he couldn't hit a lick, a welterweight with knuckles like potato chips, and he stayed in parochial school and mastered the multi-plication and logarithmic tables and sines and cosines and dollar signs and won scholarships to Regis Prep and then to Fordham and Fordham Law and now he talked about maximizing profit potential for Morris Lefkowitz, a man James Francis Riordan, had he remained a pug in Yorkville, would have called a sheeny cocksucker, he cuts the tip off his prick, the Jew bastid.

"One plus one equals twenty-one," Morris Lefkowitz said. "Blackjack. Everybody a winner."

"It's just a question of calibrating the terms," Jimmy Riordan said carefully, his tone implying what in truth he actually thought, that Jacob King was perhaps not the most effective of calibrators, his handling of the Philly Wexler situation the only example he needed to make his case.

Jacob King picked up the hint of reservation in Jimmy Riordan's voice. "Sure. Just like buying Manhattan Island from the Indians." He did not mask the taunt. It was the eternal struggle between the man of action and the numbers cruncher. "I offer twenty-four dollars, throw in a couple of beads, we close the deal . . ."

But Jimmy Riordan was rising from his chair, not paying attention. "Walter," he said, "what takes you out of the Cub Room on a cold night in January?"

"The chance to see Philly Wexler's best boyhood pal," Walter Winchell said.

"Philly Wexler was a deviate," Jimmy Riordan said, for the record. It was the first time that any principal in the Lefkowitz organization had ever been known to take a moral position. "You know Lillian King, Morris Lefkowitz, Jacob I know you know, we've been saving a seat for you, Walter, it's our press seat . . ."

Walter Winchell pulled back the chair and sat down. "I know your father," he said to Lillian King. "Mendy Aronow, right? The accountant for the Keith circuit. Could multiply three-, four-digit numbers in his head like it was two times six equals twelve. Carried a torch for Gina Hennessy that was in the Follies and married Fergus Choate, the elevator company Choates, he was a homo."

Lillian King preened. Her pedigree was not a public record written on yellow sheets, as was her husband's, and no interest in it had ever before been publicly expressed. That Walter Winchell was aware of her family tree, and had spun from it an urban parable in four sentences, was a bonus she had not been expecting on that evening when her husband was celebrating his acquittal of murder in the first degree, and it revived her spirits.

"That was my late Uncle Mendel. He was my late father's brother. My father was—"

"Whatever," Walter Winchell said. "So, Jake, something nice happened to you today." His eyes were constantly on the move, checking to see who got what table, who was coming, who was going. "I bet Billingsley a fin you wouldn't go to Ossining when it came out about Philly and his sister. The pervert got what perverts deserve."

Jacob King offered no opinion on Philly Wexler's sexual culpability. "You sure you want to sit down with a small-time shooter, Walter?"

"It wasn't me that said that, Jake. I was just quoting one of my sources."

"Unnamed. You want to give me his name, Walter, I'd really appreciate it."

Even Morris Lefkowitz laughed.

"So you're a big-time shooter," Walter Winchell said. "I protect my sources. Like I'm entitled in the United States of America. Which is why the United States of America is the greatest country in the world. And why we got to get rid of the swishes and degenerates like Philly Wexler and the pinko-stinkos to keep it that way." Without missing a beat, he leaned toward Morris Lefkowitz. "So how's the fur business, Morris?"

"Legitimate," Morris Lefkowitz said.

As if he were broadcasting to Mr. and Mrs. United States and all the ships at sea, Walter Winchell said, "And that's how Morris Lefkowitz has stayed out of jail for fifty years."

A look of pain crossed Morris Lefkowitz's countenance. "I'm just a simple furrier," he said.

Winchell was not listening. He focused on the stage, where Helen O'Connell was finishing her set. "Whatta set of pipes on Miss Helen O'Connell," he said to no one in particular, as if composing an item for his column. "Every note a treat. Swellegant. The stems aren't bad either." On the back of an envelope he jotted the words *pipes* and *stems* and *swellegant,* then turned back to Morris Lefkowitz as the stage curtain rose and the house band arrived on a turntable, playing a routine with a Latin beat. "The scoop is you're sending Jake out West, Morris. You trying to keep him on ice. Out of the newspapers for a while. Or does he just need a little sun after his stay in the Tombs?"

Morris Lefkowitz turned his dead, deadly eyes on Winchell. "You want a little Russian sable, Walter? For you I can get it wholesale."

"What would G-man Hoover say if I did that, Morris?" Walter Winchell said, his furtive gaze now moving to a commotion at the maître d's station. Flashbulbs popped. "Blue . . ." Winchell was on his feet, and he was gone, pushing past the adjoining tables, the gel in the stage lights catching his bald spot, making it gleam blue and then pink, Morris Lefkowitz left behind, just another old Jew at a ringside table who tipped too much. "You finished the picture, I hear it's phantabulous," Winchell shouted, and then to a man blocking his view, "Who let you in here, get out of the way," clearing a path by elbowing the man onto his wife's lap, and then again solicitous, "When are you and Arthur middle-aisling it . . ."

"I should worry, I should care," Blue Tyler half sang, half whispered, "I should marry a millionaire. . . . Arthur, do you qualify?"

◄○►

Arthur French remembered:

Or tried to remember, given the slippages of age, or was evasive, and perhaps even lied a little.

I embroidered:

She was almost eighteen, or perhaps nineteen, considering the uncertainty about her date of birth. She was wearing a black evening dress and a full-length red fox coat, and she was accompanied by two bodyguards, three Cosmopolitan Studio publicists, and Arthur French. She smiled and waved at the photographers, their cameras loving her and she loving their cameras in turn, the cameras wiping the teenage sulkiness from her face, Blue always in motion, posing, vamping, cooing, "I'd walk a mile for a man who walked a mile for a Camel." Joe Romagnola, the maître d', produced a cigarette, offering a light from his silver Tiffany lighter, a gift from Frank, who when he played the Paramount gave Tiffany lighters to all the maître d's at all the gin mills where he drank, and Arthur French just as quickly removed the cigarette from her mouth. "J.F. says you're too young to smoke in public," he said, and Blue said, "I'm too young to do a lot of the things I do with you, Arthur, in public and especially in private, it's called statutory something, isn't it?"

More flashbulbs as she threw her arms around Arthur French, kicking one leg behind her, Arthur, who she had fucked a few hours earlier in the top-floor corner suite at the Plaza (Arthur said that it was Blue who only liked to make love in the afternoon, not he, in his late seventies still unable to say the word *fuck*, irritable that I would even ask such a thing). Blue mimed a kiss at Walter Winchell, "Walter, love you, how's June?" not stopping to hug him, and moving behind a phalanx of bodyguards and captains and publicity men she let her red fox coat slip off her shoulders onto the floor, where it was immediately picked up by a bodyguard and handed to the coat check girl. The band eased into a rhumba and before she reached their table she drew Arthur French onto the dance floor, Arthur a game escort but no Chocolate Walker Franklin as a dancer, and as he whirled and dipped, Blue doing the leading and not he, tico tico teek, tico tico tock, Arthur spotted Morris Lefkowitz looking at them and he favored Morris with an almost imperceptible nod. Blue followed his gaze and first she saw the old man with the liver marks at the ringside table and next to him the small man with the wary eyes and the broken nose and next to him the woman with the hard angular face tearing into her steak and then she saw the man who seemed to be with the woman demolishing the steak, the not-quite-tall man with the lacquered black hair and the prominent chin and the look of someone to whom no sexual experience was foreign. He was staring at her, she who men had stared at since she was four years old, men who would look at her on the screen and put their hands in their pockets to fondle their cocks and send her fan mail crusted with their semen, but he was different, he was a man who made her feel embarrassed.

-◄◊►-

"Who's the guy?" Jacob King asked Morris Lefkowitz, his eyes not leaving Blue Tyler.

"What guy?"

"With the actress."

"Moe French's boy," Morris Lefkowitz said.

"Arthur French," Jimmy Riordan said. "His father, Moe, runs Cosmopolitan Pictures."

"They call Moe J. F. French out there in California," Morris Lefkowitz said. "When I first know him on the Lower East Side he was Moses Frankel. He was in haberdashery, and then he bought a nickelodeon. Fur is forever, and suits. But film . . ." He pronounced it "fillum," as if it had two syllables, and even saying the word made him look as if he had bitten into something that tasted bad. "So, Jacob, you understand what you're going to do in California?"

"Let me get the feel of it first, Morris," Jacob King said, rising from the table, leaving Lillian with her steak and Morris Lefkowitz without an answer and Jimmy Riordan uneasy. He walked across the dance floor and tapped Arthur French on the shoulder. A studio bodyguard moved to cut him off, but Arthur shook his head, and Jacob took Blue in his arms, more fluid on the dance floor than Arthur French, as the other dancers moved away, giving them room.

"My name is Jacob King. I'm on my way to Los Angeles"— he pronounced it with a hard *g*—"and I want to get to know you better. I want to get to know you very well."

"You're a very good dancer, Mr. King. You know all the moves."

"I know all the moves," Jacob King said. "That's very funny."

"The studio lets me date, if that's what you mean," Blue said. "Arthur . . ."

Arthur French had retrieved Blue's fox coat from the hat check girl and was moving toward them. "Mr. King is coming to Los Angeles, he says it like it's 'angle us' so I guess he's never been there, but he says he wants to get to know me better, and he has such good moves," Blue said. "I am very flattered, Mr. King. Ta ta. I'm not in the book."

She danced away from Jacob King and into the fur coat Arthur was holding out for her, did it in one take as if she was on a soundstage and knew where the marks were that she had to hit. It was a star turn, and as she danced toward the exit the house band struck up "California, Here I Come," and she waved and was gone.

◄◦►

"Did she mention him?" I asked Arthur French.

"She'd never heard of him. But then again she'd hardly heard of Winston Churchill either." I had the sense nearly fifty years after the fact that Arthur French might conceivably be implying that Blue Tyler had occasionally been rather tedious in her self-centeredness.

"And you told her?"

"I told her he was somebody she should stay away from. That he killed somebody. Wrapped him up in duct tape."

"That wasn't Philly Wexler."

"So it was somebody else. There were so many, does it make any difference? Anyway. She was never going to see him again."

"Your mistake."

"My mistake."

"But was she interested?"

"The way it turned out I'd have to say she was."

I I

THE NIGHT BEFORE he left for Los Angeles, Jacob King fucked Lillian, and then in the morning he fucked her again, positioning her as he performed his conjugal duty so that her legs were over his shoulders and he could stare out the window in his upstairs Bay Ridge bedroom at the fog-shrouded Statue of Liberty. As always, Lillian King copulated and fellated with zest, if no particular skill or peculiarity. That she was angry with him, and she always seemed to be angry both with Jacob and the world at this juncture of her life, was never a deterrent to her pleasuring. But she seemed to understand that in some deep pocket of his mind, Jacob was already entertaining the notion that this view of Miss Liberty was one he was not likely to see again, during coitus or otherwise. When he left the house in Bay Ridge, he gravely shook hands with Matthew King, kissed Abigail and Lillian King, and then was gone. Gone from their lives; of that Lillian Aronow King was sure, and it was not for her a cause for mourning.

◄○►

In his office in the fur district—LEFKOWITZ FOR FUR was the name painted on the front door, M. M. LEFKOWITZ, PROP.—Morris Lefkowitz bade Jacob King good-bye and made him a present of a custom-tailored vicuña overcoat, double-breasted, with a belt that tied instead of buckling.

"Morris, no," Jacob King said. "I'm going to California where the sun shines, you follow?"

"Take it, I want you to have it," Morris Lefkowitz said, admiring the stitching and the hang, running his hand over the soft weave. "It's South American, from the Andes, that's the mountains they got down there. The same family as the guanaco, but smaller, and the wool is more delicate. The other one, the guanaco, is for the savages that raise the goats those people eat." He smoothed a bubble at the shoulder blades. "You're going out there to represent Morris Lefkowitz, and I don't want Lilo Kusack and Benny Draper thinking Morris Lefkowitz got poor."

"We have to go, Morris," Jimmy Riordan said. "The Limited leaves on the dot—"

"So let this Limited wait," Morris Lefkowitz said without concern. He was a man used to having his wishes honored, and it did not cross his mind that the conductor of the Twentieth Century Limited would dare thwart those wishes. The conductor was after all a man who wore a uniform, and to Morris Lefkowitz it was a given that any man who wore a uniform was a man who could be bribed, especially when it was for so trivial a task as delaying the departure of a train carrying his personal emissary to the West Coast. He took a belt and fed it through the vicuña overcoat's generous loops. "Tie it, Jacob, once. Don't knot it. It wrinkles it's so soft. I hope you realize the opportunity this is."

"I had a dollar for every time you told me that, Morris, I'd be a rich man."

"You have the friendship of Morris Lefkowitz. That makes you a rich man. Jimmy . . ." Morris Lefkowitz turned to Jimmy Riordan. "You have the figures for the train?"

Jimmy Riordan patted his briefcase. He checked his watch once more, then walked from Morris's office, through the cutting rooms and the showroom to the reception area. On the front door, LEFKOWITZ FOR FUR, M. M. LEFKOWITZ, PROP. was in black lettering because M. M. Lefkowitz, Prop., thought gold was too ostentatious for a simple furrier.

"I don't hug you, it will ruin the drape," Morris Lefkowitz said to Jacob King.

Jacob nodded. "Morris," he said, a kind of obeisance, and then he too headed out past the cutting tables to the reception area. Jimmy Riordan was waiting by the front door. "Morris," Jacob King said as he opened the door, pointing to the words M. M. LEFKOWITZ, PROP. "All the years I know you, I never asked what the second *M* stood for."

"Menachem," Morris Lefkowitz said, and then, "*Mazel,* Jacob."

◄◊►

"I'll just ride to a Hundred and Twenty-fifth Street," Jimmy Riordan said when Jacob was settled into his Pullman compartment on the Limited. He looked out the window at the red carpet laid down for the Limited's passengers. On the burled-wood foldout desk his briefcase was open, and in the briefcase were stacks of crisp new bills, neatly packaged, ten thousand dollars to a package, twenty-five packages in all. "You know, New York before the goddamn war, before Franklin Delano Pain-in-the-Ass Roosevelt even, you had a town then. Thirty thousand joints. You walk in a club, you're anybody, it wasn't unusual you sat next to the guys. Sometimes the guys shot each other. Like it was part of the floor show, or something. You'd eat in a place, go to a club, grab a show, and end up in Harlem at five A.M., eating ribs and chicken wings and listening to Cab Calloway or Bill Basie. But now . . ." Jimmy Riordan made a rude noise. "New York is dead, you ask me."

Jacob King was washing his face in the compartment's tiny bathroom. "I didn't."

"Didn't what?"

"Ask you."

It was as if Jimmy Riordan had not heard. "Nobody goes to Harlem anymore," he said. "Even in broad daylight. Particularly in broad daylight. I say the reason is the LP record. You had the seventy-eights, you had to get up to change the goddamn record every few minutes. Up and down, sooner or later you'd get irritated, you'd go out, see a show, tie on a load. With the LP, you just sit there like a turnip. It's like the whole town's on the nod. Count your blessings you're getting out, you ask me."

"I didn't ask you that, either."

Jimmy Riordan closed the briefcase and handed it to Jacob. "You want to count it?"

"No. You're not going to cheat Morris. Or me. You value living too much."

The train gave a bump and then began to move slowly down the tracks.

"Look, Jake, this is really a straightforward proposition," Jimmy Riordan said. "*A-B-C. A* is, the California guys are building a place in Las Vegas—"

"La Casa Nevada—"

"*B* is, we think we have the means to assist them—"

"—in maximizing their profit potential. You told me that. What's *C*?"

"*C* is, what's your problem?"

"It's not the way I'd play it. Morris wants Nevada, I can give him Nevada. Take over La Casa Nevada. How far can I push is what I want to know."

Jimmy Riordan closed and locked the briefcase and flipped the key to Jacob King, who attached it to his watch chain. The train was gathering speed. "You're not going out there to take over La Casa Nevada," Jimmy Riordan said quietly. "You're not going out there to push. You're going out there to make nice. Make a few friends."

"And what happens when Benny Draper and Lilo Kusack and them tell me they got all the friends they need?"

"Jake. One step at a time . . ."

"Walk before I run," Jacob King said.

"That's it exactly," Jimmy Riordan said. If he caught the

sardonic edge in Jacob's voice, he chose not to acknowledge it. "It's a question of cooperation. Negotiation. Accommodation. If you anticipate a negative resolution, then the conditions become favorable for a negative resolution. I give you the seed money. I lay out the figures for you. I take you to the train just so I can give you the five-year projection, the ten-year projection, what more do I have to do to make you understand?"

Jacob smiled and straightened his loosened tie. "I love to hear you Fordham guys talk."

The Limited had come out of the Grand Central tunnel and was speeding toward the 125th Street Station. Jimmy Riordan put on his jacket, his hat, and his overcoat. "You get to Chicago, the train pulls into the LaSalle Street Depot, then you pick up the Chief at the Dearborn Street Station, you got a three-hour layover, so go to the Pump Room, you want, but just don't miss the goddamn train, the Dearborn Street Station, not LaSalle Street, LaSalle Street's where you get off the Limited, and make sure they get your luggage on the Chief, it's the Chief you pick up, the Super Chief, not the Limited, you just got off the Limited."

"And went to the Pump Room," Jacob King said. "I listen to you, I think you think you're sending me to that summer camp all you *goyim* send your kids to. Put a tag around my neck, Jimmy, so the *schwartze* porter knows what train I'm supposed to be on. And where my valises are supposed to go. His name is George, by the way, see, I already found that out, you can go home now."

"Whose name?"

"The *schwartze*."

"Jake, all the coloreds on the train are called George. On this train and all the other trains. They call them all George so you don't have to waste any time trying to remember them by their colored names." Jimmy Riordan paused. "What I'm trying to say is, you don't know as much as you think you know."

Jacob put on Morris Lefkowitz's vicuña coat and followed Jimmy Riordan down the corridor to the door of his car. On the

125th Street platform, Jimmy gave the porter a ten-dollar bill, then another ten. "You get to Chicago, George, you make sure Mr. King's bags get on the Chief, you hear?"

"Yessir."

"I know you for a long time, Jake," Jimmy Riordan said, shivering in the early evening cold. "I know what you're like. You're always looking to hit the ball out of the park. That's how you'd play it. So I want you to understand something. This isn't your play. We're building an organization. We're planning on leaving a legacy. Morris isn't sending you out there to push. To build an empire for yourself. Morris is sending you out there because we want you to show the L.A. people, illustrate to them, that the kind of security and management an asset like Nevada requires can best be achieved by national cooperation. As it were."

"So long, Fordham," Jacob King said. He watched Jimmy Riordan walk to the stairs and disappear down the steps leading to 125th Street. The porter was clapping his arms against the cold. "Hey, George," Jacob said, removing his coat.

"Yessir."

Jacob handed him the vicuña coat. "Take it."

"Take it where, Mr. King?"

"It's yours."

"I couldn't take it, Mr. King."

"You know any poor people?" Jacob King said, climbing back aboard the Limited. "Then give it to a poor person."

◄○►

Morris Lefkowitz placed a call to Los Angeles even before the Twentieth Century Limited had cleared the New York City limits. Person-to-person, Morris never being one to waste money on long distance if the party he was calling was not at home.

◄○►

Jenkins, the butler, said, "A Mr. Lefkowitz is calling from New York City."

Rita Lewis looked at Lilo Kusack, who peered over the top of the legal brief he was reading, thought for a moment, and then nodded. "See what he has to say," Lilo Kusack said. He was wearing white swimming trunks, and his face and legs and his hairy chest glistened with suntan oil. Like many affluent men in Southern California, he appeared to have stopped aging at forty, which made it difficult to guess exactly how old he was. Rita Lewis sat in a chair next to his chaise painting her fingernails as she waited for the butler to bring the telephone and plug it into the poolside jack. She was a woman of some mileage but she was well kept, like a classic automobile. Her figure filled her bathing suit, and she shielded her face from the sun with a wide-brimmed straw hat and sunglasses, off which the sun-dappled water in the swimming pool was reflected. The butler plugged in the telephone and handed her the receiver. "Morris," Rita Lewis said, holding the phone carefully so that her nail polish would not run, "it's been a long time."

"You make me wait, Rita," Morris Lefkowitz said. "You never used to make Morris wait."

"This is California, Morris. I'm talking to you from beside the swimming pool. Taking in the sun. I go inside, then I miss the sun, get a chill. So Jenkins brings the phone out here from the house. It takes time. It's not like New York, Morris."

"Who is this Jenkins?" Morris Lefkowitz said.

Rita put her hand over the receiver and trying not to laugh, she said, "He wants to know who Jenkins is."

"Tell him Jenkins is my whacker," Lilo Kusack said. "He'll understand that."

"The butler, Morris." Lilo Kusack beckoned her and she took the telephone and sat on the edge of his deck chair.

"Little Rita has a butler?" Morris Lefkowitz said. And then he said, "If that's Russian sable, then I'm Mrs. Eleanor Roosevelt."

"Who are you talking to, Morris?"

"My grandnephew Mickey. I'm trying to teach him the fur business."

"He's teaching his nephew the fur business," Rita whispered to Lilo Kusack.

"Because fur is forever," Lilo Kusack said. "Fur is legitimate.

That old man's been spinning that line since before I got my first piece of ass."

"Nice talk for a lawyer," Rita Lewis said. "Yes, Morris, I'm still here, it's not a bad connection." She screwed the brush back into the nail polish bottle. "Now, listen, Morris, I know you didn't call just to tell me about your nephew in the fur business."

"Rita, I'd like a favor."

"You know, Morris, I figured that out all by myself, that this wasn't a social call, just to bring me up to date on what you've been doing, maybe invite me out to look at the family jewels."

"You still got a mouth on you," Morris Lefkowitz said. "You always had a mouth, I give you that." He paused. "Jacob is coming to California, Jacob King, you know Jacob, he was a friend of yours." He paused for effect. "A special friend of yours."

"I hear he's coming out," Rita Lewis said. "So what's the favor, Morris?"

"It's important to Morris that Jacob meet the right people," Morris Lefkowitz said. "Remember, Rita, it was Morris that took you out of the showroom, allowed you to make something out of yourself. I want Jacob to meet nice people, the right people . . ." Before she could answer, she heard Morris Lefkowitz say, "How do you expect to learn this business, Mickey, if you think dyed mink is Russian sable." Suddenly he began to cough so hard that she had to hold the telephone away from her ear. As she did, Lilo started to move his thigh up and down against her back. "No," she said softly. "The lotion stains my suit." Lilo smiled, put down his brief and began stroking his crotch. "So I buy you another suit." Then Morris was back on the line. "Rita, you I know would never think dyed mink is Russian sable. Morris gave you your first mink, Rita. And Morris gave you your first sable. Morris would be extremely grateful, and if Morris is grateful, Morris is prepared to be extremely helpful—Mickey, some seltzer water for Morris, for the indigestion you give me—extremely helpful."

"Oh, swell, Morris. That's all we need out here is another

hood from New York who beats a murder rap because a witness just happens to have an accident, like running into a bullet when he's sitting on the can. I bet that cost you more than a sable."

"That California's made you cynical, Rita. It must be the sun. It wrinkles the skin. I didn't know it wrinkled the brain cells, too."

"I'm not getting cynical out here, Morris. I'm getting realistic. You don't get the distinction, I'm sorry."

"So, Rita, you don't owe Morris a favor?"

On the lounger, Lilo Kusack's stroking had produced a bulge in his trunks.

"All right, Morris, give it a rest, I'll introduce him around. How about Chuckie O'Hara? He's a fairy, but he's a war hero, you remember the war, Morris, and what the Nazis did to the Jews? You bought Jake a 4-F is what I hear, so he didn't have to fight the Nazis that were gassing your people."

"It was the flat feet Jacob had."

"Flat feet. My mistake. How about Jack Ford then? The Sons of the Pioneers. Adolphe Menjou? Jacob's not a Communist, is he? Adolphe hates Reds. Gangsters are okay, gangsters are party favorites this year. I'll give a costume party. Everybody can bring a gun."

"You didn't used to always make with the jokes, Rita," Morris Lefkowitz said quietly. "Not when I was around."

In truth, Rita Lewis would not have dared talk this way to Morris Lefkowitz if there had not been three thousand miles separating them. She knew it, and she knew that Morris knew it, too.

"All right, Lilo, too. I'll get Lilo to see him, it's so important to you." A well-honed survival instinct told her that it was time to make amends. She had a new life, but she knew it was pointless and perhaps even dangerous to continue insulting an important player from her past life, that even from three thousand miles away Morris Lefkowitz had the ability, if he had the inclination, to make her new life unpleasant. "Lilo's like the chamber of commerce. Lilo sells the advantages of California." Next to her Lilo began to laugh, and tried to place her free hand on the bulge in his trunks. "A land of fresh starts."

"You're a good girl, Rita."

"I'm always a good girl, Morris. That's how I got out of your showroom. All those nice old guys trying to goose me and feel me up. When all I wanted to do was save myself for you. It makes me wonder if that's why you gave me the mink coat."

"Thank you for the favor, Rita."

"Morris, no more favors. I figure I paid enough for that fur already."

Rita Lewis stood up, and walking on her heels to protect her pedicure, she placed the telephone back on the wrought-iron pool table, then sat down again on the chaise next to Lilo Kusack, who was still sunning and stroking himself.

"What I want to know is how close were you and Jake King anyway?" Lilo said.

Rita removed Lilo's hand from his crotch. "No closer than I am to you," she said.

◄○►

Rita would shag anyone with a pulse, Chuckie O'Hara said. She'd fuck anywhere. Once in an elevator going to the Top of the Mark in San Francisco. She loved to talk fucking with us old queens. She was on her way up to meet Lilo and on a whim she pressed the stop button. What'd you do that for, ma'am, the elevator man said, but before he had the words out of his mouth she was unbuttoning his fly. She was like that. They were alone, and she liked his elevator-man uniform, it was claret-colored, with a little pillbox hat and chin strap, like Johnny in the Philip Morris radio commercials, you know, the midget who said "Call-for-Philip-Mor-riiiiiissss," it was so sexual. She was wearing a Mainbocher jacket in ridged black wool, and a black wool Mainbocher dress set off by a white chiffon guimpe. No one would ever mistake Rita for Elsie de Wolfe, darling, but she did have a kind of gun-moll chic, and Lilo made sure she dressed well, Mainbocher, Adrian—his real name was Adrian Greenberg, you knew that, of course, *quelle drôle*. Anyway, when she was finished, she buttoned his fly, the alarm bell was ringing by now, then she pressed the Up button and they went straight to the Top, where Lilo's waiting for her. What took you so long, Lilo said, and she said, I sucked off the elevator man, that's what took me so long, I always suck off the elevator man at the Mark, you ought to know that by now.

She had this thing for mob guys, Chuckie said. Al Capone. Morris Lefkowitz. Jacob. Lilo. It was Capone that sent her to Morris. A kind of lend-lease offering between Chicago and New York. She was only seventeen when she was with Al, she said he had a piano player always on call, he liked to listen to the piano when he fucked, so twenty-fours a day this guy was on duty, Al said if he didn't show up he would kill him, and Rita said she didn't think he was kidding. The stories about her. When she was called to testify at the Kefauver hearings on organized crime, the senator from New Hampshire, I think his name was Tobey, he wanted to know how and why Rita happened to have been so close to so many of the top gangsters, and there she was in her Adrian suit, the one with the geometric stripes that was on the cover of *Life,* I mean, there had never been anyone so well turned out at a Senate committee hearing, and Rita said to this senator from New Hampshire, Are you sure you really want to know, Senator Tobey, and the senator said, I want to know, Miss Lewis, and the American people want to know, and Rita said, Are you really sure, and Senator Tobey said, I am waiting, Miss Lewis, and Rita said, Well, then, Senator, it's because I'm the best cocksucker in the world. My dear, there hadn't been that much chaos in a committee room since I took off my leg. Of course the committee couldn't cite Rita for contempt because she gave a legitimate answer to a legitimate question, and there was more truth than fiction in what she said.

◄○►

It was a story I had heard for years, but when I looked up the exchange in the *Congressional Record,* here is what it actually said:

Senator Tobey: Miss Lewis, how is it that you happened to get so close to so many of the top and most vicious gangsters in America?

Miss Lewis (after consultation with counsel): Senator, on advice of counsel, I will stand on my rights under the Fifth Amendment and will decline to answer that question on the grounds that it could tend to incriminate me.

They must've cut it out of the transcript then, Chuckie O'Hara said. I mean, you don't really expect the *Congressional Record* to use the word . . .

None of the newspapers mentioned any unusual exchanges either, I said.

I prefer my version, Chuckie O'Hara said.

III

I WRITE WITH a keen awareness of the imperfections of history, and the opportunity these imperfections present to a facile imagination. While I am neither so grand nor so self-absorbed as to call myself a social historian, especially insofar as I occasionally yield to temptation and take inductive narrative liberties to fill in history's gaps, I see it as the duty of the historical narrator to try to piece together why what happened did happen, to lend what happened a sense of inevitability, to create the most plausible scenario for whatever appointments were to be kept in Samarra. It is well to remember here, as the Super Chief sped Jacob King and his briefcase filled with two hundred and fifty thousand dollars in legal tender across the Arizona desert, that he and Blue Tyler, she not even nineteen years old, were agents, and again victims, of a past that was fast becoming inoperative. In fact, when Jimmy Riordan complained in Jacob's drawing room on the Limited about the way the LP record was changing America's leisure habits, he was only venting some inchoate feeling that new technologies and new venues in combination with old, dangerous ideas were navigating both the country and the various satraps of crime and entertainment that he represented into uncharted waters.

Television was a new technology, scorned by the motion picture industry, its possibilities underestimated in much the same way as the moguls twenty years earlier had underestimated the potential of sound ("like putting lipstick on Mona Lister," J. F. French had said at the time, as if Lister was the surname of Leonardo's model), underestimated it in part because to these unlettered immigrants, uneasy in the language of their adopted country, sound and wordplay they did not entirely understand were threats to their hegemony, and its concomitant tyranny. If the LP record kept people at home, pictures seen on a small screen in the living room would also keep them at home, a heretical idea to executives and producers whose livelihoods were dependent on an audience with a habit of moviegoing twice a week, like sex in marriage. It was true that people did not go to Harlem anymore, but less because it was dangerous than because tying on a load after hours was no longer so appealing without any action, the action that was a by-product of the war and the good times the war had produced, the need for danger a high, if only the financial high of betting money you did not have. This was where Nevada came in, and it is to Morris Lefkowitz's credit that he understood this, as did Jimmy Riordan and Lilo Kusack. Nevada would be a new venue, where the ribs might be lousy and the chicken wings, too, but the tables would be in play day and night, and it would be possible to win or lose ten thousand dollars on the turn of a card, and get fellated in the bargain by a house hooker, a bonus for the winner, lagniappe for the loser.

What was called patriotism had kept the lid on labor unrest during the war, patriotism and a president who would not hesitate to take over any union that threatened the war effort, as John L. Lewis and his United Mine Workers found out. The making of motion pictures was seen as an integral part of that war effort, pictures that explicitly furthered the notion of a nation united, all for one, one for all, against a common enemy that had made the mistake of stirring the American melting pot —"when those dirty yellow bellies meet the Cohens and the

Kellys," as one wartime song lyric put it. The motion picture
unions were run by Benny Draper, who came out of Chicago
claiming Capone connections, and by use of muscle and extortion and the Capone name he hammered together a consortium
of nine unions that he called the Organization of Motion Picture Craft Employees—the OMPCE. Benny Draper had a simple formula for maintaining labor peace: When a contract
expired, he informed the studios of the cash payment to him
that it would take to avert a strike, and if they balked, then he
would bring out his projectionists or his stagehands, closing
down all the theaters in a given city or all the soundstages at a
given studio. "The math is simple," Benny Draper was fond of
saying. "It will cost you more not paying me than it will cost
you paying me. You need product for your theayters, and I can
stop you making that product, or I can stop you showing it in
your theayters, your choice, I don't give a shit." This was a
direct quote given to a California state senate labor subcommit-
tee investigating union corruption in the motion picture industry by one of Benny Draper's own dissident members, who
testified in open session before the panel wearing a paper bag
over his head so that he could not be identified. The union
witness was later identified through his dental records as Matty
Stivic, an electrician as well as an officer in OMPCE Local 11;
the identification was made some months after his testimony,
when his body was discovered in a shallow grave in the desert
outside Barstow, his face destroyed by a claw hammer. The official explanation tendered by the San Bernardino County sheriff's department was that Matty Stivic had fallen among bad
companions, most likely Hell's Angels, when he went off-road
motorcycling one weekend in the Mojave.

If Benny Draper's own OMPCE members were sullen at not
sharing in the largesse directed into his pocket, they were not so
sullen as to be mutinous, his reputation for violence, vide the
example of Matty Stivic, enforcing solidarity. For a union man,
Benny Draper was a remarkably effective strikebreaker. Any locals that resisted his offer to merge with the OMPCE he would

label as Communist-infiltrated, and if they struck he would lend
enforcers to break the arms of those Cohens and Kellys who had
beaten the dirty yellow bellies and who now had the misplaced
idea that it was their turn to climb aboard the union gravy train.
However the studios complained about the cash payments to
Benny Draper, they also realized that his was a sweetheart deal,
and if he needed money to buy a house for a girlfriend or for a
union executive who had gone to the penitentiary for charges
that could not be made against Benny Draper himself, a loan
could be arranged that would look like, but could never be
proven to be, a bribe, even when said loan went unpaid. At the
same time, his OMPCE pension fund was the lender of last
resort to certain studios when the Bank of America cut off its
loan spigot, and at rates that approached, but did not cross over
the line into, usury.

Benny Draper was not alone in invoking Communism to describe his enemies. Witch-hunting was in the air. "If the witch is
a Communist, you can call me a witch-hunter, and I'm proud of
it," J. F. French told the trade papers. "If the person I am
baiting is a Red, then you can call me a Red-baiter, and I am
proud of it." With Rabbi Baruch Tyger, whose Temple Beth
Israel on Sunset Boulevard had been constructed to have the
look and proportions of a fifteen-hundred-seat theater, and
which Barry Tyger, as he preferred to be known, called the
Roxy of Judaism, and with Hugh Cardinal Danaher, the arch-
bishop of the Roman Catholic archdiocese of Los Angeles, J. F.
French had founded the I Am an American Foundation for the
Preservation of American Ideals. "The American motion picture
industry is, and will continue to be, held by Americans for
Americans," read the foundation's manifesto, written by a
screenwriter named Irving Page, who also crafted secular ser-
mons with titles like "The Stuff Dreams Are Made Of" for
Rabbi Tyger and who later appeared before the House Un-
American Activities Committee and identified 291 toilers in the
Industry as Communists, "and is dedicated to the interests of
America and the preservation and continuation of the American

scene and the American way of life." J. F. French had other reasons for backing America for Americans. "The *goyim* hear 'Jew,' they think 'Communist,' " he told Lilo Kusack. "People don't like us, so we got to use our heads. All the talk you hear about this Holocaust and the suffering of the poor Jews. The goddamn fools, they don't realize the more you tell gentiles nobody likes Jews, the more the gentiles say there must be a reason for it. That's why I hate these kike Communist bastards. I'm ashamed of the money I made off their pictures. I'd give it all to charity if the pictures weren't cross-collateralized. To an American charity. The Red Cross. The USO. The chamber of commerce. The March of Dimes for those little babies with the braces on their legs that are such good anti-Communist Americans."

I heard all of this fourth-hand forty-five years after the fact from Chuckie O'Hara, who never really tried to disguise his anti-Semitism (he was too fastidious and too aware of who employed him ever to use words like *kike* or *sheeny*, but in selected purlieus and with selected acquaintances he often talked about "the chosen" or "our chosen friends"), and Chuckie's version came from Rita Lewis, who because of some unspecified sexual misdemeanor in the past was never enthusiastic about J. F. French, and as a writer I added some fine-tuning of my own. When I repeated the story to Arthur French, he only smiled and said it sounded more or less like his father except for the March of Dimes line, but even that had J.F.'s resonance, and his father would have added it had he thought of it, even though he hated Franklin Roosevelt.

J.F. would have put you under contract, Arthur said, comedy polishes on all the Cosmo scripts.

I never met J. F. French. When I arrived in Los Angeles he was already senile, living alone at Willingham, cared for by a staff of twenty-two, one of whom, it was said locally, was a professional woman who once a day tried to find heft in his phallus. J.F. finally died, peacefully, during an afternoon nap in the solarium at his house, his flaccid member, according to Industry lore, cradled in the palm of the professional woman. Arthur was unable to attend the funeral because a horse had thrown him a week or so before his father's death, the accident breaking both his legs, making it impossible for him to travel up from Nogales, and so out of friendship (I think as a matter of fact that I was as close a friend as Arthur ever had, in spite of the twenty-plus-year difference in our ages) I attended the nondenominational service at the Westwood Mortuary, a pricey little cemetery surrounded by high-rise buildings in the heart of Westwood.

Did anyone show up? Arthur asked when I called him in Nogales after the service.

Of course.

Anyone you recognized?

Not offhand, I said.

Were you the only one there?

It was a moment before I replied. How did you know?

He was ninety-four, Jack. If he died twenty years ago, as he should have, they would have had the service on a soundstage at Cosmo, and the whole town would have turned out. Like they did at Harry Cohn's. On the lot at Columbia. SRO. Stage Seven. Chuckie O'Hara was at Harry's funeral, and he said you give the people something they want to see, they'll show up.

I'm sorry, Arthur.

It's a kettle of very different fish, Arthur said.

What?

It's something J.F. used to say. He used to mangle the language pretty good. He'd want to say a very different kettle of fish, and it would come out . . .

Arthur fell silent, and I knew he was trying to compose himself, that in the end when all was said and done and however loathsome a shit J. F. French most certainly was, his father was still his father.

Arthur, I said finally, the obituaries never said what the initials J.F. stood for.

Nothing.

Nothing?

Nothing. When he first got into the nickelodeon business, he was always looking for product to steal, and he saw this English play, it might've been by Freddy Lonsdale, or someone like that, and there was a character in it named J. F. Something-or-other, and so Moe just appropriated it.

It was the first time I had ever heard Arthur refer to his father as Moe.

He was too busy to think of names to go along with it, Arthur said. You asked him to come up with a name for a four-year-old Cosmo was considering putting under contract, and without even thinking he'd come up with Blue Tyler. It was only his own name he had trouble with.

Joseph Fennimore French, I said suddenly.

Now I know he would have put you under contract, Arthur French said the day of his father's funeral, many years ago.

◄○►

Lilo Kusack had as a matter of course told J. F. French that Jacob King was on his way to California as Morris Lefkowitz's special economic negotiator, as he had also told Benny Draper, whose OMPCE pension fund was a heavy investor in La Casa Nevada, which Lilo and Cosmopolitan Pictures were fronting. Benny Draper said there was no fucking way that Morris Lefkowitz was going to muscle into Nevada and the best way to make that clear was to whack Jacob King on the Super Chief before he ever set foot in California, he knew people he could call right that fucking minute, would pick up the Chief in Albuquerque the next afternoon and get the job done before Phoenix, and nobody would fucking know, a meal for the fucking coyotes is what Jake'd be, they'd pick his fucking bones clean, hey, making their bones, I like that. It was the kind of talk that made Lilo Kusack uncomfortable, not out of any scrupulosity or respect for human life, particularly Jacob King's, nor even because it would have put him legally at risk in the event that talk was translated into action. The main reason for his discomfort was that a move on Jacob King promised immediate retribution and then at least a nominal examination on the part of the authorities, thus adding onto the cost of the Nevada operation the additional expense of payoffs, as well as construction delays until the heat died down, and so he told Benny Draper not to worry, he had already taken steps to neutralize Jacob King, and perhaps even co-opt him. I don't know from co-opt, Benny Draper said, I just know the only fucking thing Jakey King understands is a big fucking hole behind his ear, you remember I told you that, Lilo, it's the way of the world, you guys with manicures don't like to think that, but that's the way it is.

That's the way it *was*, Lilo Kusack thought to himself, a thought he did not share with Benny Draper.

Of more immediate concern to J. F. French than the anticipated arrival of Jacob King onto the local scene was Blue Tyler, who in the first week of shooting on *Red River Rosie* was making trouble on the set. Chuckie O'Hara was directing the picture, in which once more she was playing a teenager of indeterminate years, but certainly no older than fifteen. Blue wanted to grow up, and she wanted to graduate into adult roles without observing the rite of passage that Hollywood traditionally demanded of its child stars. A child actress was supposed to marry at eighteen, as Elizabeth Taylor and Shirley Temple had, marry a slightly older contemporary associated at least in some tangential way with the Industry so that he could be vetted, his credentials checked to see that he was not just some kind of fortune hunter or troublemaker with a big cock; someone with whom she shared a passion for hamburgers or Frank Sinatra ballads, which the fan magazines said made their love inevitable, and from whom she could be easily divorced at nineteen, the divorce sanctifying her transition from child to adult, she now a woman who during her year of matrimony had engaged in sexual intercourse, perhaps even oral and anal intercourse, which finally allowed her to be the object of sexual intention on film, and perhaps even a collaborator in sexual license, so long as it did not go unpunished.

The meeting on *Red River Rosie* took place in J. F. French's private screening room on the Cosmopolitan lot. J. F. French was present, and Arthur and Chuckie O'Hara and Lilo Kusack and Blue's agent and her press agent and her accountant and her business manager. Frick and Frack and Flack was how Chuckie O'Hara referred to Blue's support team, and as their names meant nothing to me it is what I shall call them as well. Onscreen the dailies of *Red River Rosie* from the day before were being run. In the take, a close-up, Blue was wearing a gingham dress with puffed sleeves and a high-necked collar and she clutched a bouquet of roses to her bosom as she expressed dismay at the advances of an unseen suitor. The take ended, and onscreen a clapper appeared:

Red River Rosie
Scene 52
Take 23
Dir: O'Hara   Cam: Sklar

"Lights," Blue Tyler suddenly said in the darkened screening room. "Turn it off." The film wound down, the house lights came on, and Blue stood up. "You still want to know why I walked off this picture? Because this picture's a piece of shit, that's why I walked off this picture."

J. F. French puffed on a cigar and said nothing.

"Well," Blue said. "That's all I get? Silence?"

Frack looked at J. F. French and, when no one spoke, cleared his throat. "What I think, Blue, is, and when I say 'I,' I mean all of us here, Arthur and Chuckie and Mr. Kusack and Mr. French, who has given up a great deal of his valuable time to be at this meeting when he has a studio to run, and an entire menu of pictures to cast, not to mention dealing with un-American subversion from that bunch of Communists in the Directors Guild, present company excepted, Chuckie, and then since you don't seem to be aware of it, there is the possibility of a strike that could shut the entire Industry down, isn't that right, J.F.?"

J. F. French sat like a sphinx, not acknowledging Frack's question with even a flicker of the eye.

Frack plowed on. "I suppose what I'm saying, what *we're* all saying, Freddy and Maurice and Sidney and Gary and all of us who have your best interests at heart, is that by walking off *Red River Rosie,* as you are threatening to do, perhaps, just perhaps, you don't really comprehend the exigencies of the business . . ."

"J.F. doesn't make these decisions cold, Blue," Arthur French said after a moment's silence. "We've done considerable testing . . ."

Lilo Kusack was conciliatory. "There's no problem, Moe, about Blue finishing *Red River Rosie,* but—"

"Lilo, who's paying you?" Blue Tyler interrupted. "Are you here as my lawyer or what?"

Lilo shrugged and lit a cigarette.

"Lilo's talking business, Blue," Arthur said, "and you don't seem to understand business."

Blue took a deep breath. "Listen, Arthur. And Moe." She was the only Cosmopolitan contract actor who would dare call him Moe, which always seemed to amuse him. "And Lilo. And Chuckie. And Gary and Stan and whatever the fuck the rest of you people are called. I am the number-five box office attraction in America. I have been in this business since I was four years old. I make twelve thousand five hundred dollars a week, forty weeks a year, and my price bumps to fifteen when my next option gets picked up next month. So believe me, when you talk business, I know what you're talking about."

Chuckie O'Hara put his hands behind his head and stared at the ceiling. He wondered if his missing leg would ever stop itching. Time and again he would reach to scratch and only hit the plastic prosthesis, but still it itched, as the doctors had told him it would. Chuckie knew he was present only as window dressing, and while he would agree with Blue's opinion of the script, he was quite pleased with what he had shot. However the meeting turned out, he did not wish to antagonize his star by saying anything that she could use to make his life difficult when she came back to work, as come back to work he knew she would.

"What the business seems to be saying, Blue," Arthur said, "is that perhaps the present climate is not the best time for you to be making a crossover picture. Isn't that right, J.F.?"

"Arthur, why do you always call your father J.F.?" Blue said. "His name is Moe."

J. F. French permitted himself a small smile.

"Moe, the fact of the matter is I'm almost nineteen years old," Blue said. "You can't keep casting me as a fifteen-year-old cherry until my tits start banging off my belly button."

J. F. French roused himself to speak for the first time. "Nice talk from America's favorite teenager."

"That's exactly my point. I'm not a fifteen-year-old cherry anymore. You can't keep me playing one."

"That's where you're wrong, Missy," J. F. French said. "Fifteen-year-old cherries happens to be what Mr. and Mrs. America and all the ships at sea want to see you play."

"Chuckie," Blue said. "Tell Moe why you made me carry the bouquet in that shot. To cover my nips. They're like fucking acorns."

"Very effective, Chuckie," J. F. French said.

"Thank you, J.F.," Chuckie O'Hara said. There were times he would call J. F. French Moe, but this was not one of them.

"Arthur," J. F. French said without turning, "are you responsible for those acorns when you know she's got a five A.M. call?"

Arthur did not reply.

"You can't sell me in this shit anymore, Moe. The public won't buy me as little Miss Priss with her knees welded together. You're always telling me how you can't fool the public. Well, you're trying to fool them when you give me a bouquet in every shot so my boobs don't show. You're the one that sent the memo to wardrobe. 'Do something about Miss Tyler's tits.' "

"Arthur, you showed that memo to her?"

Arthur sank farther down into his seat. Chuckie O'Hara bit his tongue and tried not to laugh. Blue's tits were a problem, and her nipples looked as if she were nursing twins. Pad the nipples and it only made her breasts look larger, and there were only so many trees he could hide her behind.

"I'm almost nineteen—"

"You said that already—"

"—and I can have a valuable career at Cosmo until I'm thirty, maybe even thirty-five, if you start letting me play grown-up women."

"Who are these grown-up women she keeps talking about?" J. F. French said.

No one spoke for a moment. "Blue means bad girls, Moe," Lilo Kusack finally said.

The color began to rise in J. F. French's face. "What bad girls," he shouted.

"Blue means bad girls in general, J.F.," Lilo Kusack said. He was an expert in mood changes, and he knew that at that moment familiarity would not be politic. Had he not known him so well he might even have said "Mr. French," a lawyer's trick. "She means that maybe, in her next project, she gets a shot at a bad . . . at a more adult role."

J. F. French rose from his seat. "We let Shelley Winters play the bad girls. We let America's favorite teenager play Red River Rosie." He headed for the door of the screening room. "You," he said to Blue. "Stage Nine. You already cost this studio half a day's shooting. If you weren't America's favorite teenager, I would deduct it from your salary."

Blue waited until he opened the door. "Moe, who is Jacob King?"

J. F. French stopped. He turned and stared at Arthur. "You take your fiancée to New York, and that's who you let her meet?"

Arthur looked thoroughly miserable. "It's all right, J.F. No-body took any pictures."

"He's a good dancer," Blue said.

"She wanted to go dancing, I should've sent her to New York with George Raft," J. F. French said to his son, almost shouting.

"So who is he?" Blue asked again.

"One of Morris Lefkowitz's guys," Lilo Kusack said after a moment.

"Who is Morris Lefkowitz?"

You have to remember, Chuckie O'Hara said years later, that for all her tough mouth and tough business sense she was a true innocent. She had been brought up in the Industry and so sheltered by it that she knew virtually nothing of the world outside it.

"You don't want to know," J. F. French said. And then he said the wrong thing. "And something else you don't want to know. You definitely don't want to know Jacob King."

That the Frenches, first Arthur in New York and then J.F. at the studio, had both told her to stay away from Jacob King only stimulated that anarchic spirit that in her was like an erogenous zone. "I was only thinking a dinner date?"

"Dinner date?" Lilo Kusack said. "A lot of people had their last supper with your dinner date."

"Last supper, like in that picture about Jesus and them that Mr. DeMille did?" Blue said.

J. F. French's gaze suddenly took in Frick and Frack and Flack. This was a conversation that had unexpectedly gone into areas not covered by their pay grade. "Out," he shouted. "What are you doing here anyway? Who asked you? You. You're fired. You. You're fired. You—"

"I don't work here, Mr. French."

"You're fired anyway. You don't come on this lot again. Ever."

"Arthur," J. F. French said when the room had cleared. Then he saw Chuckie O'Hara, who supposed he had been included in the dismissal order, but who because of his leg had difficulty scurrying out. "O'Hara. You're a war hero. War heroes can stay. Arthur," he repeated.

"Sir."

"I think after *Red River Rosie* we let your fiancée grow up. I think we start setting the date for you and Blue to get married. We do it on a stage. White confetti. Bluebirds of happiness. Cosmo Newsreel." He moved over and put his arms around Blue. "I will give the bride away."

MAURY

I

FOR FIVE DAYS Melba Mae Toolate had talked.
Nonstop. She swore. Cried. Laughed. Hit me twice.
Nearly killed herself once. Not deliberately. Although in
these arias I had on tape (and on the tapes of her own that she
finally retrieved, reluctantly, on that fifth day, several of which
she let me listen to) she always seemed to be courting violence
and danger so assiduously that I thought she might be something of a death lover, albeit one who thought the actual dying,
in the event the outcome of the courtship could not be fore-
stalled, would be done by a stunt woman, with the star available
for the close-up. She divided random violent death into two
categories, those that would make a good visual and those that
would not. She was particularly taken by a wire-service report I
read to her from *USA Today* about an elderly woman in Chicago, wearing a mink coat and carrying a Chanel bag containing
only a single hundred-dollar bill and no identification, who had
placed herself snugly against the right rear wheels of an eighteen-wheeler transcontinental Allied moving van stopped at a
traffic light on Michigan Avenue, and when the light turned
green, the truck moved forward and the four huge wheels flattened her, the driver in the cab noticing only a slight bump he

attributed, in the press report, to a pothole. A good visual, Melba Mae had said.

She always did want to direct, Chuckie O'Hara said when I told him about the woman in Chicago, he like Blue contemplating the master and the coverage, I on the other hand wondering what made the unidentified woman do what she had done, and whether it was spontaneous or planned.

This is the way Melba nearly killed herself. I was listening to her tapes, straining to hear because of their bad quality (she often re-recorded over an existing tape, and she usually seemed to be drunk when she did), which made her monologues difficult to follow, and she had fallen asleep on the king-sized bed with the Indian blanket. It was cold in the trailer and she had turned the Sears electric heater at the foot of the bed up so high that when the blanket rubbed against its grill it caught fire. I was in the middle section of the trailer and it was a moment before I noticed the smell. I took my jacket and smothered the flame, then pulled the seared and smoking blanket off her and ran it outside onto her tiny patch of brown lawn, where I could finally stamp the embers completely out. When I came back inside, she was awake and lighting a cigarette, as if nothing had happened. You're going to burn yourself to death, I told her, get so deep fried they'll only be able to identify you with your dental charts. A crispy critter. She thought "crispy critter" was a cute phrase. *Cute* was her word. I told her it was what a napalm victim was called in Vietnam when I was a reporter there. It turned out she did not know what napalm was, and Vietnam, she said, that was that war we were in, right? In any case, she was never really interested in my back story. Are we talking about me or you? she would say irritably. This was a woman, after all, who I doubt had ever spent eight consecutive seconds not thinking about herself.

Selectively.

Chuckie O'Hara knew enough of her history to fill in some of the blanks. He knew she had fucked Chocolate Walker Franklin. Resulting in the first of the two abortions Lou Lerner, M.D., the studio doctor, had performed on her. *The first when I was fourteen, and is that a story,* she had said elliptically, a tease in Hamtramck. *Not now. Maybe not ever. Too many skeletons I don't want to rattle in too many closets.* Not knowing that Chuckie would give the bones a good shake. Walker was one of the all-time great swordsmen, Chuckie said, he'd fuck a jar of Skippy's peanut butter if there was nothing else around. Moe French said he'd run Walker Franklin out of the Industry when he finally found out about him and Blue. It was Lilo who told him. Lilo was the keeper of the secrets, he doled them out like communion wafers whenever it served his purposes. I never knew what his particular purpose was in telling Moe about Blue and Walker, but he did, five or six years after it was over, right after Jake was killed and I got my subpoena. Moe was true to his word. Walker never worked in pictures again. And Moe made sure he couldn't grab a job in nightclubs or on Broadway either, so Walker went to Paris, the only French he knew was "sit on my face," *asseyez-vous sur mon visage,* I think it was. Jean Gabin taught him that, they were fuck buddies when Gabin was at Fox, but after he got to France he danced at the Follies and the Crazy Horse and he had a good run as a fancy man until he was killed in a car crash on his way to Deauville to meet some vicomtesse he was boning—a colorful Afro-American phrase, they always have the best words for it, don't they, and a natural sense of rhythm—Brigitte de Freycinet, remember her, Jack, wasn't she one of your father's girls, too? The Maserati he totaled belonged to a Monegasque princess he was also boning, Léonie Grimaldi, a minor scandal at the time.

So said Chuckie O'Hara.

A couple of things Chuckie didn't know. One way Melba supported herself was via phone sex. She had a listing with a service she had found in the Personals of a local fuck sheet and guys would call her up and she would talk them off. His cock, her cunt, how wet she was getting, bingo. A couple of her regulars checked in when I was there. She wasn't embarrassed by it. Her telephone name was Mona. Just a minute, hon, let me take off my panties, she would say, and cover the phone and ask me to fix her a cup of instant coffee with Preem, and then back on the phone, You want to smell Mona's finger, I just put it up there, lick it. This was a woman after all who as a child had been sent fan mail caked with come; for her, dirty talk on the telephone was just a natural way for the older woman to make ends meet. How did you get the job, I had asked. I sent them a tape. A demo. It was the voice. I don't think they'd've hired me if they'd known how old I was.

She also had a tattoo. A pair of eyes just above her pubic line, looking down at her bush. The tattooed eyes had mascara and eye shadow, and the eyebrows were thick, modeled on hers. She wasn't sure when she got the tattoo. Or where. It was when she was out of it, she knew that. When she fell off the planet earth. Baby, I just fell off the planet earth, she said for the fourth or fifth or ninth time. It took me a while to realize that she wanted some variant of "Baby, I just fell off the planet earth" as the title of the autobiography she thought I was going to ghost for her. She really liked that tattoo. It's like the eyes are checking out how good you're doing, she had said. The tattooed eyes were disconcerting, and that's all I'm going to say about that.

◄◦►

On the sixth day she was gone.

The door to the recreational vehicle in Slot 123, Forsythia Lane, was unlocked, and the inside stripped of the more valuable appliances, the thirty-inch television set and the VCRs and the microwave oven and the Cuisinart, even the pack of ribbed Trojan-Enz condoms. The Sub-Zero freezer was open and had defrosted, leaving pools of water on the floor, and the frozen food thawing. The manager of the Autumn Breeze trailer park and recreational vehicle encampment, Mr. August Johnson, said that Mrs. Toolate had rented her mobile home furnished, was paid up until the end of the month, and had left no forwarding address. She had asked August Johnson if anyone had tried to gain entrance to her RV, her things had seemed disturbed, and August Johnson had told her that a detective from the Detroit police department had been asking questions about her, it was a police matter. She had become abusive, August Johnson said. Did he have a warrant, she wanted to know, he had to have a warrant, she knew that from watching *Hill Street Blues,* and August Johnson had told her not to call him the dirty words she was calling him, and that the Autumn Breeze would have to ask her to vacate her vehicle at the end of the month, the management did not wish any trouble with the Detroit police department, this was a camp of law-abiding citizens.

The randy old fart with the prostate cancer in Slot 122 said a minivan cab had come to pick her up in the middle of the night, and she had loaded all her things in it, the GD&WC Cab Company was its name, for Greater Detroit & Wayne County, and he had tried to help her, and she had called him a randy old fart, and he did not think that was neighborly, he had the prostate cancer after all. The old prune with the Alzheimer's in Slot 124 said a Negro had been living in Slot 123, a Mr. Roosevelt by name, there had never been a Mrs. Toolate there, and if Mr. Roosevelt was gone, then Autumn Breeze would be a safer place that night, she had never gone out because she was afraid of Negroes, you read the paper, you know why. Father Vaclav Paciorek, the pastor at St. Anton the Magyar Roman Catholic Church, said Mrs. Toolate had left her dog in the church, she knew I liked dogs and she must've known I'd take care of it. Father Paciorek said he had never been entirely convinced that Mrs. Toolate was even a Catholic, but so few people came to church these days, he was not going to pry too closely, most came because they just enjoyed the companionship, and that was why he had named her chairperson of the Shut-in Committee, it would give her someone to talk to. She had once been an actress, he had been told, although he had never heard of Melba Mae Toolate, and he liked to see all the Broadway musicals when they traveled through Detroit on tour.

Herb, the manager at Farmer Dell's, said he had not seen Melba, she was some shopper, you see her, give her a kiss for me, and the offer still stands for her to get her picture in the Farmer Dell's employee newspaper, the number-one shopper at location twenty-seven.

I I

"YOU NEVER TOLD ME you killed that nigger in New York."

It had been nearly a week since I had seen Maury Ahearne, and I had almost succeeded, until the events of that day, in forgetting about him, forgetting that he was the putative reason I was even in Detroit. Melba Mae had been more on my mind. My mistake. I should have known Maury Ahearne was not going to forget me. I was his ticket out. He was in my room on the seventy-third floor of the Renaissance Plaza when I unlocked the door that night. Looking through my notebooks and file folders. I might have been a felon brought back in handcuffs to the scene of his crime for all the concern he showed about getting caught in the act. He took a newspaper clipping from one of the folders and ran a finger over the headline. "Billionaire Broderick Heir in Racially Motivated Murder Investigation." Maury Ahearne made a clucking noise with his tongue. "You forgot to tell me you were rich, too. You don't tell me that, then where's the trust you should have with your collaborator. We're still collaborators, right?"

I silently cursed the impulse that had made me save those damned clips. And bring them with me. As if I needed another scrapbook, a memento of still another five minutes of the fame, or infamy, we are all supposed to be allocated.

He glanced at the clipping again. "Shaamel. Boudreau. You really took him out with a load of sheets?" He gave an approving nod. "Got to remember that. Bet it didn't leave a mark on him." He replaced the clipping in a folder, picked up a notebook, and waved it at me. "What's all this guilt shit in here about? You really feel guilty for whacking him, or are you just saying that because you think that's how you're supposed to feel?"

He had a gift for getting to the point. No frills, no beating around the bush. Change the subject. "How did you get in here?"

"Showed the badge," he said. "Told the assistant manager you were suspected of being Mr. Big."

"Mr. Big in what line of work?" Even as I said it I knew he would have an answer that would make me regret having asked the question.

"Kiddie porn." Explaining the furtive look I had received from the desk clerk when I asked for my room key. "The video king. Little boys with tight assholes. Sucky-fucky. I told him I'd be discreet. Keep the hotel's name out of it." There were three empty miniature Chivas Regal bottles from the minibar on the night table, and an empty can of Planter's cocktail peanuts. Meaning he'd been there a while. And probably gone through everything in the room as if it were a crime site. "That's all they're worried about." His frigid smile. "I'll tell them it was a mistake. All you got to do is tell them you're going to sue their ass and they'll probably pick up your tab." An expansive shrug. "Not that Billionaire Broderick's got to worry about his hotel bill. That ought to make that cheap sheeny out in California happy, though. You getting comped, and all."

Marty Magnin. I had forgotten about him, too. Marty would not mind the ethnic slur. It was just a cost of doing business. "What are you doing here, Maury?"

If he picked up the chill in my voice, he chose to ignore it. "I got some ideas. For our project." The project. For a moment I pulled a blank. It would come back to me. Think. Ah. *Murder One*. The short white homicide cop and the black seven-foot ex-basketball player. High concept. Which translates into shit. A translation I was not prepared to share at that moment with Maury Ahearne. "I ever tell you about Hughie McIntyre?"

I shook my head.

"I thought I did."

I still did not reply.

"Used to be in homicide, Hughie. Went to Wayne State at night. Law school. He finally graduates, but he's not the swiftest guy around, it takes him four tries to pass the bar. He's forty-three years of age, so he takes his pension and sets up shop, Hughie McIntyre, attorney-at-law, he'll make a buck out of the shit he used to put away, you know what I mean?"

I stared at him without speaking.

"The thing is, he's good at it. Better than he was a cop, you want the truth, the guys like him, they steer him cases, court-appointed stuff." He suddenly faltered. It was a rare moment, and had I not been so angry I might have enjoyed it more. He plunged on. "That was Hughie handling Emmett, the guy in court the other day when you come by, you want me to check out that old broad in Hamtramck."

I was certain that the old broad in Hamtramck was the reason I had found Maury Ahearne going through my room.

"Emmett was the guy that smoked the Cuban selling vacuum cleaners. Hughie walks him."

Emmett who had smoked the Cuban just to see if his new gun worked. With a courtroom outcome exactly as Maury Ahearne had predicted. I opened the minibar.

"I'll take a Chivas," he said.

"You cleaned out the Scotch."

"A vodka, then."

I tossed him a miniature vodka and opened a can of beer for myself. He poured the vodka over the dregs of his Scotch. "You know, I could get used to this living on the expense account."

It did not require a response.

"What were we talking about?"

No help from me. My silence was making him uncomfortable. He lined up my notebook carefully on the night table, next to the book of Weegee photographs Melba Mae had stolen from the Hamtramck library and given me.

"Oh, yeah, Hughie. He gets along with everybody, Hughie. Except the Church. You know, the Catholic Church. You're a Catholic, right?"

Three times married, twice divorced, and probably thrice if that Fiat Spider had not spun into my Porsche at Sunset and Anita and sent Lizzie through the windshield. A committer of most of the mortal sins, homicide excluded, a major offender in coveting my neighbor's wife, daughter, granddaughter, sister, au pair, aunt, and next-door neighbor, but yes, I suppose I was still a Catholic.

"He's married twenty-six years, Hughie, to this Polack, banging her would be like fucking a meatloaf, you ask me, and I guess one day Hughie comes to that opinion too, and he takes off, who can blame him? The thing is, he wants to get married again, and his new one, also a Polack, he's got this thing for piroshki, I guess, anyhow, she says she can't marry a divorced man, he's got to get an annulment. No problem, Hughie says, he's a lawyer, he'll work it out. The thing about annulment is, you get one if you're one of Princess Grace's fuck-up kids that gets knocked up by some guy with a *schlong* like a fire hydrant, she can get the money on the table and her divorce scrubbed, but if you're Hughie McIntyre that's only making a yard and a half for walking shit like Emmett, the cardinal says, Uh-uh, you were banging the meatloaf for twenty-six years, you're jerking my chain you think Holy Mother the Church is going to grant you an annulment, get out of here, come back when you got the kind of bread Princess Grace and the Kennedys and them give to the foreign missions, then you can drown the meatloaf for all we care, like Teddy there, have him give you some drowning lessons, we'll give you absolution, an annulment, tickets to the Super Bowl, that's what you want. So the second meatloaf, she takes off, and Hughie, he should be saying good riddance, but he blames the cardinal, and . . . you follow me, so far?"

I had to admire the performance element. He could almost make me believe that telling me about Hughie McIntyre was the real reason he had broken into my room.

"You want to tape it? I see you got a new tape recorder?"

Replacing the one he had thrown out the window of his car. And thrown me out right after it. Had he not done so I would not have ended up in Lily White's bed. Or in Melba Mae Toolate's RV. Cause and effect. Circumstances and coincidence. I suspect he had been listening to my tapes, too. On my new tape recorder. I returned his stare.

He shrugged, then continued. "So Hughie, he decides to stick it to the cardinal, he's so pissed he doesn't get his annulment. There's this nun, Sister Felita, she strangles this other nun with her rosary beads, the big kind nuns used to wear, hanging off their belt, it looks like a noose. When I was a kid at St. Cyprian's, this sister, she used to whack me with it."

His face darkened, and I had the feeling he was wondering why he had not punched out the nun at St. Cyprian's. Or perhaps he had. That Maury Ahearne might be a psychopath, one with a badge, had occurred to me more than once.

"When's the last time a nun's been charged with homicide in this country? You should look it up. Never, I bet. Because the D.A.s are all harps and wops is the reason why. Then this Sister Felita comes along. She's pissed because the other nun, her name was Brittany, or something like that, a funny name for a nun, you ask me. Anyway, Sister Brittany—you know, I got a hard time saying that, Sister Brittany—she was wearing lipstick and a short skirt, they don't have to wear a habit anymore they don't want to, the sisters, and this is what pissed Sister Felita, like it wasn't holy, and so she wraps her beads around Sister Brittany's neck, and did that thing like Clemenza did to Connie's husband in *The Godfather* . . ."

"Garroted her."

"That's it, that's what she does. Naturally the cardinal says, No need to go public, she just went kind of crazy, her mind went. Fuck that, Hughie says. He represents Sister Brittany's family, and he says Sister Felita was sweet on Sister Brittany, was trying to go down on her pretty young snatch, that was going to waste in the convent, when all Sister Brittany wanted to do was make novenas and the Stations of the Cross and shit like that. Well, you can imagine how much the cardinal likes to hear that, the papers and the TV will lap it up, like Hughie says Sister Felita was trying to lap up Sister Brittany's pussy . . ."

The litany of human frailty seemed to reinvigorate him, and even piqued my own resistant curiosity. In spite of myself I had been absorbed by his tawdry and meretricious tale. As I was meant to be. Maury Ahearne's smoke screen.

"Naturally he gets a settlement. Six hundred grand. Hughie got a third. The lawyer gets a third when he takes the case on a . . ." He snapped his fingers, searching for the right word.

"Contingency."

"That's it. So Hughie says to himself, two hundred grand, easy as eating chocolate cream pie, there must be more where this comes from, and he becomes a specialist in banging it to the Church."

I looked out the window, at the lights of Detroit spreading out in every direction seventy-three stories below, and wondered if any of the lights belonged to the Autumn Breeze recreational vehicle and trailer park in Hamtramck. I took a deep breath. "So what are you really here for, Maury?"

"Another client of Hughie's is this guy Rodney," he continued, as if I had not spoken. "A fag with piles."

I was beginning to lose control. "I don't give a fuck about Hughie. Or the fag with piles either."

He screwed the top back onto the empty vodka miniature, then suddenly arched it into a wastebasket. The crash of the bottle into the metal basket made me flinch. "So." He sized me up for a moment. "Why's your nose out of joint?"

"If you wanted to tell me about Hughie, you wouldn't need to break into my room. It'd wait until morning. Hughie was your backup—"

"Is that right—"

"—in case I got back here earlier than you thought, and caught you going through my things. Or maybe you're such a great storyteller, you don't need a backup, you just make it up as you go along."

After a moment he said, "You know, you're not as dumb as I thought you were."

My father had said that to me once. He had meant it as a compliment, too. "I suppose it was you that broke into Mrs. Toolate's RV."

He did not blink. "Easier than I got in here. Those old farts respect law enforcement."

"Why?"

"Because they're old. They're afraid of the Emmetts of this world, there's more of them than—"

My voice rose. "I mean, why did you break into her RV?"

"Oh." The incipient tantrum elicited a tight smile. "You got to look at it from my point of view. I don't see you for a week, and I got all these stories you don't seem to give a shit about anymore, the ones I thought would be a nice little nest egg for my old age—you sure you don't want to hear about Rodney and Father Len with the spandex tights?"

"No."

". . . and old Father Lujack, Father Len's pastor that gets busted for indecent exposure because of Rodney and Len?"

"Goddammit, Maury—"

"Okay. Okay." He sucked up the melting ice cubes in his glass, then wiped his lips with the sleeve of his jacket. "So naturally I'm a little curious about this Mrs. Toolate, lives out there in that RV park in Hamtramck. That all of a sudden you're so interested in you drop me like a bad habit." The swagger was back in his voice. "You had me look her up, remember? With all the husbands and no state aid and a drug bust in Ypsilanti, charges dropped, and I begin to wonder what this bag lady's got that I don't, so I decide to check things out."

I was getting very tired of Maury Ahearne. "She split."

"So." Maury Ahearne cracked his knuckles, elaborately unconcerned. "She'll be easy to find. You check the GDWC dispatcher, he gives you the driver, and the driver'll have a trip ticket that says where he dropped her, she's not going to get far, even you could find her."

I tried to keep my temper. In fact, I had already talked to the GD&WC cabdriver. My old police reporter training. A twenty was my way in, with a promise of another twenty depending on what he had to tell. His name was Lorenzo McNally and he said he had brought her to the bus station in downtown Detroit. Trailways or Greyhound? The dog, Lorenzo McNally said. Where she had negotiated with him. She had sold him the two VCRs for a hundred dollars, the thirty-inch Panasonic for seventy-five, the Cuisinart for fifty, the gelato maker, the microwave oven, and the six-slice toaster for another seventy-five, three hundred bucks in all, and he had tossed in the fare, what the hell, it was the least he could do, it was like hitting the jackpot on *Wheel of Fortune,* she wasn't no Vanna White, this lady, but she wasn't bad, you like the older stuff. This shit isn't hot, is it, Lorenzo McNally had suddenly asked, and I had said, no, it wasn't hot, consider it your lucky day, Lorenzo, and gave him the second twenty. I wondered what he was doing with three hundred in spare cash anyway, what kind of scam he was running, but that was for someone else's story, not mine, I did not have enough room for Lorenzo McNally, maybe it was just Melba's lucky day, too. All she had was a suitcase, Lorenzo McNally said, this old beat-up suitcase practically coming apart at the seams, it was so heavy she was dragging it behind her, she had this piece of heavy twine that she had wrapped around the handle. *I don't need much myself,* she had told me that first day. *I got one suitcase, that's it. If it gets heavy, I just get rid of stuff. The story of my life.*

She was just getting rid of stuff. Moving on. With Lorenzo's three hundred and whatever else she could lay her hands on. It was not as if it was the first time she had done it. By now she was an expert at it.

"Maury, what did you do that spooked her? You take something. Disturb something?"

"Who's Mona?"

Oh, shit. "You answered the phone?"

"It was a guy. I said he had a wrong number. He called back a minute later. He said he had a hard-on. I told him where he could stick his fucking hard-on."

I did not want to know what else Maury had said to the caller with the erection. Maybe it was he who had alerted Mona. Melba. Blue. "Anything else?"

"I looked around."

"What'd you find?"

He waited for a moment before answering. "Some tapes."

"Where?"

"In the frig." That's where she kept them. In the freezer compartment in empty packages of Stouffer's macaroni and cheese crimped at the open ends. Meaning Maury Ahearne had done a thorough search.

"You take them?"

"Played a couple." He laughed. "Of yours, too, for that matter," he said, pointing at the tape recorder. Another laugh. "So that's who she is."

"You ever see her?"

"I watched her take out the garbage. You know, she went through other people's trash cans, looking for shit."

There was no point in getting into that. "I mean when she was a movie star."

"No. Heard the name. That's it. She was like Shirley Temple, right?" A leer. "A Shirley Temple who gives head."

I let it pass. "Anything else."

He hesitated for a moment, then took several postcard-sized photographs from a jacket pocket and handed them to me. They were copies of a single exposure, a young girl scarcely into pubescence, certainly no older than sixteen or seventeen. She was naked, sitting on what appeared to be an ottoman that was almost lost in shadow, her arms clasped behind her, hair cut short, head in profile facing right, eyes looking down, her body still developing, her thighs held tight together, as if protecting her pubic triangle. She was shockingly, innocently beautiful, this naked child, in the manner of a Botticelli Venus or a Man Ray nude photograph, and I wondered who she was and who had taken the picture, and why Blue Tyler had kept so many copies of it.

"These were in the frig, too," he said. "Stuffed in an empty box of rice." He seemed quite proud of himself and his discovery. "Anyone you know?"

I shook my head.

"Kind of old-fashioned looking."

He was right. There was something dated about the photograph, and the *fin de siècle* pose of its youthful subject. I took a copy and handed the rest back to him.

"Take another one," Maury Ahearne said equably. "She had a lot of them. A whole boxful." He handed me another picture, then a third. "I left her some. I guess she gets off looking at the chick's pussy. Maybe when that guy with a hard-on calls Mona."

He was trying to goad me, for no other reason than that he enjoyed confrontation, but I was not about to play his game. "Is that all you found?" I said.

"Sure," he said. Even if he had found something else, I knew he would not tell me. Full disclosure was a concept foreign to Maury Ahearne. What he might know that I did not was always negotiable.

◄○►

I showed the photograph of the naked young woman to Arthur French the first time I went to Nogales. He said he did not know who she was. The picture is the third of the three photographs I keep on the bulletin board in my office, but I did not pin it there until later.

Much later.

PART TWO

PART TWO

NOVEL
&
SCREENPLAY

ENTER RUPERT HAYES.
 His is a name you will read only three times in this narrative, and he is of no importance to it. He was an Australian reporter, one of those large beefy red-faced types from Sydney or Melbourne, who called everyone "mate" or "monsignor" and drank prodigiously and talked too loud, usually about the venality of Australian journalism, a venality of which he thoroughly and boisterously approved, often in song. On first or eighth or twelfth meeting he would repeat endlessly:

> *You cannot hope to bribe or twist*
> *The Aussie journalist.*
> *But given what the man will do,*
> *There's no occasion to.*

He lived in a brothel in Hué, as he never tired of telling you, where the girls said he was a little quick on the trigger and usually couldn't even pull it, as he never bothered to tell you. End of psychoanalysis. I avoided him like the plague, but in January 1968, we happened to fly into Khe Sanh together and that night we shared a bunker during an artillery barrage, a thousand rounds from dusk to dawn, between us and mortality only that hole in the ground and six thousand sandbags. The bunker belonged to Bravo Company, 3d Reconnaissance Battalion, 26th Marines, and the jarheads had told us it was the safest place on the hill, a trick to initiate newcomers, neglecting as they did to add that the Bravo bunker was bordered by an ammo dump, a flight line loading area, and the regimental CP, in other words the fucking bull's-eye for incoming. (Don't ask how I had washed up in Vietnam. A tricky divorce, war as material, trying to make a reputation, the usual bullshit.) In any event I was there, and that night, January 26, 1968, I thought I was going to die. As indeed did Rupert Hayes. So much so that in the morning when the noise died down and the night's dead and wounded were being tallied, he said he was flying out on the first C-130 that touched down, and touch down is all they did, they didn't even switch off their engines, they pushed out the cargo and the empty body bags, picked up the passengers and the loaded body bags and took off, total time on the ground maybe four minutes. Fuck this, monsignor, he said, this is your war, not mine, and I don't intend to get dead in it. How are you going to file, I said, with that commitment to the facts (truth even then I knew to be something else altogether) that I still thought was important for a reporter (while wishing to Christ I had the nerve to get on the C-130 with him)—in other words name, rank, serial number, home town, casualties, different kinds of ordnance, how bright the light at the end of the tunnel, how much the doggie in the window. In the great tradition of Australian journalism, mate, he said. Make it live. Make it sing. Make it up.

Exit Rupert Hayes. Back to his whorehouse in Hué. Just in time for Tet. When he got dead.

I don't think I've thought of him since.

Make it live. Make it sing. Make it up.

I never did forget that.

◄○►

This is what I have.

Chuckie O'Hara and Arthur French. Two old men with convenient memories, one overestimating his impact on the story, the other pretending he had none at all, both eminently useful in dressing the set.

What else?

The tapes I made in Hamtramck. I suspected that Maury Ahearne had stolen Melba's own tapes, the ones she kept in the freezer compartment of her refrigerator, maybe even had duped them, although he denied it, and was keeping them, as she had been, as bargaining chips, his grasp of the main chance as tentative as hers. It turned out I was right, not that it really mattered, because Melba Mae Toolate was scarcely the most credible analyst of the life and times of Blue Tyler.

What else?

As do most writers, I like to research more than I like to write. It is comforting to sit in cramped library microfilm rooms or in front of a computer scrolling through Nexis listings; it gives the illusion of accomplishment and nourishes the idea that you are not just busy but actually working. Finding Walter Sklar, the cameraman on *Red River Rosie,* long since thought dead, alive and well in Santa Fe Springs, with a senior handicap of fourteen at Torrey Pines, is useful, even if all he had to say was that he heard Blue Tyler died in Cleveland in 1966, and that not many people knew it but Chuckie O'Hara was a fairy. There is as well always the long shot of discovering a nugget streaked with gold; the inconsistencies in a police investigation are perhaps more apparent now than they were forty years ago, unless of course (and speculation is the aphrodisiac of compulsive research) the inconsistencies were part of a cover-up. A long-forgotten police casebook becomes available, and its forensic photographs suggest that someone might not be telling the truth.

So:

Make it live.

Make it sing.

Make it up.

II

IT WAS RITA LEWIS WHO, the same afternoon as her conversation with Morris Lefkowitz, rented Jacob King the gated house on St. Pierre Road in Bel Air, decorated by William Cameron Menzies, with six bedrooms, a projection room seating sixteen, eighteen rooms overall, a six-car garage with servants' quarters above it, a swimming pool tiled in onyx, north-south tennis court, a championship croquet green with a gazebo for spectators, a three-month lease with an option for an additional three. The house was a permanent rental kept for New York and English actors and directors in town for a picture, or for upper-level Industry people in the midst of divorces or trial separations. It came with four cars, including a Cadillac convertible and a Lincoln Continental coupe, and was fully staffed with butler, cook, chauffeur, three maids, full-time gardener, and twenty-four security. Coincidentally Chuckie O'Hara had once leased it while he was remodeling his house on Kings Road in the Hills, and it was he who described it for me, referring to the photographs Cecil Beaton had taken for *Vogue* when the Oliviers were living there one season in the sun, the house having long since been torn down and replaced by a faux Regency monstrosity that stretched from property line to property line.

Renting the house for Jacob King had in fact been Lilo Kusack's idea, his supple mind beginning to operate even while Rita was fellating him by the pool after Morris Lefkowitz's call. Morris will think it means we'll do business, he said, and Jake will see all the cooz and forget about business, I don't know what Jimmy Riordan was thinking, sending Jake out here, maybe Jimmy just wanted to get him out of New York, let him work on his tan while he eases Morris out of the picture, he can't really think we'll do business together, Jakey's just a shooter with a big dick.

Morris, Lilo said when he called Morris Lefkowitz back, adjusting his genitals inside his swimming trunks, Rita said you called, I'm sorry I was out, it's been too long, Morris, we'll take care of Jake, get him set up out here, have him meet a few people. I know a nice house, just the place, we'll make him comfortable, let him see southern California hospitality up close, don't you worry about a thing, Morris.

It was precisely when Lilo Kusack said not to worry that Jimmy Riordan, listening on the extension in Morris Lefkowitz's office, began to worry, but he kept his own counsel, wondering to himself what was potentially more dangerous, Lilo Kusack underestimating Jacob King, or Jacob King underestimating Lilo Kusack, either eventuality a volatile prospect. He was also sure that Morris Lefkowitz was thinking along the same lines, Morris in his eighth decade as always immune to smooth talkers, which is one reason he had reached his eighth decade with so few scars, but he too kept his own counsel. It was in these pregnant silences that Jimmy Riordan and Morris Lefkowitz communicated.

◄◦►

According to both Chuckie O'Hara and Arthur French, it was also Rita Lewis who met Jacob King on the platform when the Super Chief pulled into Union Station in downtown Los Angeles. He was all in shades of beige, with no tie and a beige shirt that buttoned to the neck, and a beige jacket with no lapel, and brown-and-beige shoes, and in his hand he had a roll of bills from which he was liberally distributing tips to the porters wrestling with his five suitcases and two wardrobe trunks.

"So, Rita," Jacob King said when he spotted her leaning against a baggage truck the way minor contract actresses did when they were photographed at the beginning or end of a publicity junket.

"Lilo called that one right," Rita Lewis said. "He said you'd get off the Chief flashing bills like a two-bit hood."

"You got a funny way of saying hello, Rita," Jacob King said. "How long's it been?"

"Seven years," Rita Lewis said. "Lillian got pissed off, remember? She didn't think we should be fucking when she was pregnant. I can only say if she thought that, she didn't know you very well." She ran her fingers down the inside of his jacket. "Is this your idea of resort wear?"

"What's the matter with it?"

"You don't know, Jacob, then I can't tell you. Another thing. Stars get off the Chief in Pasadena."

"Why?"

"They do, that's why. That's why they're stars, they know things like that. But if you're going to get off the train looking like a Good Humor man, maybe it's better you stayed on." She looked at the pile of suitcases. "Planning on staying awhile?"

"Awhile," Jacob King said pleasantly, staring past Rita at a large man in a dirty white linen suit across the platform who seemed to be watching him.

"Let me guess," he said to the man in the white suit. "You're a cop."

"Frank Crotty, Mr. King," he said, moving toward them. "Lieutenant Frank Crotty. Vice."

It occurred to Rita that in all the years she had consorted with men of crime she had never really seen a policeman up close, except when one was giving her a traffic ticket. She liked to be out of town when bad things she thought might happen did happen. In another city. Or another state. Or another country. Switzerland was the country she liked best. Switzerland in the winter when the mountains were covered with snow. In Switzerland she would hear about the blood she was escaping and imagine it making a scarlet pattern on the virgin ski trails. There were no Lieutenant Crottys in Davos or Klosters or Gstaad. Lieutenant Crotty looked like an overweight avuncular rattlesnake, his large belly stretching the buttons of his soiled double-breasted suit. She wondered who had tipped him off that Jacob would be arriving on the Chief, and that Jacob would not know enough to get off at Pasadena. She knew it was not Lilo. Lilo would never tip his hand, and he did not believe in vulgar intimidation. She wondered if she would tell Lilo that the policeman had met Jacob at Union Station, and decided he would already know, because it was the sort of thing he made it his business to know. Not to tell him would introduce another element of distrust in a relationship already complicated by the fact that Lilo was only a middleman who defined for his clients the frontiers between the legal and the illegal, and it had been Rita's history since puberty that she was always attracted to those who had crossed the boundaries into the criminal without a passing thought, her current alliance with a coordinator like Lilo, a facilitator, a factor more of age and a concomitant instinct for survival than of the recklessness to which she had so often been prone.

"Is this an official welcome, Lieutenant Crotty?" Jacob King said.

"Unofficial," Crotty said. "You're planning to stay awhile, are you, Jake?"

"That's funny, that's exactly the question my friend here just asked.

"Lillian Aronow," Jacob King said after a moment spent counting his bags, then nodding toward Rita, "this is Lieutenant Crotty from Vice, who starts off calling me Mr. King and now we're such pals he calls me Jake."

Crotty turned his rattlesnake eyes on Rita. "Pleased to make your acquaintance, Miss Lewis."

Now she knew she would tell Lilo. It was dumb of the detective to show he knew her name, there was no advantage in it.

"The vice officers are very quick in Los Angeles, Rita," Jacob said. "You forgot to tell me that." He smiled at Crotty. "So, Lieutenant, what can I tell you you don't already know, you're so smart?"

"Maybe what're you going to be doing here, with all these grips?"

"I don't think that's any of your business, but I want to be a good citizen my first day in Los Angeles. I used to say Los Angle-us, but then a lady I met said it's An-juh-lus, so that's how I say it now. Los An-juh-lus. So how about this? I'm an investor. I believe in the accumulation and utilization of capital. I'm looking for investment possibilities." He leaned close to Crotty. "I'm an easy guy to make friends with. I'm interested in everybody I meet. I notice little things about them." He picked at the buttonholes in the sleeve of Crotty's linen jacket. "For example, your suit. It needs dry cleaning, it looks like soy sauce here, maybe moo shu pork, anyway you should use a napkin when you eat. But I also notice it's custom-tailored. That interests me. Most police officers get their suits off the pipe, two pairs of pants and free alterations.

"This is quality goods," he said as Crotty brushed at a spot on his sleeve.

"Sydney Greenstreet wore it in *Across the Pacific*," Crotty said, explaining when he did not have to, as Jacob knew he would. "I know a guy at Warner's, he gets me all Sydney's suits."

"I had a custom-made vicuña coat, I gave it to the Pullman porter on the train. George his name was. A colored." Jacob smiled. His tabloid smile. The smile Rita Lewis had so often seen when he was setting someone up. "I knew you were in the market for secondhand clothes, Lieutenant, I would've saved it for you. I think it's probably wasted on a *schwartze*."

I wonder if he smiles when he does a hit, Rita Lewis thought.

"But then I didn't know I was going to be met by a welcoming committee, my mistake, I'm sorry, what're you going to do? Your bad luck."

Over the public-address system, there was a trumpet fanfare, and then the station announcer called all aboard for the Del Mar Special, departing at eleven-fifteen, track fourteen, post time for the first race at one-thirty, all aboard, please.

Crotty waited until the announcement was finished. "If you want to make friends here, Jake," he said carefully as the porters wrestled the suitcases and the two trunks onto the baggage truck, "you got to remember to show respect for other people's interests. People here, they've got various interests. Of a business nature. They don't like other people butting in. You should remember that."

Jacob nodded, as if taking the words to heart. "Frank . . . It is Frank, isn't it?"

Crotty nodded.

"That's good advice, Frank. I'll try to remember that." He peeled a hundred-dollar bill from his roll. "You want to help the red cap with the bags?"

Crotty shrugged, then turned and walked up the platform toward the waiting room.

Jacob King watched him for a moment. "Who sent the flatfoot, Rita?"

It was the kind of question that for most of her life she had conditioned herself never to answer, nor even to surmise a possible answer. It was an article of faith with her that what she did not know, or claimed not to know, would not hurt her, while at the same time in the more realistic lobe of her brain she understood this to be a comforting fantasy rather than an empirical fact. "Who do you think I am, the Answer Man?"

"For old times' sake," Jacob King said.

She felt herself weakening. "I had to make a guess, I'd say it was Benny Draper, it's his kind of dumb play."

"So, Rita. You missed me?" Jacob King said.

◄○►

You have to realize, Chuckie O'Hara said, that Jacob just took to this place as if he had been born to it, that was one thing Lilo was dead-on about. He loved that house in Bel Air, he loved the gates and the cars and the servants and the swimming pool. He made Rita take him all around the grounds. He said he'd learn how to play tennis, he'd hire the best coaches to teach him, and that croquet was just stickball with a mallet, and this is the real scream, the pièce de résistance: Rita is showing him through the house and they run into the butler. He's in his daytime livery, black-and-yellow stripes, polishing silver or something, and Jacob grabs him by the neck and throws him up against the wall and puts a gun against his head. Who the fuck are you? he says. How'd you get in here?

I'm the butler, sir, the butler says with that kind of piss-elegant butler savoir faire, as if he'd picked up his manners butling for C. Aubrey Smith.

Needless to say, Jacob was terribly embarrassed. Oh, I'm Jake King, he says. What's your name?

Woodson, sir, the butler says.

I mean, your first fucking name, Jacob says.

And Rita said, You don't call a butler by his first name, Jake. He's just Woodson.

And Jacob said, Well, beat it, Woody.

Chuckie waited for my reaction. I'm not sure that plays, I said after a moment.

Why not?

Well, let's say Jacob arrived at the house with Rita. And he had all these bags and the two trunks. So obviously there must have been servants around to take the bags inside and upstairs to unpack them. One would just have to assume that Woodson, if that was the butler's name, would have been there to supervise, and Jacob would have had to have seen him.

You can be such a bore, Jack.

But I'm right. Right?

It ruins the scene, Chuckie O'Hara said.

—◇—

"I see you still take a shower after you do it," Rita Lewis said when Jacob King emerged from the bathroom into the master bedroom of the house on St. Pierre Road, a towel around his waist, slicking his hair back. She was smoking a cigarette and wondering exactly how much money it was he had taken from his briefcase and put in the wall safe behind the fake Remington in the sitting room next door.

"So I smell like a baby the next time," Jacob said. He went to the open French doors and waved at the Japanese gardener in the rose arbor below. "You know what I'm going do? I'm going to repaint this room in peach. I hear that's the color this year. Then I'm going to hire a guy. All he's going to do is play the piano."

"That's what Capone had," Rita said. "I told you that a long time ago."

"I keep forgetting, Rita. Al was a special friend of yours, wasn't he?"

It was a gibe she had heard too often to let it disturb her. "Capone doesn't play out here, Jake. Neither does peach. Peach was last year."

"So I'll learn. You can teach me. You've come a long way, Rita. I hear that when you and Lilo give a party, out-of-work kings show up."

Rita let the sheet fall away from her body, and as if by rote idly began flicking a thumb over the nipple of her left breast. "Just how much money did you put in that safe next door?"

"You saw that?"

"Money interests me. Especially in large amounts. So, yes, I did see that."

"More than you ever carried for Al. Or Vinny D." He checked the whiteness of his teeth in the mirror. "I always wanted a safe behind a cowboy picture. Class."

"It's a Remington, and it's a fake."

"You could've fooled me."

Rita started to say, It's not all that hard to do, but caught herself in time. She was careful about putting herself in a position that could result in her getting beaten up, the violence inherent in so many of her sexual partners a factor in their attractiveness to her, her talent for fellatio and the more exotic forms of intercourse her primary means of keeping that violence under control. If she was beaten up, she was honest enough to apportion some of the blame to herself, both for a tongue quicker than it should be (in conversation if not in sodomy) and a failure to have a heavy object, a Steuben ashtray, say, within reach to balance the odds. Considering the men she had bedded, she thought herself fortunate to have been beaten up as few times as she had, and never once badly enough to be hospitalized, a black eye easily disguised by sunglasses and bruises fading with time. Further evening the odds was the fact that there were men who might have beaten her up in the past who would be quite willing to maim and perhaps even kill other men who would beat her up in the present, were she only to ask. If nothing else, Rita Lewis was a realist; it had been a half dozen years since she had last copulated with Jacob King, and she was not quite in touch with his current level of volatility. Not knowing exactly how far she could push, and having experience of his fists, she kept her tongue in check.

"So, Rita, if I want to get rid of that phoney what's-his-name . . ."

"Remington."

". . . then how much does the real thing cost?"

"What you put into the safe."

"I'll keep the fake. Who the fuck'll know?"

"I did. How are you fixed?"

"Lilo tell you to ask me that?"

"Sure. Just like Lilo told me to blow you. He'll want me to tell him all about it."

Jacob King ran his hand over his stomach, then pinched his waist looking for excess flesh. "I'm fixed okay," he said when he had satisfied himself of his physical fitness. "The race wire pretty much runs itself. Only a fucking idiot would try to skim off the top, it's a sure way to get capped." Jacob snapped his fingers. "Except I'm not supposed to talk like that. It sends Jimmy Riordan right to the Pepto-Bismol bottle. And Morris owns a chain of laundries out here I'm supposed to look after. And a linen business. Perfectly legitimate. All the nightclubs use it. There's the, uh, the, uh . . . give me a little help, Rita . . .''

"The Trocadero. Ciro's. The Mocambo."

"That's it. They all do business with me. If they know what's good for them." He took the cigarette from her hand and used it to light one of his own. "You know what I'm going to be, Rita?" He handed back her cigarette. "One of those millionaire sportsmen Winchell is always writing about."

"Laundries and sportsmen don't go together, Jacob. It's not a good fit."

Jacob King shrugged.

"Let me spell it out for you, Jake." Rita got out of bed and stubbed out the cigarette. She stared for a moment at her reflection in the mirror. Her entire life she had liked to look at herself naked. She was an enthusiastic masturbator, and loved the perfect triangular thickness of her pubic hair, and that gravity had not yet worked its will on her breasts. "I'm not supposed to, but I will anyway. For old times' sake, like you said before. Lilo says if you're out here to make a case for Morris, you can save your breath, there's no case to make, the desert is closed. No trespassing."

He seemed elaborately disinterested in what she had to say. Few men and no women had ever been able to tell him how to run his life. "You had your jugs lifted?"

Rita tried again. "It's not like New York. It's not the Brooklyn docks. You don't cap a bunch of people here no one cares about. Just because these people are smooth, don't make the mistake of thinking they're not tough."

Jacob let his towel drop and put his arms around Rita Lewis. His thick-veined cock rubbed slowly against her buttocks until it came to rest in her crack. "I bet Lilo never had a piece of ass like you."

"Lilo used to be Joan Crawford's lawyer," Rita Lewis said. She made a perfunctory attempt to escape his grasp, then gave in to the inevitable and began to rotate her ass rhythmically against his member.

He walked her out onto the balcony over the rose arbor, the two of them naked in the warm afternoon sun, he already with another hard-on. Below, the gardener tending the tea roses pretended not to notice their pre-coital fondling. "God, I'm going to love this town," Jacob King said.

III

THE EVIDENCE IS ANECDOTAL, and when what happened actually did happen is subject to dispute, but there is reason to suggest that Jacob King, for whatever his motives (and it may have been as simple as taking him at his word when he said he was going to love this town), did heed, at least at the beginning, the advice of Jimmy Riordan to proceed slowly, to make nice, to avoid antagonisms, to turn the other cheek, as he had at Union Station when confronted by the police detective Crotty, who was probably Benny Draper's man, as he had when he ignored Rita Lewis's warning that there was no case for Morris Lefkowitz to be made, although it could be said that to have coitus with Lilo Kusack's mistress three times the afternoon of his arrival might be construed as reckless behavior, a statement in itself. Whether it was by accident or design that Jacob met Blue Tyler again in Los Angeles depends on the teller, and whether he ran into her before or after he had reconnoitered the desert is also open to debate. I can only make what I will call an informed speculation, subject of course to my own prejudices, my main prejudice an allegiance to narrative, however fragmented.

I said earlier that there were two biographies of Jacob King, equally mendacious. Both were also, it turned out, written (for two different publishers) by the same man, a true crime writer named Harold Pugh, who in the course of a given year would crank out a half dozen such criminal biographies under as many different pseudonyms; Raul Flaherty was the pen name he used on *Jake: A Gangster's Story*, Waldo Kline on *Messenger of Death: The Life and Times of Jacob King* (its epigraph from Proverbs 16:14: "The wrath of a king is as messengers of death"). Such was the facility of Harold Pugh (sadly long since gone to his eternal reward), and his good-natured propensity for charlatanism, that he had Waldo Kline flatly contradict Raul Flaherty on a number of points, and then engage in a loud public dispute with him in the low press, alleging among other things plagiarism. It is instructive nevertheless to inspect these volumes, if only because they supply Jacob King with a personal style, however vulgar (because of course they are taken largely from the tabloids of the period), and offer a chronology of his later Hollywood years, both of which I can then amend on the basis of my conversations with Blue Tyler herself, and with Chuckie O'Hara and Arthur French, none of whom volunteered any insights to the pseudonymous Waldo Kline and Raul Flaherty, and who to me, it must be said, offered largely the stuff of lonely, restless, inventive, and self-absorbed minds.

There is Jacob the vain, who oiled his skin with lotions and potions and facial creams, and kept the line of his chiseled features intact by sleeping with an elastic chin strap attached to a black net nightcap. There was Jacob the vulgar, who put Carrara marble throughout his house on St. Pierre Road and concealed, for the benefit of his guests, a row of slot machines behind the sliding teak bookshelves in his library, slot machines with an automatic payoff he could control so that his friends would never go home without a nest egg of silver dollars. There is Jacob the arriviste, who learned to play polo and golf and tennis and joined Hillcrest, where every Saturday afternoon in the game room he played gin with Shelley Flynn and Moe French and Chuckie O'Hara. Jacob the gambler, who bet ten thousand dollars on the turn of a card, and Jacob the philanthropist, who contributed to the United Jewish Appeal and the I Am an American Foundation, at whose dinner he was photographed with Rabbi Baruch Tyger and His Eminence Hugh Cardinal Danaher. What is interesting about this curriculum vitae is that it would seem to incorporate ten years of rich full living, when in fact, from the day Jacob King arrived at Union Station in Los Angeles to the day of his assassination, less than two years would transpire.

◄◦►

Blue Tyler said Jacob King did not play polo, it was Arthur who played polo, Jacob just liked to wear boots and jodhpurs, he thought he looked good in them, he'd wear them to the polo matches and watch Arthur and Spencer Tracy and D.Z. play, and he had begun taking riding lessons shortly before the accident (she always called his murder "the accident"), he said if Arthur could ride a horse so could he. She said she could not remember if he wore a chin strap or a nightcap to bed, but she tended to doubt it because he liked to fuck in the middle of the night, if he got up to pee he couldn't go back to sleep without a fuck, and she would remember going down on anyone wearing a chin strap and a nightcap, she thought it would make her lose the urge to help him get it up.

Blue said Eddie Schmidt did Jacob King's clothes. Who was Eddie Schmidt, I said. Tailor to the stars, Blue said, without a hint of irony.

Arthur said it was Willingham, his father's house on Angelo Drive that had the black Carrara marble, not Jacob King's. Chuckie said every Industry house on the west side of Los Angeles had black marble, and naturally he called it Crakow chic.

Real estate records show that Jacob King bought the house on St. Pierre Road the week after his arrival. The deed was in the name of JFR, Ltd., a subsidiary of Lefko Enterprises. JFR was James Francis Riordan. Lefko was Morris Lefkowitz.

Chuckie O'Hara said that Jacob had plans drawn for the slot machines he wanted installed behind sliding teak bookshelves at the house on St. Pierre Road. He died before the slots could be installed.

Arthur French said Jacob King was not a member of Hillcrest. He said he would have blackballed him.

Au contraire, Chuckie O'Hara said. Every Saturday when he wasn't shooting he would play gin at Hillcrest with Jacob and Shelley Flynn and J. F. French.

Moe French wouldn't have let Arthur blackball Jacob, Chuckie O'Hara went on. Moe would say Jump, and Arthur would say How high. I thought you liked Arthur, I said. Moe's errand boy, Chuckie said. Take away Moe and what do you think Arthur would have been?

The records made available to me by Hillcrest's resident manager (at Arthur French's request) resolved the dispute over Jacob King's club membership by showing he had a permanent guest card; his sponsor was Shelley Flynn and his seconder was Chuckie O'Hara. Chuckie claimed (and as in most matters he put a pederast's spin on his motives) that he only wanted to be available in the locker or steam rooms in the event Jacob ever lapsed from the theology of heterosexuality.

It is also true that Jacob King did try to insinuate himself into the community. Went to temple. Met and embraced Barry Tyger with an open checkbook. A total of forty-two thousand dollars, according to the audit the Internal Revenue Service conducted of Jacob King's tangled finances after his murder. Rabbi Tyger was an artifact of the times, one who saw himself less a spiritual leader than an envoy to the *goyim* and a high priest of secularism. He took voice lessons and sold religion the way his flock sold their motion pictures, avoiding piety as if it were a sin, even offering absolution to the moguls for their sexual transgressions. Having intercourse with a shiksa was a lesser transgression than traffic in the ideas of "Reds, pinks, and pseudo-liberals" (the words taken from *The Collected Sermons of Barry Tyger,* with a jacket photo of the author in a double-breasted blazer, open-necked shirt, and foulard ascot). He believed nothing was served by invoking the ghettos of Eastern

Europe from whence so many of his congregation came. "What's so great about Minsk or Pinsk?" he asked an interviewer. "What virtue is there in ethnic emphasis? We have beautiful Jews and we have stinkers, and so does everybody else. This roots, roots, roots, it's all baloney." Except on the Sabbath, he was a regular at the high-stakes gin games at Hillcrest, in effect his second synagogue, where Jacob King, Chuckie O'Hara said, saw to it that he was a regular winner.

Baruch Tyger refused to officiate at Jacob King's funeral. Asked by the *Los Angeles Herald Express* if he had anything good to say about the deceased, Rabbi Tyger said, "He's dead."

◄○►

Therefore:

Proceeding from guesswork, my sources at best tainted and working on agendas of their own, I have Jacob King driving fast across the desert, his destination some four hundred miles to the northeast—Las Vegas, Clark County, Nevada. The urban sprawl that is Los Angeles County today would then have petered out long before the San Bernardino County line, and the ribbon of two-lane blacktop would not have been a modern freeway with parabolic exits and interchanges. He would have been behind the wheel of either the Cadillac convertible or the Lincoln Continental coupe that came with the house on St. Pierre Road; if the Cadillac, the top of course would have been down and the sun beating on his bare head, because the wind would certainly have sent a hat, had he been wearing one, bouncing across the desert sands.

I must assume that the Mojave was the first desert Jacob King had ever seen. It was the conceit of Raul Flaherty in *Jake: A Gangster's Story* that he immediately perceived that the Mojave offered an even more advantageous body dump than Sheepshead Bay, where in the Flaherty version Pittsburgh Pat Muldoon had been deposited, that the blistering sun and the shifting sands would quickly erase all a body's identifying characteristics, and what remained would be a meal for coyotes and snakes and vultures and scorpions and desert predators of all sizes and shapes, an arm here, a leg there, even the head a moveable feast. Always shameless, Harold Pugh as Raul Flaherty further claimed that Jacob King used the desert as his own private outdoor cemetery on any number of occasions. It is a conceit I tend to doubt, because I suspect a boy born in Red Hook and accorded only a fifth-grade education would not be natural historian enough to be easily familiar with the flesh-eating habits of desert scavengers and carnivores, and furthermore he was practiced killer enough to realize that a drive of several hundred miles or more with a body going rank in the trunk, and with all the possibilities of vehicular malfunction as well as desert sheriffs who supported themselves with the income from speeding tickets, was a risk not worth taking.

─◇─

Consider Fremont Street in downtown Las Vegas that spring evening when Jacob King pulled into town. He would park his Lincoln Continental across the street from the Pioneer Club's Vegas Vic cutout sign, its arms rocking against the night sky, its cigarette puffing and glowing. Correction: There was no "downtown" Las Vegas that season, there was just Las Vegas, a tired anything-goes honky-tonk for the construction workers who had worked on Boulder Dam and stayed on as maintenance personnel, small-time action and small-time whores and twenty-four-hour heat. Jacob King knew exactly where he wanted to go, a nondescript casino called the Bronco down the street from the Pioneer Club. He went inside, looked around to see who if anyone was looking either at him or consciously away from him, and then sat down at a blackjack table. The dealer seemed bored. He was a man about Jacob King's age, with thinning black hair plastered to his skull, a short muscular body, expressionless eyes, and protruding from under the right cuff of his white shirt the bottom of a tattoo, what appeared to be the locks of a woman's hair. The two other players at the table, turbine managers from the dam in cheap cotton pants, short-sleeved shirts, and straw cowboy hats, watched without comment as Jacob slid a thousand dollars in hundred-dollar bills at the dealer and asked for ten one-hundred-dollar chips. The dealer shoveled the cash down the chute and stacked the hundred-dollar tokes in front of Jacob King.

"And another thousand in hundreds," Jacob King said after a moment, passing the bills across to the dealer. The other two players looked at each other, then shook their heads. "Too rich for me," one murmured as they gathered their chips and left Jacob King alone at the table. Jacob put five chips down.

The dealer dealt a hand to Jacob King and one to himself. "Dealer holds on seventeen," he said.

Jacob King gestured for another card, then another. He turned his cards over. Twenty-two. The dealer raked in the chips.

"Morris told me you might be coming in, Jake," the dealer said quietly as he dealt out another hand.

"What else did Morris tell you, Eddie?" Jacob King said.

"He tells me I owe him one," the dealer said. His name was Eddie Binhoff and like the late Philly Wexler he had known Jacob King most of his life. "He's right. The genius of Morris Lefkowitz is, you always end up owing him one. You live to be a hundred and sixty-two years old, you get a call from Morris, he's two hundred and ten years of age, he points out you still owe him one. So what are you here for, Jake?"

"Blackjack," Jacob King said.

"Fuck you," Eddie Binhoff said, paying nineteen. They talked softly, always playing, Jacob winning or losing, Eddie Binhoff raking in or paying out chips, the hundred-dollar game scaring off the casual players.

"You've always been a very suspicious guy, Eddie, you know that?" He doubled down and let his eyes wander over the down-at-the-heels casino. "I figured out here, the sun shines, everybody says howdy, you'd loosen up, get less suspicious. But no. You're the same coiled-up guy you were in Red Hook, we were kids, you know that?"

"I been in the joint twice since I leave Red Hook. Nine years total. I even got a tattoo in the joint, it gave me something to do, a chick named Roxanne.

"That's her on my arm," Eddie Binhoff said, showing Jacob

the bottom of the tattoo. "Except I don't know no Roxannes. What the hell. It helped pass the time." He moved cards crisply out of the shoe, and flicked his over without looking. "The guy who give me the tattoo, he says I got to pay him in skull, so I broke his fucking skull is what I did. That's the beauty of doing a guy in the joint. You're already there, nobody gives a shit, it's one less mouth the state has to feed."

"Hit me," Jacob King said.

"I get out last time, Morris makes some calls, sets me up, that's how I get to owe him one," Eddie Binhoff said. "Bingo, I'm a solid citizen. I even got this little bungalow with a porch out front. So I sit on my porch and read about you in the papers. I want to jerk off, it makes me so happy reading about you, a kid from the same neighborhood as me. You want to cut up old touches, we'll cut up old touches."

Jacob turned around and watched the stage, where a woman singer wearing a Levi's shirt missing two buttons and showing dark roots under her blond dye job was trying to lip-sync "Don't Fence Me In," mechanically snapping her microphone cord as if it was a lariat, and smiling in the direction of Eddie Binhoff's table.

"You banging her, Eddie?"

"A couple of times. She's a little stringy."

"So," Jacob King said. He had a jack and a deuce showing. Eddie Binhoff slid him an eight of clubs. Twenty. "Lilo Kusack's new place. La Casa Nevada. What do you hear about it?"

"Jake. I don't have three ears. I hear what everybody else hears. Lilo's fronting it for Benny Draper, Benny's pension fund's putting up the construction costs. You know all that before you leave Penn Station."

"Grand Central. You been away from New York too long, Eddie. You take the Limited to Chicago from Grand Central, not Penn Station, get off at LaSalle Street in Chi, grab something to eat at the Pump Room, go over to Dearborn Street, pick up the Chief, George makes sure your grips are on the train."

Eddie Binhoff dealt himself a seven. Twenty-one. "Who the fuck is George?"

"The colored guy on the train. All the colored guys on the train are called George. That way you don't have to remember their colored names. I guess they didn't teach you that at Attica." Jacob King nodded for another game. "You pull into L.A., you get off at Pasadena. Stars get off at Pasadena. You ought to remember that, Eddie, you ever take the Chief to L.A., you'll want people to think you're a star."

"You know something, Jake," Eddie Binhoff said. He was never overly talkative, but if he did choose to speak, he always said what was on his mind, with no fancy elocution. "I'm beginning to think maybe you didn't whack Philly Wexler, it was some other guy, it was a bad rap, even Morris is clean, he had nothing to do with that fucking poinsettia that blew Ruthie away." He kept staring at Jacob King as he raked in four one-hundred-dollar chips and laid out the next hand. "A guy who tells me stars get off the train in Pasadena, I'd say that guy don't have the temperament to be a hitter."

Jacob King cracked his knuckles, his olive-complected face darkening even more. Eddie Binhoff had seen the look before, and the mayhem that usually followed. There was a bas ball bat under the table, but he knew that Morris Lefkowitz would not consider his using it to counter an assault by Jacob King as payment for the favor he already owed. Morris Lefkowitz would take it amiss, and Morris Lefkowitz did not let things he took amiss ride, even when there was twenty-five hundred miles between where he was and where what caused him offense had taken place. Jacob did not take his eyes off Eddie Binhoff. "You always did have a smart mouth, Eddie," he said finally. He lit a cigarette and inhaled deeply. Then he smiled. "So what else you hear about Lilo's place."

"It's going to be a money machine with marble crappers," Eddie Binhoff said, steadying the bat with his knee. Morris Lefkowitz or no Morris Lefkowitz, he knew he would not have let Jacob King come across the table. "Or so some people say. I don't see it myself."

"Because you got no vision, Eddie. People saying anything else?"

"Some people say Morris is blowing smoke up his ass, he think's anybody's going to cut him in." Another player sat down at the table. "Beat it," Eddie Binhoff said to the new player, and when the player made no move, he repeated the order, his voice barely a whisper. "I said beat it."

The player looked at Eddie Binhoff, then at Jacob King. "I want to play. I got the money." He put a twenty on the table. "Give me some chips. Or get me the pit boss."

"Good, call the pit boss, that's your right," Jacob King said. "And when you do, I'll take this cigarette here . . ." He flicked the ash into an ashtray, leaving a burning ember at the end of the butt. He pinched the cigarette and put the ember under the chin of the other man. ". . . and I'll put it out in your eye."

"It'll hurt," Eddie Binhoff said.

The player twirled in his chair and scurried away, leaving his twenty-dollar bill on the table. Jacob beckoned a drinks waitress, gave her the player's twenty, and added a hundred. "Give it to that scared little guy over there looks like he's going to wet his pants." He took another bill from his roll. "And here's a hundred for you, sweetheart."

"Thank you, Mr. King." She smiled at Jacob. "I'm free later, you got nothing to do."

"Even in a shithole like this they know you, Jake," Eddie Binhoff said.

"Christ, most of the broads in this place are older than Morris," Jacob King said, as if the waitress was not still at his elbow. She flounced off. "You got time to show me around, Eddie?"

"I got twenty-four hours a day, it's such an interesting place."

"I don't have all that many guys from the neighborhood out here, Eddie." It was as close as Jacob could come to admitting there were some hands he was not willing to play alone. "I need somebody to watch my back."

Eddie Binhoff clapped his hands to show the pit boss he was not palming any chips, then pulled off his apron. "You must be getting out of practice, Jake. There's been two guys on your back from the moment you walked into this joint."

"So you like being back on the payroll, Eddie?"

IV

JUST VAMPING NOW, I said to Chuckie O'Hara.

Vamp, Chuckie said. We were sitting in the beamed two-story living room at his house in Carmel Highlands, with the ocean crashing against the rocks below. Occasionally I heard a noise from the study next door, and when I turned to look, I could see the wraithlike figure of Vera O'Hara, Chuckie's mother, trying to hide behind the huge oaken door, afraid she might be caught eavesdropping. She was over ninety, and so deaf that had we had put our conversation on loudspeakers she could not have heard it, but it still did not stop her from trying to listen. She had loved Blue Tyler. Charlton should have married Blue, Vera O'Hara yelled at me when Chuckie told her I had seen Blue in Hamtramck, they would have made such a perfect couple, and I would be a grandmother and even a great-grandmother today. It's true that Charlton was a little older, but he was exactly what Blue needed, a stabilizing influence, the loss of his leg would not have made any difference at all to her, she was so adorable, but Charlton just preferred those men friends of his, Charlton, I have never understood you, you were the catch of Hollywood, not to mention the women here in

Carmel, but they're just fortune hunters up here, and I don't know what you ever saw in that Johnny person anyway.

Gianni Pontecorvo, Chuckie said to me in a conversational tone, confident his mother could not hear a word he said. And then to Vera, enunciating every word carefully, Because Gianni had a palace in Venice and the most beautiful boys I have ever seen, dozens of them.

Well, then, Vera O'Hara said, he had children and you didn't, that's one good thing you can say about him, and I never even thought he liked pussy.

The word caught me by surprise.

She does that, Chuckie O'Hara said. It's hilarious. Her mind. Slips in and out. I didn't even know she knew those words until she was eighty-six. I bet she's a tomb of dirty stories. Then loudly to Vera, Aren't you, Mother? And I want to hear every single dirty one.

What? Vera O'Hara said, but it was time for her nap and a nurse took her away.

Vamp, Chuckie repeated.

All right, I said. This is tricky, because no one really knows what happened. Jacob is in Las Vegas, checking out La Casa Nevada. That we have to assume. And that's where Morris arranges for him to find Eddie Binhoff . . .

A wonderful character, Eddie Binhoff, Chuckie said.

Absolutely. A find.

Real?

Absolutely. In the essentials.

A composite.

Well, I said, you look at the clips, and Jacob seems not to have known anyone except the women he was fucking, and Morris Lefkowitz and Jimmy Riordan, who were back in New York, and the people who didn't want him out on the Coast . . .

Moe and Lilo and Benny Draper, Chuckie said.

And there had to be someone he could trust, someone he could talk to . . .

234 · JOHN GREGORY DUNNE

The Walter Brennan part, Chuckie said. Someone he could bounce ideas off of . . .

His muscle . . .

I understand. Perfect . . .

. . . and there was this guy named Eddie Binhoff who had done some work for Morris . . .

In Nevada?

I would think so. Probably. Yes. In Nevada. And other places.

(In fact, I had found Eddie Binhoff's name in *The Index of American Crime and Criminals,* cross-referenced both to Jacob King and to Morris Lefkowitz. The authorities claimed he had hit Rocco Mingus and Dominic Conti, among others, for Morris Lefkowitz, and had served two terms at Attica State Penitentiary in New York for manslaughter and aggravated assault. He seemed to have known Jacob in Brooklyn, and on one of her tapes, Blue had mentioned an Eddie, although she couldn't remember his last name. That Eddie person, she called him, I think he was Jacob's shooter, he was always around, he gave me the creeps. There was no Eddie Binhoff in either the Raul Flaherty or the Waldo Kline biography. The records of the Nevada Gaming Commission, however, indicated that an "Eddie Binyon," sometimes known as "Allie Lazar," formerly a blackjack dealer at the Bronco Club in Las Vegas, had been sought for questioning in connection with Jacob King's death, but he had not come forward voluntarily and his whereabouts were never discovered.)

I have no problem with Eddie Binhoff, Chuckie O'Hara said. I think we go with him. There was some strong, silent, dangerous type always with Jake, his name could have been Eddie, I can't remember, and you've fleshed him out. It's an under-the-title part anyway.

(I could not help noticing that he was now talking in the first person plural, as in "We go with him." Directors never change.)

We'd only be taking a few liberties, Chuckie said. It's the inner truth that matters. After all, Cary did play Cole Porter. And she played her butch, my dear.

(I wondered how he had gone from Eddie Binhoff to Cole Porter, but didn't press it.)

I see them, Jake and Eddie, Chuckie said, going out to the site of La Casa Nevada. It's night, of course. Wonderful images, night shooting in the desert. And we have those people who are following Jake, we mustn't forget them. And Jake has to be formulating a plan . . .

◄○►

Jacob King peered through the darkness beyond the chain-link construction fence. Instinctively he wiped the dust from his shoes against his trouser legs, as if there in the sand he could maintain their gloss. Caught in the high beam of the Continental's headlights, he could make out the outlines of a complex in the initial stages of construction. The contractor's sign read:

LA CASA NEVADA
GRAND OPENING DECEMBER 31ST
HEADLINING SHELLEY FLYNN IN THE MOJAVE ROOM
HAPPY NEW YEAR

Eddie Binhoff had positioned himself behind the open door on the passenger's side of the Continental, the door offering a shield of sorts. He tensed as a car sped by, and then another, but neither one slowed down. A white Cadillac convertible had followed them from the Bronco to the city limits, then had turned off. A dumb fucking car to use as a tail. Maybe they just wanted Jacob to know they were there. As if Jacob would give a fuck. That was one thing that hadn't changed. He had never given a fuck about anything. Behind him he heard Jacob King curse, and when he turned he saw Jacob at the top of the chain-link fence, examining a rip in his pants. Eddie Binhoff smiled. Jacob hated any imperfection in his wardrobe, and even claimed that an allergy to dry cleaning fluid justified his endless purchases of new clothing. As Eddie watched, Jacob jumped from the top of the fence and disappeared into the darkness.

The night was turning cold. There were few things that frightened Eddie Binhoff, but the outdoors was one of them. He hated the desert, hated its vast emptiness and the creatures he imagined populating it. Of all the places where Morris Lefkowitz might have exiled him, he could not think of a worse place than Nevada. He heard the sound of another car and felt reassured. He was comforted by the weapon in his belt, comforted as well by his ability to inflict pain without remorse. He almost wished the car would stop, offering him an opportunity to threaten and cause hurt, but like the others it did not even slow down. Somehow it reminded him of the night he did Dominic Conti over in Jersey. On the spur of the moment, before he buried Dominic in a lime pit in Essex County, he cut his hands off and threw them in the trunk of his car. When he got back to Brooklyn, he wrapped up the hands and put them on ice at Curly Aderholt's delicatessen in Brighton Beach. Curly was too scared to complain. Then when he did Albert Torrio, who had taken out Jack Caplan and had to be whacked, he placed the prints from Dominic Conti's gun hand on the piece he left at the scene. The *Mirror* said that its police sources had privately indicated that Dominic Conti was a prime suspect in the murder of Jack Caplan. And all that was left of Dominic was in a lime pit in Essex County, New Jersey. It was nice the way things worked out sometimes.

A noise behind him, and then Jacob King was scrambling back over the fence. More cursing as he once more tore his trousers. Then he was at Eddie Binhoff's side. "The place is nothing. Unless you're a fucking rattlesnake."

"Nothing?" Eddie Binhoff said, yanking his thumb back toward the construction site. "I've been in penitentiaries smaller than that."

"That's what it looks like. Exactly. A fucking pen. It's got no pools. It's got no golf course. It's got no tennis courts. It's nothing."

"Jake, the game out here isn't fun in the sun. The game is gambling."

"I told you, you don't have any vision, Eddie," Jacob King said, again examining his trousers. They were so torn that his undershorts were showing. He suddenly turned and kicked the fence, as if it was responsible for tearing his pants. The display of temper seemed to calm him. "Say you wanted to talk to the union guys on this," he asked deliberately, "who would you talk to?"

"You know who you see. You see Lilo. In L.A. And Lilo sees Benny Draper."

"I mean here. I mean, say you wanted to talk to them direct?"

Eddie Binhoff suspected he knew where Jacob was heading and tried to contemplate the ultimate cost of the favor he owed Morris Lefkowitz. "Lilo talks to them direct."

"I mean, say you wanted to go around Lilo. Say you wanted to slow things down."

"I wouldn't do that," Eddie Binhoff said. "I'm too attached to my kneecaps."

"Who?"

It was exactly as Eddie had suspected. "You told anyone you're thinking this way, Jake? You told Morris? You told Jimmy?"

"Who would you see?" Jacob King insisted.

Eddie wondered if Jacob was carrying. Something he should have checked out. Something he would have checked without even thinking about it if he was still in New York. He thought the desert sun was making him brain-dead, even though he rarely went out in it. What he heard was that Jacob did not carry regularly anymore. Like Morris. He was a fucking executive now. When his piece used to be like a second dick. A good bet he wasn't carrying, then. A good bet but not a cinch bet. And he never did anyone unless it was a cinch. Give it a chance. Think it through. He could do him out here, put him in the Continental, drive back to Vegas, leave the car on the street, catch a bus out. To Elko. Elko was a place Morris Lefkowitz might not know someone who owed him a favor. No. Morris would know someone even in Elko. Or he'd know somebody who knew somebody who knew somebody in Elko. And who the fuck would want to die in Elko? Another car. Eddie raised his hands against the glare of the headlights. I've been in the desert too long, he thought. The old days I would have had all this figured out. Like when he put Dominic Conti's hands on ice. An investment in the future. He watched as the car took the curve without braking. The driver was a born wheelman. A professional's appreciative appraisal.

To business.

"Who would I see?" Eddie Binhoff considered Jacob King's question. "Jackie Heller. He tells the locals here what to do."

"Jackie Heller," Jacob said, snapping his fingers impatiently. "His brother Leo used to work for Morris, right? He got whacked out."

"I took out his hitter," Eddie Binhoff said slowly. "Willie Posner. That was my second time in the joint."

"So let's go see Jackie." A smile creased Jacob King's face. "He owes you one."

HELLER, JACOB ("JACKIE")
Union Organizer, Racketeer (1903–1948)

BACKGROUND: Born Jacob Hiss, Hunt's Point, the Bronx, New York. Minor public education. Younger brother of Leo (Hiss) Heller, reputed hit man for Morris ("The Furrier") Lefkowitz. Leo Heller was found shot to death outside Yankee Stadium on December 25, 1939, with a note attached to his body saying "Happy Hanukkah." The murder of Leo Heller was never solved, although the fatal shootings of Wilhelm ("Slow Willie") Posner and Dino Montepulciano in the week between Christmas and New Year's in the Brownsville section of Brooklyn were said to be in retaliation for his death. DESCRIPTION: brown hair, brown eyes, short, well built. ALIASES: none. RECORD: many arrests, no convictions. Active as an enforcer in the construction trades and on the New York docks. Reportedly beat a man to death with his fists on a Hoboken pier in 1935. The victim, Terry Mulvehill, was said to be trying to organize the longshoremen. Fourteen eyewitnesses testified that Mulvehill had fallen from a ladder even after the Hudson County medical examiner said the traumas were not consistent with a fall from a six-foot ladder. In 1940, for reasons of health (he was diagnosed with tuberculosis), he moved to Las Vegas, Nevada, and formed Heller Sanitation Services, which on a contract from local authorities hauled all the garbage in Clark County. Heller was found shot to death in the desert outside Las Vegas in February 1949. His body was badly decomposed, and desert animals had carried off most of his appendages. He was identified from dental records. No one was ever charged with his murder.

ALSO SEE, LEFKOWITZ, MORRIS; DRAPER, BENJAMIN; KING, JACOB.

The Index of American Crime and Criminals

Jackie Heller lit Jacob King's cigar. He had the general dimensions of the Coca-Cola machine that sat in one corner of the dispatcher's office overlooking the Heller Sanitation garage. "You like that cigar, Jake? It's Havana. You're interested in casinos, Havana's the place. I was down there over New Year's. Definitely. Havana. That's where you want to go."

In the background, the dispatcher was ordering Heller Sanitation's garbage trucks into line for the nightly pickup.

"I've been to Havana, Jackie," Jacob King said, drawing deeply on his cigar.

"Rum and Coca-Cola. Beautiful señoritas, regular Latin spitfires. Action like you never—"

"I'm not interested in Havana," Jacob said, his face disappearing behind a cloud of smoke. "Morris doesn't feel he can make a contribution in Havana."

Eddie Binhoff stood at the door and watched Jackie Heller and Jacob King. He knew he made Jackie Heller nervous, favor or no favor owed him. He always felt better when he made people uncomfortable. More in charge.

"So, Eddie, tell me about Dom Conti's fingerprints, I nearly shit when I heard about it . . ."

"We're not here to talk about Dominic Conti," Jacob said.

"Right," Jackie Heller said, "you were asking about—"

"La Casa Nevada."

"What you were asking . . . this question of possible labor problems . . . on a job like La Casa . . . you are speaking hypothetically, right?"

Jacob King smiled. "Hypothetically. Right."

Jackie Heller went to the window, picked up a microphone, and yelled to a trucker below. "Off your butt, Two-oh-seven, I docked you last night and I'll dock you again. Two-oh-four, you cover Boulder, move it the fuck out." He came back and sat down across from Jacob King, wiping the sweat from his face. On the garage floor the diesels began revving up. "It's only driving a fucking garbage truck, it's not like they're working on the atom bomb, you know what I mean, Jake?"

"No."

"It's the fucking desert." Jackie Heller began to cough. His tubercular cough. It was always a good way to play for time. "There's no organization," he said finally. "By the time you count out the guys who just don't show up because they got something pressing to do, like getting laid, I'm lucky I can get one crew out." He turned to Eddie Binhoff, wiping the phlegm from his lips. "You agree with that, Eddie?"

"No."

"He's a fucking whacker, what does he know from organization?" Jackie Heller whispered to Jacob King.

"Enough to do Leo's hitter," Jacob said pleasantly. He rolled the cigar between his fingers, then held it under his nose, sniffing the aroma. "Stop stalling, Jackie."

"Jake. Word of honor. Not stalling." He chose his words with care. "You ever been in the Tombs?"

Jacob King did not reply.

"That's right, you just did four months in the Tombs," Jackie Heller said. "Well, then. So you know. You want a blanket in the Tombs, you got one. It costs you five dollars. Another buck, you get disinfectant. To delouse the blanket. Your mother write you a letter? No sweat, you're in the Tombs, you'll get it delivered to you. For another dollar. You want a five-dollar bottle of booze? It'll cost you ten, but you got it. You got a broad coming to visit? You got twenty-five dollars, the hacks are going to let you screw her on the lower tier. You get laid in the Tombs, Jake? I did once, I got the fucking crabs."

"Meaning anything is possible, Jackie?"

"Hypothetically speaking."

"At a price?"

"That's why we don't live in Red Russia, Jake."

Jacob leaned close to Jackie Heller. "How much is Benny Draper paying you to run things here?"

"You can't pay it."

"I can do better. I can offer you a seat at the table."

Jackie Heller looked at Jacob, then at Eddie Binhoff. "A piece?"

"Exactly."

Jackie Heller wiped his brow. "You don't have anything to give me a piece of."

"I would if we built our own place. And opened it first."

"You don't have a site."

Jacob shrugged. "I don't want to be the second guy across the Atlantic, Jackie. The one you remember is Lindbergh. But who was second? Tell me that, Jackie."

"Morris wouldn't do that." Jackie Heller's voice was almost plaintive. "This is L.A. territory."

"Jackie, where is it written?"

"Jake. It's only natural it's L.A. You build a place out here, you got the entertainment angle. Benny and Lilo got it all sewed up, they got Moe French. Moe French wants the lights to go on when he makes his pictures, he plays ball with Benny. It's cozy. He bitches, then he pays. Through the fucking nose. Benny threatens to strike him, what else is he going to do?"

Jacob tapped his cigar against the edge of Jackie Heller's desk, leaving a pile of ash. "He could let Benny strike him." He looked at Eddie Binhoff and smiled. Now he plays the card, Eddie Binhoff thought. Jake is very good at that. He did not know what the card was, but he knew Jacob would play it, and he knew it would make Jackie Heller sweat. "He could let Benny strike him," Jacob King repeated slowly, and then, after the words had sunk in, he said, "Then you could break the strike."

Jackie Heller began to sweat. He went to the Coke machine and banged it until a bottle slid down the chute. He opened the bottle and drained it as Jacob and Eddie Binhoff watched.

"Look at it this way, Jackie," Jacob said. "You could make Moe French very grateful. I bet Moe would get so grateful he'd see the advantage in stopping Benny Draper from siphoning the entire state of Nevada into his pension fund."

"I did anything like that," Jackie Heller said, "I'd need a definite message from Morris. A definite message he was behind me."

Eddie Binhoff doubted that a definite message would be coming, a definite message was not Morris Lefkowitz's way. He considered the possibility that if Morris had not given his blessing to what Jacob was proposing, perhaps he would not then have minded if he—Eddie—had taken Jacob out earlier that evening at La Casa Nevada. On the other hand, Morris Lefkowitz was a gambler, and maybe he had given Jacob the free hand he seemed to be playing.

"Morris is deeply committed to the future of this desert," Jacob said. "He wants to see a thousand blossoms bloom here. Anything you could do that would help . . ."

"It's Benny I'm worried about . . ."

When it's Jake King you should be worried about, Eddie Binhoff thought.

"A doorknob's got more brains than Benny Draper," Jacob said.

"Look, Jake." Jackie Heller looked doubtful, then began hyperventilating. "You want to do business here, there's some people downtown you're going to have to see, and I'm not sure they'll see you."

"Of course they will, Jackie," Jacob said softly. "You just tell them Jacob King wants to see them. That ought to do the trick." He smiled and locked his arm around Jackie Heller's neck. "I think they'll make the time. I think you can count on it." He tightened his grip. "Set it up."

◄◇►

From the continuing testimony of Lyle Ledbetter, appearing before the federal grand jury impaneled in Las Vegas, Clark County, Nevada, to investigate matters pertaining to the shooting death of Jacob King o/a December 1, 1948. Court was called to order at 9:11 A.M., May 25, 1949, in Department C, U.S. District Courthouse, Las Vegas, Nevada, the Honorable Lucius Klinger, presiding. Stanley Prince, assistant United States attorney for southern Nevada, appeared for the government:

THE COURT: Mr. Ledbetter, you are still sworn. Mr. Prince, you may proceed.

MR. STANLEY PRINCE (hereinafter referred to as "Q"): Now, Mr. Ledbetter, you served five terms as a county supervisor, is that correct?

MR. LYLE LEDBETTER (hereinafter referred to as "A"): Until March of this year, that is correct, yes.

Q: When you resigned?

A: That is right.

Q: And the circumstances of your resignation were not what we would call voluntary, is that right?

A: That is correct.

Q: The circumstances being that you were informed that you were under investigation for the acceptance of, uh, gratuities, and in the event that you cooperated with the state, the court might look with favor on the disposition of any charges that might be filed against you.

A: I answered that yesterday.

Q: But this is today. Answer the question, please. You don't answer the questions, then the court might be less likely—

A: I get the picture. Yes, I agreed to cooperate for the reasons you stated yesterday, today, and probably tomorrow, too.

Q: It always helps when a cooperating witness gets the picture, Mr. Ledbetter. Especially in the looking-with-favor department. Now, when court adjourned yesterday, you were about to tell us the circumstances of your first meeting with Jacob King. So why don't you tell us in your own words, the more details the better, I bet you're a very good, a top-notch storyteller, and I and His Honor here love nothing better than to hear a good story well told.

THE COURT: You made your point, Mr. Prince. Proceed, Mr. Ledbetter.

A: Well, I get this call from Jackie . . .

Q: Let the record reflect that Jackie is the late Jackie Heller, formerly owner of Heller Sanitation, is that correct, Mr. Ledbetter?

A: Right.

Q: The same late Mr. Heller who gave you a cashier's check in the amount of five thousand dollars if you could swing the board of supervisors into awarding an exclusive garbage-hauling contract for Clark County to Heller Sanitation.

A: How many times I got to answer that?

Q: A pretty song you never get tired of listening to, Mr. Ledbetter. So sing it again, Sam. *(Laughter.)* It's a line from the movie *Casablanca*, Mr. Ledbetter. Actually the line is "Play it again, Sam," but you don't mind if I put my own interpretation on it, do you?

A: No. And, yes. Yes, I accepted five grand from Mr. Heller . . .

Q: As a campaign contribution . . .

A: Yes . . .

Q: And you were able to convince your colleagues to award the garbage contract to Mr. Heller's company . . .

A: Yeah. To Jackie's company.

Q: So Jackie Heller called you . . . just proceed in your own words, Mr. Ledbetter.

A: And Jackie said that a Mr. King wanted to see me, he had a proposition.

Q: Did Jackie Heller identify Mr. King?

A: He said he was Morris Lefkowitz's right-hand man. I knew who he was. I read the papers. I knew who Morris Lefkowitz was, too. Who doesn't?

Q: And knowing this you still agreed to see Mr. King?

A: You got to be nuts you think I'm not going to see Jacob King. I value living too much.

Q: So Mr. King turns up at your office. Tell us what happened, Mr. Ledbetter.

A: That's what I been trying to do, but you interrupt all the time.

Q: I take your point, Mr. Ledbetter. In your own words now.

A: He makes me look out the window and not at him. And he asks me to tell him how I see Las Vegas. And I say to Jake, Mr. King, I say, the way I see it, we've got a city in its takeoff phase. A city determined to pull itself up by its bootstraps. It's L.A. twenty years ago, and I'm determined not to let it make the same mistakes. And he says to me, You want clean air. And I say to him, That's my franchise, that's why I was elected, I want a community with clean air. A decent place to raise a family. And so naturally I have some concerns about making sure that this grows into that kind of city. And he says, Where a kid can have a paper route, unbothered by undesirable elements. And I say to him, I say, Jake, I can see we're on the same wavelength . . .

Q: You're still looking out the window? At the splendor of the Las Vegas of the future?

A: Right. I can see it. And I say to him, I think of Las Vegas as an unspoiled natural resource, and I'm looking for a way to protect that resource. And he says, You're looking for a feedback on that resource. And I say, A feedback would definitely address my concerns, Jake. And in the window of my office I can see his reflection . . .

Q: And what do you see in that reflection?

A: I see this guy with a briefcase, Jake, of course, and he's taking bills out of the briefcase, and the wrappers are still on the bills, and he's laying the bills on my desk. And he says to me, Lyle, you are creating a wonderful business climate here, and I know if I want to buy some property you will make sure I got no trouble with the zoning, and you will speak to the liquor authority, and I'm sure you got pals on the gaming commission, and I say, Yeah, I know somebody I can call. Then he says, When you turn around you'll see two piles, the small pile on the left is to get Matty Cassady off my back.

Q: Let the record reflect that Matty Cassady is Matteo Cassady, the sheriff of Clark County. What exactly was the relationship between Matty Cassady and Jacob King?

A: Jake said Matty had his people tailing him from the moment he arrived in Clark County. In a big-ass white Cadillac you couldn't miss, that was the point of it, I guess, so that Jake knows they know he's there. I talk to Matty and he tells me that Benny Draper doesn't want Jake King in Clark County. Anywhere. Over and out.

Q: And that presented a problem?

A: A big damn problem.

Q: Unless the price was right?

A: Let me put it this way. Matty's a guy, he never liked his right hand to know what his left hand was doing.

Q: So his right hand was taking money from Benny Draper and his left was prepared to grab some of Jacob King's money?

A: Or the other way around. *(Laughter.)*

Q: Let me make the jokes, Mr. Ledbetter. How much money did Jacob King leave on your desk?

A: Twenty-five thousand dollars.

Q: And how much of that was to go to Matty Cassady?

A: The twenty-five was for me. To help move things along. Condemn a site, that sort of thing. Matty's pile was seventy-five hundred.

Q: But in his court case, Mr. Ledbetter, Sheriff Cassady stood accused and was convicted of receiving only six thousand dollars.

A: Well, there was a kind of finder's fee, if you know what I mean.

V

I T WAS A SUNDAY when I heard that Jake King was in Vegas, Arthur French said.

How can you be sure it was a Sunday, Arthur?

Because we played polo on Sunday. At Will Rogers's place. And I remember I was playing polo when I heard. So it had to be a Sunday. J.F. told me Lilo was upset. He—Lilo, not J.F.— had this man in Vegas, I think it was the sheriff . . .

Matty Cassady . . .

I can't remember his name. He was on some sort of retainer to Benny Draper . . .

The U.S. attorney called it a bribe.

Jack, I'm not interested in details like that, you can find that in the newspapers, it was, what, forty-five years ago? You said you wanted ambiance, the *mise-en-scène.*

I would say polo was a definite *mise-en-scène,* Arthur. Polo. At Will Rogers's. Who else played?

Tracy. Zanuck. Howard Hawks. Everyone was there. It was what we did on Sunday. J.F. Chuckie. Blue. Lilo and Rita. Jack Ford sometimes. Mitch Leisen. Kate, if Spencer was playing. Charlie Feldman. Jean Howard. Jean's got some wonderful pictures of those polo Sundays, you should call her. David and

Jennifer. One Sunday after polo, we were having lunch—Nancy and Eddie Clanahan always catered—and Jennifer led a conga line into the pool. All of us with our clothes on. Even J.F. Jean has the photograph in her book.

Okay. Now how does Matty Cassady figure in this?

Matty who?

The Clark County sheriff Benny Draper had on retainer.

Oh, yes. Well, apparently this Matty called Lilo that Sunday, and he said the Jake was over in Vegas spreading some money around. For what reason we didn't know. Although we found out soon enough. And Lilo was upset. It was just another problem he didn't need. Benny Draper was also there that Sunday. Benny and J.F. were having a fight over whether the OMPCE would strike Cosmo or not, and J.F. thought Benny was becoming too expensive a proposition . . .

—◇—

"Since when are you a lawyer, Matty?" Lilo Kusack said into the telephone. He and Benny Draper were sitting at a glass-topped table under a peppermint-striped umbrella. At the next table, J. F. French, in an oversized Panama hat, sat next to Blue Tyler, who was wearing a sleeveless dirndl dress and ostentatiously chewing gum, pretending to watch the match but more intent on checking out who was looking at her. She waved at Chuckie O'Hara and Shelley Flynn and belatedly joined the smattering of applause as Arthur French backhanded his mallet and sent the ball bouncing away from his goal. "You're just a cop . . ."

"A cop I buy, remind him," Benny Draper said to Lilo. He caught Blue's eye and lewdly flicked his tongue over his lips.

"Don't spout the law at me, Matty," Lilo said into the telephone. "I know Nevada's a state, I know Nevada is part of the United States, I know being in Nevada is not a chargeable offense, and I know anyone can go there, even Jake King." He listened for a moment, then said, "All right, okay, he belches, I want to know what he had for dinner. Okay? I'm interested, Benny Draper's interested, Benny's right here, he wants me to remind you he wants something for the money he pays you, you got that?" He listened. "We understand each other then."

"I remember the days when you bought a cop, he stayed bought," Benny Draper said when Lilo hung up the telephone. "Now you rent them by the day, like nigger help." He pointed to the polo teams galloping up the field. "You know what that is out there? It's baseball, on a horse. A slow horse. I like my horses faster. I like them to run around this way"—he traced a track in the air—"and I like to know who's going to win before I put a bet down."

"You want to hear about Jake King?" Lilo Kusack said.

"So he's in Nevada, so what?" Benny Draper said.

"Jake King in Nevada means Morris Lefkowitz wants in," Lilo said.

"Morris Lefkowitz comes into Nevada, even the whoooores won't work for him," Benny Draper said. "He's yesterday's newspaper, an old man who can't get it up anymore. You know how he does it now? He puts on a fur coat and watches girls do it." He looked up as Rita Lewis sat down at the table with a plate full of food. "The one here," he said, nodding in Rita's direction, "is the last one he boffed, right, sweetheart? You were Morris's last fuck, when was it, twenty years ago?"

Lilo Kusack watched Rita, ready to mediate in case she decided to pour her glass of wine into Benny Draper's lap, and follow it with the plate of pasta. Putting up with Benny, he always told her, was the price of doing business with him, but putting up with anybody or anything was not something that came naturally to Rita Lewis.

"Was that before Capone, Rita, or after?" Benny Draper said.

Rita picked up her plate and her glass of wine. For an instant, Lilo thought everything was going to land on Benny, but then Rita smiled. Her killer smile, Lilo Kusack thought. Her one-day-I'll-get-even smile. "It's always a pleasure seeing you, Benny."

"Hey, Rita," Benny Draper said to Rita's back as she moved toward Blue Tyler's table, "you remember what Al died of?" He punched Lilo Kusack on the arm and then exploded into a fit of giggles. "The syph."

"Who's this Al with the syph, Rita?" Blue Tyler asked as Rita sat down, Blue's hormonal antennae as always quivering at the faintest signal of sexual indiscretion.

"A mensch," Rita Lewis said. She unfolded her napkin and drained her wineglass, then amended her answer. "Compared to Benny."

"Benny's just been sitting there looking at my boobs all afternoon," Blue said. She lifted her hair and turned around so that the back of her dress faced Rita Lewis. "Fix my bra, would you, Rita? I think the strap in the back's all tangled up, that must be why the wire in the cup's so tight, and I don't want to get cancer of the tits or anything like that, Lou Lerner, the doctor at the studio, he says I got to watch out for my titties all the time."

"Call wardrobe, you want your fucking bra fixed," Rita Lewis said, taking another glass of wine from a waiter. She put up with Blue for Lilo's sake, and then only reluctantly. Rita had little tolerance for being patronized, and condescension was second nature to Blue, a perquisite of a box office deity, one adopted automatically for dealings with lesser mortals in the universe of film.

"What're you so pissed off at?" Blue Tyler said, one hand reaching into the back of her dress as she tried to straighten the strap, bewildered and angry that Rita should take offense at what seemed to her only a reasonable request of her lawyer's aging mistress. "I can't help it if your friend Al had the syph, does Lilo know?"

More or less to herself, Rita said, "Afternoons like this, even Morris's showroom looks good."

"Morris?" Blue Tyler said, her inquisitiveness overriding her anger. "You mean that old man in New York Moe says I'm not supposed to mention."

J. F. French roused himself. "Shhhh. Watch the polo."

"Moe," Blue said, "you ever heard of the Pledge of Allegiance?"

"Why you ask?" J. F. French said, alert and suddenly suspicious. If ever he thought his loyalty to his adopted country was under question, or his knowledge of its institutions less than perfect, his grammar became uncertain and the accent he had tried so hard to lose more pronounced.

"I got to say it, that's why. At the I Am an American dinner next week at the Ambassador you said I had to go and introduce that Congressman What's-his-name, and now Barry Tyger thinks it'd be great if I lead the audience in this pledge. I hear it's long. Do I have to memorize it? Or can I have cue cards?"

"It's easy," J. F. French said. He seemed visibly relieved, as if a challenge to his patriotism had been successfully met. " 'God bless America' is how it begins."

"Oh. Like the song that fat lady sings," Blue Tyler said. "That's cinchy."

J. F. French stood and clapped as Arthur galloped down the field and pounded a loose ball into the goal.

"Look at Moe," Benny Draper said at the adjoining table. "When his name was Moses Frankel, horse was something he ate. If he was flush." He whistled to get J. F. French's attention. "Hey, Moe, you know what they say? Poland to polo in one generation."

J. F. French turned and whispered something to Blue, then moved over to Lilo's table and sat down next to Benny Draper.

"So, Benny," J. F. French said, removing his Panama hat and wiping the sweat from his brow. "We got a deal?"

"What Benny was just explaining to me, Moe," Lilo Kusack said, "is that the offer on the table is not currently acceptable."

"Lilo," J. F. French said. "Tell Benny bribing him is becoming a fucking luxury."

"Lilo," Benny Draper said, "tell Moe to take a strike then. Either way he pays, and my way is cheaper. Easier to explain to his board in New York, too. And I hear he's already in enough trouble there, with all those Red Communists he's got under contract."

"Listen, you fuck . . ." J. F. French said, his face turning purple.

"Moe, Benny," Lilo Kusack said soothingly. "The Bolsheviks aren't the issue here."

"Lilo, what can I do?" Benny Draper said. "My people want

a strike. The cost of living is going up, I'm having a hard time keeping them in line, with this penny-ante offer Moe and the other studios are making."

J. F. French started to answer, then thought better of it. "Lilo, you take care of this," he said, getting up, "I want to watch the polo."

Lilo fiddled with his fountain pen until J. F. French was out of earshot. "No strike for the life of the contract," he said, "what's it going to cost?"

"You deaf? You got wax in your ears? I keep telling you, two million. In cash." Benny Draper watched J. F. French take a seat beside Blue Tyler. "Maybe a million if . . ."

Lilo waited for the other shoe to drop.

Benny Draper pointed to Blue Tyler. "If Moe lets her sit on my face."

"I think Moe might think that's a little steep."

Benny Draper got to his feet. "You tell Moe, steep is when he can't sleep at night because he don't know who I'm going to pull out in the morning." He perused Blue Tyler. "On second thought, it's still two million. That one don't look like she'd be all that hard to get to know."

There was a gasp from the crowd as Arthur was thrown from his horse, and applause when he got up immediately and captured the horse's reins.

"He rides like he's still in Poland," Benny Draper said.

"I'll talk to Moe," Lilo said. "We'll get together."

"You want to get hold of me, I'll be at Santa Anita," Benny Draper said. "Watching midgets who know how to stay on a horse."

V I

I HAVE ALWAYS been partial to what Oliver Goldsmith called the "Advertisement" he placed at the beginning of *The Vicar of Wakefield*. "There are an hundred faults in this Thing," he wrote, the Thing being his novel, "and an hundred things might be said to prove them beauties. But it is needless. A book may be amusing with numerous errors, or it may be very dull without a single absurdity." Without wishing to compare myself to Oliver Goldsmith, I can only say there are a hundred faults in this Thing, and numerous errors and absurdities.

To wit:

To the best of my knowledge, Jacob King perpetrated no act of violence resulting in loss of life during his initial foray into the Nevada desert. This opinion, and it is no more than that, is based on a close reading of the Nevada newspapers and law enforcement case files during the period when Jacob King was first said to have been in Las Vegas, as well as the period immediately thereafter. In this time frame, there were five deaths classified by municipal and Clark County authorities as homicides, all of which resulted in arrests, with the accused then taken to trial and in every case convicted; three of those convicted were subsequently executed in the gas chamber at the Nevada State Prison in Carson City. The other two victims were a murder-suicide (a pit boss at the Fremont who shot and killed the keno girl with whom he was living because she had taken up with a cocktail waitress at the hotel, and then killed himself by firing into his mouth the Smith & Wesson .38-caliber pistol he used to kill the keno waitress, severing his medulla oblongata). Even the fecund Harold Pugh (in either his Raul Flaherty or Waldo Kline manifestations) could find no evidence of a homicide that might have been attributed to Jacob King. There were also a half dozen deaths in the surrounding desert that the authorities categorized as suspicious, but one was a snake bite and a second a fall down the shaft of an abandoned talc mine and a third a hit-and-run victim and a fourth a driver with a blown tire who waited in his car with the engine on to keep warm in the frigid night air and was asphyxiated; and there were two gunshot suicides, one with a note, the other a woman with a history of mental instability.

◄◄◘►►

That Jacob King appeared innocent of any act of violence in this Nevada sojourn was not good enough, however, for Marty Magnin and Sydney Allen. Having sent me to Detroit in the first place, Marty wanted some return on what he called his investment, that is, the two weeks I had spent on expenses at the Renaissance Plaza milking (Marty's word, not mine) Maury Ahearne for the proposed screenplay about the homicide detective and his new partner, the black seven-foot-two-inch NBA center forced into early retirement because of his bad knees. When I expressed to Marty a lack of interest in continuing with the project, he finally wormed out of me, in his dogged way, that I had in fact found Blue Tyler, a nonperson for four decades, and to Marty this was an idea with more potential than any possible high-concept story about a cop and his sidekick, and far less problematic as there are not all that many seven-foot-two black leading men. Fuck the spade is what Marty said, wiping his hands of that project, and then he said, I laid out a lot of money to you, kid, you owe me, give me this one, I'll option it, you want to do a book, then okay, you do the book in the morning and the screenplay in the afternoon, we apply what I already paid to your fee, this story's a natural. Knowing Marty as I did, I said I would only do it on spec, and when I finished, then we would work out a deal. Any day he did not have to lay out any money was a good day to Marty Magnin, and he readily acceded.

The story was also a great announcement. An announcement is what producers and directors make when they do not have a picture with a start date and above-the-line pay-or-play talent. The announcement in the trades read "Magnin and Allen to Team Again in Top-Secret Show Biz Biopic Epic," the "top-secret" Marty's way of mollifying me by not mentioning Blue Tyler's name. The Allen of "Magnin and Allen" was of course that top-seeded shit Sydney Allen, top-seeded because after a stunt man named Chesty Warren was killed in an elaborate and unnecessarily dangerous helicopter gag on one of his pictures, Sydney spoke at the funeral and said that while life was short, film was forever, and that Chesty would live for as long as there were still theaters to show *Angel's Flight;* needless to say, *Angel's Flight* was the name of The Sydney Allen Film that Chesty had died on. Sydney's so little he wears a woman's watch, I once said about him, and the remark in true Hollywood fashion was immediately reported back to him, reinforcing his opinion of me, which was no better than mine of him.

—◦—

"Sydney thinks the story should be a little more . . ." Marty Magnin said.

"Piquant," Sydney Allen said.

"Explain *piquant,*" I said.

"I see Jacob as a man trying to contain his rages," Sydney Allen said, "but occasionally he boils over. And I feel that at this point in our piece we need to see him boil over. See his furies erupt."

"How?"

"Sydney thinks he should kill somebody here," Marty Magnin said.

"It adds complication to his character," Sydney Allen said. "And shading."

"He didn't kill anybody in Vegas that time."

"But he has the essence of a killer," Sydney Allen said. "I see it as his taint. The mark of Cain. As it were."

"And because you see this mark of Cain, then he should kill somebody he in fact didn't kill. As it were."

"We're not certain he never killed anybody, Jack," Marty Magnin said. "What about that guy in the mine shaft."

"He was eighty-seven years old according to the newspapers," I said.

"The hit-and-run victim then?" Marty persisted.

"A guy wearing a dress," I said. Again true, from the police reports.

"We're talking nuance here, Jack," Sydney Allen said.

"We're talking murder, Sydney." I could not believe that I was taking the side of Jacob King, acting as if I were his defense attorney.

"We're talking I want it," Sydney Allen said. His lips seemed to disappear into his teeth when he was angry. "And I want you to give it to me."

I could not help myself. "Life is short, but film is forever, Sydney."

"I want you to give it to me tomorrow," Sydney Allen said.

◄O►

This is what I gave him.

◄O►

EXT. LA CASA NEVADA NIGHT

ANGLE ON THE STRUCTURE
looming out of the darkness, etched against the sky.

ANOTHER ANGLE—JACOB KING AND EDDIE BINHOFF
driving past, looking at it, Jacob at the wheel of the Continental.

EDDIE BINHOFF
in the passenger seat, adjusts the rearview mirror.

ANOTHER ANGLE
The omnipresent tail seen in the rearview mirror.

> EDDIE BINHOFF
> We've got company.

> JACOB
> I have had this shit.

EDDIE BINHOFF
looks sharply at Jacob, then removes his pistol and makes sure it
is in working order.

JACOB KING
suddenly revs the convertible up and careens down the empty
highway at a dangerously high speed.

ANOTHER ANGLE
The tail gives chase.

ANOTHER ANGLE
Jacob suddenly slams on his brakes and the Continental skids
into a U-turn. Jacob then heads back down the highway in the
wrong lane, directly at the chase car.

> EDDIE BINHOFF
> Jesus, Jake . . .

ANOTHER ANGLE
A look of horror on the two men in the tail car. Desperately the
driver crosses the highway trying to get out of the way of Jacob's Continental.

ANOTHER ANGLE
Jacob's car hits the right rear fender of the second car, spinning
it around.

ANOTHER ANGLE
The passenger tries to get off a shot at Jacob and Eddie Binhoff.

ANOTHER ANGLE
The car takes off across the desert, Jacob's Continental in pursuit. The car cannot find purchase in the desert sand and is once more clipped by Jacob's convertible. It stalls.

ANOTHER ANGLE
Jacob lines up the other car and then heads his Continental straight into it. A horrendous crash. Jacob backs up for one more shot.

ANOTHER ANGLE
The man in the passenger seat staggers out of the car. He tries to get a shot off, but then seeing the Continental heading straight for him takes off across the desert.

ANOTHER ANGLE
Jacob wheels after the fleeing, running, stumbling man.

ANOTHER ANGLE
The man stands his ground and tries to squeeze off a shot.

ANOTHER ANGLE
Jacob driving as fast as he can on the desert sand hits the man squarely.

ANOTHER ANGLE
The man flies over the hood of the Continental, blocking Jacob's vision for a moment, then slips off the hood.

ANOTHER ANGLE
The man dead in the desert sand.

ANOTHER ANGLE
Jacob wheels around and heads back toward the stalled second car. Once more he slams into it.

ANOTHER ANGLE
The driver dazed and bleeding, his head resting on the steering wheel.

ANOTHER ANGLE
Jacob bolts from the Continental, followed by Eddie Binhoff, gun in hand.

ANOTHER ANGLE
Jacob yanks open the battered door of the second car and pulls the bleeding driver out. Jacob is in an uncontrollable rage.

> JACOB
> Give me your fucking gun, Eddie.

EDDIE BINHOFF
hands his weapon to Jacob, who sticks it up the nose of the driver.

> DRIVER
> *(whimpering)*
> Jake, I'm begging you, please . . .

JACOB KING
fires one shot. The shot tears off the end of the driver's nose.

THE DRIVER
weeping uncontrollably, bleeding profusely from the spot where the end of his nose had been.

JACOB KING
now sticks the gun into the driver's ear. He is still enraged.

> JACOB
> You fuck, you're not worth killing. You just go back
> and you tell Lilo and Benny we are here to fucking
> stay. You understand that?

THE DRIVER
nods.

JACOB KING

lays the gun against the man's ear and once more fires. The noise is thunderous.

THE DRIVER

claps his hands over his ears, deafened by the roar of the gun.

DRIVER
You're crazy . . .

JACOB KING

leans close to the weeping man and screams into his ear.

JACOB
You fucking tell them that, too.

CUT TO:

◄◦►

"Great," Marty Magnin said.

"Interesting," Sydney Allen said.

As much as I would like to claim that the desert homicide sprang from the dank and darker subbasements of my own inspiration, Blue had in fact mentioned in her tapes that Jacob did tell her once he had run over some guy of Benny Draper's in the desert, and shot the guy's partner (I should say here that whenever Blue had cause to mention any of Jacob's putative homicides, she would always refer to the victim as this guy or that guy, the anonymity of the word *guy* eliminating the necessity of the guy having a name and a personality and a father and a mother and women he fucked and maybe even children), first shooting off the guy's nose, then his tongue and his ears and his thumbs and his kneecaps, and finally blinding him, his plan being to leave this human husk as a message to his employers, without the motor facilities to identify his tormentor, but finally he killed him with a bullet in his ear because, Jacob had told her, no man deserved to live out his remaining years in such misery. In crime's Camelot, this seemed to pass as honor, and she was willing to accept it as such without question. To say the least, the revelations appeared indiscreet on Jacob King's part, especially from a man otherwise so circumspect about the murders attributed to him, a man used to admitting nothing and denying the same, so I do not know if I believed her tale or not (it took only fourteen seconds on the tape, and was parenthetical to a meandering story about a *Little Miss Marker* knock-off she was once meant to do on a loanout to Warner's, with Bogie and Jim Cagney). I did find the specificity of detail intriguing, but then she was always a woman with a fertile imagination, especially when it came to story, and I have been in enough story conferences to recognize the lust to embroider and punch up a sequence, a word here, some business there. In any event the scene I concocted on demand for Sydney Allen, even though it was never filmed, became just another story that attached itself to the ongoing and ever growing legend of Jacob King, and in time was even accepted as truth.

As it were.

VII

I COACHED HER on the Pledge of Allegiance, Chuckie O'Hara said. Gave her line readings, told her where to breathe and where to pause. I used to do it with her on every picture. You shouldn't forget, she couldn't read when she became a star, she was only four, remember, and her scripts had to be read to her, that's how she learned them, and she never really stopped doing it, she'd come to me for line readings even for the pictures I didn't direct. And so I said to her, I pledge allegiance—pause—to the flag—pause, breathe—of the United States of America—pause, breathe—and to the republic for which it stands—pause. Chuckie, she said, why not a pause after "to the republic," and I said, Because the clause shouldn't be broken up, and she said, What's a clause? Apparently they never got around to clauses in the English grammar course at the studio school. If they even taught grammar. The Little Red Schoolhouse. It was on Stage 11. I think the only geography she ever learned there was the map of movie star homes. The funny thing was, when she was called to testify before the Committee, she was asked if it was called the Little Red Schoolhouse because it was teaching Communist propaganda. It's true. You can look it up. Needless to say, Moe French closed it down right after that. Red is for apples, not Communists, he liked to say. None of us had any idea what he meant, but we would all sit around in the executive dining room at the commissary, everyone agreeing right and left, That's right, J.F., red is for apples, not Bolsheviks. Then all of a sudden Blue said, Why aren't you going to the dinner, Chuckie? You're not one of those Communists Moe is always talking about, are you? My dear, the chill that ran up my spine. I wondered what she had heard, and I even considered going to the dinner. I had bought a table anyway to keep on the good side of Moe, but told him I couldn't go because I was shooting. Moe didn't seem to care if I went or not, he thought I was solid, I'd shot this short for him against Upton Sinclair in the 1934 election for governor, all the studios shot them and then showed them in their theater chains and pretended they were newsreels. It was the first time I ever used a hand-held camera, so it would have a grainy, man-in-the-street look. Mine had Walker Franklin's cousin Esmeralda something, Nixson, she was a part-time actress and full-time maid, telling the camera she was voting for Sinclair because he would show California how well Russia really worked, and that he was going to build low-income housing for the colored in Beverly Hills. I have to admit it's not a picture I include in my filmography. My God, I voted for Landon in 1936, and I have never told anyone this, you must never repeat it to a soul, for Hoover in 1932. I could not stand that cripple, waving that cigarette holder of his. Think of Jack Barrymore sober, with braces on his legs, and you've got him. A ham actor is all he ever was. So why did I join the Party then? Love's mission. I was enamored of someone, so I joined as proof of my undying ardor. I loved it. All those fervent young revolutionaries, ready to try anything, even me.

—◇—

I have a copy of Blue Tyler's testimony before the House Un-American Activities Committee. She was never asked if Cosmopolitan Pictures' Little Red Schoolhouse was so named because it taught Communist propaganda.

—◇—

It was Mr. French who wanted me to be at that dinner, Melba Mae Toolate said. I had an early call the next morning, and he said he would get Chuckie to rearrange my schedule, it was important that the biggest stars in the Industry be there, and I was Cosmo's biggest star, I would introduce the main speaker, some congressman who was investigating Reds in the Industry, and afterwards I'd say this pledge. The real reason I didn't want to go was because that rabbi guy, Barry Tyger, was always trying to feel me up, he'd put his arm around my waist and then let his thumb knock up against my boob, copping a cheap feel is what he was doing. At least the Catholic guy, the what do you call what he was . . .

The cardinal.

That's right, I knew it had a bird name, at least the cardinal kept his hands to himself, but he must've been at least a hundred years old, I don't think pussy was on his mind. Anyway he was wearing this swell outfit, kind of an orangey-red with buttons all the way down the front, neck to ankle, and a yarmulke, did you know Catholics wore yarmulkes? I thought it was just a Jew thing.

It's called a biretta.

It looked like a red yarmulke, you ask me. I think if Mr. French knew that Jacob was going to show up that night, he would've said go home, you got an early call, we don't want to get behind schedule on *Red River Rosie*. Mr. French was always telling me not to let Arthur get fresh if I had an early call, he meant I shouldn't let Arthur fuck me.

How did Jacob know enough to show up?

Well, there were these big billboards on Sunset and all over, with my picture about fifty feet high, and the lettering saying "I Am an American Day" in red, white, and blue type, Jacob couldn't have missed seeing it if he tried. I guess he just wanted to see me again, I don't know, I really hadn't thought of him much, except I kept hearing Rita was fucking him, and Chuckie said he heard he had a dick that belonged in a circus, it was the eighth wonder of the world. It was all right, I suppose . . .

━○━

Arthur French had a copy of the invitation squirreled away in the scrapbooks of his Hollywood years that he never liked to admit he still kept and, I suspect, browsed over in the small hours when sleep was difficult and bad memories and minor treasons laid siege and assaulted:

COSMOPOLITAN PICTURES AND J. F. FRENCH PRESENT
THE "I AM AN AMERICAN" DINNER
HONORING CONGRESSMAN THEODORE WILDER
RECIPIENT OF COSMOPOLITAN PICTURES FIRST ANNUAL
"I AM AN AMERICAN AWARD"
INVOCATION: HIS EMINENCE HUGH CARDINAL DANAHER
THE AMBASSADOR HOTEL   FEBRUARY 19, 1947
BLACK TIE   COCKTAILS   DINNER
DANCING TO THE MUSIC OF BOB CROSBY AND THE BOBCATS

Arthur also had the clips, and the accompanying Cosmopolitan publicity photographs of his father embracing Theodore Wilder and introducing him to Irving Berlin and Sam Wood and Victor Fleming and Blue Tyler, and photos of Blue with the congressman's wife, LuAnne Wilder, and with Shelley Flynn and Clark Gable and Walt Disney and Adolphe Menjou and Ginger Rogers and Barry Tyger, and with the cardinal, in his full ecclesiastical robes. It was Barry Tyger who in fact had suggested it might be better if the cardinal delivered the invocation rather than he because one of the congressman's aides had inquired if there would a large Hebrew element attending the dinner.

There were no photographs in Arthur's scrapbooks of Jacob King at the "I Am an American Dinner," but he did have a copy of Congressman Wilder's address:

"Communism is older than Christianity. It is the curse of the ages. It hounded and persecuted the Savior during His earthly ministry. Inspired His crucifixion. Derided Him during His dying agony, and then gambled for His garments at the foot of the cross. Communism has spent more than nineteen hundred years trying to destroy Christianity and everything based on Christian principles. Communists are now trying to take over the motion picture industry, and howl to high heaven when our Committee on Un-American Activities proposes to investigate them. They want to spread their un-American propaganda, as well as their loathsome, lying, immoral, anti-Christian filth, before the eyes of your children in every community in America."

A headline in the next day's *Los Angeles Mirror:* J. F. FRENCH TO FILM INDUSTRY AT EXTRAVAGANZA: "BACK ANTI-COMMIE CRUSADE."

Another headline, in the same day's *Herald:* BLUE TO LOUELLA: "I'VE BEEN AN ANTI-COMMUNIST SINCE I WAS FOUR."

"My first exclusive," Louella Parsons wrote. "Blue Tyler, who has thrilled movie audiences since she was four years old and has grown into a beautiful young woman, told me at the 'I Am an American' dinner last night that she has been an anti-Communist since her very first picture, the delightful *Sunny Face.* 'In Russia, Louella,' Blue told me, 'they tell you what to do, but in America anyone can become a star like I have.' Wise words, Blue. Blue also said that she wanted to talk to high school students about the importance of home life and good citizenship. And to think this True Blue American is still two years short of casting her first ballot, for an anti-Communist, this pillar is sure."

Arthur remembered the Bob Crosby orchestra playing a syncopated dinner-music version of "America the Beautiful." He and Blue were at the head table with his father and Chloe Quarles, from whom J. F. French was more or less separated, but who he thought a more appropriate dinner companion than his current attachment, a French Filly younger than Blue Tyler. Chloe was living in Montecito in sapphic bliss with a former Filly, a situation J.F. had not anticipated when he invented the Fillies, and the stable became in effect his own private brothel, but she was always available to be with J.F. on public occasions. The Wilders were also at the table, as well as Lilo Kusack and Rita Lewis, her breasts generously displayed in a Mainbocher dress, and Benny Draper (at Lilo's invitation, his reasoning being that it could not hurt to have Benny and Moe breaking bread at the same table), Benny the only man in the ballroom not wearing a tuxedo, apparently his idea (this from Arthur in his droll mode) of solidarity with the workers. Blue was seated on Congressman's Wilder's right, pretending to be interested in what he had to say. What he had to say, according to Arthur, seemed to be about the Jews.

"Your industry, Mr. Frankel—" Congressman Wilder said.

"French," J. F. French said.

"Excuse me," the congressman said. "I must have been thinking of somebody else. Mr. French. French. Of course. Mr. French, your industry has got to be serious about this secret infiltration of all those Reds—"

"And pseudoliberals," J. F. French interjected.

"They're bad for the Jews, Moe," Lilo Kusack said, inhaling his cigar and then blowing perfect smoke rings past the congressman's face. The whole evening seemed to entertain him.

"Exactly," Congressman Wilder said, waving the smoke away. "Exactly right, Mr. . . ."

"Kusack. K-U-S-A-C-K. I come from Vilna."

"Where is that, Mr. Kusack?"

"Tennessee," Lilo Kusack said, not missing a beat. Rita Lewis tried not to laugh. There were times when she almost liked Lilo, and this was one of them.

"Did you know, Mr. . . ."

"French."

"Did you know, Mr. French, that Edward G. Robinson's real name is Emmanuel Goldenberg?"

"Nooooo," Lilo Kusack said, drawing the word out. "Is that

right?" He poured the last of a wine bottle into his glass and snapped his fingers at a waiter for another bottle. "Did you know that about Eddie, Moe?"

J. F. French stared impassively at Lilo Kusack.

"I didn't know that, Lilo," Blue Tyler said. "It takes up a lot of letters on a marquee, that must be the reason Eddie changed it." She paused, counting on her fingers as if computing the number of letters in both names. "But Edward G. Robinson is only a couple of letters less than Emmanuel . . . what did you say his name was?"

"Goldenberg . . ."

"It really doesn't matter with Eddie. He's below the title anyway. I don't know why he changed it then."

Congressman Wilder turned and looked at Blue in puzzlement, as if she might have been pulling his leg, but irony, as Arthur always assured me, and as I learned in my brief acquaintanceship with her, was a tactic not included in her arsenal of dissembling.

"You're so cute," Blue Tyler said. She pursed her lips, placed her hand under her chin, and blew the congressman a kiss off her fingers. "It's a good thing you're so happily married to what's-her-name over there, or I'd steal you away from her." She mouthed the words, You make me wet, and then aloud said, "You going to eat that spud?" Before he could answer, Blue had speared the last roast potato from his plate and stuffed it into her mouth. "Rita," she said, chewing noisily. "Arthur told me you used to fuck some Italian gangster in Cleveland when you were a kid."

Rita Lewis regarded Blue without speaking. She knew it was a waste of time and energy to dislike Blue, a child-woman who had never really been a child but from the age of four only a capital asset. When she was still a little girl, grown men had looked at her in a way she knew they were not supposed to, in a way that made her understand, years before puberty that her body, especially the part between her legs, had a greater currency even than money. The language she talked was that of the film crews she worked with. She said *fuck* and *cunt* before she knew what the words meant, and now that she had learned, she used them because of the effect they had on the people who would control her. Her every whim was catered to, her willfulness indulged. She had never been held accountable for her actions, and she knew implicitly that as long as she continued to be the star she was she never would be.

"Arthur," Blue said, waving her napkin in his direction, "what was the name of that gangster you said Rita used to ball in Cleveland?"

Arthur French pretended not to hear and bent close to Congressman Wilder. "I think what the Industry needs is a statement of principles about this menace."

"What menace is that, Arthur?" Blue said. And then to Rita: "I mean it's exactly the kind of picture I want to do now. You're fifteen years old—did you say Rita was fifteen or sixteen, Arthur?" There was no response from Arthur French. "Say sixteen then, and you're screwing this ginney from Cleveland, and then you end up out here. In Hollywood. The stuff in the middle, Arthur will hire a writer."

Across the table, LuAnne Wilder was looking numbly at Blue Tyler, as if she did not quite believe she was hearing what she thought she was hearing. "I'm very good on story," Blue said to her confidentially. Turning back to Rita Lewis, she said, "Maybe I'll give myself a kid. So I have something to lose in the last reel. Because J.F. is always saying money doesn't buy happiness. That's bullshit, look at all this," she said, her hand sweeping around the Ambassador ballroom, taking in the hundreds of people in evening dress. "They don't look unhappy, Clark and Ginger and them. I'm not married to the kid, either, but the writer can work out something I can lose." For a moment she was lost in thought, going over the possibilities for emotional loss. "Maybe a mother. Or a brother. Who's crippled." A satisfied smile. "I really like that." In her mind, she seemed to be mulling over the crippled brother who would die in her screenplay, and how she would play his death scene. "I was born for this part, Rita, what do you say?"

"I would say it was Chicago," Rita Lewis said slowly. "And I was fourteen." She took a compact from her purse, examined her face, then snapped it shut. "And I think it'll be a while before you grow into the part."

"That shows how much you know," Blue Tyler said. "If we put it in Cleveland, we won't have to pay you for the rights then." She leaned across the table. "Arthur, do you want me to show you how bad girls kiss?"

"Actually, no, Blue," Arthur said.

Blue winked at LuAnne Wilder. "But I want to, Arthur."

Arthur French pulled a bill from his pocket and handed it across the table to Blue. "Why don't you go powder your nose, Blue."

Blue snatched the bill away from him. "Arthur, you're always sending me off to the potty."

"Because you act like you're not potty-trained," Rita Lewis said.

"Well, fuck you," Blue Tyler said.

◄o►

There were photographs of Jacob King's arrival at the dinner in the morgue at the *Los Angeles Times*, and other photos from newspapers long since dead in the microfilm room at the UCLA library.

"King," Jacob King said to the young woman at the registration desk. He caught a glimpse of himself in a mirror, surreptitiously checked both left and right profiles, shot his cuffs, flicked an invisible piece of lint from the silk collar of his double-breasted dinner jacket, and finally ran his tongue over his teeth, searching for any food particles that might have lodged between them. Several of the reporters and photographers waiting in the ballroom's annex for the evening to end moved closer to check out the late-arriving stranger paying so much attention to his appearance. Filtering through the closed doors, the rising voice of Congressman Wilder could be heard inveighing against the Communists who had stage-managed the crucifixion. "Jacob King."

"I'm sorry, Mr. King," the young woman said, suddenly and

unexpectedly flustered. There was a sexual component to the man smiling so knowingly at her, as if he knew what she looked like without her clothes on, knew she was having her period and wanted to escape to the ladies' room to change her sanitary napkin, and knew that she knew what he was thinking. "I can't seem to find your name on the list."

Jacob removed a roll of bills from the pocket of his tuxedo jacket. As the reporters watched, he peeled off five hundreds and fanned them out on the table as if he were laying out a full house. "I'll buy a table then."

"The tables have all been subscribed, Mr. King," she said, reluctant to reach for the money. "But I know the committee and all true Americans will be extremely grateful to receive your generous contribution . . ."

"A true American." Jacob nodded appreciatively. "That's the way I like to think of myself."

Suddenly one of the reporters said, "You're Jake King, aren't you?"

He turned to the photographers and smiled. "You boys are a little slower than they are back in New York."

There was a blaze of flashbulbs. "Be nice, fellows, only my good side," Jacob King said.

The young woman at the registration desk looked perplexed. The man with the polished hair was getting as much attention as Clark Gable had when he arrived earlier, but then everyone knew who Mr. Gable was. As Jacob moved toward the door of the ballroom, trailed by the photographers and reporters shouting questions, he turned and flashed his knowing smile, the smile she would remember later that night and wonder what it would feel like to lose her virginity. "You see, sweetheart, it's okay."

◄o►

The houselights in the ballroom dimmed, and then went out. Only the candles on the tables flickered. The conversational hum slowly died down until there was no sound except for nervous coughing and waiters rushing their trays toward the kitchen. Then suddenly in the center of the room, framed by a spotlight, the face of Blue Tyler.

"I pledge allegiance . . ." Pause. ". . . to the flag . . ." Pause. ". . . of the United States of America . . ."

Jacob King stood just inside the ballroom door, transfixed, staring at Blue's spotlighted face, her hair backlit, giving her an almost celestial appearance.

At the head table, J. F. French whispered to Arthur, "She got it wrong, the little whore, it's God bless America."

"No, no, she's got it right, J.F.," Arthur said, "just repeat it after me. '. . . one nation . . . under God . . .'" The invoking of the Almighty, then not included in the pledge, had been a concession to the cardinal, although Barry Tyger, devout secularist that he was, later told J. F. French he was not all that thrilled with His inclusion, it being his considered opinion that God should be confined to the Sabbath.

Rita Lewis lit a cigarette and as she took a first deep drag, Lilo Kusack reached over and removed it from her lips. "'. . . indivisible,'" Lilo said, crushing Rita's cigarette into an ashtray, then smiling at her, "'with liberty and justice for all.'"

The houselights came up, and J. F. French rose as if propelled, vigorously leading the ovation. "That's my little girl, one take, that's all it took, that's why her pictures come in on time and under budget. Rita, get up, clap, be a good American like little Blue."

"I'm going to go pee," Rita Lewis said, ignoring him. "Lilo, is it okay if I grab a smoke in the can, I can smoke there, can't I?" Lilo nodded with a benign smile. Rita was trying to pick a fight, and he never argued with women, it was a waste of time, and only occasionally did he hit one. "Order me a Rob Roy then," Rita said. "On second thought, two Rob Roys." She caught Mrs. Wilder staring at her. "Were the Commies really at the foot of the cross? I never heard that at St. Leo's in Chicago, and the nuns there taught all sorts of weird shit." Rita favored LuAnne Wilder with her most dazzling smile. "You want to come to the can with me, honey?"

LuAnne Wilder shook her head back and forth, as if in a catatonic trance. She seemed to have forgotten how to blink.

At the microphone Blue Tyler linked arms with Congressman Wilder. "I told Ted Wilder . . ." She turned to the congressman and winked ostentatiously at him. "I can call you Ted, can't I . . . Teddy?"

There was another burst of applause.

"Timing," J. F. French said. "My little girl's got perfect comedy timing."

"Anyway," Blue said, "I told Ted if he kept his speech short, I would give him the first dance. The first dance to the first winner of the first annual Cosmopolitan Pictures 'I Am an American' award." More applause. "And then he gets up here and yaks for twenty-two minutes." She paused. "It didn't take twenty-two minutes to burn down Atlanta in *Gone With the Wind*." It did not seem entirely suitable to make fun of a foot soldier in the front line against Communism and there was only a smattering of nervous laughter. Blue did not seem to notice or care as she shielded her eyes from the lights and peered out into the audience. "Clark, that is still such a good picture." Then she turned back to Congressman Wilder. "Come on, Teddy, let's cut a rug. Cheek to cheek. Ten cents a dance."

Immediately the orchestra struck up "You Ought to Be in Pictures," and Blue whirled Congressman Wilder onto the dance floor. All over the ballroom, other couples began dancing. At the head table, Lilo Kusack was left momentarily alone. He was always most perfectly comfortable in his own company. People and their demands interrupted the reasoning process. He cut the end off another cigar with a gold clipper and, as he lit it, watched J. F. French trying to maneuver LuAnne Wilder into a foxtrot. It was like watching elephants fornicate, he thought. Even Benny Draper was dancing, with Chloe Quarles. The invitation to join Moe and the nitwit congressman at the head table had not seemed to make Benny any more tractable, but nothing ventured, nothing gained. The contract problem would not go away, and Moe was on a short fuse. Maybe, Lilo thought, we can throw Chloe into the deal. She doesn't look bad for her age. Even up the ante a little. Chloe and her girl-friend. A perfect triple-decker. Benny was so bent he might even consider it.

"Hello, Lilo."

Lilo looked around as Jacob King pulled out a chair and sat down beside him. "Jake, what a nice surprise," Lilo said equa-bly. Part of his success was predicated on his never being fazed by the unexpected. "Rita said something about you being in town. I been trying to get hold of you."

"Really."

"I knew you were free I would've asked you here tonight. It just didn't occur to me the Red Menace was in your line."

"I'm here on business."

Lilo removed a leather cigar case from his jacket and offered a cigar to Jacob King. "Cuban. Great town, Havana."

"Someone just told me that. Offered me a cigar, just like you did. Havana, this person I am acquainted with said. Rum and Coca-Cola. Beautiful señoritas. Regular Latin spitfires."

"Whoever told you that told you right."

Jacob King watched the dance floor for a moment. "I was thinking more along the lines of Nevada."

"You were?"

"This new place you got out there. I think you call it La Casa Nevada."

Lilo Kusack contemplated his cigar. "Actually we call it ours."

"You do?"

"Yes."

"I'm told you have a cash flow problem trying to finish it."

"You were told wrong . . ."

"A cash flow problem Morris is willing to help you solve with all the resources he has available."

Lilo Kusack regarded Jacob, then cupped his ear and cocked his head toward the orchestra. "What's the name of that song they're playing?"

" 'Bewitched,' " Jacob King said immediately. " 'Bothered and bewildered.' Why?"

"You can hear it, then?"

"Sure."

"Oh. I thought you were hard of hearing is why I asked."

"What makes you think that?"

"Because you didn't hear me when I said we had no cash flow problem." Lilo rolled the cigar around in his mouth. "You know, they're working on this new quiz show over at NBC Radio, you ought to think about it, Jake, you know all the songs. *Name That Tune,* I think it's going to be called." He removed a piece of loose leaf from the cigar. "If it works, they're going to put it on the television. You'd be a natural." When Jacob King did not reply, Lilo mimed spraying the ballroom with a tommy gun. "The *Hit Parade,* though. Maybe that's more your line."

Jacob King took a handful of walnuts from the nut-and-fruit-bowl centerpiece and began cracking them one by one in his fist, never taking his eyes from Lilo Kusack. Suddenly he felt a hand on his shoulder.

"Mr. King," Blue Tyler said. She was standing beside his chair with Arthur French, who had his arm around her waist, as if ready to pull her away if Jacob made a move.

"Miss Tyler," Jacob King said, brushing the walnut shells from his hands and trying to rise.

"Please, stay where you are," Blue said. "You forgot to tell me Mr. King was going be here tonight, Arthur, you should remember to tell me these things." To Jacob she said, "You were such a good dancer. Is your dance card full?"

"Yours is, Blue," Arthur French said quickly. "J.F. wants his driver to take you home. Chuckie says you have to be on the set by eight tomorrow."

She made no argument. "It's nice to see you again, Mr. King." Her throaty voice as always held the promise of deviant behavior. "Arthur's told me so many . . ." (a Chuckie O'Hara line reading) ". . . interesting . . ." (a second, almost imperceptible, pause) ". . . things about you. Maybe you can come out to the studio and watch me shoot."

"I'd like that, Miss Tyler. It's nice to see you again, too."

Lilo Kusack watched as Arthur guided Blue toward the ballroom door. "You made an impression, Jake. Remind me to ask Arthur what he told her about you. He should tell her you've seen a lot of shooting in your time." He pushed his chair back and stood as Rita returned to the table, followed by Shelley Flynn and J. F. French. "You know, Rita, Jake. Of course, you know Rita."

"Bet the house he knows Rita," Shelley Flynn said in a voice one had to strain to hear. Sotto voce was his normal conversational tone so that in the event anyone took offense at one of his gibes he could always claim to have been misunderstood.

"And Shelley Flynn, I know you know Shelley. From the Latin Quarter. All you New York guys know one another." Shelley Flynn nodded equivocally at Jacob King. He owed his livelihood to J. F. French and he would wait to see how J.F. and Lilo reacted before any demonstrative welcome. "J. F. French you don't know. J.F. is Cosmopolitan Pictures . . ."

"This is not exactly a social visit, Lilo," Jacob King said quietly.

"I didn't think it was, Jake," Lilo said. "So let me lay it out for you so there's no misunderstanding. The place in the desert is ours, it's closed, hands off."

"It's also unfinished," Jacob King said. "So let me"—he paused for emphasis—"lay it out for you. We can help you finish it. Or"—he leaned closer to Lilo—"we can build our own joint that'll make yours look like a pizza palace."

"I see definite problems with that, Jake. Here's Benny," Lilo said, as Benny Draper took a seat next to J. F. French and glowered at Jacob King. "Benny can help me explain it to you. Benny, Jake was just saying he might build a place in the desert, so tell him how hard it's going to be."

Arthur French slipped quietly into the empty chair beside Rita Lewis. Onstage Bob Crosby had put on a red-white-and-blue skimmer and was doing a buck-and-wing, singing, "I'm a Yankee Doodle Dandy . . ."

"I thought you had security, Lilo, keep New York shit like this out of here," Benny Draper said over the music.

". . . Yankee Doodle do or die . . ."

Jacob reached and took an apple from the fruit bowl. As the rest of the table watched, he polished it carefully on the lapel of his tuxedo, then suddenly tossed it to Benny Draper, who bobbled it as if were a hand grenade and let it fall to the floor.

"For such a tough guy, Benny, your coordination isn't much," Jacob King said.

". . . a real live nephew of my Uncle Sam's . . ."

Lilo put his hand firmly on Benny Draper's shoulder to keep him in his chair.

". . . born on the Fourth of July . . ."

"Jake, you're not being diplomatic," Lilo said. "You come out here like you own the place, you start making waves, you go over to Vegas—"

"What're you going to build over there, a sand castle?" Benny Draper said. "I run every union between here and Chicago. A hammer don't hit a nail over there I don't give the say-so. A waiter don't pick up a tray, a truck don't get loaded, except I give the okay. Jakey King don't get the okay, you understand that, you fuck?"

". . . I am the Yankee Doodle boy . . ."

"You see the problems, Jake," Lilo said soothingly. "Say you managed to build a place. Who's going to play it? Shelley, you going to play Jake's place?"

"Whose place?" Shelley Flynn said. He now knew what side to come down on. "The only place I see is La Casa Nevada. What're you going to call your joint, Jake. Casa Lefkowitz?"

Benny Draper exploded into laughter. "Shelley, you got to stop, you're going to make me wet my pants. Casa Lefkowitz, oh, Jesus . . ."

Bob Crosby and the Bobcats segued into a patriotic medley. "Over there, over there . . ."

"Moe," Lilo Kusack said. "What kind of talent you going to make available to Jake?"

"When I was in theaters in the Lower East Side, I had a dog act once," J. F. French said. "Danny Doberman and His Pinschers. It might still be available. Arthur, make a note, check it out in the morning." Arthur stared at his father. "I said make a note, Arthur."

"Right, J.F." Arthur took a pencil and scribbled something on the inside of a matchbook.

". . . the Yanks are coming, the Yanks are coming, the Yanks are coming over there . . ."

Rita Lewis took a lighter from her purse, tapped a cigarette on her case, and waited to see how Jacob would respond. He seemed contained, even faintly amused. It was the way she suspected he would be before he hurt someone. Moments like this excited Rita. It was like watching a cockfight. She would like to get a bet down on the outcome. She would bet Lilo was doing something he rarely did, overplaying his hand, and she wondered if it was because he knew she had fucked Jacob when he got into town, and was wondering if she was still fucking him. He wouldn't ask, and would not believe her if she said no, which in fact was true.

"So, Jake," Lilo said, "let's enjoy ourselves. We'll order some champagne, I'm buying." He whistled for a waiter, took a money clip from his pocket and laid it on the table. "This is a swell town to visit. Grab a little sun, go down to the beach, I have a place out past Zuma, get a broad, take her out there, you'll go back to New York a new man, you can tell Morris thanks, but no thanks, we don't need his money."

With a flourish, Bob Crosby sang, ". . . and we won't be back till it's over over there," then, without a pause for breath, moved into "It's a grand old flag, it's a high-flying flag . . ."

Jacob picked up Lilo's money clip and removed a hundred-dollar bill.

"If you're a little short, Jake," Lilo said, "I'll be glad to help you out, we like to give our tourists a good time."

Benny Draper giggled. Everyone else at the table watched but did not say a word.

"Give me your lighter, Rita," Jacob King said.

Rita passed him her lighter without hesitation. Jacob lit it, looked at the flame, and then held it under Lilo's nose. "I'm going to tell Morris . . ." He took the hundred-dollar bill and lit it with Rita's lighter.

"What the fuck're you . . ." Lilo said.

Jacob removed the rest of the cash from the money clip and set it on fire with the burning bill.

"I'm going to tell Morris that you people out here've got money to burn."

Bob Crosby whipped his microphone cord. ". . . the land I love . . ."

"You act like you're still on the fucking Brooklyn docks," Lilo said, as he tried to stamp out the flames and save what bills he could.

Jacob King rose and looked at Lilo. "Don't you ever forget it," he said.

As Jacob King walked toward the exit, Arthur French remembered, Bob Crosby said, "Everybody join in," and all over the ballroom, voices were raised.

". . . the land of the red, white, and blue . . ."

—◇—

Arthur, I said skeptically. Not really "A Grand Old Flag."

Well, it could've been "Praise the Lord and Pass the Ammunition," Arthur French said. You read the clips. They all said it was an evening full of patriotic songs. And there was this enormous American flag and I remember Jake walking out underneath it.

You remember it, or that's the way you'd shoot it.

Jack Ford always said print the legend.

—◇—

Marty Magnin had a more direct concern.

Speaking as a filmmaker, the producer of twenty-one major motion pictures, and for Sydney Allen, an auteur, one whose films had garnered three best-picture Oscar nominations, although none had ever won, the reason he had never been a winner, always implied by Sydney but never stated outright, being the Industry's bias against a New York director who would not tolerate the usual Hollywood bullshit interference, he had only one question:

When are Jake and Blue going to fuck?

VIII

BLUE REMEMBERED IT happening the night after La Casa Nevada burned down.

Mysterious was the adjective most often used in the newspaper accounts of the predawn fire that consumed and destroyed La Casa Nevada. *Mysterious* is a word encouraging speculation of the wilder sort, and at the city desks and in the gossip columns and in the studio commissaries and at the gin rummy games at Hillcrest and at Brenda Samuel's whorehouse in the Hollywood Hills, where the Industry elite gathered to fornicate in an ambiance of complete privacy and where it was said that Jacob King was a volume customer, much of the speculation had to do with the same Jacob King.

Jacob King would always claim that he had never met Brenda Samuels, and that he had not paid for a piece of ass since the two dollars he gave at the age of ten to Philly Wexler for the use of his sister.

It was Chuckie O'Hara who was the source of this information. While I am willing to accept the first part of the claim, I have trouble with Jacob taking Chuckie into his confidence about Ruth Wexler.

The headline and accompanying story in the *Times* about the fire was discreetly placed on page eight, below the break:

MYSTERIOUS EXPLOSION LEVELS NEVADA PLEASURE PALACE
AUTHORITIES SEARCH RUBBLE FOR CLUES

Cosmopolitan Pictures' Weekly Newsreel offered a series of shots of the still-smoldering construction site; in the background, fire and police officials could be seen picking through the embers and talking to Lilo Kusack and Benny Draper, who were unnamed and who I was able to identify only by running the film slow-motion, and then freeze-framing and technically enhancing the footage. In the stentorian tones that the commentators on those old studio newsreels all seemed to favor, a voice-over said: "A propane leak is the cause given for the explosion that destroyed what was to be America's number-one gambling palace, La Casa Nevada, in the Mojave Desert near Las Vegas. Authorities here discount rumors of arson or other foul play. Here is Clark County Supervisor Lyle Ledbetter."

There was a cut to Lyle Ledbetter, in an open-necked shirt and a straw cowboy hat: "I have been assured by Fire Chief Ben Hawk that his department's initial investigation has indicated there is no truth to the speculation that this was anything else but what it was—a fire. These things happen . . ."

Then over a final shot of the still-smoking sign saying, GRAND OPENING DECEMBER 31ST—HAPPY NEW YEAR, the commentator's voice: "There is no immediate word as to when construction will begin again on La Casa Nevada. And now for a change of pace, the French Fillies promenade at the Easter parade . . ."

◄○►

Jacob King was called in for questioning by the Los Angeles Police Department on the matter of the fire at La Casa Nevada. He appeared voluntarily without an attorney, and although he was fingerprinted and a mug shot was taken, he was neither charged nor held in custody. The police refused to be quoted even off the record, but I have culled all seven newspapers publishing in Los Angeles at the time, and by incorporating the remarks each paper claims Jacob King made, and by throwing out repetitions and inconsistencies, I am able to draw together one coherent statement: "I'm a businessman. I can't take those New York winters any more. My health. I'm looking for investment possibilities. Someplace where I don't have to shovel snow. I say to Lieutenant Crotty, I'm having a little trouble here. Maybe you can help me out. This so-called felony you keep referring to. It occurred in Las Vegas, right? And Lieutenant Crotty, he says, Right. So I say to him, What are you guys in Los Angeles doing, bringing me in and mugging me and printing me on a Las Vegas case? You want to arrest me, arrest me, send me over to Vegas in leg irons. But you don't do that, I say to him. So I keep reaching the same conclusion. You got nothing on me. And one last thing, I say to him. Under Section 516 of the California penal code, all photographs and fingerprints must be returned to the accused if no charges are brought and the accused has no prior conviction in this jurisdiction. You can look it up, I say to him. I did."

In fact, Jacob King's reading of Section 516 of the California penal code was accurate. Both the mug shots and the fingerprints were returned to him, and were found among his effects after his death. I find Jacob's having the California penal code at his fingertips almost as interesting a comment about him as the homicides he is alleged to have committed. It bespeaks both an intelligence and a sense of humor that I had previously been unwilling to concede.

◄◦►

Morris Lefkowitz was eating lox.

"This was not the deal, Morris," Jimmy Riordan said. "We wanted a nice straight business arrangement. Now a hotel burns down. I don't want to know who did it. I don't want to know how the person did it. I don't want to point any fingers. All I know is Jake is putting us into the construction business, and we're going to have to build our own hotel."

"So we're in the construction business," Morris Lefkowitz said. "A new business, a new challenge."

"You don't just go out there, torch their operation, not expect another shoe to drop."

"Sometimes it's important to keep your eye on the big picture, Jimmy," Morris Lefkowitz said, "not think all the time about shoes dropping."

Jimmy Riordan approached from another angle. "And we got to deal Jackie Heller in."

"His brother Leo was a nice boy. Did what he was told. No questions. Jackie will do what you tell him to do, Jimmy." Jimmy Riordan did not miss the point. He would be the messenger bearing Morris Lefkowitz's message to Jackie Heller. "It runs in the family."

"What do you want to cut him in for?"

"Chump change," Morris Lefkowitz said.

Jimmy Riordan wondered if he should try again, because that was his advocate's obligation, but he knew that Morris Lefkowitz had already made his mind up. Nevertheless. "Morris, Benny is not going to let this happen."

"Tell me, Jimmy," Morris Lefkowitz said, selecting another slice of pink lox, smelling it, and then laying it on his plate as if it were a sable pelt, "would you rather be in business with Benny Draper or with Jackie Heller?"

Morris had already worked it through, Jimmy Riordan thought. As usual. In the best of all possible worlds, it was no contest. Jackie Heller was a boob who could be bought, as Morris knew, for chump change. Benny Draper was a crazy boob, with a significant piece of the action, the greed to want more, and a willingness to use violence to see that he got it.

"Have some lox, Jimmy," Morris Lefkowitz said.

"Morris." One last time. Explore all the options, as he had been taught at law school. Explain the possible repercussions. "Believe me. This could mean bad stuff."

"You know what, Jimmy? I've seen bad stuff before, and I'm still eating lox." He picked his teeth with the silver toothpick he kept on his watch chain. "Jacob's there. We're here. Go with Jacob."

◄○►

Blue Tyler was dancing by herself to the music of *Pal Joey* on Jacob King's Victrola when she looked up and saw him framed by the French doors leading into the living room of the house on St. Pierre Road. She wondered how long he had been there, watching.

"I know this house," she said. It was as if she felt no explanation was needed to explain how she had been allowed entry, and as if she knew he would not ask for one. "It used to belong to Chuckie O'Hara."

"I don't know any Chuckie O'Hara."

"Well, then, you don't know anything, do you?"

"That's possible."

"The director. He's done three of my pictures. And now *Red River Rosie*. Chuckie's a fairy. You know what a fairy is?"

She amused him, and amusement had never before ranked high in his pursuit of the carnal pleasures. "I think I know what a fairy is."

"His boyfriend was the butler. Withers, I think his name was."

"Woodson," Jacob King said.

"Anyway I saw them necking in the kitchen at the wrap party for *Lily of the Valley*. Chuckie directed that, too. I was eleven. No, twelve. I came out of the kitchen and I said to my mother, 'Withers is in the kitchen kissing Chuckie's penis.' "

"You think you know a lot, don't you?"

"I know that Arthur says you burned down La Casa Nevada."

"If I burned down La Casa Nevada, it was stupid of you to come here."

"Did you? I mean, burn down La Casa Nevada?"

"I was here last night."

"Getting laid. By one of Brenda Samuel's girls. Arthur says that was your alibi."

"What else does Arthur say?"

"Arthur says you're a gangster. Are you a gangster?"

The question did not faze Jacob King. It was one he had been asked most of his adult life by reporters and assistant district attorneys and by people ostensibly on the right side of the law, and he understood the frisson they received by asking, and the power he had over them by not minding that they had asked. "That's a newspaper word. Some people use it. It's like *movie star*. It doesn't mean anything."

"*Movie star* does too mean something," Blue said quickly. It was as if Jacob King had challenged her entire value system, the only one that held any meaning for her. Usually she was in control, and here was a man she suddenly suspected would be difficult to control. "It means people don't care what I'm in, they come to see me. *Movie star* means I can make any picture I want."

"*Gangster* means I can shut it down."

She was walking around the room now. There was a photograph in a silver frame. "Is this your wife?"

He nodded.

"Arthur told me you were married. Arthur said you killed people. What do you say about that?"

"I'd say Arthur leads a secondhand life. And I'd say you're getting pretty sick of that."

She looked at him for a moment, then turned, walked out of the living room, across the foyer, and slowly began to climb the main staircase. She had loved staircase shots since *Lily of the Valley*, when she, a poor servant child, was pretending to be the lady of the manor, only to be discovered and banished from the main house as a thief. She tried to have a staircase sequence in every picture. She knew where the camera should be placed, and how it should track her up the stairs, one long traveling shot and no cutaways.

After a moment Jacob followed her. When he got to the second-floor landing, he watched her disappear into the study next to the master bedroom down the corridor.

"The safe's behind that painting," she said when he walked into the study. "Chuckie told me that."

"It's a Remington, and it's a fake," Jacob King said.

"Who's Remington?"

"A famous painter."

"What do you keep in the safe? Your tommy gun?"

Jacob pressed a button and the painting disappeared up into the ceiling. "It's open. Open it."

She pulled open the door, and gasped. The safe was full of loose cash and stacks of bills still in their paper wrappers. "You keep this kind of money in an open safe?"

"It's one of the advantages of being a gangster. No one's going to take it."

She kept looking at the money, as if it were the fruit in the Garden of Eden. "How much is it?"

"A hundred grand. Maybe two hundred."

She scooped a handful of cash from the safe and held it in her hands. "For my sixteenth birthday, I signed a seven-year contract that made me the highest-paid teenager in America. I make twelve thousand five hundred dollars a week this year, but I never see it. My agent sees it. My lawyer. My business manager. My accountant. I've only held a hundred dollars in my hands once in my life. And that's when I made a contribution to the March of Dimes on behalf of the Industry. Mrs. Roosevelt thanked me."

"Take it," Jacob King said.

Suddenly she threw the money into the air, then watched it drift down, her childlike avarice almost as highly developed a sense in her as sex. "I don't want your money," she said finally as the bills dropped off her like snow.

"What do you want?"

"What do you think I came here for?"

—◦—

"Are you lucky?" Blue said later. She could see the full moon shining through the open French doors in the bedroom.

"So far. Why?"

"Arthur said if you didn't watch out, you were going to get killed."

Jacob did not reply.

"That's why you should stay with me," Blue said. "Because I'm lucky."

"How lucky?"

"Very lucky. During the war, I was fourteen, I was on this war-bond tour with Carole Lombard. She was great, Carole. We talked all the time. Usually about men. I mean, she treated me like a grown-up. I told her some things I never told anyone, and she told me she really loved Clark, but that Ted Fio Rito, you know the bandleader . . ."

Jacob nodded.

". . . she said he was the best she ever had." She rolled over and brushed her lips over Jacob's cock. "Like you with me." It was a line she would have insisted on saying if the Hays Office allowed fuck scenes. He lifted her up into the crook of his arm. "Anyway. The tour was a big success, we sold over two million dollars in bonds, I said I would kiss any man who'd buy ten thousand dollars' worth of bonds, and Carole said she'd kiss anyone who'd buy fifty thousand dollars' worth, and if you bought a million dollars' worth, well, you just think about what she'd do for that. It always got such a laugh. I said, Carole, what if someone buys a million, and she said, someone's going to get the fuck of his life. But finally we just wanted to get back home, we'd been away so long, the whole trip we'd been on a train, and so we decided to fly instead. TWA. A DC-3. It made a stop in Las Vegas. A gas stop. I got off, I didn't think it was going to leave so quickly, and it took off without me. And crashed into a mountain. Everyone on board was killed. Including Carole."

Jacob King took a deep breath. "That's lucky." He ran a finger down her stomach. "I guess I'll stick close to you. Try and buy a piece of your luck."

She rolled over and looked at him, as if debating whether to say something more. "Actually . . ."

"Actually what?" Jacob said.

She rose from the bed without answering and went to the doors leading to the balcony. Tears were welling in her eyes and she did not want him to see them. She did not like to think about the crash, because the crash made her think about why she had missed the plane, the reason she had never told anyone, not even Arthur, and with Arthur she shared her worst secrets, even those that hurt him most. It was a reason that saved her life, but there were moments, rare, it should be said, when she wondered if she might have been better off had she been on the plane when it smashed into Potosi Mountain, and rescue crews were dispatched to bring down the bodies, and then she wondered if she would have had a bigger funeral than Carole. She knew everyone would have cried. Even Moe. She tried not to cry now and, as always when she did not want to yield to emotion, searched for an appropriate line of dialogue from a favorite movie. That was the thing about movies. There was never a situation that had not been anticipated in some picture. High in the night sky she could see the stars.

"Oh, Jerry," she said, turning to face Jacob. "Don't let's ask for the moon, we have the stars."

He looked at her quizzically, then got up from the bed and joined her at the window. He had an erection. She had never known any man, not even Walker Franklin, who got so many erections. "My name isn't Jerry," he said, and she thought perhaps he might be a little angry.

"It's a line from a movie. *Now Voyager.*" A pause. "Jacob." The "Jacob" was offered with a slight emphasis, so that he would not miss the point.

"I never saw it."

"With Bette and that German guy, Paul, that was in *Casablanca.* He played Jerry."

"I didn't see it."

"Well, you didn't see anything, did you?"

"I had things to do," Jacob King said, enveloping her in his arms. After a moment, he said, "You know, the first time I ever saw the stars I was ten years old."

"What?" she said. Carole and the plane crash and her imagined funeral were forgotten. "What do you mean, ten years old? Were you blind or something?"

"You don't see the stars in Brooklyn. I got sent to this juvenile farm, it was upstate, in the mountains. I stole a car, and I couldn't even drive. I just hot-wired it. I hit three cars in the block, then this old fart, he was crossing the street, how was I supposed to see him, I couldn't even see over the wheel. I'd already been laid, but I'd never seen the stars. And there they were, at this juvey farm."

It was a story outside her realm of experience, but it freed her to talk about herself, the subject with which she was most comfortable. "When I was five I went to the premiere of *Angels on Parade* . . ."

"What's that got to do with the stars?"

"Wait. Let me tell you. And after they ran it, Mr. French took me onstage and introduced me and said Let me present someone who is going to be Cosmopolitan Pictures's brightest star. And I started to cry. Because the stars were in heaven. And when he said I was going to be a star, I thought he meant I was going to heaven. You know, like dying?" She burrowed into him. "I'm not even afraid of dying anymore. You know what I'm afraid of instead?"

He tightened his hold on her. "You're afraid of walking into someplace and nobody gives a shit, nobody knows who you are, you're a nobody."

Blue twisted out of his arms and looked at him. This was not the way she would have put it, but it was more or less what she meant. "How do you know that?"

"Because we're alike, you and me."

"No, we're not," she said with a hint of petulance. He was not an actor, nor a director, nor a producer, nor did he own a studio, like Moe, nor was he a son, like Arthur. These were the only categories of people she really knew, and he fit into none of them. And a writer would certainly never live in a house like this. She did not know where production managers and makeup men and hairdressers and wardrobe mistresses lived, although she tried to remember them by their first names, and gave them all Christmas presents that the studio paid for and charged to the production number of whatever picture they had worked on with her. "Because I'm famous."

He smiled, and it occurred to her that he must be famous, too. In his way. Whatever that way was. Famous enough so that his presence made people nervous, people like Mr. French and Lilo and that awful Benny Draper, men whose business was making other people not just nervous but fearful. "Well, anyway," she amended, "I've been famous longer than you."

A shrug, still smiling. "Yes, we are alike," he said gently. "We're in different lines of work, you and me, but we're out there in the spotlight, because that's where we want to be."

That was it. That was it exactly. How did he know that? "What kind of work are you in, Jacob?"

"I'm a sportsman," Jacob King said.

IX

THERE IS VERY LITTLE in this narrative that Blue Tyler, Arthur French, and Chuckie O'Hara, each with a personal and totally self-absorbed perspective, could agree on, but they all agreed that the downfall of Benny Draper, leading to his violent demise, began the day he ordered a wildcat strike that pulled the gaffers off Cosmo's Stage 7, the largest on the lot, where Chuckie, in the last week of shooting on *Red River Rosie*, two days behind schedule and hearing about it from J. F. French, who was threatening to replace him with Victor Higgins, Metro's equally homosexual director of big-budget musicals (an idle threat, because J.F. would never pay a loan-out fee to L. B. Mayer, who he wished would choke on a fishbone), was preparing the production-number finale. Of course I looked up the trade papers for that day. The page-one headline in *Daily Variety* read, ALAN SHAY IDENTIFIED AS RED, while the *Reporter*'s front page was bannered with DIRECTOR SHAY TAKES FIFTH 47 TIMES; in both papers, the story of the ongoing negotiations with Benny Draper's OMPCE was buried on page five: PROGRESS REPORTED IN LABOR TALKS, reported *Variety*, LABOR SETTLEMENT REPORTED NEAR, said the *Reporter*.

It was our Manhattan Towers number, Chuckie O'Hara said. Rosie's run away from the Red River Valley and come to New York, and she's all the rage, of course, so down and dirty, a fifteen-year-old Texas Guinan, but the sophisticated New Yorkers just love her, and she has this society fiancé, who doesn't know how old she really is, Billy Teasdale played the part, oh, how I loved that boy, but he was a monogamous fag, if you can believe it, he and Victor Higgins were together for years, Victor was always out on the town, playing the field, but Billy was just Miss Stay-at-Home, gardening and cooking, nothing says lovin' like something in the oven. Anyway. Enough of unrequited amour. Blue was supposed to dance down the floating staircase of this penthouse apartment, one hundred and two steps, my dear, the bannister swathed in chiffon, Blue singing "Anything Goes," ba ba bababa bum, "In olden days, a glimpse of stocking . . . was looked upon as something shocking . . ." It takes four and a half hours to light the master, Walter Sklar was the slowest cameraman on the lot, but he was Moe French's nephew, and I always got stuck with him, I think his main job was to tell Moe if I was prancing around with anyone below the line. So it's eleven-thirty and we haven't had the first setup yet, and Blue's acting cunty with wardrobe and makeup, she wants to show cleavage, she wants her knockers squished together, and I say to her, Blue, you're playing fifteen, I know you're nineteen, we'll compromise, I'll show just a tiny little hint of cleavage and see if I can prevail on Moe to run an ad campaign that says, "Blue's Got Tits and Billy's Got 'Em." Anything to get a laugh out of my star. And she says, Billy wouldn't know what to do with them. *Quelle vrai.* You have the rag on, dear, I say, or a little preggers, are we? You see, I had met this new gentleman friend, and I'd heard that Arthur was on hold, and that Arthur was being such a good sport about it, Arthur was born being a good sport, and he'll die being one, it's like he came over on the fucking *Mayflower,* he's such a good sport. Fuck you, Chuckie, she said in that winning way of hers, but by that time the shot was finally ready, and the A.D. said, Places everybody, and the chorus boys and those loathsome French Fillies took their places, and Blue rode to the top of the staircase on a boom, and the A.D. said, Music ready, and I said, Rolling . . . and . . . action . . .

◄o►

I hated to lip-sync, Melba Mae Toolate said, and so in all my musical numbers I'd do the songs to a live mike, and then in postproduction I'd rerecord. I hated that picture. I never minded Chuckie being a fairy, but I never had to do love scenes with him, not that I had any love scenes with Billy Teasdale, because I was only supposed to be fifteen, and he didn't know that, or his character didn't, and so the thing was, was he going to kiss me or not, the jerk-off factor, Chuckie called it, the jerk-off factor was what made me a star. Billy was nice, I suppose, but I was always asking him if Victor was the husband and he was the wife, or vice versa, and he would tell me I had bad breath. Fuck him. I didn't go to his funeral. He had a stroke or a hemorrhage or something bad in his head, he was on location, and they couldn't get him to a hospital in time, Victor threw himself on Billy's casket at the funeral, that's the only reason I wish I'd gone, to see that, it made Clark Gable furious, he said Victor should be barred from the Industry. He was such an asshole at times, Clark. One time he told me that my being with Jacob set a bad example for the Industry, and I said, What about all those old bags you married for their money and shit before Carole, Carole told me she thought you were cherry when she married you, she didn't say that, but that got to him. Fuck him, too.

Give me a little grapefruit juice, and while you're up, throw a little vodka into it, put the juice in first, then the ice, then the vodka, and don't stir it, that way the juice is like a chaser. Anyway, I'm up on this staircase waiting for Chuckie to say Action, and I look down and see Billy Teasdale picking his nose and looking at it, it really got me in the mood. I'm pissed off at Arthur, too, he's being so fucking noble, he says this is just a phase I'm going through, I say, What's just a phase, getting it twice a night regular, which I shouldn't have said, then I get to look at Billy snacking on a little piece of snot, no wonder he had a fucking hemorrhage, the boogers clogged up his arteries, then Chuckie says, Action. The music starts, I start coming down the staircase, "In olden days, a glimpse of stocking . . ." Left foot over right foot, right food over left foot. ". . . was looked upon as something shocking . . ." I'm halfway down the stairs, when the whole stage goes dark, pitch-black, and I'm scream- ing, Will someone get me off these fucking stairs. I was making over twelve thousand dollars a week, I was the most valuable piece of property on the lot, and none of those people whose job depended on me knew how to get me off those fucking stairs. I thought I was going to die, and I thought it would've been a better ending going into that mountain with Car- ole . . .

◄○►

Arthur French was playing tennis at Hillcrest when his father's secretary called the club and had the manager go to the courts and tell him that the electricians had walked out and he was to return to the studio immediately. Arthur always obeyed his fa- ther and went back to Cosmo without changing out of his ten- nis whites. Not changing was a mistake, he realized as soon as he walked into J. F. French's office. J.F. was in a rage, and Arthur knew that sooner or later he would be the target of opportunity.

"What do you mean, wildcat strike?" J. F. French was screaming at Lilo Kusack. "I don't see no wildcats, I just see a bunch of bums, and that bunch of bums was walking out, that bunch of bums Benny Draper gets paid to keep in line. What the fuck I been paying him for, they won't even follow orders?"

"They are following orders, Moe," Lilo Kusack said. He had assumed his reasonable, lawyer's tone, speaking so low it was difficult to hear him. "They're following Benny's orders. That's your problem."

"My problem is we got no product for the Christmas season,

this keeps up . . ." J.F. stopped, as he seemed to see Arthur for the first time. "Lilo, who's this tennis player just walked in here without knocking? Bill Tilden?" He ran his eyes over Arthur. "He's a *fageleh*, Bill Tilden, you know that? You a *fageleh*, too? I should call you Bill, the way you let that little girl working her ass off down on Stage Seven get porked by that gangster man from New York . . ."

"It's just a phase," Arthur French said.

"Phase," J. F. French said. "He's got a dick bigger than your racket, I hear . . ."

"Moe, Moe," Lilo said soothingly. He knew Arthur would never defend himself against his father.

"Don't Moe, Moe me, Lilo," J. F. French yelled. "I hear he's sticking his racket into Rita, too."

Lilo inspected the shine on his shoes. There was no point in interrupting this tirade, or taking offense either. He knew history was on his side. Someday J. F. French would lose control of his studio, as all the oldtimers had lost control of theirs, Laemmle and Schulberg and Fox, all of them, and Lilo would make sure he was there to kick him when he was down. And kick him once more for good measure. As for Rita, she was who she was, at least she wasn't fucking the poolboy anymore, she wasn't a wife, there was no point in trying to put her on a leash, and he doubted any man would be capable of that. Even her fucking Jacob might prove useful in the long run, a way to wean Blue away from him when the time came, as come it must. Blue was the client whose viability he must protect. After that service was performed he would start thinking about getting rid of Rita. It was time he should be getting married again anyway, and Rita was not wife material. Nor was it a role she sought. Getting rid of her would sadden him. Rita's brain might be in her pussy, but there were few men and no women whose brain he valued more.

"You got nothing to say?" J. F. French said belligerently.

"The electricians could be back this afternoon, Moe," Lilo said evenly, "if you just let me bring Benny in and we make his deal."

"Such a tough guy, this Benny. The gangster man burns down his hotel, your hotel, Lilo . . ." J.F.'s hand shot out, his forefinger like an arrow, his voice rising, strangled, almost inarticulate, the artery in his neck pulsating. Lilo thought he might have a stroke right there, and that would be something he would enjoy. ". . . *my* hotel, and what does Benny-tough-guy do about it? He calls this wildcat thing against me. Better he should let his wildcats chew up the gangster man that's fucking everyone I know. I think Benny's wildcats got no teeth, is what I think."

In fact, Benny Draper had tried to tell Lilo of the plans he had for Jacob King, all of which involved cutting off his genitals, and one with hammering a pipe up his anus and pouring red hot battery acid in it. I am not hearing you, Benny, Lilo had said, I am an officer of the court, if I heard what you were saying, I'd have to report you or be charged with misprision of a felony. I am not hearing you, I will not be party to a conspiracy, but if you do anything to Jacob King right now, even the federal attorneys you've got in your pocket couldn't stop a grand jury from indicting you. In truth Lilo was surprised that Benny had not done something stupid already. Quick and brutal vengeance was instinctive with him, a signature. He did not think Benny was getting any smarter, so perhaps Moe was right, perhaps Benny did talk the talk now better than he walked the walk. In which case a call to Jimmy Riordan might be in order. Not just yet. But a possibility.

Down the line.

To establish ground rules.

And the length of any leash attached to Jake King.

"I have the figures, J.F.," Arthur was saying when Lilo focused back on the matter at hand. Arthur had picked up the numbers from business affairs before coming to his father's office. The papers were sticky from his still-sweaty tennis clothes. "Make the deal now, the stoppage only costs ten thousand for the morning . . ."

J. F. French looked at his son in wonderment. "I send Bill Tilden here to the University of Southern California, and you know what he learns? He learns 'only.' Like in 'only ten thousand.' Like it's his money."

"Moe, with the insurance, you'd come out okay," Lilo Kusack said.

"Insurance." J. F. French's voice was beginning to rise again. "You must've been the one teaching Bill Tilden 'only' at the University of Southern California."

"The fact is, J.F.," Arthur said, "it doesn't matter when we settle. Because we *are* going to settle." It was as if Arthur thought he could impress his father by taking the realistic approach. "We haven't got any options . . ."

The color was beginning to rise in J. F. French's face when his secretary buzzed from the outer office.

"You're fired," J.F. shouted. "I said no calls."

"Miss Tyler from Stage Seven," the secretary said coolly. She had already been fired once before that morning, and she would be fired again that afternoon, and she would return the following day to be fired once, twice, or even thrice more. She had worked for J. F. French for eleven years, and she had stopped counting the number of times she had been fired, and she no longer cared that he was serious every time he dismissed her, always in a fury, or that he seemed not to know her first name. As a result she had never told him that her husband had polio and was confined to an iron lung in a Culver City hospital, because if he knew that he would have fired her for certain, it would make him obligated, and he despised obligation to other people, particularly those subservient to him. He expected her to keep his secrets, but she had as little interest in his women and what they did to him as he had in her private life, and its sorrows. Her name, the name J. F. French never bothered to learn, the name Arthur years later told me, was Dorothy Warnick—she was Miss Warren to J. F. French and sometimes she was Miss Warner and occasionally Miss Warnick, but never Mrs. anything—and often Dorothy Warnick contemplated what she would do if her health failed to the point where she could no longer take care of her husband, if indeed visiting him in his iron lung could be said to be taking care of him (this again from

Arthur, who would talk to her, and call her Mrs. Warnick, but never Dorothy, this woman who had felt his father's wrath as often as he, although J. F. French and his discontents were never mentioned). She dreamed of killing her husband in this eventuality, perhaps with a gun secured from the property department, and then killing herself so that her body fell by his infernal machine. I know this because Arthur had told it to me when we were working together on our heart-transplant screenplay, he thought it was something we might find a use for. I of course wanted to know what had happened to her, but Arthur of course had no idea, not being as unlike his father as he preferred to think, or pretend. "She says it's urgent," Mrs. Warnick said.

J. F. French picked up the telephone and without a greeting began to yell. "You want to show your titties, I hear about it already." Lilo Kusack marveled at the way J. F. French knew what was happening every minute on every stage and in every office. "Show your titties to your gangster man, if you want, I don't want titties showing in a J. F. French production. We put out entertainment for the whole family." He listened for a moment, then whirled his chair around so that neither Arthur or Lilo could hear what he was saying. "He said what?" he whispered into the telephone. "What else did he say?" He nodded and said, "All right" and "Where?" and "When?" and then he listened some more, and said, "All right" again, "Let me know," then hung up and turned back to Lilo and Arthur, a look of satisfaction on his face.

"Moe, the clock's running," Lilo said finally. "What do you want me to tell Benny?"

J. F. French rose from behind his desk. "You tell Benny to go fuck himself."

"Moe . . ." Lilo began.

"Out," J. F. French said. "And take Bill Tilden with you."

◄○►

Blue said her instructions from Jacob were to ask J. F. French to meet him at the beach, in Malibu, and to tell him that perhaps he could offer a solution to the labor problems burdening Cosmopolitan Pictures. When Jacob called the set, she was still caught halfway up the floating staircase, screaming imprecations, paralyzed with fear, a darkened soundstage suggesting to her only that the Communists were at fault, perhaps even Alan Shay, although she did not know what the Fifth Amendment was that he had taken forty-seven times the day before, only that it was un-American, as Mr. French was always saying, and anyway Alan Shay was a terrible director, he had been replaced on *Cotton Candy,* he doesn't know how to direct children, he's mean, she had complained to Mr. French, and Alan Shay had been fired, her wish a command, which was perhaps why he had become a Communist. She thought war with Soviet Russia was at hand, and that she was going to die on a fake staircase, surrounded by a bunch of fairy chorus boys in silver tails, at least when Carole died it was quick, one moment she was alive, the next she wasn't. Then someone rigged a generator, and the lights came on, and she rode the boom down to the stage floor, her makeup blotched by tears, her mascara staining her long white gloves. When she got to her trailer, the telephone was ringing, and it was Jacob, he had already heard about the gaffers walking out and he listened patiently to her talk about the Reds and what they were doing to the Industry, and then he told her to call Moe and give him a message. She did not want to call Mr. French, he was mad at her about Arthur and the way she was treating him, and she wondered why Jacob called him Moe if they had never met, Moe would not like that, but Jacob said some dirty things to her over the phone, and she made the call. It was not until she hung up that she began to wonder how he had known about the strike so quickly, but of course Jackie Heller had told him it was coming up, and Jacob knew immediately that it was an opportunity.

◄○►

"You got a funny way to get in touch with me," J. F. French said. He hated the beach and especially the constant, crashing sound of the waves. It was something he could not control, and he insisted on total control. "Why not just call?"

"I wouldn't get through," Jacob King said. "I didn't want to talk to one of your yes-men."

"I don't have yes-men. I have no-men."

"You say no, they say no."

J. F. French smiled. "A smart boy. So why am I here getting sand in my shoes?"

"Because, Mr. French, you're up to your neck in shit. Your studio is shut down and Benny Draper wants two million to let you start it again. It's you today, it'll be Fox tomorrow, Paramount the next day. Until you come up with that two million. And what that buys all of you is two years without a strike. Unless Benny gets up on the wrong side of the bed one day and starts to squeeze."

"You mean I get sand in my shoes to hear something I already know."

Jacob King picked his words carefully. Jimmy Riordan did not give him much credit, but he had watched Jimmy talk and he had watched Morris talk, and with them each word meant something, and too few words were often better than too many. "I can have your studio operating again by Thursday morning," Jacob said. "I've got the people available. No more strikes anyplace for the length of the contract."

"And what do we have to pay you for all those bones I think you're going to have to break?"

"Nothing."

"So who are you, Prince Charming? I made that picture already. Another fairy tale I don't need. What's it going to cost? I need a price. Free means trouble."

Jacob King looked up at the Pacific Coast Highway. For a moment he watched J. F. French's chauffeur following behind them in his employer's Bentley. Jacob had never seen a car before with a right-hand drive. It was something he would like to have, and the driver, too. "I want to go into Nevada," Jacob King said slowly. "I want to build my own place. I want your support. I want Lilo Kusack out of my hair. I want you and the other studios to supply the entertainment. Your best people. I want a break in the price. If I can let the right people know you're not going to try and stop me, then that's like money in the bank, Mr. French. I'll take care of the rest."

"By the right people you mean Morris."

Jacob King did not reply.

"Did Morris tell you to burn down my hotel?"

Now it was Jacob King's turn to smile.

"So you burned it down yourself?"

"Prove it."

"Okay, we let sleeping cats lie," J. F. French said, his command of metaphor as always insecure. "You think Benny Draper's going to let you get away with this?"

"I don't lose any sleep over Benny Draper."

"He wants to stick a pipe up your ass."

"I heard that. He's free to try."

J. F. French turned and waved to his chauffeur. The car stopped on the highway, and the chauffeur got out and held open the right rear door. "Benny wanted to fuck that little girl who's going to marry my son."

"That little girl's old enough to make up her own mind who she's going to fuck, Mr. French."

"So I hear," J. F. French said, heading up the sand toward the Bentley. "You talk to Morris, I'll talk to Lilo."

◄◦►

According to Arthur French, Jacob King told his strike-breakers they were to carry no firearms, no knives, and no explosives. It was Eddie Binhoff, wielding a baseball bat, who led Jackie Heller's electricians, all of whom were carrying ax handles, through the OMPCE picket lines outside the Cosmo studio gates. The Cosmo Newsreel showed a montage of labor violence, invoked the Red threat, and then showed a scene of Benny Draper, screaming obscenities and with blood gushing from a cut over his eye, being arrested and led into a paddy wagon by studio policemen who had been made special deputies by the Los Angeles Police Department, Lilo's doing. The headlines in the trade papers told the story:

SPLIT IN OMPCE RANKS
DISSIDENT FACTION SEEKS TO OUST DRAPER

Then:

HELLER PLAN CHALLENGES UNION BOSS DRAPER

Then:

UNION BACKS HELLER PLAN
SETBACK FOR DRAPER

Finally:

STUDIOS SET TO SIGN NEW LABOR PACT

◄o►

He lit a cigarette. By the light of the match she could see that he had shaved after the last time. He smelled of baby powder and shaving lotion. Now he had her doing it. Afterward she would sit on the bidet and let the water spray up into her. It made her feel sophisticated. Like a grown-up. She did not have a bidet in her own house on Tower Road, and she would have to ask Arthur who she could get to install one, a plumber she supposed, anyway it was the kind of household detail she left to Arthur.

She seemed so small. "There's something I want to tell you," Jacob King said, blowing a perfect smoke ring in the darkness. "Don't ever come here if I'm not here."

"Why?" Blue Tyler said. "Because of Benny?"

Jacob did not reply.

"Remember I said I was lucky."

"You're not that lucky."

X

THE *VALIANT* WAS a gambling ship that operated off San
Pedro just beyond the three-mile limit, and thus beyond
the jurisdiction of Los Angeles municipal and county authorities. It had Panamanian registry, but in fact it was a buried
asset of the national racing wire Morris Lefkowitz had given
Jacob King to supervise. Acting through layers of intermedi-
aries, Jacob King was lavish in the gratitude he dispensed to the
appropriate officials in the appropriate agencies of government
for not seeking redress against the motor launches that took
guests from the Santa Monica and Paradise Cove piers to the
Valiant and back, guests who would never return to the *Valiant*
should the authorities seek to intercept these water taxis while
within the three-mile limit, and book the passengers into county
jail for violation of various anti-gaming statutes.

It was Blue Tyler who broached to J. F. French the idea of
holding the wrap party for *Red River Rosie* on the *Valiant,* the
inducement being that Jacob King would comp the studio, with
everything on the house, or on the ship, as the case would be.
Moe's such a cheapskate, he'll love it, Blue said, he squeezes a
nickel until the buffalo craps. While J. F. French appreciated a

PLAYLAND · 307

bargain, he was a cautious man, and before he agreed to Jacob King's offer, he had Lilo Kusack check his sources downtown to make sure there would be no watery police raid that would bring embarrassing headlines about Cosmopolitan Pictures, and also to find out what Benny Draper was up to, he did not want Benny doing something rash. My people downtown say they never heard of the *Valiant,* Lilo told J. F. French, so you're clear there, and Benny's having dinner in Boyle Heights with his Chicago guys, they're giving him a lot of heat, more than he can handle, but I'm not so sure you should do this, Moe, you can afford a wrap party, pay for it yourself, don't get too tight with Jakey King, it might look bad.

So pay for it yourself, you're so rich, Lilo, J. F. French said, and he told Blue that the *Red River Rosie* party would be held on the *Valiant,* no expenses to be incurred by Cosmopolitan Pictures.

That Jacob had made the offer was in itself a small surprise, as he himself had never even been on board the *Valiant,* the reason being that he was susceptible to seasickness, the slightest rolling motion while under way putting his stomach in a turmoil, and he hated any situation where he appeared not entirely in command. But on the night of the party, he stood at the top of the gangplank, resplendent in a white dinner jacket, greeting his guests as they came aboard, Blue at his side, and just behind her Eddie Binhoff, wearing a midnight-blue tuxedo, Eddie Binhoff, who Jacob did not introduce to anyone and who Blue told one and all was Jacob's bodyguard, Eddie Something. Chuckie O'Hara was there, and both J. F. and Arthur French, Arthur reluctantly, but under orders from his father to attend, and Chloe Quarles and Shelley Flynn and Walker Franklin, and the French Fillies, and the boys in the chorus, and Billy Teasdale with Victor Higgins, and Reggie Ford and Sonya Rose, the screenwriters, and Walter Sklar, the D.P., even Lilo Kusack and Rita Lewis, as well as the A.D.s and the set decorators and the camera loaders and the grips and the best boys and the makeup men and the wardrobe mistresses and the script girls. Everything was free, the champagne and the food, and everyone was given a pile of chips, no one was to take the launch back to the Santa Monica pier a loser. There were fireworks and there were staterooms below for those who wished to grab a Filly or a chorus boy for a quick fuck. Jacob King was a most extravagant host, and he danced with Blue, and he also danced with Sonya Rose, the writer, all two hundred pounds of her, and with Chloe Quarles, several Fillies, both script supervisors, and with Blue's personal maid, Rosalia Jefferson. Blue danced with Chuckie and Arthur and Billy Teasdale and Reggie Ford, but it was with Walker Franklin that she was at her most energetic, tap dancing alongside him, all energy and splits, matching him step for step, almost competitively. It was funny, Chuckie said. On a picture, Walker was never supposed to make eye contact with Blue during a dance number. J.F.'s orders. Eye contact with a white woman wouldn't go down in the South. So I always designed the sequence in such a way that Walker was looking at the extras or at Shelley Flynn but never at Blue. No eye contact, only cock contact, it turned out. A little secret Blue shared with Aunt Chuckie. The performance was clearly distressing and distasteful to J. F. French, who was thankful that it was taking place on this boat and not in a more public venue where photographers might be present. There's something you got to tell Blue, he whispered to Lilo Kusack. There's only two kinds of colored people. Entertainers and dangerous.

—◦—

It was around ten o'clock when mal de mer began to ravage Jacob King, and Blue and Eddie Binhoff took him out on deck, where he leaned over the rail and threw up, gallons of puke, Melba Mae Toolate remembered four and a half decades later, perhaps more graphically than the situation actually warranted. It was green-and-yellow barf, it really fucked up that white dinner jacket, Melba Mae said, and his breath was so bad this Eddie guy gave him some Sen-Sen, you don't really like to see the guy who went down on you last night and who you thought was going to go down on you again tonight puking over the side, his hair all matted with sweat, and he stunk, you know that puke smell that stings your nose.

In other words, Jacob King was on the *Valiant* in full view of two hundred people the night that Benny Draper was shot in the face by Schlomo Buchalter.

Buchalter, Schlomo
Syndicate Gangster, Hit Man (1890–1947)

BACKGROUND: Born Schlomo Bookhouse in Manhattan's Lower East Side, distant cousin of Louis Bookhouse, later Louis ("Lepke") Buchalter, head of Murder, Incorporated. Description: 5'7¹/₂", brown hair, brown eyes, stocky. Education ended 1906 at Oneida State Reformatory for Boys, to which he had been remanded in 1901 for assault with intent to do bodily harm, i.e., with lug wrench, on one Wong Fat while robbing complainant's laundry on Mott Street in lower Manhattan. No occupation other than crime. Upon release from Oneida Reformatory, became free-lance murderer and Syndicate hit man performing contract assassinations for Murder, Inc., and reputedly for Morris Lefkowitz and various crime families in Chicago and New Jersey. Alias: "Round Trip," so called because he would take a contract any place in the United States, and return to New York immediately thereafter. Because of his fear of betrayal, his modus operandi was always to work alone. Law enforcement agencies estimate that over the years Buchalter carried out at least forty contract hits, but while often arrested for murder, he was never formally charged with the crime. Served three-year term in New York's Attica State Penitentiary for bookmaking, then an additional five-year term for assault with intent to kill, to wit, a guard at Attica, the assault taking place on the day of his release for his first offense. Also served three-year term in Joliet State Penitentiary (Illinois) for arson, the bombing of a labor union local opposed to Chicago Labor Leader and Mobster Benjamin ("Benny") Draper. Upon release from Joliet, Buchalter became Draper's chief enforcer. When Draper moved his activities to California to consolidate his hold on the corrupt Organization of Motion Picture Craft Employees (OMPCE), Buchalter followed, continuing his enforcer role. Ill health subsequently forced him to curtail his activities. Then on April 2, 1947, Buchalter shot and killed Draper in a Mexican restaurant in the Boyle Heights section of Los Angeles, and was in turn shot and killed by Draper's bodyguards. The dispute allegedly involved Draper's failure to fulfill the monetary terms of a contract hit Buchalter had carried out for his former mentor some years previously.

ALSO SEE, DRAPER, Benjamin; BUCHALTER, Louis ("Lepke")

The Index of American Crime and Criminals

◄◊►

The fate of Benny Draper was sealed two weeks before the wrap party, and the night after the OMPCE had backed Jackie Heller's proposals both to strip Benny of his plenipotentiary powers and to seek a new three-year agreement with the motion picture studios. It was a defeat that Benny could not afford to take without a response, especially considering his failure to take action after La Casa Nevada burned down. If he was a figure of fear to many in the Los Angeles community, Benny was still responsible to his masters in Chicago, who had an investment to protect, and in Benny a kind of colonial governor who kept his position as long as he was able to maintain order, and profitability. This Lilo Kusack implicitly understood, and so to a lesser extent did J. F. French, and certainly Morris Lefkowitz and Jimmy Riordan, men of business all. However satisfying Benny Draper might have thought it to take out Jacob King as the source of all his difficulties, and however many exquisite tortures he might be contemplating for him, the powers in Chicago would never take kindly to any homicide that focused the glare of attention so directly on Benny, and ultimately onto themselves. But move he thought he must, if only to reestablish his reputation for retribution, and if he could not move against Jacob King, there appeared to be no cordon sanitaire around Eddie Binhoff. He came within the rules of engagement. The man watching Jacob King's back had no one in turn watching his back. Hitting Eddie Binhoff would be a statement. A discreet announcement that Benny Draper was still a player.

◄◊►

"They were amateurs, jerk-off artists," Eddie Binhoff said contemptuously of the two men with shotguns who tried to kill him outside the underground garage of the residential hotel in Hollywood where he had taken an efficiency apartment. It was after midnight when he had pulled up to the garage. His gun was out of its holster and resting in his lap, just in case, considering the situation. He honked his horn, saw the small window in the door open and close as he was checked out, and then the main door slide up on its rollers. But instead of the attendant usually on duty, there were the two men with shotguns who moved toward the Studebaker Jacob King had given him from his own motor pool of four cars, blasting away at the windshield. Eddie Binhoff resisted the temptation to duck and shoot, and instead hunched low over the wheel and floored the accelerator. The Studebaker rocketed forward, sending the two men flying like ten pins. One lost his shotgun and ran, while the other took off, skipping and jumping on a bad leg as the Studebaker crashed into the far wall of the garage, and began spitting rust-colored water from its radiator. Gun in hand, Eddie Binhoff rolled out of the car, into the patchy grease on the floor, but the men were gone. His suit was covered with muck, there were pieces of windshield glass in his forehead and eyelid, and his chest hurt from where he had been pinned by the steering wheel. He picked the shotgun up from the driveway and closed the garage door.

"Jerk-off artists," Eddie Binhoff repeated the next morning in the catwalk office occupied by Jacob King at the Acme Linen Supply Company, one of the businesses that Morris Lefkowitz owned in Los Angeles and that Jacob ostensibly ran. The noise outside the glassed-in aerie was deafening. A huge dryer tumbled table linens and an industrial pressing machine belched steam. On the floor shirtless workers yelled back and forth in Spanish. "They didn't know what they were doing. You want to do the job right, they get you inside the garage, they close the door, then they drop you when you're getting out of the car. A guy getting out of a car is helpless. You leave him by the front door, blood all over his suit, it makes a hell of picture in the paper the next morning."

"You're an artist, Eddie," said Jacob King, who had left Philly Wexler by a mailbox in Washington Heights, making for a hell of a picture in the *Daily News* the next morning. "What'd you tell the people in the building about your car?"

"I said I had a load on, the attendant wasn't there, I opened the door, and when I got back in the car, the chick with me, she put her foot on the accelerator, she was drunker than I was, I had to get her home, she was somebody's wife, and that somebody wasn't me. They love hearing that kind of shit."

"What about the attendant, the one who's usually there?"

"You know, I already thought about him, Jake, I thought about him a lot, even without your help."

Jacob King smiled.

"His lucky night. His wife had a baby. Twelve-oh-one A.M., Queen of Angels Hospital, she went into labor at seven, he got the night off at seven-thirty, and yes, I did check out the hospital, Rosario Ynez Guttierez Cano, eight pounds thirteen ounces, the father was there."

"Or you would've whacked him."

Eddie Binhoff shrugged. Murder was his profession and he did not make jokes about it. "So we got a problem," he said after a moment. He squeezed his cheek and pulled a shard of glass from it. "The problem's name is Benny Draper. And the problem's not going to go away until we take care of it."

"Not by you, Eddie, and not by me."

"Then who? The people in this town, they think you do a garage hit outside the garage. It's the fucking sun is the reason, it bakes the brains out."

Jacob King paused. "You remember Schlomo Buchalter?"

"Round-trip Buchalter, right? He started out with Morris. Christ, who didn't start out with Morris? Jack the Ripper, maybe."

"You wanted to take somebody out, it was the price of the hit, plus two round-trip tickets to Havana or someplace warm for Schlomo and a chick. You saw Schlomo at Hialeah, you knew somebody'd just been iced someplace cold."

"Used to be Benny Draper's shooter. I thought he was dead."

"Dying. Cancer of the bowels. Poor bastard weighs about

thirty-five pounds. He lives with his sister someplace out in the Valley."

"What valley?"

"The San Fernando Valley, Eddie. If you're going to live out here, you got to learn the geography. Think of it this way, the Valley's like Queens, you know Queens, right?"

"Woodhaven Boulevard I know," Eddie Binhoff said. He had done someone once on Woodhaven Boulevard, but it was so long ago he couldn't remember the someone's name, only the name of the street where he had done him, and how. The someone was in a gin mill on Woodhaven Boulevard and had left his car outside. A Hudson Terraplane. Eddie Binhoff remembered that, too. And he remembered it was raining. It was only the someone's name he had trouble with. He had lifted up the Hudson's hood, and yanked out its battery cables. Then he waited down the block in his own car. A long wait, but finally the someone comes out of the gin mill with a pretty good load on, and of course he can't start his Terraplane. Eddie Binhoff drove over, got out of his car, and said, I got some jumper cables, you want some help? And the someone said sure. The last thing he expected to find on Woodhaven Boulevard at three o'clock in the morning in the rain was someone with a set of jumper cables, wanted to help him out. It made the someone feel good and not nervous. Exactly the way Eddie had planned it. Then he pulled out his piece, and said, Actually, I don't have no jumper cables, and proceeded to shoot the someone a lot. Rocco, that was the someone's name. Rocco . . . Rocco . . . Rocco . . . Mingus. Remembering Rocco Mingus's name made Eddie Binhoff feel better. Like he wasn't getting old. "So he lives in this valley, Schlomo. You checked him out already, didn't you, Jake?"

"I think we go see Schlomo," Jacob King said.

-◄◊►-

Schlomo Buchalter was sitting in a wheelchair in the sitting room of his small but immaculate Pacoima bungalow, a lap robe over his knees. His sister, Ada Buchalter, sorrow etched into her long plain face, hovered nearby, constantly wiping her hands on her apron. "It won't be long now," she mouthed to Jacob King, who had told her his name was Shimon Solomon, from the Temple Emmanu-El in Van Nuys. Both Jacob and Eddie Binhoff, who Jacob introduced as Leo Rivkin from Reseda, wore yarmulkes. What he and Leo wished to do, Shimon Solomon told Ada Buchalter, was to take Mr. Buchalter out for a ride, let him get a little sun, see some sights outside the home, they understood he rarely left the house, and such a pleasant house it was, too, Mr. Buchalter was fortunate to have so devoted a sister. They were not in the burial plot business, they assured her, they understood that the plans for his funeral service and interment had already been provided for by his layaway plan, and they would of course be available to fill out a minyan if the need arose. It was just they had both once heard the famous Rabbi Baruch Tyger say, when he was the guest rebbe at Temple Emmanu-El, that the younger healthier members of any congregation owed an obligation toward the elderly, the frail, and the less fortunate, a reaching out. As proof of their good intentions Jacob King gave Ada Buchalter the autographed copy of *The Collected Sermons of Barry Tyger* that he had bought with a fifty-dollar bill, keep the change, from the pile on sale in the lobby at the "I Am an American" dinner at the Ambassador Hotel.

◄○►

They parked on a hill overlooking the Pacoima Reservoir. Eddie Binhoff retrieved the wheelchair from the trunk of Jacob King's Cadillac convertible, then lifted Schlomo Buchalter from the open back seat, and placed him gently in it. Jacob pushed Schlomo to the top of the hill.

"I pushed a guy off a hill once," Schlomo Buchalter said, staring down past the scrub at the placid waters of the reservoir. His voice was raspy and weak. "A very high hill. Outside Salt Lake City, in a state called Utah. You know what I remember about Utah? They shoot you there, you get the death penalty. That's the only state they do that in. I done people in states where they got the electric chair, where they got the gas chamber, and where they hang you. I was very interested in Utah. What they do is, they tie you to a chair, they put a blindfold on and then a target over your heart and then they shoot you. You're dead before you ever hear the shot. I like that. You got to go, then I think I like the way they do it in Utah best."

The effort had weakened him, and his head rested on his chest. "The doctors, they say I got six weeks at the outside," Schlomo Buchalter said. "I worry about Ada. She takes good care of me. I shit in a bag and Ada cleans it out, she never complains. The house is paid for and I got a little laid away for her, but not much."

"Ada know how you made your living?" Eddie Binhoff said.

"Ada just wishes I got married," Schlomo Buchalter said, not answering the question. "So I had kids or something she could take care of after I'm gone. That's what Ada does best, she takes care of people. You take a look at Ada, you know why she never got married. A telephone pole is better-looking than she is."

"I got a proposition, Schlomo," Jacob King said.

"I didn't think you brung me all the way out here just to show me the reservoir, Jake. I see you and Eddie come into the house wearing your yarmulkes, I think I'm going to get whacked, and Ada's going to see it, I was wondering what I did to deserve that."

"Benny Draper," Jacob King said.

"You been giving him a lot of trouble, I hear. And I hear he used two fairies who tried to take you out, Eddie."

Eddie Binhoff grunted.

"Benny's a putz," Schlomo Buchalter said presently. "I did a guy for him, some guy giving him static in the union, testified against him wearing a paper bag over his head. Benny says his name was Stivic, and he wanted me to hurt him. The claw hammer was his idea. I used a piano wire in my time, a regular screwdriver, a Phillips screwdriver, a baseball bat, never a claw hammer until this time. Then Benny says put a bag over his head. I said fuck that, you put a bag over his head, everyone knows it's Benny Draper that placed the order, they're going to come after

Benny then, and Benny's going to give me up, bet on it. I am very careful when I do somebody, that's why it's the cancer that's going to get me, I'm going to die in bed. So I do the guy, and drop him in the desert, but I don't put no bag over his head. The deal was five large and two tickets on the Lurline to Honolulu, me and Ada, it would give her something to remember. Benny comes up with three large and no tickets on the Lurline, he says I got cancer, what do I want to go Hawaii for, none of the pineapple whores'll want to fuck some guy who shits in a bag."

The unmistakable voice of Benny Draper. No one could ever make it up.

"Then you can't get close to him?"

"Sure I can get close to him. I don't get mad, I get even. I say, you're right, Benny, you wanted a bag over his head, I don't give you no bag, I don't deserve no tickets on the Lurline, my motto was always if you do a guy, follow orders, do him right, and this time I fucked up. You ought to retire, he says, and I liked that, a guy in this line of work doesn't get to retire much, so I retire. I see Benny, though. He goes to this joint in East L.A., Obregon's, it's called, every Monday night, and I go there sometimes, I like the Mexican food, and Benny, he does, too, when he sees me, he picks up the tab and sticks a fifty in my pocket, like I'm some kind of charity ease. So, Jake, you want me to do Benny, I'll be glad to do Benny, if that's what you have in mind.

"Ada will piss and moan, and I'll say I'm dying, let me do what I want, and what I want is some Mexican food, it gives you gas, Ada, I don't like to watch someone eat Mexican it gives gas to. I'll take a cab to Obregon's, the cabdriver pushes me inside, I always have a table in the back by the kitchen, force of habit, I like to see who comes in, who goes out, and I can always scram out through the kitchen, I see something I don't like. They know me there, they place my wheelchair so I can see all the action in the joint, and when Benny comes in, he'll come over, he'll tell Mama Obregon it's on him, and when he sticks the fifty in my pocket and leans over and pats me on the cheek, that's when I'll do him, I'll have the piece in my lap under the blanket, I'll get him right under the jaw, it'll take off the back of his head."

"You got a piece?" Eddie Binhoff said.

"You got a dick?" Schlomo Buchalter answered.

"Is it clean?"

"If what I think is going to happen does happen, it don't matter if it's clean or dirty, does it?"

"You know you got to get him with the first shot," Jacob King said. "His people'll take you out before you can get a second one in."

"I figure it'll be like Utah, Jake, better than in a hospital with tubes up your nose, and one of those catheter things in your dick," Schlomo Buchalter said. "I got some numbers in mind."

Schlomo Buchalter said he wanted ten thousand dollars, in advance and all cash, small bills, and he would put the money in a safety deposit box he had taken out in Ada Buchalter's name at Federal Savings, the Glendale Branch. Ada was also to receive two round-trip tickets to Hawaii on the Lurline. "Is Morris still in the fur business, Jake?"

Jacob King nodded.

"She always wanted a beaver coat, Ada. I don't know why, it's hotter than shit out here, but I see her looking at the *Life* magazine, at the model wearing a beaver coat, and I think she'd like one."

"That shouldn't be a problem, Schlomo."

"I think I better go home now, Jake. It's been a nice day, a nice outing, but I'm getting a little tired."

Schlomo Buchalter was silent as Jacob King wheeled him back down the hill to the parked convertible. Eddie Binhoff picked him up from the wheelchair and deposited him in the back seat, then replaced the chair in the trunk.

"How about a week from Monday?" Jacob King said. "I was thinking I'd go out and pay the *Valiant* a visit that night."

Schlomo Buchalter's head bobbed up and down. "One thing

I should ask you," he said as Jacob started the engine. "What happens if I lose my nerve?"

·"Eddie'll whack you," Jacob King said without hesitating. "If you're in the hospital with tubes up your nose, then he'll whack you there."

"That's what I thought," Schlomo Buchalter said. "I always liked to know all the angles." He seemed to be counting the utility poles as they sped by. "You remember Leo Spain, Jake? Got his tongue cut out in a whorehouse on Fort Washington Avenue?"

Jacob King shook his head.

"You always got credit for that one, but it was me."

DISPUTE OVER MONEY LEADS TO MOB SHOOTOUT

LOS ANGELES—(AP)—The bloodbath shootout Monday in an East Los Angeles restaurant that led to the deaths of labor leader Benjamin Draper and reputed Mob murderer Schlomo Buchalter was said to be the result of a dispute over money Draper had not paid to Buchalter for the alleged murder two years ago of Matthew Stivic, a dissident member of the Organization of Motion Picture Craft Employees. Buchalter, who county medical examiners say was terminally ill with . . .

XI

"OF COURSE I READ the newspapers, Jimmy," Morris Lefkowitz said into the telephone, folding that afternoon's *Journal-American* over to a photograph of Jacob King, in black tie, entering the Ambassador Hotel for the Academy Awards dinner arm in arm with Blue Tyler, who was to present the best-picture Oscar. A dark-haired model in a floor-length red fox coat pirouetted before his desk, swishing the fur as if it were a tail. "And I see Jacob with this Blue or this Green. What kind of name is that for a girl?"

"It's not a name like Lillian is the kind of name it's not, Morris," Jimmy Riordan said. "I go to see Lillian in Bay Ridge Tuesday, and when I'm there, Matthew comes in—"

"Who is this Matthew?" Morris Lefkowitz said. The model began untying the belt on the coat.

"Matthew is your godson, Morris. Matthew King, son of Jacob King and the former Lillian Aronow . . ."

Morris Lefkowitz was silent. He had little appreciation of sarcasm, and none when it was directed at him.

". . . and Matthew asks his mother if they were millionaires," Jimmy Riordan said, instantly translating the disapproval in Morris's silence and reducing the level of his sarcasm. He

hated having to invoke Lillian King. She was a chronic com-
plainer, but via Lillian perhaps he could rein in Jacob. "And
Lillian says why do you say that. And Matthew says because the
Mirror is calling Papa a millionaire sportsman. And he shows
Lillian the picture of Jake with this girl."

"Jimmy, stop talking like a priest," Morris Lefkowitz said, as
he switched the telephone from one ear to the other. "So he's
sticking it into this Blue or Green, he also stuck it into Benny
Draper. Next week he breaks ground in Nevada. And that is the
point, that is why we sent Jacob out there in the first place."

"Agreed, Morris, agreed. But he's calling this place Playland,
he never checked that out with us." A pause. "Morris." Jimmy
Riordan tried to control his voice. It was beginning to rise, as it
never had before when he talked to Morris Lefkowitz. It was
Lilo Kusack who had let him know what Jacob was proposing to
call the new hotel in the desert. Lilo Kusack who called Jimmy
Riordan every day or so now. Jimmy did not trust Lilo Kusack
any more than Lilo trusted him, but with Benny Draper's timely
demise and with Benny's successor, Jackie Heller, indebted
both to Morris Lefkowitz and to Jacob King, Lilo Kusack did
not have too many ears into which he could whisper anymore,
and whispering was his key to the kingdom. "It's like he's a lone
wolf out there. He could've used Lilo's plans for La Casa Nevada, we could've worked it out, Lilo was willing, but no, Jake's
got to get a new architect, he says Lilo's hotel was going to look
like Attica, you don't want a hotel looks like a pen, he says, you
want a joint people will feel comfortable in. Well, you don't call
a place in the goddamn desert Playland either." Lilo Kusack's
opinion, passed on to Morris as Jimmy's own. "You call it Eldo-
rado. You call it Rancho Diablo, the Pyramid. Playland sounds
like Seventh Avenue."

"I am Seventh Avenue, Jimmy," Morris Lefkowitz said. He
motioned the model to the side of his desk, then reached up
and finished untying her belt. "That's Jacob's little joke. He
knows I'd understand."

The model let the red fox fall from her shoulders. She was
naked underneath it.

"We will talk, Jimmy. Playland. I like the sound of that."

Morris Lefkowitz hung up the telephone and examined the naked young woman. "The secret of being a successful showroom model," he said, "is posture."

"Yes, Mr. Lefkowitz."

"You got to remember that. Posture."

"Yes, Mr. Lefkowitz."

"In fur, tits are secondary," Morris Lefkowitz said.

—◦—

"I talked to Morris," Jimmy Riordan said over the telephone to Jacob King in Los Angeles. "He likes the name you picked out for this place."

"Playland, Jimmy," Jacob King said. "Say it. It comes out easy, you won't choke on it. It'll grow on you."

Jacob's pushing, Jimmy Riordan thought. When there was no need to push. It was his history. Success in itself was never enough to satisfy him. He always wanted more. Toward those he conquered Jacob was never benevolent. That yesterday's enemy could be tomorrow's ally was a concept he could never comprehend. Take no prisoners, sack the villages, kill the women and children. These were the rules under which he operated. It was time to let him know the new guidelines. "I've been talking to Lilo," Jimmy Riordan said.

Jacob took his time answering. "You been talking to who?"

"Lilo," Jimmy Riordan said. "Morris asked me to." A minor prevarication. In fact it was he who had suggested it to Morris, when Morris was enjoying the fruits of Jacob's triumphs in an almost unseemly way. He could read Morris, he had spent most of a professional lifetime reading Morris Lefkowitz, and Morris was what Jacob was not, benign in victory. "Lilo and I reached an understanding—"

"Lilo and you? You making Morris's decisions for him now, you telling me Morris is an old man, can't think for himself anymore?"

"Lilo and Morris," Jimmy Riordan said quietly, correcting himself. It was a tactical mistake of the kind he rarely made. In the background he could hear a rhythmic sound that was familiar but that he could not quite place. "Morris is cutting Lilo and his people out there in. You run the operation, California takes part of it."

How large that part was, and the form it was to take, Jimmy Riordan deliberately neglected to say. The concept of oversight, insofar as it meant control over the purse, was not one to which Jacob King would ever agree willingly. He would accept, if grudgingly, Morris Lefkowitz controlling the purse, but he had a history with Morris, a history that had added significantly to Morris's power and profit. Oversight from Lilo Kusack was something else again, even though Lilo would only have the power to recommend, not the power to order. Whatever fealty Jacob King felt he owed Morris Lefkowitz, whatever his sense of obligation to him, he would never accept orders from Lilo. Even Jimmy recognized that, and he hoped Lilo did, too. Jimmy liked Jacob, even trusted him to a point, as a staff officer must trust a commander in the field or fire him, and he neither liked nor trusted Lilo Kusack. Yet he wondered, if push came to shove, whether he would back Jacob or Lilo, then banished the thought as idle speculation. Speculation, however, and thinking the unthinkable, were what Morris Lefkowitz paid him handsomely for. Morris would as always be the court of last resort, and he retained the absolute power to overrule Lilo, and anyone else in the deal.

"Partners," Jimmy Riordan continued. "No more rough stuff. All we ever wanted out there was a deal. Now we've got the deal we wanted in the first place."

The deal we should have had in the first place was what Jimmy Riordan actually meant, and Jacob did not miss the implicit rebuke. "Rough stuff got us this far."

He was like a victorious general who, having won a war, discovered he had no aptitude for peace, Jimmy Riordan thought. "Perhaps," he said.

"Fuck perhaps," Jacob said, "it's not going to work, this partners thing."

"It's your job to make it work, Jake." The quietness of Jimmy Riordan's voice did not mask the warning in his words.

"There's no way I go to Lilo with my hat in my hand," Jacob said truculently. Or if he did, there would be a gun in his other hand.

"Of course not." The smooth Jimmy Riordan. "You have a free hand." He paused. "Within reason."

"What's within reason?"

"Morris decides." Two words that ended argument. Morris was like Moses, inventing commandments as he went along. Even sitting at Morris's right hand as he had these many years, Jimmy Riordan still did not fully comprehend how Morris Lefkowitz computed all the factors by which he arrived at a decision. "You know there's a built-in flexibility in every budget, Jake. For the unexpected contingency." Jimmy was careful not to define the extent of the flexibility, or what might be construed as an unexpected contingency. Give him something else to think about. "By the way, I'm coming out for the groundbreaking."

"It's a long fucking way to come just to see a steam shovel pick up some dirt," Jacob King said. But of course he knew why Jimmy Riordan was coming, and it did not improve his disposition. To dot the *i*s and cross the *t*s. Blessed are the peacemakers.

"Morris thinks a New York presence would be advantageous," Jimmy Riordan explained. A thought Jimmy had impressed on Morris. To let the locals know, and Jacob King as well, that for all his laurels, Jacob was just a consul, not a monarch. Jimmy could still hear the rhythmic banging, *thwonk, thwonk*, behind Jacob King. It offered an opportunity to change the subject. "What's that noise I keep hearing, Jake?"

"A ball," Jacob King said.

"Against a backboard?"

"Yes."

He had a sense that Jacob was being evasive. Even in middle age with a daily trim and a weekly manicure, Jimmy Riordan still had the soul of the prosecutor he had years before left Yorkville for Fordham to become. His ability to cross-examine once he smelled evasiveness or sensed a flawed argument, a failed excuse, was one of the things that made him so valuable to Morris

Lefkowitz. Another *thwonk,* and another. It was suddenly important to him to identify the sound positively, if only to keep his talents in shape. "Stickball?"

"No."

"Someone's playing catch?"

"Tennis," Jacob said after a moment.

"You play tennis?"

"I'm having a lesson."

—◇—

About the groundbreaking ceremony for Playland, there was little I could find on file in the newspaper microfilm rooms, and if Melba Mae Toolate's memories were vague, Arthur French's were opaque. Melba Mae remembered that it was boiling hot, and that Shelley Flynn was funny, he was wearing a midnight-blue tuxedo even though it was the middle of the day, but she could not recall anything he had said, it was, she said, the usual Shelley nightclub shit. She also remembered that it was the first time she had been to Las Vegas since Carole Lombard died. Arthur French had refused to drive over, one of his few acts of rebellion against his father, Arthur could be such a pill sometimes, Melba Mae said, but Arthur's story was that he was supervising Chuckie O'Hara's director's cut of *Red River Rosie* so that it could meet its release date. Melba remembered that Jacob King wore a new white suit, the color of milk, sewn up especially for the occasion by Eddie Schmidt, tailor to the stars, and that he had wanted to wear a black silk shirt and a white silk four-in-hand with it, but Rita Lewis, that cunt (Melba's words), said it made Jacob look like a gangster, it wasn't the image he was trying to project. The gossip columnist in the Hollywood *Reporter* itemed that Blue Tyler would attend the groundbreaking in the company of "mysterious Manhattan Hotel Investor Jacob King," and in his column Jimmy Fidler wrote, "Manhattan Hotel Investor Jacob King (the big bux behind new Nevada hotspot Playland, breaking ground today) is burning to branch into pic biz with his True Blue!!!!!" In the Los Angeles *Express,* there was a photo of Blue showing more leg and bum than the studio usually let photographers shoot, a shot that to J. F.

French's consternation went out over the wires, after which J. F. French fired the entire publicity department. The Las Vegas *Review-Journal* featured two full pages of Blue Tyler photographs and one picture, on page seven, of Clark County Supervisor Lyle Ledbetter digging up a shovelful of desert sand. Jacob King appeared in just a single photo, a group shot with Blue, Shelley Flynn (in a dinner jacket, as Melba had remembered), and Lyle Ledbetter, but the picture was cropped in such a way that only Jacob's white-sleeved left arm and a quarter of his face showed. In the caption he was identified as "Manhattan Hotel Investor Jacob King, who put together the financing for this new enterprise in association with L.A. Attorney Lilo Kusack."

Whose idea was "Hotel Investor?" I asked Melba Mae.

Chuckie's, Melba Mae said.

Well, yes, of course, it was my idea, Chuckie O'Hara said. I thought it had a certain panache. Like "actress-model" for hooker.

◄○►

"I see the sun, a great blistering orb," Sydney Allen said. "Space. Panorama. Kitsch. Giant earthmovers gouging out the landscape. Ecological murder in the service of corrupt mammon. Let your imagination run riot, Jack."

I refrained from saying that ecological murder was not the direction in which my imagination ran riot.

"One other thing. I want Jacob in that white suit with the black shirt and the white tie."

◄○►

EXT. PLAYLAND CONSTRUCTION SITE DAY

LYLE LEDBETTER
the Clark County supervisor, holding a shovel in his hands on a makeshift stage, is making a speech in the blinding midday sun.

LYLE LEDBETTER
I see Las Vegas as a city in its takeoff phase, an
unspoiled national resource . . .

It is the dialogue from his grand jury testimony when he recalled JACOB KING trying successfully to bribe him.

ANOTHER ANGLE—AN ARCHITECTURAL RENDERING
of Playland resting on an easel next to Lyle Ledbetter. It is a modernistic building surrounded by grass and palm trees, and shows tennis courts and swimming pools.

> LYLE LEDBETTER
> . . . a community with clean air, a decent place
> to raise a family . . .

ANGLE ON JACOB KING
He stands with Jimmy Riordan, Lilo Kusack, Rita Lewis, and Blue Tyler. The presence of Lilo Kusack and Jimmy Riordan, both wearing ties and silk suits, seals the armistice between the two factions.

ANOTHER ANGLE
Red ribbon surrounding the building site.

ANOTHER ANGLE
A sign that says:

> PLAYLAND
> WHERE THE FUTURE IS NOW

ANOTHER ANGLE
Earthmoving equipment in the distance ready to move in and begin work.

ANOTHER ANGLE
Reporters taking notes.

ANGLE ON BLUE TYLER
posing for photographers more intent on snapping her picture than Lyle Ledbetter's or Jacob King's. Blue wets her lips, arches

her neck, lifts her skirts, all the poses of a star doing a day's work.

ANOTHER ANGLE—SHELLEY FLYNN

in full evening dress—tuxedo, ruffled shirt, patent-leather pumps in spite of its being high noon. With a buck-and-wing, he bounces to stage center, elbows Leo Ledbetter aside, and takes the shovel from his hand.

> SHELLEY FLYNN
> Good evening, ladies and gentlemen, welcome to my first show here at Playland, what a beautiful gang you are . . .
> *(a beat)*
> So I'm early. That's how excited I am to be here . . .
> *(conspiratorially)*
> I also don't have another gig.
> *(into a routine)*
> Appearances are everything, right? Take a look at me. Pretend I'm a lifeguard. How far out would you go?
> *(as if hearing applause)*
> What an audience, jeez. What an audience. Listen up. Right here, on this spot, Jake King—Jake, take a bow—Jake is going to build the biggest goddamn hotel in the state of Nevada . . .

ANGLE ON JACOB KING

who acknowledges the smattering of applause.

ANGLE ON LILO KUSACK

> LILO KUSACK
> *(quietly)*
> *We* are going to build . . .

ANGLE ON JIMMY RIORDAN

who looks at Lilo but makes no response.

ANGLE ON JACOB KING

who winks almost imperceptibly at Rita Lewis.

> JACOB
>
> Opening night, Lilo. You and Rita. The honey-
> moon suite. On the house. And you know what
> else?

> RITA
>
> Don't tell me. Shelley Flynn in the big room.
> You're going to comp us.

ANGLE ON SHELLEY FLYNN

> SHELLEY FLYNN
> *(shoots his cuffs)*
> . . . you see sand now . . .
> *(shaking the shovel)*
> . . . but in six months you're going to see a
> fucking paradise, excuse my French. Swimming
> pools. Fountains. Tropical plants. Those big pink
> birds they got in Florida. Music. Hotshot sing-
> ers. Me, Shelley Flynn. Star of stage, screen, ra-
> dio, bar mitzvahs, I'll go to the opening of a
> door . . .
> *(milking imaginary applause)*
> Guys in tuxedos every night of the year, and I
> don't mean fucking headwaiters, or bandlead-
> ers . . .

LYLE LEDBETTER

seems slightly discomfited. This is not the churches-and-schools
line he had hoped Jacob King would take.

> SHELLEY FLYNN
> . . . all the broads are going to get out their
> diamond bracelets, they come here. Satin sheets,
> if you want them. Bathtubs you can swim in.
> Gold fixtures . . .

ANGLE ON LILO KUSACK

> LILO KUSACK
> *(sotto voce to Jimmy Riordan)*
> It's supposed to be a casino, not a fancy
> whorehouse.

ANGLE ON JIMMY RIORDAN
who again does not respond.

ANGLE ON JACOB KING
focusing on Shelley Flynn as if Lilo had not spoken.

> SHELLEY FLYNN
> . . . class games. Crap tables, sure, but baccarat . . .

ANGLE ON BLUE TYLER
now bored, stifles a yawn and looks at her watch. She flashes a
smile at Jacob King, then leans toward Lilo Kusack.

> BLUE TYLER
> *(whispering)*
> Lilo, my new contract. I want it in writing. No
> close-ups when I'm having my period. You can
> always tell.
> *(puffs out her cheeks)*
> I look like this.

LILO KUSACK
takes a leather notepad from his suit pocket, and with a gold
pencil jots down Blue's instructions.

SHELLEY FLYNN
wipes the sweat from his brow.

> SHELLEY FLYNN
> . . . behind those braided silk ropes they used to
> have in places like Europe . . .
> *(a beat)*
> Hey, I'm just wasting time . . .

(to Jackie Heller)
. . . Jackie, let's get those guys of yours working, time is money, time is money . . .

ANOTHER ANGLE
The earthmoving equipment moves toward the site, rolling
over the red ribbon, and then carving out great hunks of sand
from the desert.

ANGLE ON THE GROUP
all turning away except for

JACOB KING
who lingers, gazing at the site.

ANGLE ON JIMMY RIORDAN & LILO KUSACK
who look back at Jacob King. They look at each other word-
lessly, then get into their chauffeur-driven car for the ride back
to Los Angeles.

HOLD ON JACOB KING
as he removes the architect's rendering of Playland from the
easel.

DISSOLVE TO:

XII

MONTAGE:
It was Chuckie O'Hara who dubbed Jacob King The Great Gatzberg, and the name stuck, to Chuckie's initial dismay and horror, for it was accepted as sacred writ in the film community that Jacob did not suffer perceived slights with equanimity. In the past, it was whispered, bones had been broken for less, but because battery was not considered a viable social option for a guest member at Hillcrest, a member of the congregation at Barry Tyger's Temple Beth Israel, it was now said that husbands who uttered any public slur about Jacob King, his origins or his reputed profession, would be quietly cuckolded, their wives fucked up the ass as punishment. Although Rita Lewis and Lilo Kusack were not joined in matrimony, theirs was the example most commonly given, albeit sotto voce, since Lilo's documented capacity for retaliation—if only economic career-ending retaliation—was said to equal Jacob King's. Jacob, however, took Chuckie's remark as a compliment, a comment on the style and stylishness he was trying to affect, although I find it difficult to believe he had ever read or even heard of *Gatsby,* or seen the movie. Someone however must have told him about the book, probably Blue. She was an

avid, if primitive, reader, sliding her forefinger slowly along each line of type, her lips moving as she read, two habits that the teachers at Cosmo's Little Red Schoolhouse could never break her of, habits she still had when I met her as Melba Mae Toolate. She was less an autodidact than a seeker after romance, or, to be precise, romantic parts she thought she could play, Jane Eyre or Elizabeth Bennet, say, or best of all Joan of Arc, especially (according to Arthur French) if the Maid of Orleans could have a couple of love scenes. In her reading of *Gatsby*, Blue identified with Jordan Baker; in her opinion (and this too was via Arthur, and so open to question), Daisy Buchanan was "a cunt."

──◦──

They were gorgeous together, Chuckie O'Hara said. He was always buying her things. Emerald earrings. A diamond necklace. I remember the premiere of *Red River Rosie* at Grauman's. Real Hollywood stuff. The searchlights crisscrossing the sky, a big crowd in the bleachers. Blue being the star of the picture, her limo was the last to arrive. Moe had wanted to ride in the same car, but she said only Jake or she wasn't coming, and if Moe insisted on riding in her car, she'd tell Jimmy Fidler, who was doing the live radio feed, that she had cramps, and she would've done it, too, Moe knew that. Jake got out of the car first, and he was wearing tails. Nobody wore tails to an opening, but he could bring it off. He helped her out of the car, and they walked up the red carpet into the theater, Blue blowing kisses, the flashbulbs exploding. You remember what Nick Carraway said about Gatsby, that there was a romantic readiness about him that he had never found in anyone else? Well, that's what Jake had. Usually the stars slipped out of the theater after the houselights went down, but Blue always stayed, she just loved looking at herself on screen. There was a party afterward at Moe's, everyone was there, Elsa Maxwell and Cole Porter, Noel Coward, my date was Hedy Lamarr, if you can believe it, Moe didn't like guys to come with guys, except Noel, and I always thought Elsa was in drag. I liked Hedy, she was fun, she said,

Chuckie, I'm having my period, we can't do it. That huge fucking house of Moe's, three bands rotating so the music never stopped. Jake and Blue never seemed to leave the dance floor. It was as if they were alone out there, and everyone was watching them, but what I remember best was Lilo. His face was almost totally shrouded by cigar smoke, and he never took his eyes off them. It was scary.

◄○►

Chuckie again:
Jake and Blue would have these croquet luncheon parties every Saturday at the house on St. Pierre Road. For all the sports he tried to learn, croquet was the only one he was any good at, he used to love to slam your ball out of the way, as if he was trying to knock it into Ventura County or was paying back someone who'd done him wrong. There was a violence about it, about croquet, for God's sake, you got a sense that he was only truly master of his own fate in the world of violence. He'd play in these high-stakes games with Howard Hawks and Louis Jourdan and Mike Romanoff, Reggie Gardiner, people like that, all decked out in his white flannel slacks, and he seemed to be surrounded by this aura of mystery that they didn't have, a distance. It was as if he knew everyone was talking about him, and they were a little afraid of him. He liked that. He was a celebrity in the kingdom of celebrity, and nobody is more fascinated by a celebrity than another celebrity.

◄○►

Still Chuckie:
Jake and I always got along. I never knew exactly why. He didn't like fairies, we made him nervous. I don't mean in any sexual sense, that sexually ambivalent psychocrap that's always dropped on studs. He just didn't understand men who liked to fuck other men. Maybe in the joint, he said, if it's a long stretch, but even then I think I pass. So I suppose our getting along had something to do with my losing my leg, it wasn't a fag thing to do. He asked me if it hurt, and I said no, I was in shock, I didn't even know the leg was gone until I woke up on the hospital

ship, and then he asked if I thought I was going to die, and I said yes, and he said did that make you scared, and I said I couldn't remember, but probably, yes, I was scared the whole time I was on Peleliu. Both days. So why'd you do it then, he said, you could've gotten out of it. As if I was stupid not to. He meant because I was queer, not because I'd been a Communist. God, I didn't tell anybody that. That was around the time Alan Shay committed suicide after testifying, and all us old Commies were scared to death. Anyway I didn't have an answer. It was as if he was trying to find out how his victims must have felt, those twenty or thirty people he was supposed to have murdered. Or maybe he thought it was going to happen to him one day, and he wanted to know how to behave, or how he should behave, he certainly would like to behave as well as this fairy movie director.

◄◌►

Meta liked to say—

Meta?

This girlfriend I had at the studio school, Melba Mae Toolate said. She wasn't in the business.

And she said what?

Meta said that dancing is a vertical expression of a horizontal desire, you ever hear that?

I heard that.

Well, Jacob was the best dancer I ever knew, outside of Walker Franklin, he made dancing like balling, you danced with him you couldn't wait to ball after. You'd think someone who was such a good dancer would be athletic, but he wasn't. Arthur could hardly do the two-step, but he was a good athlete, and this drove Jacob crazy. He thought if he bought all the right clothes, that was all he needed. Arthur rode, so he had to ride too. He had jodhpurs made and a hacking jacket, and he bought a polo helmet and some mallets, and he even had this artist guy painting a portrait of him in the jodhpurs and laced-up knee boots, he was going to give it to me as a present, but I saw it, and I laughed, big mistake, Jacob didn't like people laughing at him.

What'd he do?

He fired the painter, said he didn't know how to paint worth a shit.

What happened to the portrait?

It ended up over at Playland.

Unfinished?

Yeah.

What happened to it after . . .

Listen, I don't know. Jesus, you ask a lot of fucking questions, it's none of your fucking business.

Okay.

How about topping off my drink?

You sure?

What're you, my fucking keeper?

(I opened another half pint of vodka and splashed some into her glass. She took a swallow, then a second. In the freezer, I found a frozen macaroni-and-cheese dinner, popped it into the microwave, and set the timer. By then her mood had lightened.)

The first time he got up on a horse, the horse threw him, and he took out his gun, I thought he was going to shoot it.

Really?

(A cryptic smile. In other words, it was a better story with the gun. Even in Hamtramck, she hadn't lost the knack of juicing a scene.) He tried tennis, too, right?

All he could do was hit the ball hard, when he didn't miss it. But I could beat him, and that was too much for him. I'd say to him, Jacob, you've got to set your feet like this, and you've got to be ready to move toward the add court or toward the let court, and he'd say, okay, okay, let's do it, and I'd slam one by him. One day he flung his racket away, and he says you know what kind of game tennis is, and I said what kind of game is it. And he said it's the kind of game Arthur plays, I bet he's really good at it. And I said Arthur played in college. And he turns me around right there on the court, puts his hand up under my shirt over my boob, and he says, well, tell me something, did Arthur play this in college, was he as good at this as I am? So he took lessons every day, not from some club pro at Hillcrest, but from Lanny Todd, he was in the semifinals at Wimbledon in 1936, on our own court, because he didn't want anyone to see how bad he was. He'd practice and he'd practice, he willed himself into being a tennis player good enough to beat me. He liked beating me, it was as if his life depended on it. Finally I said to him you play like a fucking gangster, and he said no, I played like a gangster when you were beating me. And then he said if I'm a gangster, what does that make you. And I said a gangster's moll.

What else did you do?

We fucked a lot. All the time, actually. I gave him a locket from Tiffany's once. A silver locket. With his initials and my initials on it. I put a couple of my pussy hairs in it.

(I nodded, and my absence of response seemed to make her rethink what she had just said.)

Listen, just say I put a picture of me in it. Don't mention the pussy hairs. I was only kidding anyway. We kidded a lot. And gave each other lots of presents. With him it was always jewelry, you know, diamonds and shit. I remember a pair of emerald earrings. I didn't tell him, but I had copies made, and then cashed in the real things. You see, I was always afraid I was going to be without money one day, broke, like I am now, and I wanted to have some stashed away.

Did he ever find out?

(She waited a moment.) Yes.

How?

Why the fuck do you have to know that?

(I did not reply. For a moment or so, neither one of us said a word. The buzzer on the microwave went off, and I removed the macaroni and cheese. It was so hot, I dropped it on the floor. My clumsiness had a soothing effect on her. As I was cleaning up the mess, she began to talk again.)

He brought them in to get insured, and the insurance guy said they were paste.

What'd he do?

I was at the studio, and I came home, and there was all this jewelry on the living-room floor. He didn't say a word at first, he just got up and stamped it all under his feet, crushing it all to shit, and then he began to scream, if you wanted money, you just had to ask me for it, and I began screaming back at him, I threw a shoe at him, I think, and I said I never asked anybody for anything, and I'm not going to start with some fucking gangster.

What happened?

We ended up fucking, that's how all our fights ended.

Did he hit you?

Never. Not once. I would've been out of there if he had. The funny thing is, we were having all these people to dinner that night, to see a picture, and we went through with it as if nothing had happened. You got to understand about Jacob, he wanted to know everybody. He'd say let's have a few people in for dinner next week. And he already had a list made out. Eddie G. Robinson, he'd say, Ida Lupino, Linda Darnell, Arthur, I want to make a tennis date with Arthur sometime, Marvin Le-Roy.

Mervyn LeRoy, I'd say.

Okay, so it's Mervyn LeRoy, he'd say. Chuckie, too.

And I'd say, You can't have both Mervyn and Chuckie.

Why not? he wanted to know.

They don't like each other.

Then fuck Marvin LeRoy, he said.

Mervyn, I said again.

You know the money in that safe upstairs? he said. I'll bet it all he was born Marvin. You want to bet.

No, I said. I'd seen him bet. Once when he was playing cards and I was watching behind him, he reached up and put his hand between my legs, then raised ten thousand. One weekend he took a hundred sixty-five thousand off Moe French. The next weekend he lost it back, and ten grand more. I said bad cards? And he just smiled.

Meaning he let Mr. French win?

Meaning he smiled.

Playland was under construction by now, I said.

Yes.

Did he spend much time in Nevada?

He had this guy Jackie in charge over there. Jacob would talk to him every day, sometimes two or three times a day.

But he didn't go over much?

Not at first, no. But he wanted the place finished so he could open up New Year's Eve. And there were a lot of shortages. Wartime regulations or something. And he'd start yelling into the phone, what do you mean wartime regulations, the war's over two years, for Christ's sake, don't give me shortages, Jackie . . .

Where was he when this conversation was taking place? Out by the pool? At the tennis court?

This was why I remember, it's so cute. He was getting fitted for the tails he wore to the *Red River Rosie* premiere, he had all the measurements taken at the house, he had a three-way mirror in his dressing room, and the tailor was saying, you dress left or dress right, that meant what side of the pants did he want his balls to hang on . . .

I nodded.

And Jacob would be screaming we need copper, we need pipe, lumber, cement, all the shit it took to build a hotel, and at the same time he'd be saying to the tailor, I think the crotch is too low, and this guy Jackie thought Jacob was talking about his crotch, and Jacob said, no, no, Jackie, pay what you got to pay, pay black market you got to, who do you think I am, Cardinal Spellman, I'm going to worry about that? Who was Cardinal Spellman anyway?

The Catholic bishop of New York.

What'd he have to do with it?

It was just a saying.

He have any money in it?

I don't think so.

Oh. I read in a magazine that they had all this real estate, the Catholics. So I thought he might have had a piece of Playland.

(It was something I truly wanted to believe: Francis Cardinal

Spellman and Morris "The Furrier" Lefkowitz in a joint venture.) Could be.

Anyway. Jacob said he'd settle with those guys later. The guys who were jacking up the prices, I guess.

What do you think he meant by settling with them?

That he'd hurt them.

(She seemed to accept without question that to cross Jacob King would be to incur physical retribution.) Was there ever any time you were with him, I asked carefully, when you were afraid?

Once, she said after a moment.

What happened?

We were watching a picture at the house. That's what we'd do nights we didn't go out. Woodson would serve us dinner on a tray in the screening room, and I'd make some popcorn, it was the only thing I knew how to cook. Jacob liked to watch old gangster movies . . .

Really?

Yes, and Mr. French had found an early one Bogie had made . . .

◄◦►

"I thought it was great," Blue Tyler said when the lights came up. She was stretched out on a couch, her head resting in Jacob King's lap. "I love Bogie's lisp, it's sexy."

Jacob took a handful of popcorn and dropped a piece in her mouth.

Blue yawned, and then seemed to realize Jacob had not replied. "You got nothing to say?"

He tried to drop another piece of popcorn into her mouth, but Blue turned her face away and it fell to the floor. Suddenly she rose from his lap and stared belligerently down at him.

"Well, what'd you think?"

"I thought it was all right."

"Come on, Jacob, I want to know what you really thought."

"Then I really thought it was a piece of shit," Jacob King said quietly.

"You're a critic now?" Blue said defensively. The movies were her turf, and suddenly that turf was under attack from a civilian who didn't know how hard it was to make a film. It was so easy to be critical, it always made her furious.

"Okay, then I thought it was great."

"No, I want to know what you didn't like, Mr. Bosley Big Deal Fucking Crowther."

"Who's he?"

"He's the critic for *The New York Times*. You don't know anything, do you?"

"I know a couple of things."

"Like what?"

From the projection room, the projectionist said good night, he would see them next week.

"Like what?" Blue repeated.

Jacob slapped his hands together, wiping away the popcorn crumbs. "Like the scene in the car," he said at last. "The one where Bogie takes the guy out. He just pulls out his piece and starts blasting."

"And that's not how you do it."

"No, that's not the way you do it."

"Well, how do you do it then?"

"Look, it's not important . . ."

Blue was insistent. All her life she had gotten her way, all her life every caprice was satisfied, all her life there had been legions of retainers at her beck and call to do what she wanted done, however trivial or mean, and she was not about to be thwarted now. "No, I want to know."

Jacob stared at her for a moment without speaking. "The way I hear, you do it this way," he said finally, his voice so soft she had to strain to hear it. "You say, Let's go out and get a bite to eat. You get a driver, you put your boy in the front seat next to him, you sit in the back. Everything nice and easy. You talk about the ponies, you talk about the Giants, you talk about the fried calamari at Mario's, What you do is, you squeeze some extra lemon on it, it's a real treat. Let's go to Mario's, you say.

"Except you take the long way," he said after a pause. She

was staring at him, her eyes not blinking, and he wondered if he should continue. "The quiet way. The guy's still thinking about the calamari with the extra lemon, he can almost taste it, when bang, the guy in the back seat puts one under his ear. You open the door, you push the guy out. You wipe your piece clean, you drive over the Williamsburg Bridge, you drop the piece in the river, then you go looking for some of that fried calamari." He was still staring at Blue. "That's the way I hear it's done."

Blue shivered, then sat back down next to him on the couch. "You scare me sometimes. I'm not used to being scared."

"You want to leave?"

"No," Blue Tyler said.

XIII

MAURY AHEARNE checked in periodically from Detroit. Always after midnight California time. I had a feeling he had trouble sleeping. His calls were always collect. I wondered what he would have done if I did not accept the charges.

"I checked her old telephone records," he said one night.

"Is that legal?"

"You want to find her, or not?"

I did not reply.

"Nothing there," Maury Ahearne said after a moment. "Local calls, no long distance. The church, the drugstore, never even used up her message units."

"I suppose something will turn up." I was not hopeful.

"As a matter of fact." I should have known he would save the best for last. "Remember I told you once she wasn't on any kind of public assistance?"

"Yes."

"Well, I checked out the banks in Hamtramck. It took a while, but I found out she had a savings account at First Federal Trust. There seemed to have been regular payments into the account. On the first and the fifteenth of the month. Seven-fifty each time."

I did not wish to know the level of extortion and intimidation Maury Ahearne must have used to get that information. "Account in her name?"

"M. M. Toolate."

"How was the money deposited?"

"By wire. Money orders."

"Still coming?"

"Stopped the first due date after she left."

"How did she withdraw it?"

"Cash. A hundred bucks a pop. Four twenties, a ten, a five, three ones, and eight quarters. Never varied."

This from a woman who before she was twenty years old was making fifteen thousand dollars a week. "Anything still in the account?"

"Took everything out the day she left. Didn't close it, though. So she owes a finance charge. Five bucks a month. You got to keep a minimum amount."

"It's a start."

"I'll keep on top of it."

I was sure he would.

◄○►

"Arthur, she seemed to be on a kind of remittance," I said when I talked to him in Nogales on the telephone the next day.

"What do you mean?"

"She wasn't on welfare."

"What about Social Security?"

"She would have just been eligible. Anyway that doesn't explain the earlier years. It wasn't a lush life, but it was more than subsistence."

"You mentioned the shopping coupons she used at the grocer's." Arthur must be the last man in America to use the word grocer, as if there were still active family purveyors tugging their forelocks, By Appointment to J. F. French. "That was an inventive way to stretch her budget."

He had a gift for being insufferable. "Did you have her on some kind of annuity?"

"Why do you ask?"

"Because it seems there were twice-monthly payments into her savings account."

"You are a romantic, Jack," Arthur French said.

"Does that mean no?"

"It means I have a mare about to foal, and that's of more interest to me than some cock-and-bull speculation about a bag lady's annuity."

"Even if the bag lady is Blue Tyler."

"If it's a colt, I'll name him Broderick," Arthur French said as he hung up.

—◇—

Maury Ahearne again.

"I checked the bus schedules for the night that cabdriver took her to the bus station downtown. The dispatcher on the dog remembered a bag-lady type, not bad-looking, she only had one suitcase, and it was falling apart. Couldn't lift it, it was so heavy, she was pulling it behind her with a piece of rope or something."

Exactly what the cabdriver had told me.

"Got on a bus to Kansas City. I got hold of the driver finally, he remembered her, all right, she sat right behind him the whole trip. Wouldn't let him put the suitcase in the baggage compartment. Never slept. Humming songs the whole way. They get to K.C., he had to carry the suitcase for her, and it fell apart, spilled out all over the platform . . ."

"He remember what was in it?"

"Shit, mostly."

I had the feeling that Maury was holding out. "Anything that wasn't shit?"

He waited for a moment. "You remember that dirty picture of the little girl?"

The naked child in the strangely erotic old-fashioned photograph Maury Ahearne had stolen from Melba Mae Toolate's RV. The postcard-sized photograph Melba Mae had so many copies of. "Yes."

"She had a bunch of them in the bag. The driver tried to cop one, and she took a swing at him."

I got one suitcase, that's it. If it gets heavy, I just get rid of stuff. The story of my life.

If she was on the run, why would she bring those photographs. How did they fit into the story of her life?

"What happened then?"

"The cops came. I checked someone I know in the department down there. They wanted to book her for vag loitering, but she had over five hundred cash with her. And the bus driver didn't want to press charges. I showed him a copy of the picture. It was the same one."

"So it was her."

"Looks that way."

◄O►

The trail went cold after Kansas City.

It was then that I took the photograph of the unknown nude woman from my desk and pinned it on my bulletin board alongside the two pictures of Blue Tyler, the one in the conference at the William Morris Agency with her covey of managers, and the other of her dancing at Ciro's in the arms of Arthur French on the night of Jacob King's funeral.

XIV

W HEN DID IT BEGIN to go wrong? I asked Chuckie O'Hara.
I suppose I should have seen the signs when I went over
there, Chuckie said.

◄○►

Jake wanted me to see Playland, and he wanted Blue to come
over too, she'd only been there once since the groundbreaking.
She said it was boring, there was nothing to do, it was like
watching grass grow, except there was no grass. What Jake was
trying to do was run the building from L.A. He'd left that
gorilla of his in charge over there . . .

Eddie Binhoff . . .

Whatever his name was, and the construction guy . . .

Jackie Heller . . .

. . . and he thought that would do it, there was no real need
for him to be over there all the time, he wasn't going to take a
hammer and start banging nails, after all. He kept the architect's
drawing of the place in the living room at the house on St.
Pierre Road. It was the first thing you saw when you came in,
and he'd tell you how it was going, this was done, that was
done. It was as if he thought it was the Sistine Chapel, and he
was Michelangelo. He didn't really want to be in Vegas, there

was no place good enough to stay, and he was having too good a time being this millionaire sportsman he was supposed to be, with the croquet parties and the gin games at Hillcrest and the box at Santa Anita, and his picture in the paper all the time. So what he was going to do was rent a little plane and we'd all fly over, but after Carole Lombard died, you couldn't get Blue near a plane, so I drove over with her and Jake. It was a miserable drive, a lousy two-lane road, six or seven hours in the heat.

How was Blue?

A pain in the ass. She didn't like the sun, she thought it gave her freckles, like Kate Hepburn, for some reason she never liked Kate. And she hadn't figured out a way to tell Jake yet she was going back to work . . .

On *Broadway Babe*?

I was supposed to direct it, it was a nice story, the script needed some work, but I couldn't put my mind to it, because someone had told me that Irving Page, that no-talent little prick, had named me to the Committee in closed session.

He named two hundred ninety-one people.

Well, I didn't give a rat's ass about the other two hundred ninety, I was just worried about me. If you were named in closed session, you couldn't find anything out, they wouldn't tell you, you didn't want to check too closely, and you didn't want to get a lawyer yet, it might look suspicious, like you were guilty.

So you really didn't know if you'd been named or not until you got a subpoena?

Right.

Who told you you'd been named?

Reilly Holt. (Chuckie paused.) The screenwriter. (Another pause.) I suppose today you'd call him my significant other. Or more significant than the others, if truth be told.

And he was in the Party?

My dear, the Grand High Poo-bah. He hated my enlisting in the Marines after Pearl Harbor. He said I was a capitalist tool and was only going to be cannon fodder in capitalism's employ.

Reilly always did have a certain gift for prognostication. But then when I came back, he was absolutely besotted by my stump. I thought that was rather weird, even by my recherché standards.

How was Jacob on the trip over?

Sullen. And talkative. Too talkative. Dropping names. It's an art, name-dropping, and with Jake it was always a little too obvious.

Whose names?

Sam and Frances Goldwyn, for starters. He and Blue had gone up to Laurel Lane for a screening. Or, to be accurate, Frances had asked Blue, and she brought Jake without checking with them. Frances wasn't too happy about it, the Harrimans were the guests of honor, a pair of trophies is more like it. I bet it was the only time in his life Averell was in the same room with someone who'd made his bones. I was there that night, and Lilo was too, and Lilo said, Tell Ambassador Harriman who your biggest hit was, Jake. He could be a cunt, Lilo. Sam, of course, got Jake's name wrong, par for the course, he thought his name was King Jacob, and he told Jake he'd met King Carol of Romania and King Victor Emmanuel of Italy, but never a King Jacob, what country was he from? Jake just laughed, he'd been around long enough by then to do that when something went over his head. Anyway, Sam gave him the name of his tailor in London, Huntsman, and pretty soon Jake was going around saying he thought he'd buy some suits in London, he'd heard Huntsman was the best, Sam Goldwyn used him. He even brought it up again in the car on the way over, but then he got sullen when Blue said be sure to have the tailor make the jackets extra large so his holster wouldn't show. She was kidding, but there were some things Jake didn't think were funny anymore. I thought he was going to throw her out of the car right then and there, but just at that moment we came up over a rise, and there it was, in the distance, in the dusk, Playland.

The night work lights already were on, and the night crews were unloading materials, and there was this haze of dust as the trucks drove in and out, but you could see the shell of what would be the hotel and the casino beginning to take shape, beginning to look like the rendering in Jake's living room. The sun was going down behind us, and it was starting to get cold, but Jake wanted to pull off the road so we could stop a moment and look down at it. We got out, and Blue put her arm around his waist and burrowed up against his jacket. She was trying to make amends, I guess, for her smart mouth, until finally, without a word, he unbuttoned the coat and wrapped it around her. It was like she was part of him. I think it was the closest I ever saw them.

◄○►

"Who ordered the double crews, Jake?" Eddie Binhoff said. He was wearing a white shirt and a black string tie, the uniform he wore when he was dealing blackjack at the Bronco Club, except now his sleeves were rolled up, and in his hand he held a work schedule attached to a clipboard.

Jacob King gave no indication he had heard Eddie Binhoff's question. In the dirt and noise of the work site, he seemed peculiarly alone, surrounded by his own presence, oblivious to Eddie and to Chuckie and to Jackie Heller, who was poring over a blueprint outside the construction trailer, oblivious to everyone except Blue, who appeared to be playing hide-and-seek with herself in the framing of an adjoining structure, nature's child. Jacob rotated slowly, three hundred sixty degrees, taking in his new domain, missing nothing. He seemed transfixed, Chuckie would remember, as if Playland had opened for him a future he had never contemplated.

"You know what I like best about it?" Jacob King said. It was not clear to whom he was addressing the question. Perhaps only to himself.

"Jake," Eddie Binhoff persisted, scratching the purplish bruise of the tattooed tribute to Roxanne that curled around his forearm. "Do Lilo and Jimmy know about these extra crews?"

"What I like best about it is that it's mine," Jacob King said quietly to no one in particular, still ignoring Eddie Binhoff. The words chilled Chuckie O'Hara. Or was it just the cold desert night air that made him shiver? Then Jacob added a quick smile, the trance broken.

"Jake, I'm supposed to okay this," Eddie Binhoff said. "You say it's okay, I'll sign, we'll put them on the payroll. But I can't do it on my own."

"I don't check things out with Lilo, you know that, Eddie," Jacob said. He initialed the work order, then stepped through the rubble to a pile of marble Blue was now examining in the building where she had been playing. She pointed to the marble, then whispered something into Jacob's ear. He examined the billing slip, then whistled sharply through his teeth. "Hey, Jackie, what kind of fucking marble is this?"

Jackie Heller folded his blueprint and walked toward Jacob King. "Domestic, Jake." He looked at Blue, then at Chuckie, as if waiting for an introduction. "I showed you the samples," he continued when no introduction was forthcoming. "You said it was okay. Eddie, Jake said it was okay, right?"

Eddie Binhoff shrugged.

Again Blue whispered into Jacob's ear.

"Blue says domestic is shit," Jacob said. "I want Italian marble."

"You know what that costs, Jake . . ."

"Jackie, I don't give a fuck what it costs, I want Italian marble," Jacob said.

"Who the fuck's going to know it's Italian or not?" Jackie Heller said.

"I'm going to know, Jackie. Blue's going to know. Chuckie's going to know. My friends are coming to this joint . . ." Jacob paused, his face mottling with rage. He hefted a piece of marble, as if testing its capacity to be a weapon. "My friends are coming to this hotel"—a subtle change, *joint* to *hotel*, *joint* belonging to the old Jacob King, *hotel* to the new—"and my friends are the kind of people who know the difference between fucking domestic marble and fucking Italian marble, you fucking understand that?"

It was the first time Chuckie had ever seen the volcanic side of Jacob King's temper, the side people talked about when he was not around. He thought Jacob was going to brain Jackie Heller with the piece of marble, and Eddie Binhoff seemed to think so too, moving into Jacob's path to prevent an assault if one came.

Jackie Heller took a deep breath, not a man to give up easily. "It means we're going to have to reorder."

Jacob watched Blue as she wandered away into the framed corridor of the adjacent building. She grabbed an unfinished upright and began to swing around it as if it were a maypole. "Then reorder, Jackie."

"We don't just give this stuff here back, Jake. And it means another delay."

"Jackie," Jacob said, once more back in control, and in control even more dangerous, it seemed to Chuckie O'Hara, with every word a warning. "Just do what you're told."

"Jacob," Blue Tyler suddenly moaned. She was sucking on a finger.

"What's the matter, what happened?" Jacob King said.

"I have a splinter in my finger," Blue Tyler said, holding her finger out to him. "Kiss it away." She fell into the lascivious movie pout Chuckie O'Hara had shot so many times, tears gathering in the corner of her eyes. She always could cry on cue, fifteen takes with never a miss, and cry again in all the coverage. With most actresses he would say, Think of something sad, but never with Blue, if the script said cry, she cried. What dark thoughts brought her so easily to tears he did not wish to know. It was enough that she did it. "Then we'll do something dirty later that Chuckie doesn't know how to do." She paused. "At least with a girl."

Jackie Heller looked at Eddie Binhoff, whose face betrayed nothing. Jackie seemed at the point of apoplexy.

Jacob King squeezed Blue's finger until a spot of blood appeared, then removed the splinter.

"Jacob," Blue said, licking her finger, "you think this ceiling's maybe . . . a little low or something?"

Jacob looked up, then stood on his tiptoes, and finally jumped, pushing the flat of his hand against the ceiling.

It was too much for Jackie Heller. "That ceiling is here to stay."

"What do you mean, the ceiling's here to stay?" Jacob King said.

"I mean, the whole building is framed at this height," Jackie Heller said. "You didn't like how high the ceilings were, you could've changed the fucking plans. Two months ago is when you should've done it, not now, it's too fucking late, that's a fact."

"If you raise it another foot," Blue said serenely, "you wouldn't get that . . . that Brooklyn tenement feeling."

Jacob examined the ceiling once more. "Raise it another foot, Jackie."

"Jake." Jackie Heller was almost pleading. "You want me to tear the whole place down and start over, because she says it looks like a fucking tenement? In Brooklyn? Where she's never even fucking been?"

"I grew up in Brooklyn, Jackie. Tear it down. Do it right. It's simple."

"For your information," Blue said to Jackie Heller, "I did P.A.s for *Carioca Carnival* in Brooklyn. So there."

"P.A.s?" Jackie Heller said after a moment. "I don't know P.A.s."

"Personal appearances," Blue said. "No wonder the ceiling's so low, you don't know anything." She turned her back to Jackie Heller, and said, "Jacob, I'm hungry, can't we go get something to eat?"

◄◦►

It was during dinner downtown at the Bronco that Blue let slip she was going back to work. Jacob had wanted to go to the Fremont, but Blue refused, she said it was awful, and Jacob said how did she know, she had never been there, and Blue said she'd been there the night Carole Lombard's plane crashed, and it was a bad-luck place, and she wasn't going to eat there, if

Jacob wanted to eat there, he could eat there alone, she'd have dinner with Chuckie.

"Chuckie," Blue said over her shrimp cocktail, "the new script doesn't work, have Moe put that fat writer on it, Sonya whatever her name is."

"What new script?" Jacob King said.

Blue looked at Chuckie, then at Jacob. "Arthur's sent me a script. I mean, I haven't even really read it yet.

"All the way through," she added evasively when she sensed her denial was not playing. "I just know the story. I mean, this could be the crossover picture." She was talking fast now. "This could be where I grow up. So when I'm thirty-five years old, like you are—"

"You going to direct it, Chuckie?"

Chuckie sliced his steak and nodded.

"Maybe I can produce it, then," Jacob King said suddenly. That Blue had not told him about the new script now seemed secondary. "When the hotel's finished, I'm thinking of branching out. Into new areas. I'd like to produce, I think I'd be good at it."

"Jacob, you don't even know the story."

"So tell me the story."

"Well, in it I play this musical comedy star, see, queen of Broadway, everybody claps when I walk into Sardi's, blah blah, and I fall in love with a big-time mobster, see, and there's this great scene when I'm in my dressing room, opening night, flowers, telegrams, blah blah, and my maid—who loves me like a mother, black-mammy Hattie McDaniel type—she tells me he's been killed. Mob shoot-out. Big tragedy. Love-of-my-life-type thing. Camera comes in close on me, putting on my makeup—"

"No close-up if you're having your period," Chuckie O'Hara said lightly, watching Jacob's face.

"—and what happens is, I go on with the show," Blue said, pressing on. "Triumph. Great reviews. 'Last night on the stage of the Belasco Theater a legend was born,' et cetera. And only

I know the price I paid. I live with the tragedy. Do you love it?"

"It needs work," Chuckie said.

"Jacob, aren't you going to tell me what you think?"

"You lost me after 'he gets killed,'" Jacob King said.

◄◦►

The announcement that Blue was to star in *Broadway Babe* was big news in the trade papers. BLUE TYLER SET FOR *BROADWAY BABE*, *BROADWAY BABE* MARKS CAREER SHIFT FOR BLUE, and BLUE TYLER—YESTERDAY'S BABY, TOMORROW'S BABE were three of the front-page headlines I found in the microfilm room at the UCLA library. The press conference announcing the new picture was held at the Brown Derby, with Blue and Chuckie taking questions and posing for photographers, and Jacob King so discreetly in the background he was not mentioned in the news stories. J. F. French was nominally the host, but it was Blue's moment, Chuckie remembered, and she made the most of it. She was clearly in charge, a child-woman with the movie star's contempt for the reporters who covered the Industry, free to be outrageous because she knew that nothing outrageous she said would ever be printed in their newspapers.

It was like I wasn't even there, Chuckie said. And thank God for that, because I was afraid someone might ask me about the hearings, and whether I was going to be called or not. If Moe had heard the rumors, and I'm sure he had, Lilo had a tap on the Committee, of course, he never let on. I suppose it was a collateral benefit of having my leg blown off. That meant I couldn't have been a Communist. But Blue was simply off-the-map that day. I think that as Jake was becoming more circumspect, she was taking on a little of his wildness, and she was wild enough to begin with.

◄◦►

"Blue," a reporter asked, "you've been working steadily since the age of four, so you must really like to work, is that right?"

Blue Tyler shielded her eyes from the flashbulbs. "Like to work?" She giggled. "Let me put on my Industry spokesman face." She knit her brows. "I want to be known as the hardest-working star in this Industry to which I owe so much, and which gives so many people a release"—she paused, then giggled some more—"from their drab, unhappy, crappy, shitty little lives. Jesus, you guys are trying to make me sound like fucking Loretta Young—"

A studio press agent interrupted, trying to restore some kind of decorum. "What Blue means is that for the first time in the history of Cosmopolitan Pictures—"

"What Blue means," Blue Tyler said, "is what Blue just said." She peered at the press agent. "Stanley, what are you making that cutting gesture across your throat for? Are you trying to cut me off? These reporters are my friends. They're not here just to stuff their faces with Cosmo's booze and some lobster Newburg. You are my friends, aren't you, guys?"

The reporters laughed.

"What Blue means is that for the first time in the history of Cosmopolitan Pictures—"

Another question broke through the press agent's spiel. "Blue, do you have any hobbies?"

"I like to drown cats." She gnawed on a fingernail and stared lewdly at the questioner. "And fuck. I really like to fuck."

The publicity man was sweating profusely, the stains creating moons under the arms of his jacket, trying to prevent the press conference from further deteriorating into chaos. ". . . a former child star emerges . . ."

Nobody was listening. It was now just a question of how far she would go. "Are you at all spiritual, Blue?"

"I pray all the time," Blue said. "Just the other day, I went into Good Shepherd Church in Beverly Hills. I'm not even Catholic, but I got down on my knees and I prayed that Mr. French . . . you all know J. F. French . . ."

J. F. French raised a hand holding an unlit Havana cigar.

". . . what girl hasn't been down on her knees for Mr. French."

There was loud laughter from the reporters.

J. F. French stared impassively at Blue, then walked to the banquette where Jacob King was sitting by himself, toying with a drink.

"What did she tell you about me?" J. F. French said, the color rising in his face.

Jacob suppressed the urge to ask what Blue might have told him that made Moe so suddenly angry. It was something to remember. "Nothing."

"Good." J. F. French seemed satisfied. "Some people are ungrateful in this business. Ingrates. You got to watch out for them."

"You mean Blue?"

"Not Baby Blue," J. F. French said. "She's a good little girl." He rolled the unlit cigar under his nose and contemplated Jacob King. "So tell me, how's the hotel business? A little more complicated than"—he hesitated—"than what you used to do."

Jacob let the remark pass. "I'm thinking about producing, Moe," he said casually. "I was thinking I'd produce Blue's next picture after *Broadway Babe*. And I deliver her to you. She remains exclusive with Cosmopolitan Pictures."

"You want to become a *producer*?" The idea appeared to astonish J. F. French. "Jake, I hear you've got all the troubles you can handle with that hotel of yours." He rose from the banquette. "You're way over budget, I hear. Way, way over." He clapped his hands loudly. "That's it. No more questions. Get those freeloading bums out of here." He turned back to Jacob. "A producer." He started to laugh, the way he laughed at Shelley Flynn. "You ought to think like Morris, Jake. The fur business. Fur is forever."

XV

HE WANTED TO DO A WESTERN, Arthur French said. A Brooklyn Jew, and he wanted to do a Western. He hired Dudley
Nichols to work up a story, with Blue as the lead. Chuckie
told him Dudley had won an Oscar for *The Informer*. Needless
to say Jake had never heard of Dudley or *The Informer*. All the
while Lilo was saying where did the seed money come from.
Lilo had a way of aski.`g questions in such a way that they
became accusations.

And that was when it went wrong?

Sending him out here always was a demented idea, Arthur
said, with that uncanny ability of his to make hindsight seem
like prescience. But it really began to go wrong the day he hit
Lilo.

◄◦►

Melba Mae Toolate remembered they were doing head when
the call came that morning from Jackie Heller. Whether indeed
Blue and Jacob were engaged orally is subject to question, as
Melba tended to punctuate her memories according to the sexual acrobatics she claimed she was performing at the exact moment of the incident remembered. It was however a Saturday,
she was sure of that, because there was to be a croquet luncheon

at the house on St. Pierre Road, and croquet luncheons took place only on Saturday. And she had not intended to invite Lilo.

"Jacob, don't answer it."

Jacob King tousled her hair and reached for the telephone.

"We're never alone anymore," Blue said. "There's always all these fucking people around."

"Yeah," Jacob said into the telephone. "Jackie." He sat up in bed. "What's up?"

"Jake, where the fuck are you?" Blue crawled up on Jacob's chest. She could hear Jackie Heller shouting at the other end of the line. "You were supposed to be here yesterday. We got decisions to make, checks to sign. We're already two months behind schedule, and today my plumbing supplier says no more deliveries until he gets paid, certified check, nothing else, seventy-five grand, so I got two dozen plumbers sitting on their ass on double time, waiting for somebody to write a goddamn check that can be covered . . ."

Jacob distractedly fondled Blue's breast with his free hand. "I keep telling you, Jackie, let Eddie handle it."

"Let Eddie handle it." Jackie's voice was strangled with rage. "Eddie Binhoff's a contract killer, for Christ's sake, that's the only fucking thing he knows about contracting . . ."

Blue began sliding back down Jacob's chest. He was beginning to get angry, and seeing him angry always made her feel erotic, in command, able with her encyclopedic sexuality to calm his furies.

"Wait a minute, hon," Jacob whispered. Then back into the telephone, his quiet voice, the dangerous voice. "I'll give him a check, Jackie. I'll hire a plane and send it over this afternoon."

"It's got to be a cashier's check, Jake."

"It'll be out of my own account. A personal check from Jacob King. That's better than a cashier's check. You tell him he'll have it by tonight. If that's not good enough for him, then Jacob King will be insulted." He let the words sink in. "And then you tell that fuck to start making his deliveries or Eddie will break both his fucking arms, and then he'll stick a piece of dynamite up his ass and light it. You tell him about Dominic Conti's hands. That ought to do the trick. Don't worry about it, Jackie. I'll talk to you later."

He slammed the telephone back into its cradle.

"Who's Dominic Conti?" Blue asked. Jacob's circumcised prick stood straight up, as thick as a pepper mill. She wondered if he could balance a telephone book on it. Chuckie had once told her about some South American who could do that, but she would match Jacob's dick against anyone's. Even Walker Franklin's. Walker was not circumcised, and the folds of his foreskin had the consistency of the treads on an automobile tire. His dick always had a urine smell, and she guessed that was why she preferred Jewish men and their circumcised cocks.

"A guy Eddie used to know. Listen, come up here."

"Jacob, I'm not finished."

"We'll finish later. I need a favor."

A pout. "What?"

"I want you to ask Lilo today."

"I'll ask Lilo. It's that cunt Rita I won't ask."

"Lilo won't come without her."

"No."

"Blue. It's a favor. The first one I ever asked."

—◇—

"You've done wonders with this place, Jake."

"Thanks, Lilo."

"What do you call this thing we're sitting in?"

"A gazebo." Jacob pronounced it "gaze-boe."

"You had one in Red Hook, right?" Lilo started to laugh. "And I bet they pronounced it 'gaze-boe' in your neighborhood, too, right?"

Jacob King flushed, but he had vowed not to be provoked, and smiled.

"Rita was beginning to think Blue didn't like her, the way we were never invited here, me being Blue's lawyer, you and me being partners, she had to think that, you know how dames are."

"You're not a croquet player." He saw Blue at the center wicket check to see if anyone was watching, then move her ball slightly with her foot to get it in a better position. Cheating came naturally to her. She was playing in a mixed doubles foursome with Chuckie, Arthur, and Rita Lewis. "These afternoons are for serious players."

"So if I'm not a serious player, then how come we get this last-minute invitation?" Lilo waved at J. F. French. "Moe, you'll be glad to know, I took two tables for your Mount Sinai benefit."

"So we're even," J. F. French said. "I took two for UJA."

Lilo turned back to Jacob King. "The way of the world out here, Jake. You scratch my back, I'll scratch yours."

Jacob King took a deep breath. "We're running a little short at Playland, Lilo."

"You know, I figured there was a reason Rita and me got invited at eleven o'clock this morning, and I figured that was the reason, and not that Blue wanted pointers from Rita on how to do *Broadway Babe*." Lilo smiled at Jacob King. "We should define our terms here, Jake. One, we're not running a little short, we're running big short. And two, *we're* not running short, *you*"—he paused for emphasis—"are running short. We give you a budget, you're twice over it already. Frankly, Jake, you got a problem."

"So it's my problem."

"Your problem, right, exactly. Bottom line. We send somebody in there to pick up after you, it's coming out of your piece." Lilo rose suddenly from the table. "Shelley. Long time no see."

"I was in Chicago," Shelley Flynn said, embracing Lilo. "A gig at the Drake. My clean shit. No cooz jokes. I save my dirty shit for Playland when it opens. How you doing, Jake?"

Jacob raised a hand in greeting. It was as if he had been dismissed by Lilo Kusack.

"Chicago," Lilo said. "You remember that joint in Moline, Shelley? When you were just starting out, and I was booking bands?"

"Nino's," Shelley Flynn said, taking a place at the table under the candy-striped umbrella. "Nino's Flame Room. That was a tough joint, Nino's. Those guys"—Shelley Flynn flattened his nose to one side with a finger—"knew how to kill a guy with a newspaper. You ever heard of that, Jake?"

Jacob King shook his head, not about to offer his professional expertise.

Shelley Flynn jabbed an imaginary newspaper. "The *Chicago Tribune* was good, like a fucking Louisville Slugger. Hey, Jew-boy, they'd say, poking you in the fucking ribs, your first show was shit, you better be funny the midnight show or we'll break your fucking kidney, Sidney. Hey, I said, my name is Sheldon, not Sidney. You want to break my kidney, get my fucking name right . . ."

Lilo roared with laughter, all the while looking at Jacob.

". . . for the newspapers. 'Shelley Flynn, headlining the bill at Nino's Flame Room in beautiful downtown Moline, was murdered last night . . .'"

From an adjoining table, J. F. French said, "I should be the one breaking your kidney, the grosses on your latest."

Shelley Flynn rose and knelt down in the grass beside J. F. French. "J.F., seriously, I die tomorrow, I want my ashes spread on your driveway, so your car don't skid . . ."

Lilo Kusack wiped tears of laughter from his eyes and attacked his lunch. "That Shelley, what a guy. He gives me gas I laugh so hard." He broke a roll in two and stuffed half in his mouth. "So, Jake, Moe tells me you want to be a movie producer." A hard laugh. "A word of advice." Lilo drew his right hand into a gun and pulled an imaginary trigger. "Stick to what you're good at."

Jacob drummed his fingers on the table, determined not to be provoked. "I didn't like this to begin with, Lilo. But the deal is, we're partners."

"Look around, Jake." Lilo's hand took in the manicured lawn and the tables full of people. "This place is full of people who understand deals. Deals aren't open-ended. Ask anybody here. You had your shot. You got rid of Benny. You deserve credit for that. Digging up Round Trip Buchalter, that was genius. That kind of deal you know how to do. But you ask me, it's time we put somebody on the job over there who can add and subtract."

Blue's voice suddenly reached them.

"Arthur." Blue was trying to prevent Chuckie O'Hara from slamming her ball. "Isn't there a rule against someone playing with a wooden leg? It gives Chuckie an unfair advantage, because that thing of his is so heavy."

Lilo watched Blue for a moment. "She's not very interested in your problem, is she? And you don't understand it, because you think she's crazy about you." Lilo carefully buttered the other half of his roll. "I've been around this business a long time, Jake. I understand girls like Blue. They like to be around people like you. It makes them feel wild. It makes them feel dangerous. The fact you're a gangster is what gives her the goose. Not you. Morris pulls the plug on you, see how long she sticks around."

Jacob tried to control himself.

"So you're fucking her." He looked Jacob up and down. "Jake, who hasn't she fucked?"

Jacob King erupted from his chair and smashed Lilo Kusack in the face. Lilo's chair toppled over with him in it. Jacob sprang to his side and began savagely kicking him as he lay on the gazebo floor. Suddenly Blue appeared and jumped on Jacob's back, trying to pull him away. "Goddamn you," she screamed, "you don't hit people. They only do that in B-pictures."

Jacob shook her from his shoulder and wrenched her around, holding her by the wrist. "What exactly do you think I am?" His face was contorted with rage. It was as if no one else was present. None of the other people on the lawn said a word. On the floor Lilo assumed a fetal position, and dabbed at the blood pouring from his nose. "A hood? A mobster? You think I'm a killer? That gives you a thrill?"

"Get your fucking hands off me."

Jacob suddenly released Blue. She looked at him for a moment, then turned and fled from the gazebo.

‹o›

Quelle melodrama, Chuckie O'Hara said, *quelle dramaturge*. There were all these people milling around, pretending nothing happened. Thank God for Rita. Okay, everyone, the show's over, she said, like she was a traffic cop, ordering everyone around, go home, get laid, get a drink, tell everyone all about it, it's an event, like Pearl Harbor, you can tell people you were here that day. Arthur, you drive Lilo to the emergency room at Mount Sinai, she said, and to Jake, Where do you think you are, back at the social club in Red Hook? Even Blue didn't get off free. She was up in the house and kept on asking, What could Lilo have said that made him do that? And finally Rita was just fed up to here, and said, You wouldn't understand, Blue, it wasn't in the script. And with that, Blue bounces out the door, gets in her car, sideswipes Jake's Continental, and nearly cracks up on her way out the driveway. And in the middle of all this, Jake had just disappeared. We looked all over the house, and he wasn't there, and nobody had seen him leave. So Rita pours herself a drink, and she says, You know something, Chuckie, I wished you fucked women, because you're my type of guy. I would've loved being on that island with you. Like I loved being here this afternoon. I wouldn't have missed it for anything.

Of course, her day had a postscript.

‹o›

It was three in the morning when Rita Lewis spotted Jacob King's smashed Continental on a deserted stretch of Mulholland Drive. Jacob was smoking a cigarette at the edge of the cliff, looking down at the lights of the San Fernando Valley twinkling below. Rita parked and got out of her car.

"What did you tell Lilo?" Jacob said. He was unshaven, his shirt streaked with sweat and dust, and he looked exhausted.

"I didn't have to tell him anything. Lilo's not used to getting beat up at a croquet game. So he takes two Seconal, two shots of Scotch to calm him down, and he's out until morning. If I'm lucky, he doesn't wake up, and he remembers me in his will."

Jacob laughed. The laugh he had when he was on top of the world, Rita Lewis thought.

"What you don't understand about Blue and Lilo, Jake, is they're going to go to each other's funerals," Rita said. "This is a community here. All these people today, they all belong to it. Everybody there, except for you and me. Their kids marry each other. One of them dies, they all show up to sit shiva. Except it's with drinks, and Virginia ham, and everybody doing a little business, and Barry Tyger talking about the stuff dreams are made of. You don't understand that."

Jacob did not reply for a moment. "I need a favor, Rita."

"How much do you want?"

"How do you know it's money."

"You're not the first guy to ask me for money, Jake. Someone calls me at three o'clock in the morning, says to meet him out here, this godforsaken place, and then says he needs a favor, I can figure it out. How much?"

"Seventy-five grand."

A low whistle escaped from Rita Lewis's lips. "Why?"

"Nobody's been paid at Playland. I thought we'd be finished by now, everything would be all right." He took a deep breath. "The suppliers said no more deliveries effective Monday morning. Jackie says the crews wouldn't report for work."

"And that's what the fight with Lilo was about?"

"Among other things," Jacob said. He did not elaborate and knew Rita would not ask what the other things were. In any event, Lilo would probably tell her what he had said about him and what he had said about Blue. Lilo always had the last word. "So I wrote out a personal check this afternoon, rented a plane, and flew it over. I wasn't on the ground more than ten minutes. I don't have the money, Rita. I need you to cover it until I can talk to Morris. If it bounces, then it's all over."

Rita leaned against the car and wondered if she could count the lights below, wondered in how many of those houses people were fucking at that very second. "Why not?" she said after a moment. "It's my retirement money, Jake. For that time in my life when I have to buy myself a beachboy."

"I'm good for it, Rita."

"One thing. Your girlfriend. She turn you down?"

"I didn't ask her."

"Why?"

Jacob hesitated. Rita knew the answer even before he spoke. As far as he had traveled, as far as he wanted to go, it was only with people like her and Eddie Binhoff that he would ever feel really at home.

"I don't know her long enough, Rita," Jacob King said.

XVI

THAT WAS SATURDAY.

By Sunday morning, Lilo Kusack already had his lines out.

Jacob was supposed to have lunch at Hillcrest with Shelley Flynn, and he arrived on the dot at twelve-thirty, having decided it was best to pretend nothing had happened yesterday, it was an altercation that would be quickly forgotten and no score kept. At the desk, he was told that Mr. Flynn had just called and said he would be unavailable for lunch, and no, there was no further message, and so Jacob went into the bar and ordered a Tanqueray Gibson straight up. There were only a few people present, but no one looked up, and no one said hello. Barry, he greeted Rabbi Baruch Tyger, but Barry Tyger looked through him as if he was not there, Barry Tyger to whom in a gin game four days earlier he had fed cards that made him a seven-thousand-dollar winner. He had just taken a handful of salted peanuts when a waiter said that the resident manager wished to see Mr. King, could he come with him to the resident manager's office. Jacob signaled for a chit to sign, but the bartender shook his head, and busied himself washing glasses, while the waiter hovered close to his elbow until he finished his drink. It reminded Jacob of the way cops tried to box you in when they came to arrest you.

The resident manager's name was Nathan Krakower, and for a moment Jacob wondered if he was perhaps kin to Hyman Krakower, alias Pittsburgh Pat Muldoon, who came to such an untimely end in Sheepshead Bay the winter of 1933. Probably not. Nathan Krakower did not favor Pat Muldoon, and he was so nervous his voice threatened to break. The membership committee, Nathan Krakower informed Jacob King, had recently rewritten the articles in the club by-laws relevant to guest memberships. They were no longer open-ended, and so Mr. King would have to surrender his guest card, and while he would of course be welcome if he came to the club with an accredited member, he unfortunately had exceeded the number of guest visits allowable under the new rules, which were retroactive and included the period of his guest membership. As he handed over his guest card, Jacob said he understood the difficulty of Mr. Krakower's position, and that he had handled the matter with the tact and delicacy he had come to expect from the members and staff at Hillcrest.

There was one further item, Mr. Krakower said, and by now he was visibly perspiring. Some members, and he was not at liberty to name them, had asked for assurances that no harm would come either to the membership, the staff, or the club facilities as a result of this action.

It was then that Jacob King laughed.

-<o>-

Lilo also contacted Hedda Hopper. On Monday, her column in the *Times* began: "This editorial is dedicated to all those Hollywood stars who try to play with fire, particularly Blue Tyler. Blue, you first won America's heart as a four-year-old cinemoppet, and all your dreams should have come true by now . . ."

-<o>-

As it happened, Chuckie O'Hara was shooting wardrobe and makeup tests for *Broadway Babe* with Blue that Monday morning, even though the rewrite on the script was still not finished and the score only half written. Her eyes were all puffy, as if she had been crying all weekend, but when Chuckie asked if she had seen Jacob she told him to mind his own fucking fairy business. Everyone on the set had seen Hedda's column, and as Blue slumped at the makeup table, her hairdresser was reading it to her.

" '. . . dreams should have come true by now. You have youth and beauty . . .' "

"C.C.," Blue said to her makeup man, "I have a zit on my nose, fix it."

"As soon as I finish with the bags under your eyes, sweet," C.C. said.

" '. . . and fame and jewels,' " Gavin, her hairdresser, continued. " 'You have an army of adoring fans. You have studio scion Arthur French begging you to set the date. But let's talk frankly, Blue. Some Hollywood insiders are saying . . .' "

"Gavin, did you talk to that cunt?" Blue said irritably.

"Hedda doesn't talk to us little people, you know that, Blue," Gavin said. He continued to read. " '. . . insiders are saying your current flame is out, out, out. Blue, your fans beg you, don't persist on a romance that only means trouble, with a capital *T*. You're more royal than any king.' Well, does she have a nerve. 'More royal than any king.' C.C., is that what they call a veiled reference?" Gavin put down the paper and examined Blue in the mirror, appraising the makeup. "You need . . . something."

"What I need is a good fuck, and you and C.C. don't fill the bill," Blue said.

—◇—

I saw him first, Chuckie said. It was supposed to be a closed set, and I'd heard that J.F. had barred him from the lot. I don't know how he got on, maybe the studio police were afraid they'd get shot, but then they'd worked with him when he broke Benny Draper, and they liked him. Anyway, there he was, stepping over the cables and the stacked lumber until he got to the edge of the set. Blue was doing left profile, right profile, hitting her marks, it was uncanny, she never missed a mark in all the pictures I did with her. He didn't say a word. I think it was the first time Jake realized she had a working life that no matter what happened would always exclude him. Then she saw him. Mr. Trouble with a capital *T*. Chuckie, she said, will you please ask that gentleman to move, he's in my eyeline.

The cunt of the eon, but a star. All right everyone, I said, take five.

◄◦►

"I'm going to New York for a few days," Jacob King said. "When I get back, I'm going out to Playland. I want you out there with me."

"I'll be working," Blue said. She still had the makeup Kleenex around her neck.

"You'll be finished."

Blue took the Kleenex from her neck and wadded it in her hand. "You ever think maybe we're finished?"

Jacob watched her for a moment. Her gaze did not waver. Then without a word he turned and headed for the stage door.

"Chuckie, how much longer do I have to fucking wait around here?" Blue said.

Did she cry? I asked.

She only cried on cue, Chuckie O'Hara said.

◄◦►

It was the first time Jacob King had been to New York since he arrived in California on the Super Chief. Whether he drove to Bay Ridge to see Lillian King and Matthew and Abigail King is unknown. It is known—this from Melba Mae Toolate—that Jacob and Lillian talked more or less regularly on the telephone, business usually involving the children, or finances, or repairs on the house. Their last exchange, however, became so acrimonious that all communication between them had ceased. Soon after which a lawyer in New York contacted Jacob about working out a financial settlement for a legal separation, leading ultimately to divorce, with Lillian Aronow King having full custody of Matthew and Abigail King. The lawyer's name was Ze'ev

Boorstin, and in due course Ze'ev Boorstin was contacted by James Francis Riordan, attorney-at-law, who told him that separation and divorce were no longer contemplated, and that any expenses Mr. Boorstin had accumulated would be paid by Lefkowitz For Fur, M. M. Lefkowitz, Prop. Moreover, if Ze'ev Boorstin pursued the matter with Mrs. King further, a complaint would be lodged with the New York State Bar Association. Lefkowitz For Fur, Ze'ev Boorstin said. Is that Morris Lefkowitz? It's enough for you to know that it's M. M. Lefkowitz, Jimmy Riordan said.

What was the reason for all this sudden acrimony? I asked.

Jacob told her he wanted his brats out for the opening of Playland, Melba Mae Toolate said, and the bitch wife said I'm not sending them out to meet your new whore.

Jacob told you this? I asked.

I was listening on an extension, and I said, Who're you calling a whore, you fat bitch. I couldn't help myself.

-◁◦▷-

"Every prick out there's on overtime, twelve hours a day, seven days a week," Jimmy Riordan said. "You got plasterers in from Detroit. Detroit, for Christ's sake. Carpenters from Cleveland. Fucking Cleveland. In fucking Nevada." Profanity was an indulgence to which Jimmy Riordan rarely resorted, but there were times it got the attention he wanted it to get. "I didn't know you were trying to end unemployment in the Cleveland locals. They're having a hard time in Buffalo, too, you want to help them out. Will you just explain to me why? Why? In simple no-bullshit English?"

"You been in touch with Jackie," Jacob King said. "You went behind my back. I would've given you the figures, you just asked me. I know how much we're over. It's the price you pay, you want a Christmas opening. We got a building boom in California, everybody's short work crews, that's why we bring in Detroit, Cleveland. You just asked me, I would've told you that. But no, you go behind my back, you go to Jackie."

"Of course we've been in touch with Jackie. That's what you

do, Jake, you go four million dollars over budget. What're you going to do now? You going to work Jackie over, like you worked Lilo over? That was smart, real smart, they do that in all the big companies these days. Merrill works over Lynch, Kuhn beats up Loeb." He wondered if Jacob even knew what Merrill, Lynch and Kuhn, Loeb were. "Now I hear you want to be a fucking movie producer." He started to say Your brains are in your dick, but thought better of it. "And I hear you want to buy your suits in England."

Morris Lefkowitz sat behind his desk, hands folded in front of him, his head swiveling between Jimmy and Jacob, saying nothing, taking everything in. He had aged since Jacob had last seen him. There were brown spots on his hands and on his scalp that he did not remember from before. There was no point in carrying on an argument with Jimmy. Morris would make the final decision. "Morris . . ."

"Jimmy talks sense, Jacob."

"You know what you're telling me, Morris?" Jacob King never thought the day would come when he would confront Morris Lefkowitz. You argued with Morris, but once his mind was made up you did not cross him. Morris knew best. "You're telling me you're an old man."

Oh, God, Jimmy Riordan thought to himself, I didn't hear that. Morris Lefkowitz's subjects showed him more deference than was shown to kings and popes, or paid the price if they did not. Jacob of all people should know that, he had pulled the trigger on Philly Wexler for a less heinous heresy. Lilo's right. He's crazy.

"That's the way you speak to Morris, then don't speak," Morris Lefkowitz said with difficulty.

"I'm in touch with Lilo, Morris," Jimmy Riordan said quickly. "He can move somebody out there tomorrow, bring the thing under control. Somebody who knows how to add and subtract."

"You used to have big dreams, Morris," Jacob said. "You used to be a gambler. Now you sit here and tell me you're turning your big dreams over to the accountants. To the lawyers. You're letting the Fordham guys place your bets."

"Jacob, you are causing me such pain," Morris said.

"Your choice, Morris." Jacob was relentless. "Is that what you really want out there, somebody, the only thing he knows" —Jacob looked directly at Jimmy Riordan—"is how to add and subtract. Put it together right, and it will last long after you and I are gone."

"His idea of right will break us, Morris," Jimmy Riordan said. "Go on this way, California will pull their money out, and we're back where we started. We got to think savings."

"Savings," Jacob exploded. "What is this fucking savings you're talking about."

"It's a word you must've been in reform school the day it was taught," Jimmy Riordan said, and immediately regretted it. The ad hominem was not his style. It placed him on the same level as his antagonists, and Jimmy Riordan detested a level playing field.

Morris tented and untented his hands, rhythmically, as if keeping time. "Jimmy," he said at last. "We give Jacob some leeway."

As always Morris Lefkowitz spoke in tongues. Leeway was for Jimmy to interpret. Leeway was granted to Jacob King as it would be to an unruly son. The son Morris Lefkowitz never had. The son from whom he would ultimately exact tribute for the offense of calling him old. "I'll work out the figures, Morris."

"You work out the figures, Jimmy." He raised his hand, as a pontiff might, a sadness in the gesture. "*Mazel,* Jacob." It was what Morris Lefkowitz had said when Jacob King left this same office for California, but then it was a benediction, and now it had the sense of a farewell.

❖

The rain slanted down at La Guardia. Morris Lefkowitz's black customized four-door Oldsmobile slid into a No Parking zone outside the departure entrance, and his driver, Rocco, put a hundred-dollar bill in his lap to give any policeman who asked him to move. Jimmy Riordan raised the window between the front and the back seat so that Rocco could not hear what he had to say, then put his hand on Jacob King's arm. "Jake, I want to tell you something," Jimmy said quietly. "I haven't always worked for Morris. I wasn't always a Mob lawyer. My first job out of Fordham Law School was working for the New York State Banking Commission. I started out checking the books at the First National Bank of Oneonta, New York. I look at something that's costing too much, I get a funny feeling. A little buzz."

"You think I'm cooking the books?"

"No. Cooking the books I understand. What I don't understand is why you think you got to build the Taj Mahal out there."

Jacob almost said he wanted to be respectable, but caught himself. At his center of gravity, he knew that respectability would always elude him. He was who he was, and he would carry the tag Jacob King, with all it implied, to his last day. "Because I want to hear people say, Jake King built the Taj Mahal out there," he said finally. It was not respectability, but as close as he could ever come to it.

"At least you're honest, Jake. Okay. So let me explain something, something I didn't want to, but . . ." Jimmy Riordan lowered the window to the front seat. "Rocco, go inside, find out when Jake's plane is leaving."

"Eight-thirty, Mr. Riordan."

"It's raining, Rocco, it could be delayed."

"I got you, Mr. Riordan." The driver opened the door and ran toward the departure lounge.

"The Italians, you got to tell them things twice," Jimmy Riordan said.

Jacob smiled. It was a complaint he had heard often from Jimmy in days when life was easier, and Morris was younger. New York days.

"Jake, you want to be something you're not," Jimmy Riordan said. "You're a hood. A smart hood. In time, maybe very smart, smart enough to cross over and be like Morris. That's why Morris said okay today. Morris still believes in you. But Morris is also still a businessman. And there's a point at which any businessman . . ." Jimmy paused. He knew Jacob well enough to know that he would understand the meaning of what he was about to say. He repeated, ". . . there's a point at which any businessman will cut his losses."

Jacob King opened the car door. The rain splashed inside. "Morris is old."

"Jake, Morris wants you to be old, too. I want you to be old. Believe me."

"So long, Jimmy."

XVII

FROM THE CONTINUING TESTIMONY of Lyle Ledbetter, appearing before the federal grand jury impaneled in Las Vegas, Clark County, Nevada, to investigate matters pertaining to the shooting death of Jacob King o/a December 1, 1948. Court was called to order at 10:42 A.M., May 30, 1949, in Department C, U.S. District Courthouse, Las Vegas, Nevada, the Honorable Lucius Klinger, presiding. Stanley Prince, assistant United States attorney for southern Nevada, appeared for the government:

THE COURT: Good morning. I hope everyone had a nice weekend. Mr. Ledbetter, you are still sworn. Mr. Prince, you may proceed.

MR. STANLEY PRINCE (hereinafter referred to as "Q"): How are you, Mr. Ledbetter?

MR. LYLE LEDBETTER (hereinafter referred to as "A"): All things considered, I'd rather be in Philadelphia.

Q: I think W. C. Fields has copyright on that joke, Mr. Ledbetter. Now, before we recessed Friday, you said you would ransack your memory about the state of affairs at Playland in the weeks after Jacob King moved here more or less permanently to oversee the finishing touches of construction. Where was Jackie Heller during all of this? He at least had a construction background?

A: Correction. The joint was no longer called Playland.

Q: Explain, Mr. Ledbetter.

A: Well, when Jake gets back from New York, the first thing he does is take down the old sign that says PLAYLAND and put up a new one that says KING'S PLAYLAND. I thought he'd gone nuts. His whacker—

Q: For the record, explain *whacker*, Mr. Ledbetter.

A: His shooter. Bang, bang. It's a word the guys use. *Whacker*.

Q: For the record then, *whacker* means designated killer, would that be fair to say?

A: Yeah. I suppose. *Whacker* just sounds nicer. The guys know what it means.

Q: And you, too.

A: It's a word I hear. Where was I?

Q: Mr. King had just returned from New York and the first thing he did was change the name of the hotel from Playland to King's Playland. At which point, his designated killer, or whacker, as you so colorfully put it, said . . . what is this whacker's name by the way?

A: Eddie something. I don't even like to look at him, I mean he looks like if he hurts someone he won't lose much sleep over it.

Q: Your Honor, this will be the last interruption, but let the record reflect that Mr. King's alleged whacker has variously been identified as Eddie Binhoff or Eddie Binyon, and there is a possibility that he has also been known as Allie Lazar. We have been unable to locate him so we could serve a subpoena. You can continue, Mr. Ledbetter.

A: Okay. So anyway Jake takes down the old sign and puts up the new one, KING'S PLAYLAND, and this Eddie says to him, Jake, I hope you know what you're doing, Morris has had guys hit for less than that . . .

Q: For the record, Morris is Morris Lefkowitz of Lefkowitz For Furs in New York City. Now let's get back to Jackie Heller. Where was he?

A: Making scarce. He'd done something to piss Jake off, excuse my language, Your Honor, Jackie said it was nothing, just a misunderstanding, but this Eddie guy mentioned he'd like to rip Jackie's tongue out and have it for a sandwich, and Jake says they only do that in B-pictures, Eddie. I mean, you want to know what kind of guy this Eddie was, Jackie was no day at the beach, he killed a guy once in Jersey with his bare hands, and messing with Eddie was not on his agenda. What I hear is that Eddie once cut off some guy's hands in New Jersey, but that's only something I hear. Eventually, Jackie and Jake make up, because he goes back to work at Playland, I think if he doesn't, he thinks he'll get whacked himself, and so everything seems to be going all right, two shifts a day.

Q: Then progress was being made at the hotel?

A: When I'm there, yes. There's this decorator, he's a . . . let's just say he's a little light on his feet, he wears a polka dot bandanna around his neck, he calls everyone by a girl's name. Like he calls Eddie the whacker Edna. Not to his face, he's not that dumb. And he's showing swatches to Jake for the main showroom. Your Honor, can I say this in my own words, I hope the members of the jury won't be offended, you know what I mean?

THE COURT: I'll tell you when you're out of order, Mr. Ledbetter.

A: Okay. He says, this decorator, What I'm thinking, Mr. King, is a carpet in ecclesiastical red and the ceiling in persimmon. And Jake says, I wanted a whorehouse, I don't need some *fageleh* that's never been in one to tell me what it looks like. Scratch the ecclesiastical red, scratch the other one too, try peach, I always liked peach. And things are coming along so good, his entertainment director's interviewing showgirls for the line. It's the little things, Lyle, he says to me, I've got to know him by now, he calls me Lyle, I call him Jake, he's okay, I never saw the bad side people talk about so much. It's the little things, he says, take that chick over there, the one that says she worked at the Chez in Chicago and the Copa in New York, she's a human mattress, for Christ's sake, and he says to her, Honey, I bet the last place you worked had a carpet in ecclesiastical red. He's got this guy working for him, a vice cop from L.A. doing some free-lance, Crotty I think his name was, and Crotty's checking the girls out, and Jake tells this guy Crotty anyone with a vice conviction is out.

Q: A class operation.

A: Definitely. There was one other thing.

Q: Do tell us, Mr. Ledbetter.

A: This is late in the game. Jackie tells him a cat got caught in the swimming pool pump, caused the water in the pool to drain out. Like somebody pulled the plug in a bathtub. I'd like to tear that cat's heart out, Jackie says, we got to rip out the plumbing in the pool and start all over again. And Jake says, How long's it going to take, and Jackie says, Four days and it's going to cost a bundle. And Jake says, Two days, and one thing, Jackie, I want you to let the cat go, it's bad luck for a gambler to touch a cat.

Q: And?

A: Just at that moment, one of the construction guys comes out from the drain, he's holding the cat in his hand, and he'd strangled it.

XVIII

WHERE WAS BLUE all this time?
In L.A., Arthur French said. Preparing *Broadway Babe*.
Recording the score.

She said she hated to lip-sync.

It was a way of keeping her busy, Jack. To keep her mind on things.

And off Jacob.

I suppose you could say that.

Were you seeing her, Arthur?

Yes.

Sleeping with her?

That's a cad's question.

You're the only person I know who'd use the word *cad*, Arthur. What finally made her go over to Vegas?

Not what, who.

Who then?

Rita.

◄○►

Another polo Sunday.

Lilo Kusack was on the telephone. "All right, Jimmy." He was speaking softly, not watching the match, admiring Blue, who was wandering through the crowd, hidden behind over-sized sunglasses and a huge straw hat, sipping a piña colada. It's like she's giving the straw head, Lilo thought. Advertising her availability. Poor Arthur. In her life he would always be a utility player. In the starting lineup only until someone better showed up. She was not wearing a brassiere either. Lilo could tell. Tits like concrete. They didn't move when she walked. "Wherever Morris says," Lilo said after a moment. He had always been able to think about women and business at the same time. "He's an old man. I understand. But you understand, too. It's time. Okay? So let me know." He hung up the telephone. "I get old, I get soft," he said to Rita Lewis, "do me a favor, shoot me."

"I could arrange that," Rita Lewis said. "No trouble. I imagine there's a couple of guys out there would do me that favor." She took a lipstick and touched up her lips. She knew Lilo was on the verge of dumping her, but she would land on her feet, or on her back, she always did. Maybe she should do the dumping. It would be more flattering to her ego. Lilo was a good and steady fuck, but a fuck was just a fuck. Anyway, however it broke, she still had her nest egg. A little here, a little there, a bauble or two in the safe deposit box, her furs, the odd tip on the market, a boat race at Hollywood Park, a bonus for carrying packages and never asking what was in them, it added up after a while. Especially with the number of men who had passed through her life, and the kind of men they were. Jake had paid her back, as she knew he would. Jake would cheat a man, but never a woman. It was matter of vanity. And he had not tried to discount the amount, as she knew Lilo would have tried to do if he had been in Jake's situation. But of course Lilo would never be caught in Jake's situation. He arranged situations, he did not get caught in them. Lilo was a picker-up of pieces, many of which he had caused to be broken in the first place. "So tell me, Lilo, what do you mean, it's time."

"I mean, it's time you minded your own business for a change," Lilo said. "And in case you're thinking what I think you're thinking, forget it. I told it to Benny once, the dumb fuck, and I'll tell it to you, I'm an officer of the court. Funny stuff I want nothing to do with."

Rita knew she had pushed this particular button as long as it could be pushed, but if she was on the way out anyway, one more push couldn't hurt much. "What you're saying is, they don't play polo at Folsom."

She moved away from Lilo and sat down next to Blue Tyler, who for a moment did not acknowledge her presence. Blue sucked up the last of her piña colada, a great slurping noise, then held out the glass to a maid. "Why do horses go poo-poo so much, Rita?" Blue said. "Arthur falls off so often, I'm afraid he's going to fall into a pile of horse poo."

"I haven't given it all that much thought," Rita said. She knows everything there is to know about fucking and cock-sucking and camera angles, Rita thought, but nothing at all about the world, and how it works. Because of her Jake had cut his ties to the only organization he had ever known, and sooner or later it was going to get him killed, for as much as he might want to be a part of her world, he brought too much baggage to it, and it had no place for him. She wondered if Jake knew this, and she thought he probably did. He was never dumb, he just did dumb things. Lilo said the emerald earrings and the other jewelry that Jake had given Blue were paid for out of the Playland account, and Lilo said that's a no-no. She did not know if this was true, or whether Lilo was just saying it, trying it out on her before he tried it out on Jimmy Riordan, and once he told Jimmy, Jimmy of course would tell Morris.

"You read the rewrite on *Broadway Babe* yet? We used some of your back story, the part about you and the ginney gangster from Chicago. We didn't make him a ginney, though. Moe wants to call him Bo Lamarr."

Rita looked at Blue, all sunglasses and straw hat and boobs that didn't jiggle, and for the first time she felt old. In her whole life she had never been as young or as unwary or as protected as Blue Tyler. You could spell it out for her, but Blue would never be able to comprehend that she was Jake's only chance. Her presence would put him in a kind of protective custody, because she was too valuable and too visible to have anything bad happen to her, and if it did, too many questions would have to be asked, too many scores would have to be settled. But that wasn't in any script Blue had ever read, any picture she had ever seen. For Blue everything always worked out in the last reel, and Al Capone was called Bo Lamarr. "You've never worked without a net, have you, Blue?"

"I've worked since I was four. Which is more than you can say."

"I mean, you've always had Arthur. And his father. And the studio. On your side." She paused, certain that Blue did not understand. "Jake's over there with nobody on his side." His name caused an almost imperceptible shudder. "Some people are saying he got in over his head because of you."

Blue ostentatiously pretended not to listen, and clapped loudly as Arthur hammered a ball downfield.

"It's real life, Blue," Rita said, moving close to her. "No directors. No writers. No makeup, no wardrobe, no script. Just one man out there, walking a tightrope for you, and all the guys on both coasts making book on when he falls off. Not if he falls off. When he falls off. Because he will. And when he does, you know what I bet you'll do?"

Blue whirled around. "The only reason you even care about him is because you used to fuck him," she said savagely. Suddenly there were tears at the corners of her eyes. Rita remembered Chuckie saying that she only cried on cue. Maybe, maybe not. "What'll I do?" Blue said.

"What you'll do is, you'll go out to dinner," Rita said gently. It occurred to her, a bad moment, that she was probably old enough to be Blue Tyler's mother. "With the polo player. And his father. Like you've done once a week since you were four years old."

◄○►

What happened over there, Arthur?

She never talked about it.

Never?

Ever.

◄○►

We hold on Blue at the polo match, Sydney Allen said, no dialogue, the match going on behind her, the sound fading and her face slowly filling the screen, blotting everything else out, then we dissolve off her face into the desert, and we pick up a piece of music . . .

◄○►

EXT. PLAYLAND NIGHT

THE LIGHTS of a LIMOUSINE on the desert highway.

ANOTHER ANGLE—JACOB KING
aware of the approaching lights, ever watchful.

THE LIMOUSINE
pulls to a halt in the parking light. Its lights remain on.

ANGLE ON JACOB KING
shielded by his car, his hand going close to his gun. BLUE TYLER steps from the limo and stops when she sees Jacob.

> BLUE
> You still want me out here?

CUT TO:

INT. PLAYLAND SHOWROOM NIGHT

BLUE TYLER
alone onstage in the unfinished showroom. She is barefoot, in jeans and a sweatshirt, holding a champagne glass as a make-believe microphone as she sings "I See Your Face Before Me."

ANGLE ON JACOB KING
alone, at what will be the premier table in the vast empty showroom, watching Blue.

THE SOUND OF BLUE'S VOICE
fades but music carries over the next scenes.

DISSOLVE TO:

INT. PLAYLAND CASINO NIGHT

JACOB KING AND BLUE TYLER

dancing, alone among the empty tables, as Blue slowly begins to undress Jacob, dropping his tie on a crap table. MUSIC carries over.

DISSOLVE TO:

◄◦►

His suite was only half-decorated, with tarpaulins and sanders and sawhorses and paint cans stacked in a corner of the living room, and paint samples on the sheetrock walls, different hues of peach, none quite right, the peach had to be right. Set against one wall, unhung and unframed, was the still-unfinished portrait of Jacob in riding clothes. He liked it unfinished, it had a roughness to it, maybe that's the way he would hang it. And without a frame either. Every window looked out at the sign, KING'S PLAYLAND, ablaze in neon. In his bedroom, he kept the curtains open all night, the sign illuminating his face and helping him sleep. His bed was round, six feet in diameter, a mistake, he had concluded, it was difficult to get comfortable in a round bed stationed in the center of the room, he always felt as if he was going to fall out of it. During his stay, he had fucked three or four of the girls he had picked for the chorus line, none more than once, his heart didn't seem in it, one of the girls had said, only his dick, and he didn't want them there in the morning.

Of course Blue liked the round bed, it was her first time in that configuration, "Let's box the compass," she said.

"What does that mean?" Jacob King said. He was brushing his damp hair with the pair of silver brushes she had brought with her from Los Angeles, a peace offering. "For afterwards," she said. A cigarette hung from his lips.

"I don't know." She yawned and stretched, and rolled away from the wet spot, then back on top of it. His spunk made her feel closer to him. She did not want to take a shower, she liked the smell of his come on her. "I heard it in that Erroll Flynn picture Mike Curtiz directed at Warner's. The one about the pirate. Captain Something."

"I didn't see it."

"I bet you never even saw a picture of mine before you met me."

Jacob sat beside her on the bed. "You could make money on that bet," he said, smiling.

Blue took the cigarette from his lips and drew on it. She let her head and shoulders hang over the edge of the bed and began to blow smoke rings, knees raised, legs apart, her buttocks providing purchase. Her breasts flattened out against her chest until only her nipples seemed to protrude. Jacob leaned over and removed the cigarette from her mouth, then crushed it out in an ashtray. "The first time I ever saw you, Arthur took a butt out of your mouth. At the Copa. He didn't want you photographed smoking."

"You remember that?"

"Yeah."

"You ever think we'd end up this way?"

"It crossed my mind."

"I remember, too."

"What do you remember?"

"That you knew this was what I looked like with my clothes off."

Jacob King smiled. "Well, I wasn't surprised."

"Jacob, I never want to get old."

A shadow passed over his face, a shadow he hoped she did not see. *Morris wants you to be old, too. I want you to be old. Believe me.* "Yes, you do."

"Will you get old with me, then?"

How could he promise that? "I am old."

"No, you're not." She heaved herself upright, in perfect shape, a dancer's motion, as if she was doing a sit-up.

"Twice as old as you are. And more."

"Well, you act young."

He stacked the brushes and put them on the bed.

"Are you still lucky, Jacob?"

"I hope as lucky as you are," he said quietly. "I think about that plane a lot lately. And you missing it."

She wondered if she should tell him. She hated secrets, she could never keep them, as much as she always promised she would, but this was one she had kept for more than five years. It made her feel guilty sometimes that she had lived and Carole and the others had died, but there it was. "Jacob," she said. Her voice was grave. "It wasn't just luck."

He heard the hesitant note and said nothing. Better not to ask questions. Questions might make her retreat. Nor did he touch her. She was naked on his bed, and she smelled of him, and there might be a moment to reach for her, but that moment was not now.

"Actually, how I happened to miss the plane was because I was with Mr. French." She took a deep breath. "Moe." There. It was out. She had thought that if she ever told, the words would come bursting forth, and that she would cry as she did when she was younger and had thought about it, but she held back. She was an actress after all, nineteen now and not fourteen, a fourteen-year-old would behave differently. "He'd been getting some kind of award in Chicago, from the B'nai B'rith, I think, and he'd stopped off here in Vegas on the way home. He came here to gamble sometimes. He'd checked the studio to see where I was, and when he found out our plane was stopping over here, he left me a message at the airport to meet him at the Fremont, and so I went into town." She looked directly at Jacob. "He made me go down on him." It was the first time she had ever performed fellatio, but she saw no reason to mention that. Or that it was easy to learn. Or that she called him Mr. French throughout, and Moe called her "little girl, nice little girl," and had not removed his trousers, that was later, when they were in bed, listening to the radio, KVEG, the voice of southern Nevada, music and news. Vaughn Monroe was singing "Racing to the Moon," when there was an interruption for a news bulletin, a plane carrying Carole Lombard and Blue Tyler had crashed outside Las Vegas, and there appeared to be no survivors. Blue began to cry and then to scream. J. F. French slapped her hard across the face and said if she screamed once more she would never work for Cosmo again, and except for intermittent sobs, she stopped crying. As Moe quickly got dressed, she noticed how old he seemed and how the fleshy folds and wrinkles in his stomach made him look like a melting candle. He would die before she did, and that was a comforting thought. Wait here, he said, don't move, don't make a sound, then he went down to the lobby and reserved a room for "Wanda Nash," the name she was always registered as when she was on location or doing P.A.s, and it was to Wanda Nash's room in the Fremont that she was hustled the night Carole Lombard's flight flew into Potosi Mountain near Table Rock, Nevada. "That's how come I missed the plane."

Jacob held her close. I'll kill him, she thought he said, but she wasn't sure, it sounded like a line in a picture, not real life. He held her so tight she thought he would crush her shoulders. Oh, God, she thought he said, but again she wasn't sure, she was only sure he understood.

"I never told Arthur." She burrowed her face into Jacob's shoulder. No tears, it was just such a relief to tell someone. She had never done it with him again, she wasn't after all one of the French Fillies, who could be fired and not missed, she was Blue Tyler, she was only fourteen years old, but the failure or success of Cosmo's entire slate of pictures depended on her, Mr. French knew that and she knew that, and what happened at the Fremont gave her an edge that she never intended to lose, and from that day on she always called him Moe.

"I want you to go back to town first thing in the morning," Jacob said suddenly.

"Don't you want me anymore?"

"I'll rent a plane."

"I don't see why I have to go back."

"Just try doing what I say for a change."

"I don't have to shoot for another three weeks. You just don't want me anymore."

He had run all her pictures in the screening room at St. Pierre Road, and he knew she was doing what Chuckie called her patented pout. He wanted to say, I want you for the rest of my life, but it didn't sound like him. Some other time, perhaps. Not now. "Listen. Blue. What I do . . . you think it's glamorous." He paused. *The fact you're a gangster is what gives her the goose.* "It's not. Sometimes it's dangerous."

"Jacob. You think I don't know that."

Not some other time. Now. "I want you for the rest of my life."

◄◦►

The plane was ready at dawn, idling on the tarmac, a single-engine Cessna four-seater. Blue rummaged through her shoulder bag for a bandanna as Eddie Binhoff took her bags from the trunk of Jacob's Continental. Jacob walked over to the mechanic who was inspecting the aircraft. The pilot was already inside, looking at his charts.

"All set, Mr. King," the mechanic said. "It's clean."

"For your sake I hope it is," Jacob said. "Because you're going with her."

"I said it was clean, didn't I?"

"I always like to make sure."

"Hey, wait a minute . . ."

"Maybe you want to talk it over with my friend Eddie over there?" Jacob said.

The mechanic shuddered. He had heard about Eddie around town, and he had heard what talking anything over with him involved. He wiped his hands on his coveralls. "I guess I go to L.A."

"I'm glad to hear that."

The mechanic took Blue's bags from Eddie Binhoff and put them into the Cessna's luggage compartment. Blue knotted the bandanna, and then clung to Jacob.

"You know something? I'm not afraid to fly anymore. That's one thing you did for me."

"So call me."

"So maybe I will."

He kissed her, held her tight for a moment, then released her. She reached the door of the plane and looked back, one renegade to another, a melancholy joke between them.

"Big bad gangster," Blue Tyler said.

◅◦▻

It's funny what you remember, Melba Mae Toolate said. Do you know what I remember about that day?

What?

I remember that the fender on the Continental, you know, the one I sideswiped the day he hit Lilo, I remember it still wasn't fixed. That wasn't like Jake. He always wanted everything just right.

Do you think he knew . . .

About what was going to happen?

I nodded.

I think he knew.

And that's why he sent you back?

I think he decided when I told him about Mr. French.

Why?

You'd have to ask him.

You mean, it was about rules he didn't understand.

You'd have to ask him.

Did you call him?

Every night.

XIX

Even *The New York Times* put it on the front page:

KING, GANGSTER, IS SLAIN IN NEVADA

—Jacob King, 41, former New York gangster and associate of Seventh Avenue furrier Morris Lefkowitz, was slain last midnight by a fusillade of bullets from an unidentified gunman in his top-floor suite of the King's Playland Hotel, which was scheduled to open this upcoming New Year's Eve . . .

The *Daily News* headline said:

RIVALS RUB OUT JAKE KING, GANGLAND'S NO. 1 MOBSTER

—Jacob ("Jake") King, 42, the nation's No. 1 gangster, and pal of Hollywood celebrities, was ambushed tonight in his palatial six-room suite at the soon-to-open King's Playland Hotel in Las Vegas. Attention was focused on rivals who wanted to take over his multimillion-dollar hotel and gambling empire, although local authorities said they had no clues as to the identity of his unknown killer or killers . . .

The *Journal-American:*

JAKE MOWED DOWN BY GANG

. . . The suave, personable King was killed wearing a purple smoking jacket when bullets from an unknown killer tore him apart in front of a portrait of himself he had recently commissioned. Sources say that the portrait was splattered with the hoodlum's blood . . .

The *Post:*

JAKE'S LEGACY—NATIONWIDE GANG WAR?

—A gang war of nationwide proportions may have been touched off by the snuff-out death of Jake King, 43, mob hit man, gambler, and man about Hollywood . . .

And Winchell: "Is Blue blue??????? . . . And didja hear what they're calling that portrait Jake King's brains were splattered all over? . . . Modern art, geddit? . . . Jakey was wearing jodhpurs in his pitcha . . . Jodhpur Jakey better be riding a fast horse to get out of where he's going . . ."

◄○►

Jacob walked through the empty casino, spinning the roulette wheels and checking the quality of the felt on the crap tables. The clocks. He should get rid of the clocks. There should be no clocks in a casino, time for a gambler should stand still. He would do the kitchen tomorrow, too. A chef had told him he had found evidence of rat shit, it was that way in every new building, no big problem, just drop a little something on the inspector from the Department of Health, otherwise an exterminator would have to be called in. Exterminator, Jacob wrote on the leather-bound notepad he always carried now. Another gift from Blue. From a place in Paris. He would go there with Blue one day. It made him smile that he would call the exterminator rather than pay off the health inspector. Bribery had always been second nature to him, anyone can be bought, an article of faith learned from Morris, but Playland was going to be on the square. He pushed the elevator button, and when the light did not immediately come on, made another note to have an electrician check it out tomorrow. In the elevator he noticed some barely perceptible chipped paint. Still another note. So many details. The paint in the corridors. The brass numbers on the room doors. Jackie Heller. Jackie was playing footsie with Lilo again. Rita said she had seen them at Hillcrest. Jackie had forgotten to tell him he had gone to L.A. What else had Jackie forgotten to tell him? Eddie could handle that. When things slowed down. Where was Eddie anyway? He checked his watch. Blue would call at ten. He walked down the hall and opened the door to his suite.

Eddie Binhoff was standing at the picture window, staring out at the KING'S PLAYLAND sign.

"Eddie. I been looking all over for you, where you been, you want a drink, something to eat?"

"Come over here, Jake, take a look at this."

Jacob walked to the window. Outside the marquee, neon was lighting up the night sky. He had planted a dozen palm trees around the Playland sign, five grand a tree, take it out of my end, he had said to Jimmy Riordan, and the fronds were now waving gently in the night breeze. It was the right thing to do.

"You did it, Jake," Eddie Binhoff said.

"Goddamn," Jacob King said after a moment. "It's beautiful." He would deal with details tomorrow. Right now he just wanted to enjoy the moment. "We've come a long way from Red Hook, Eddie."

"A long way." Eddie Binhoff moved to the bar and turned on the radio. Guy Lombardo and his Royal Canadians live from the Starlight Roof at the Waldorf-Astoria, Carmen Lombardo on the vocal. I'm wild again, beguiled again . . . "Calls for a drink."

. . . a simpering, whimpering child again . . .

Jacob stood by the window, mesmerized by the sign. He wondered if the lights should blink on and off. No. They should stay on, as they were now, reflecting off his face, like neon sunlight. "Eddie, Guy Lombardo's the kind of class guy I want here, I'll call him tomorrow." He turned, and there was Eddie Binhoff standing by the bar, the double-barreled shotgun he had stored in the bar cabinet in his hand. "Oh, no," Jacob King said. "It had to be you, didn't it?"

"I'm sorry, Jake," Eddie Binhoff said, and he was sorry, even as he pulled the triggers, and the force of the shotgun pellets propelled Jacob backward against the wall, down which he slid until he came to rest against his still-unhung portrait.

. . . bewitched, bothered, and bewildered . . .

XX

MORRIS LEFKOWITZ FLEW OUT for the funeral, his first trip on an airplane. He booked under his own name on United, then under the name Schmuel Leibrandt on TWA, and of course with Jimmy Riordan took the TWA flight, sending Lillian King and Matthew and Abigail on United. Just in case. Lilo, Jimmy Riordan had said on the telephone from New York, Morris doesn't want the press there, and Lilo Kusack had said, not to worry, we put an announcement in the paper that the service will be at Forest Lawn, I know a place in Van Nuys, it's where Schlomo Buchalter was buried out of, they do a nice little service, no crowds, you don't mind if I don't show up, Barry Tyger's busy, too. Morris said that was fine, he understood Lilo's reluctance, and then, because he did not trust Lilo Kusack, made still other arrangements, under Schmuel Leibrandt's name, to hold the service at the Heyer & Sobol Funeral Home & Mortuary in Studio City, the name of the deceased being Yakov Kinovsky, whose body was to be cremated and his ashes placed in a mortuary crypt.

Lillian King and her two children, along with Morris Lefkowitz, Jimmy Riordan, and Eddie Binhoff, were the only mourners at the mortuary, except for Rita Lewis, her face hidden behind a thick black veil, and Chuckie O'Hara, who that very morning had been served with a subpoena to appear before the House Un-American Activities Committee. It was Rita who had found out where the service was actually being held, a call from a pay phone to Jimmy Riordan so that Lilo could not overhear, and the promise, Listen, Jimmy, I'm not the fucking lady in red, I'm not going to finger Morris, Jake was a friend of mine. She had called Chuckie, and he had said Jake was a friend of his, too, of course he would go, and by the way I got my subpoena today. What're you going to do? Rita had asked on the way to Studio City, and Chuckie had said, Auntie Charlton will think of something crowd-pleasing, darling, you can count on that.

The rabbi in his prayer shawl recited the kaddish, and said a few words about Yakov, a generous contributor to Jewish causes, and then the service was over. "Thank you, Morris," Lillian said, dry-eyed through the ceremony, Matthew and Abigail each clinging to a hand, neither quite sure what it all meant, and then Lillian had asked Jimmy if the woman in the veil was one of Jacob's whores, why not let him die in peace, and what about the fairy with the gimp, there were children here, they shouldn't be exposed to such things. Right, Lillian, Jimmy Riordan had said, you are absolutely right, it shows a definite lack of respect, all the while thinking the only benefit of this unhappy occasion was that he would never have to see Lillian King again.

Morris Lefkowitz hung back until after Lillian departed, then approached the urn containing Jacob King's ashes, which rested in the still-open crypt. There was a typewritten card on the door of the crypt: YAKOV KINOVSKY (1907–1948), and under Jacob's name, the words, chosen the night before by Jimmy Riordan from a dictionary of quotations, "But westward, look, the land is bright."

Morris's face was ashen, his hand unsteady, and the wattles on his neck hung over the collar of his shirt. He's going to die soon, Jimmy Riordan thought suddenly, a calculation he had disciplined himself not to entertain, even as the evidence of

Morris's physical decay had become steadily more apparent, even as, concomitantly, his fabled mental agility flashed only sporadically, like the filament in a lightbulb that blazed brightest just before it burned out. Jacob had made the mistake of calling Morris old to his face, while Lilo would only whisper it into Jimmy's ear, a messenger certain that his message would not be passed on. Loyalty was a virtue Jimmy valued, and his loyalty to Morris Lefkowitz had always been total and unquestioning. For fifty years, Morris had been a master puppeteer whose mario-nettes danced to the tune of his supple fingers, with never a misstep. Now there were too many puppets falling in a heap. First Philly Wexler, then Jacob, with all the attendant litter. Morris was on borrowed time, and if Morris, his protector, was, then so too was Jimmy Riordan. The difference was that Jimmy knew it, while Morris seemed to comprehend it only fleetingly, as when he made Jacob's funeral arrangements, Morris whose entire life had always been governed by his sense of self-preser-vation. It was for Jimmy to make the deals ensuring that Morris died in bed, a field marshal emeritus. And at the same time put into place a deal for himself, after Morris was gone, commuting his self-exile to the country of crime, where Morris Lefkowitz had reigned for so many decades as absolute monarch, and where James Francis Riordan had served twenty years and then some as the monarch's chief minister.

"Sometimes, Jimmy," Morris Lefkowitz said, turning away from the crypt, "I wish I was in another business than the fur business."

As Morris started for the door, his step faltered and Jimmy quickly motioned for Eddie Binhoff to go with him. Eddie nod-ded, then stopped, and for a second placed both hands on the ceramic urn holding the last remains of Jacob King.

Jimmy stared at the urn and made a mental note that as soon as Morris was on the plane back to New York, Eddie Binhoff should take care of the Jackie Heller problem and then get lost for a while.

As for the future, speed was as much a priority as skill. The extortioner's skill he did not doubt he possessed, and he thought that time, though short, was still on his side. First however he had to pay homage to the dead, and ask forgiveness.

◄○►

Rita told him they would all be at Chasen's that evening, she was giving it a pass, it was a show of solidarity that she did not wish to attend, a way of letting the community know that life went on, and it was at Chasen's that Jimmy Riordan found them, sitting in the first banquette on the left inside the door, Blue Tyler and her court, J. F. French on one side of her, Arthur on the other, and Lilo Kusack next to Moe.

"This little girl's starving," J. F. French said. "Get us a plate of shrimp . . . then the hobo steak . . ."

"I'm fine," Blue Tyler said, demure in Edith Head's black wool jersey, and the two strands of natural pearls around her neck, and the small hat with the *point d'esprit* veil.

"Of course you're fine," Arthur French said. "Nobody said you weren't fine." He snapped a finger. "Waiter, get us some shrimp . . ."

"Why do you think we're at Chasen's, little girl?" J. F. French said, and then answered his own question. "We're at Chasen's because you're fine."

Lilo Kusack half rose. "Jimmy," he said to Jimmy Riordan, who was sliding into the booth next to Arthur French. "Swell to see you. You know Moe and his son, Arthur. Blue, this is Jimmy Riordan from New York, Jimmy, this is Blue Tyler."

She knew she was not supposed to speak, but only nod and smile as if Jimmy Riordan was just another fan seeking an autograph, but she could not help it, she had to ask. "You were a friend of—"

"God rest him, we were all his friends," J. F. French interrupted. "Where's that shrimp, Arthur?"

"A big dreamer," Arthur French said, ignoring his father.

"A pioneer," Lilo Kusack said, "you have to admire that." He raised a glass of champagne. "Here's to him."

"Wait a minute, Lilo, Jimmy doesn't have a glass," J. F. French said. "Arthur, a glass for Mr. Riordan."

A waiter brought a champagne flute and filled it. The table was wrapped in silence. All over the front room people were looking at them, and Dave Chasen was whispering to favored customers who the stranger with the battered nose was at the Frenches' booth. Blue tried, but could not take her eyes off Jimmy Riordan. She wanted to ask him what Jacob was like in New York, and if what happened was her fault, and would it have happened if they had never met.

"To Playland," Lilo Kusack said.

"I can drink to that," J. F. French said.

Arthur and Lilo and J. F. French clinked their glasses, and so, after a kick under the table from J. F., did Blue.

"And to Jake," Arthur French said, the unspeakable finally mentioned. "He was what he was."

Jimmy Riordan tapped a fingernail against his flute but did not raise it with the others. He looked at them all, one by one, troubled not so much by the decisions he had made, even by their cost, as by a residual sense of loyalty, and guilt. He had to say what he came to say. "You know what he was?" Jimmy slid from the booth and stood, staring down at them. "He was worth this whole goddamn table. He was worth this whole goddamn town."

Lilo put his glass down, and then so did the others. No one said a word. Blue Tyler lowered the veil over her eyes, and after a moment Jimmy Riordan walked out of Chasen's.

—◦—

His *me absolvo* speech, Arthur French said forty years later, his smirk scarcely contained. The Great Gatzberg had his Nick Carraway, and his name was Jimmy Riordan.

XXI

THE PLAN HAD BEEN for her to cross over, to make that leap so many child actresses had failed to make, from children's roles to those of adult women. Blue Tyler was never cute, and that was to her advantage. There was always in her a knowingness her contemporaries did not possess, a latent sexual component that allowed the audience to fantasize that when the adults in her pictures might be getting it on, she conceivably was peeking through the keyhole. Unlike the other child stars of her time, she made her better pictures when she was an adolescent, when she had tits and a working twat, as Chuckie O'Hara later said, and the popcorn eaters somehow knew it, however much Cosmopolitan Pictures tried to disguise the fact. The plan, however, was not to be. *Broadway Babe* was postponed for a year (the official reason was that the score had to be thrown out; the real reason I did not find out until I was able to pull it out of Arthur French), and then first Chuckie O'Hara and later Blue herself became victims of history. Winchell was out front. "Say, didja hear where pinkostinko director Chuckie O'Hara lives in El Lay. In a part of Hollywood they call the Swish Alps!!!!" Preproduction was halted when Chuckie went to Washington to testify, and after he took off his leg in the

HUAC hearing room he was fired by J. F. French, and replaced by Victor Higgins. Blue then quit *Broadway Babe* in protest, and was immediately put on suspension by the studio. Some months later she too was subpoenaed and summoned to Washington. Her primary interrogator was Congressman Theodore ("Ted") Wilder, the first recipient of the "I Am an American" award, at whose dinner Blue had led the audience in the Pledge of Allegiance. The congressman was particularly interested in her performance, when she was eight, in *Little Sister Susan:*

Q: That picture was directed by Mr. Charlton O'Hara, is that correct?

A: Yes.

Q: An admitted Communist?

A: The only thing I know about Chuckie, Congressman . . . I don't know.

Q: What is the only thing you know about Mr. O'Hara, Miss Tyler?

A: Only that he was a good director.

Q: Now *Little Sister Susan* was written by Mr. Reilly Holt, is that not correct?

A: Yes.

Q: A Red Bolshevik Communist, is that not correct?

A: I never met Reilly Holt. Mr. French didn't let stars talk to writers.

Q: A very good idea, if those writers were Red writers. Now you had a line in *Little Sister Susan,* and that line was "There's a far land I dream about . . ."

A: I guess . . .

Q: And was that far land Red Russia?

A: I don't know. I mean, I thought it was just someplace, you know, else, someplace else . . .

Q: Mr. Chairman, that is the insidious nature of these Red degenerates like O'Hara and Holt. They put their propaganda filth in the mouth of a little girl . . .

In perhaps the most manic moment of Blue's appearance, she was asked if she was now or ever had been a Communist. "Mr. Tavenner," she replied to the Committee's chief counsel, "I won't be old enough to vote until next year's election."

◄○►

You quit *Broadway Babe* because of Chuckie? I asked.

And because of Jacob, Melba Mae Toolate said. Because of a lot of things.

What things?

Just let me alone, will you? Everything.

◄○►

Cosmopolitan Pictures invoked the moral-turpitude clause in her contract, an action that left the studio's highest-paid star functionally unemployable in the Hollywood community. No one seriously believed that she was a Communist, but the clause covered a multitude of sins, most of which in fact she had committed. Her earnings since the age of four had gone into trust accounts so that her financial position was not as precarious as that of others who had been blacklisted. But then neither were her funds infinite, and Cosmopolitan brought her to the brink of financial ruin through a series of legal maneuvers holding her accountable for production costs on pictures it had developed for her. She formed an independent production company and announced pictures, none of which of course were made. Then in 1951 she was subpoenaed to appear before the Kefauver Crime Committee to answer questions about the murder of Jacob King and whether it was the result of labor racketeering in the motion picture industry. Rather than testify she left the country for Italy via Mexico. Her passport was immediately revoked.

She was broke.

She was twenty-three years old.

◄○►

Moral turpitude, Arthur?

Well, there was Jake, and there was Chuckie, who was not just queer, he was a Commie on top of it, Arthur French said. And don't forget Walker Franklin. Any one of those was grounds for the moral-turpitude clause. He hesitated. Then: Plus we didn't know if she would work out as a grown-up.

Was that the real reason?

It went into the mix. Those were tough days, Jack. Television changed the whole equation. That, and making us get rid of the theater chains.

You people were all heart, Arthur.

I went along with the decision, Jack.

But she was a proven player.

It was a new ballgame.

◄○►

She made a number of pictures in Italy, none of which were released in the United States. Occasionally exposé magazines featured lurid accounts of her past and present. She was a lesbian, a bag lady for the Mob, a madam, she had fingered Jacob King, she had borne his love child, she had borne Arthur French's illegitimate daughter, she had aborted both, she had secretly married Jacob, she had secretly married Arthur, she had even secretly married Chuckie O'Hara, she was the beneficiary of hush money from Jacob's former associates, she was a call girl in Rome, she was a courier for the Italian Communist party. Her putative lovers ranged from Doris Duke to the Duke of Edinburgh, Lucky Luciano was said to be smitten, as was Senator John Kennedy, his father, Ambassador Joseph Kennedy, and my father, Hugh Broderick. In rapid succession she married and divorced a gaffer on one of her pictures; a grandnephew of Benito Mussolini; and one of King Farouk's lesser pimps. Be-

404 · JOHN GREGORY DUNNE

tween marriages she briefly took up again with Walker Franklin, but when she could not support him in the style to which he had grown accustomed, he abandoned her for a Venetian principessa. In the late fifties, more or less forgotten, she came back to New York. There was little fanfare, except for a brief flurry when a chorus girl she knew jumped out a window on West End Avenue, the story she had told me in Hamtramck. Blue Tyler's chorine gal pal, as the tabloid headlines put it. Nobody really cared except Walter Winchell, and he, like her, was a relic of another age. For two years she sang in a nightclub on Sixth Avenue, married and divorced twice more—two horn players, who also happened to be brothers—and then in the early 1960s, she simply disappeared.

She was broke.

She was unknown.

She was a drunk.

She was thirty-three years old.

As Blue Tyler, she ceased to exist.

◄◦►

Baby, she said, I just fell off the planet earth.

PART THREE

META
& THE HOUND
OF HEAVEN

I

ACTUALLY SHE DID TELL ME, Arthur French said. After a fashion. In her own way.

◄○►

On the flight to Tucson and then on the drive from Tucson to Nogales, I had debated whether I should finally mention to Arthur that Melba Mae Toolate, during our last taping session in Hamtramck, had reported matter-of-factly that when she was fourteen years old she was giving his father a blow job at the Fremont Hotel in Las Vegas that sixteenth of January, 1942, at about the time that Carole Lombard's TWA flight, with Blue Tyler supposedly a passenger on board, crashed into Potosi Mountain in Table Rock, Nevada, with no survivors. Trying to sort out Blue's life, and Melba Mae's problematic take on it, I had come to the ranch twice since my return, and talked to Arthur at length on the telephone, and again that one time in his father's orchid house at Willingham when he had come up to Los Angeles, but the topic was not one with an easy transition into it ("Oh, by the way, Arthur . . ." did not seem to fill the bill), and so I kept putting it off until I could find an opportune moment. We rode every day, I think because Arthur liked to see my discomfiture in the saddle. I don't like horses and hated to ride, and he sat a horse better than one might have expected from the son of Moses Frankel, immigrant turned haberdasher turned mogul. And also if we were riding I could not tape, and I had the sense that Arthur wanted few records kept of any discussions we might have about Blue Tyler. It was not until my last night at the ranch, as we sat on the veranda before dinner, with the sun disappearing behind the foothills and a third or perhaps even a fourth drink stiffening my resolve, that the old cop-shop reporter I had once been took charge, the one who in days past could ask the relatives of murder victims to comment on the brutal slaying of their son or daughter or husband or wife or brother or sister, and ask it without hesitation. Still it was with a certain trepidation, earned over the years of our friendship, that I finally told him what Melba Mae Toolate claimed was the reason Blue Tyler had missed Carole Lombard's plane that night. And as so often with Arthur, I was not prepared for the equanimity of his response.

It was a long time later when she told me, he said. In her own —he paused—devious way.

(For the moment, I let *devious* pass.) Did you believe her?

I knew my father. I knew his tastes.

Your father ran her out of the Industry. That could be why she said it.

She wasn't like that, Jack. You never knew Blue Tyler. You just knew Melba Mae whatever her name is . . .

Toolate.

Anyway, it was after she left Hollywood and dropped out of sight when she told me. Three, four years ago.

How'd she tell you?

You remember how I once said she always kept in touch. Out of the blue I'd get something in the mail.

Like Walker Franklin's obituary, stuff like that?

That's it, yes. Well, she'd seen this show on television. *Unsolved Murders,* I think it was called. One of those shit shows like *Hard Copy.* Re-created crimes. She sent me a review of it from some paper in the Midwest.

A show about Jacob King?

No. About someone she'd gone to school with. At the Little Red Schoolhouse. Meta . . . Arthur paused, as if wondering whether to continue; then he did, selecting each word even more carefully than usual. . . . Meta somebody who the studio publicity department said was her best friend. Blue mixing with real people was the story line. The fan magazines ate up that kind of stuff. It was bullshit.

And this woman was murdered? Arthur seemed to be putting distance between Meta and Blue, and I was curious as to why, so for the moment I chose not to mention that I had already rummaged through dusty studio files and discovered the photographs of Blue doing algebra problems with Meta Dierdorf, and reading *Little Women* with her, Meta Dierdorf, who even in death took second billing to her more famous schoolmate:

BLUE'S TRAGEDY
NON-PRO CLASSMATE FOUND STRANGLED IN TUB

It happened when I was in the army, Arthur said. Making propaganda films with Ronnie Reagan down at Fort MacArthur in San Pedro. You know, I actually outranked him. This Meta . . .

Dierdorf, I said. Meta Dierdorf.

Jack, Arthur said, scolding. You knew about her all the time, didn't you?

I came across her name. In the clips.

Yes, Arthur said, drawing the word out, even in distress never losing his ingrained capacity for irony, his eyes never leaving mine, as if demanding I ask the question that hung in the air between us.

I knew my father, I knew his tastes.

I could not avoid it: Did your father . . . know her?

Arthur nodded. Yes, he said finally. I can't say I was surprised, it was a pattern with J.F. The younger they were, the younger he felt. She was—another pause—perfect . . .

In what way?

Non-industry. She didn't know anyone we knew. Except Blue. And that was just a friendship the publicity department dreamed up. I don't think I ever heard Blue mention her.

Melba Mae talking: *This girlfriend I had at the studio school. She wasn't in the business. Meta said dancing is a vertical expression of a horizontal desire.*

Arthur continued: J.F. must've seen her on the lot. And seen the advantages . . .

Advantages?

There was always gossip about that . . . chorus line he kept. And so I asked Lilo.

Why Lilo?

It was the kind of thing he would know. What you've got to remember about Lilo is that he was always preparing a defense, for the day he might need one. Looking for an edge. When that girl died . . .

Miss Dierdorf.

I know her name, Jack, Arthur said sharply.

I did not respond.

When she died, Arthur said after a moment, Lilo told me he'd asked J.F. if he knew her.

Knowing already of course that he did.

Lilo just hated surprises. And he was also Blue's lawyer. He was watching out for her, too.

Why?

There were all these photographs of the two of them at school . . .

Arthur was prevaricating, I knew it, but at least he was talking. Better to let him continue. Double back later.

And some at the Hollywood Canteen, I said.

More publicity shots. The Canteen was for enlisted men. Blue wasn't much of an egalitarian when it came to the military. She preferred officers, but publicity said it was good for morale to send out shots of her with soldier boys and sailor boys.

Your father . . . I hesitated.

Did he kill her? Arthur said, finishing the question for me. No, I don't think so. J.F. was capable of doing a lot of terrible things, but I don't think he was capable of that. He was, and even now it's hard to say this about your own father, he was a coward.

He might have had somebody do it.

Jack, stop talking like a television writer.

It was a line meant to terminate debate. I let the silence build between us. Then: What did Blue have to say about this *Unsolved Murder* show? How did that lead into her and your father?

She didn't have anything to say about the show itself. It was just her way of telling me she knew about J.F. and this Meta girl, and she knew I knew. That's the only reason she sent it. Arthur smiled. Memories are made of this, he said softly, almost singing the lyric. Then: There was a piece of lined notebook paper with the review, the kind kids use, that seemed to have been ripped out of a spiral notebook. And on it she'd written that I was always nicer, I was always the nice one. Nicer than J.F. is what she meant without saying it. And then she said she'd been with him when that plane went in. That's all she said. That she'd been with him. Nobody had to draw me a picture. Even at the time I suppose I knew. Or guessed.

But you never asked her.

No. Arthur stared into the lengthening twilight, biting his lower lip until I thought he might draw blood, and I realized that whatever he had once felt for Blue had never been entirely erased, and never would. J.F. was at the Fremont, he said at last, and I knew she was too because she'd called me from there, I thought she was on the plane, I thought she'd died in the crash with Carole, and she called me because she wanted me to know she was all right, she was registered as Wanda Nash.

Arthur closed his eyes and pinched his face between his hands. Nobody had to draw me a picture, he repeated, his voice trailing off. Then after a moment: We came up with some medical excuse about why she missed the flight.

Strep throat . . .

You've done your homework, Jack. He was back in control, his smile as arch as ever.

So she sent you this clipping.

Our code. When we were together, what counted was not what we said to each other, but what we didn't say.

It still seems to be, I said.

You know the police never made the connection between that girl . . . Arthur paused, as if he could not bear to say her name. . . . that girl and J.F. And they never thought to ask Blue about it. Maybe Lilo had the fix in. It didn't matter. She would have lied for him.

For your father? Why?

Because he was family, Jack. We were the only family she ever knew.

I I

I KNEW THAT an unsolved homicide investigation was never closed, and so after my conversation with Arthur French in Nogales I was able, through an LAPD detective I knew (one who like Maury Ahearne was always available for a little free enterprise) to photocopy the file on Blue Tyler's schoolfriend Meta Dierdorf, female Caucasian, age 19 years, height 5'3", weight 121 lbs., eyes brown, hair brown, file A-39536 (dead body). Date: July 27, 1945. Crime: PC 187 (Homicide).

The initial report filed by the primary investigator set the scene:

At 9:45 A.M., July 27, 1945, notified by teletype from Mid-Wilshire substation that there was a dead body in bathtub at El Coronado Apartments, 8497 Fountain Avenue, West Los Angeles. Body discovered by maid upon arriving at site o/a 8:30 A.M. this date. Maid Emerald Johnson notified janitor Cletis Rivers, who notified substation. Proceeded to above location El Coronado apartments. Victim resided in Apartment G, two-floor apartment with three bedrooms and two bathrooms on 2d floor, LR, DR, kitchen and toilet on 1st

floor. Found dead body of victim lying in bathtub in bathroom on 2d floor. The head face down was at the spigot end
of tub and the left foot was resting upon the upper edge of
tub at other end. The right leg was resting in the tub. There
was no water in bathtub at time of my arrival at scene. There
was small amount of blood upon bottom of bathtub under
victim's face. Also what seemed to be dried discharge upon
lower part of buttocks. Victim's body was nude. There was a
wet turkish bath towel lying upon bathroom floor alongside
of bathtub. When assistant medical examiner arrived at scene,
body was examined, samples taken of dried blood in tub and
discharge on victim's buttocks, and cultures taken from anus
and vagina. Body was turned over in bathtub and it was then
discovered that a piece of cloth was protruding from victim's
mouth, and the teeth were clamped tightly over same. The
piece of cloth had a small red border upon it, and seemed to
have been torn or cut from the end of a towel or a roll of
bandage. A search was made of every part of the house for a
towel with a red border with a part of it missing or a bandage
box, but nothing was found. The bedroom of victim is adjacent to the bathroom. There was valuable jewelry and other
articles of value upon dresser and in closet, including camera
equipment. There were two photograph albums of men in
uniform which were collected to aid in investigation, as was
film in camera, which was sent to police lab for developing.
There was also $272 in cash in stocking drawer. Change purse
in pocketbook on dresser contained $14 in bills and $3.42 in
coins, as well as victim's driver's license, gas and food ration
cards, and card saying victim was registered as a hostess at the
Stage Door Canteen in Hollywood. A pair of pajama pants
was lying upon floor alongside of bed. The pants had a tear in
them. There was a blood spot upon carpet next to the door
that leads to the bathroom. The carpet was wet around the
blood spot and indicated that an attempt had been made to
rub it out with a wet cloth. There were no blood spots of any
kind upon bathroom floor or upon the bed. Also no indica-

tions of struggle having taken place on the bed. In room was also a diary and address book, property of victim. Attempted to question colored maid Emerald Johnson, but she was too distraught to answer questions except to say that she came to apartment to clean three days a week and that nothing of value seemed to be missing. She said that she was at choir practice at Bethany Baptist Church, 3891 Central Avenue, night before. Questioned colored janitor Cletis Rivers, who said victim's car, a green 1939 Dodge coupe, was not in basement garage where it was usually parked. Notified Mid-Wilshire substation to check DMV re registration and to put trace on vehicle. Photographs were taken of crime site and victim and then body was removed to the county mortuary for further examination and investigation and postmortem operation.

> T. J. Spellacy
> Lieutenant Robbery-Homicide
> Investigator (Primary)

It was odd, even obscene, looking at old forensic photographs of a naked dead nineteen-year-old who if she were still alive would be close to seventy, with all the attendant miseries and complaints of old age and failed expectations. Meta Dierdorf was not a pretty sight in her bathtub. Her face was battered, her nose bloodied, her lips puffed and split, her breasts bare and bruised. On the side of the tub, there were smeared traces of excrement, indicating that as she was dying her sphincter had loosened and she had evacuated her bowels, which meant that the last thing she smelled was the stink of her own shit. In one photo, taken at the County Medical Center morgue after her body had been moved there for the postmortem, a pocket handkerchief had been placed over her pubic symphysis, a peculiar daintiness, I could not help thinking, considering the circumstances of her death. Perhaps the real obscenity, however, was that I found myself getting a little turned on by the pictures, especially by the one with the handkerchief over her bush.

In spite of that, in spite of the blood and the bruises and the blackened eyes and the shit and all the detritus of violent death, I recognized almost immediately that the body in the bathtub was that of the naked young girl in those postcard-sized photographs Maury Ahearne had stolen from the refrigerator in Melba Mae Toolate's recreational vehicle at the Autumn Breeze trailer park in Hamtramck, Michigan. The photographs Blue Tyler had kept for nearly half a century. The photographs she had spilled on a Greyhound bus platform in Kansas City. The photograph I had shown Arthur French on my first trip to Nogales. And whose subject Arthur had claimed he was unable to identify.

I remembered:

I knew my father, I knew his tastes. . . . The younger they were, the younger he felt. . . . She was perfect. . . . She didn't know anyone we knew. Except Blue. And that was just a friendship the publicity department dreamed up. I don't think I ever heard Blue mention her . . .

And Blue:

This girlfriend I had at the studio school. She wasn't in the business . . .

Arthur again:

Lilo just hated surprises. And he was also Blue's lawyer. He was watching out for her, too . . .

Why was Lilo watching out for Blue?

I knew it was not because of any studio publicity pictures of Blue and Meta Dierdorf that might be floating around. Not even at my most gullible would I have believed that. Lilo wouldn't have told me, even if he could; he died of acute uremic poisoning in 1980, after he was mistakenly transfused with the wrong blood type after a prostate operation at the J. F. French Medical Center in Palm Springs.

Rita Lewis might have told me, but in 1964 she was strangled while waterskiing off Acapulco in the company of a beachboy that she had, as she had prophesied, bought as her toy. As she was trying a complicated backward turn, the ropes got caught around her neck, and broke it.

And Arthur seemed to be lying.

Why?

◄◦►

The file said that two used rubber prophylactics wrapped in Kleenex were found in a bedroom wastebasket, the foil wrappings indicating they were of the Sheik brand, and a third prophylactic wrapped in Kleenex, this one identified by its foil as a Rameses brand, was found in another bedroom wastebasket. In the medical examiner's autopsy, it was discovered that the victim was also wearing a latex pessary. According to the prescription bottles in her bathroom medicine cabinet, Meta Dierdorf's gynecologist was Milton Heifitz, M.D., of 321 South Camden Drive, Beverly Hills, and Dr. Heifitz told officers he had written the prescription for the pessary two years earlier. There were multiple semen stains on the blanket and bed sheet as well as several dried semen spots on the bathroom floor next to the toilet. The postmortem report said that while there was evidence of semen both in the victim's mouth and on the exterior of her buttocks, the specimen on her buttocks was prob·bly the result of ejaculation and not anal intercourse, as there appeared to have been no penile penetration of her anus. Chemical analysis of the semen indicated that it came from two different donors. The autopsy also indicated that the absence of bruising or edema in the vaginal passages supported the conclusion that Meta Dierdorf had not been raped either prior to or subsequent to her murder.

◄◦►

Miss Anita Rose, secretary to Matthew Dierdorf, the victim's father, told police she had cabled her employer in Bahrain about the death of his daughter, but that he had already checked out of his hotel, leaving as a forwarding address a poste restante in Ankara, and there had been no response to a cable she had sent there. Checking the records at the El Coronado Apartments,

Lieutenant Spellacy discovered that Meta Dierdorf's apartment was leased to Carlisle Properties, a company incorporated in Panama whose listed president was Matthew Dierdorf. Ten weeks before Meta Dierdorf's death, the trading of Carlisle stock was suspended on the American Stock Exchange when the company and its directors were cited for stock manipulation, with criminal charges pending. Matthew Dierdorf's listed home address was in Reno, Nevada, with a postal drop in Los Angeles, a one-room office in the Bradbury Building, where Anita Rose took his messages. Matthew Dierdorf had left the country via Mexico in April, gone to Brazil, and then allegedly to Bahrain, and rent on the apartment at 8497 Fountain Avenue had been in arrears since the April payment.

Anita Rose made all the arrangements for Meta Dierdorf's funeral. Expenses for the undertaker and the funeral service were paid out of her private bank account. There was a solemn high requiem mass at St. Ambrose's in Hollywood, attended by several tenants at the El Coronado apartments, a delegation from the Hollywood Stage Door Canteen, and a platoon of the curious, as well as by four homicide detectives, on the chance that the killer might choose to pay his (or less likely her) final respects. Interment was at Forest Lawn in Burbank. Atop the casket was a spray of lilies with a card that said, "Daddy." The florist who provided the bouquet told Lieutenant Spellacy that it had been personally selected by Anita Rose, who had signed the card herself and paid for the flowers in cash.

Lieutenant Spellacy's efforts over the years to contact Matthew Dierdorf were unavailing. These efforts came to an end in January 1951, when Matthew Dierdorf, according to a newspaper clipping from the New York *World-Telegram* included in the casebook, jumped, fell, or was pushed from the roof of the St. Moritz Hotel in New York. His body, the story said, landed on top of a mounted patrolman on the Avenue of the Americas. Matthew Dierdorf was killed, as were both the policeman and his horse, a red gelding whose name was Oscar.

◄◦►

Meta Dierdorf's address book, her daily diary, and her photo albums (the photographs mainly snapshots of servicemen identified on the black album pages only by first names written in white ink) were included in the case file. Her handwriting was childlike, all in block letters, both the periods and the dots over the letter *i* perfect little circles. The entries in the diary were mainly banal—hair appointments and manicures and pedicures and lunch dates and dinner dates and monthly references to "C," which I assumed, as I expect Lieutenant Spellacy had also, was the curse, that benighted word so in disuse in this more enlightened time. She was irregular, or at least had a dramatic tendency to think she was—"C should have started today???"—and then a day or so later—"C & cramps, whew!" There was not a single mention of Blue Tyler in her diary nor any pictures of her in the photo albums. I suppose Arthur French would have said this lent credence to his dismissal of their putative friendship as little more than an invention of the Cosmopolitan publicity department, but then Arthur had also said he had not recognized the young woman when I had showed him her photograph. Her address book, however, did contain Blue Tyler's change of address when she moved in March that year from Linden Drive in the Beverly Hills flats to Tower Road north of Sunset, as well as each new unlisted telephone number every time the studio changed it, sometimes as often as four times a year. Checking Pacific Bell, Lieutenant Spellacy found that the last of Blue Tyler's unlisted numbers had been changed just ten days before Meta Dierdorf was killed, and was recorded in the victim's book, suggesting that at least indirectly the two young women had been in contact.

There were a number of references in the diary to someone named "Vida" or "Vide"—the uncertainties of Meta Dierdorf's penmanship making each possibility plausible—and sometimes simply to "V." On close reading, one could infer (as did Lieutenant Spellacy) that she had some sort of financial arrangement with V, Vida, or Vide, to whom it appeared she lent her apartment for what seemed to be romantic trysts, perhaps even for cash. The notations were often in bad schoolgirl French: "V demain—$$$$$—bon pour le docteur," or "Vide —ici avec Monsieur Pepe La Moko, ooo la la, peut-être cinquante dollars pour Plein???" or "Vida—quelle surprise, beaucoup l'argent au médecin pour ma silence!!!" Her address book yielded several people whose first or last names began with the letter V—two Virginias, a Vergil and a Vincente, a Van Sant and a Vandergrift, but one Virginia was a hairdresser who had left Los Angeles in January 1945 for a defense job at Boeing in Seattle, and the other was a maiden great-aunt of eighty-one confined to an institution in Montecito; Vergil Harper and Vincente Simeon, decorators who shared Apartment D-2 in Meta Dierdorf's building, were at a party in Hillsborough, down the peninsula from San Francisco, the night of her murder, a party that upon investigation turned out to be a drag ball. Lemuel Van Sant, a brigadier general in a federalized unit of the California National Guard, died on Okinawa in June of acute amoebic dysentery, and Mrs. Florence Penn Crowell Persico Margolis Vandergrift had been residing in Reno for five weeks prior to the murder, attending to her fourth divorce.

—◦—

As I read her diary, it sometimes seemed as if Meta Dierdorf, that last year of the war, was a one-woman USO, with lunches and dinners and tea and drinks with soldiers and sailors and marines and coastguardsmen, both officers and enlisted men, no branch of the services scanted. On the evening of her murder, Meta Dierdorf had gone to the Stage Door Canteen at six and had stayed less than an hour, jitterbugging with several servicemen; then she had left, saying she was not feeling well, telling another hostess, Miss June Holt, that she had drunk too much punch at a luncheon earlier that day at Chloe Quarles's house for the marines assigned as extras to J. F. French's production of *Ready, Aim, Fire.* June Holt said she had walked Meta Dierdorf to her car and she appeared in good spirits, not unwell, leading Miss Holt to speculate that she had another engagement rather than actually being ill, as she had claimed. "Meta was always mysterious about who she saw," Miss Holt said in her statement to Lieutenant Spellacy. Although the rules of the Canteen stipulated that hostesses were not supposed to date the servicemen they met there, addresses and telephone numbers were routinely exchanged. Miss Holt also said that she was unaware of anyone named Vida or Vide that Meta Dierdorf might have known, or indeed of any friend whose first or last name began with the letter V.

For a period of time immediately after the murder, the leading suspect was someone identified in Meta Dierdorf's day book only as "Tommy." The entry on the day she was killed said "Tommy—7:30 chez moi, C fini!!!" Cross-checking all the names in her address book and her photo albums, Lieutenant Spellacy was finally able to track Tommy down to Mather Field, outside Sacramento, where as Captain Thomas Benedict, USAAF, he was assigned as a flight instructor to an A-20A light bomber training squadron. Lieutenant Spellacy went to Mather Field, and in the presence of a recording secretary and a Major Anders from the judge advocate general's office, he questioned Captain Benedict. The captain at first denied knowing Meta Dierdorf, then said he had stood her up the evening in question, leading Lieutenant Spellacy to lay out the seriousness of his situation and the possibility that he could end up in the gas chamber. As an interrogator, Lieutenant Spellacy did not beat around the bush. From the official record, August 3, 1945:

Q: You want it straight?

A: Yes.

Q: You fly airplanes, right?

A: Yes.

Q: A combat hero, right?

A: I flew in combat.

Q: Well, excuse me if I don't stand up and salute and say the country owes you a debt of gratitude.

MAJOR ANDERS OF THE JAG: I don't think that tone is necessary, Officer.

Q: Oh, you don't, do you? Well, listen, soldier boy, let me lay it out for you. This is a civilian offense, violation of Article 187 of the California penal code, the unlawful killing of a human being, to wit, Miss Meta Dierdorf, that this hero flyboy here says he don't know, only he can't explain how his picture just happened to show up in the photo album of this chick, unless maybe he's got a twin, for all I know, you got a twin brother, ace?

A: No. I am an only child.

Q: Well, your parents should've had a daughter then, ace, because I already got enough to arrest you, and as for you, Major whatever your name is, I got a warrant for that arrest here in my pocket, and I can dance him right off this post in cuffs, and there is nothing you can do about it, because you don't fart around with civilian authorities in a capital crime involving nonmilitary personnel. What I do is I bring him down to L.A., I charge him with violation of PC 187 and throw his ass into the county jail. Oh, will they love you in there, ace. Here comes the flyboy, they'll say, and they'll be lining up outside your cell to fly their peckers right up your brown trail, you know where the brown trail is, ace?

A: I think so. Yes.

Q: A weekend in the county jail, and the gas chamber will start looking good, so stop jerking me off, ace, and begin talking, or I'll go over to the PX there and buy you some lipstick and eyeliner and dress you up for your weekend in county.

MAJOR ANDERS: Rest assured, Officer, I will report this to the JAG.

Q: Major, rest assured, you can go fuck yourself and I'll sleep tight tonight. Or I'll arrest your ass for obstructing justice. Now where were we, flyboy, your memory improved?

It had. Captain Benedict admitted to having had sexual relations with Meta Dierdorf the evening of her death, saying he had lied only to protect her good name. He was the source, he said, of the two Sheik-brand prophylactics in the wastebasket, but not of the semen in the victim's mouth. It was, he said, the first time they had intercourse, although she had masturbated him on two prior occasions, and she seemed experienced and precise in her tastes. Asked if she had demanded money, Captain Benedict said she was not a prostitute, but came from what he called "a good family," the basis for this assumption being the luxury of her surroundings and her conversation about well-to-do people she seemed to know in the business and motion picture communities. He was unable to remember any names of the people she said she knew, although he did remember her saying she had gone to a party that day for some sailors or marines who were going to be extras in a new movie, and he had asked if she knew how he might get assigned to that detail, it would be a way for him to see her more often, and it might keep him out of the invasion of Japan everyone thought was coming up, he had done his share in North Africa and Italy and he was not looking forward to going back into combat. The captain claimed he left Meta Dierdorf's at nine-thirty the night of the murder, a claim backed up by the trip tickets of the cab company he had called from her apartment and by the cabdriver who had driven him to the air corps base at El Segundo. In his separate interrogation, the driver, Arnold Toledano, stated that as the captain was getting into his cab a young woman he later was able to identify as the victim from her photographs ran from the apartment. She was carrying a camera and the pilot's wings

from the captain's uniform, which she had apparently been playing with during the course of the evening. She pinned on his
wings, then posed him for a photograph in front of the apartment building, after which, the driver reported, they had kissed
in the street, and "a nice looker she was, she didn't seem to be
wearing any brassiere." The driver had then taken the captain to
El Segundo, where according to military flight manifests he had
boarded a ten-thirty flight to Mather Field. The film in Meta
Dierdorf's camera developed by the police lab contained the
photograph of Captain Benedict that the victim had taken, although the picture was somewhat indistinct because of the fading light. It was the last photograph on the roll of film, and
none of the other exposures, all of which were shots of the
marines at the luncheon earlier that day at Chloe Quarles's
house, were of any use in the investigation. As the medical examiner had fixed the time of death as no earlier than eleven-
thirty P.M., Captain Benedict's alibi seemed airtight, and he was
removed from the list of suspects.

There was no official complaint from the judge advocate general in the police file about the bullying nature of Lieutenant
Spellacy's interrogation.

-<o>-

Meta Dierdorf's green 1939 Dodge coupe was found abandoned the day after the murder in what the *Los Angeles Times*
called "a Negro section of Los Angeles," its gas tank empty and
the key still in the ignition. There were fingerprints on the key
and on the door handles, but they were too smeared to be of
use to the authorities. According to Cletis Rivers, the janitor at
the El Coronado apartments, Meta Dierdorf was in the habit of
leaving the key in the ignition when her car was in the garage
and often when it was parked in the street outside the building,
in spite of his repeated warnings that she was running the risk of
theft. Lieutenant Spellacy was convinced, however, that the
theft of the automobile was a coincidental matter unconnected
with the murder itself. There was no way of knowing if the car
keys were in the apartment or had been left in the car when she

parked it in the basement garage. Had it been a simple case of someone burglarizing Meta Dierdorf's apartment, the thief would have stolen not only the car keys but also the nearly three hundred dollars in cash as well as the jewelry on her dresser, which had an insured value in excess of $7,500. Had the victim come upon the burglary unexpectedly, she might have been raped or killed by the thief, but the postmortem said she had not been raped, and in any event she had engaged in sexual intercourse with two different men after returning to her apartment, leading to the conclusion that she had been there throughout the evening.

Along with his written reports, Lieutenant Spellacy had included some handwritten notes and speculations about the course of his investigation that, against department regulations, he had stuck into the casebook, as only official documents and transcribed interrogations were supposed to be in the department file. It was as if he knew that one day someone might come along, find his jottings, and be able to give them a fresh interpretation.

QUESTIONS, Lieutenant Spellacy had written, and then he had ticked them off:

1) Who is V?
2) who is the doctor (le docteur)?
3) Who pays for this apt? 19 yr old girl in 6 rm apt, no job, father broke. hook shop? vice says no. flyboy Benedict says no. neighbors say no unusual traffic. needs $. lets apt out for friends to screw?
4) Motive?
   a) extortion? V paying off? what silence? what is MD keeping quiet?
   b) screwing?
   c) just unlucky?
5) V? Vida? Vide? What is this Ooo la la SHIT anyway?
6) B. Tyler—cool customer; she knows more than she's let-

ting on; claims not to have known MD well—bullshit; Mr. Smooth, her sheeny lawyer Cusak (?), says studio handles distribution of phone #s, list not updated—don't kid a kidder.

7) brass says lay off B. Tyler. Cusak got to someone? concentrate on PC 187, not boom boom, boom boom not police business. concentrate on colored angle, stolen Dodge coupe in negro area. Screw them. Boom boom = PC 187. V = silence = key.

◄○►

I did a Nexis search of Lieutenant T. J. Spellacy on my computer and ultimately found a small obituary in the *Los Angeles Times*. He had died of coronary artery disease in 1984, at the age of seventy-eight, and was buried in Twenty-nine Palms, California, beside his younger brother, the Right Reverend Monsignor Desmond Spellacy, a Catholic priest and former chancellor of the archdiocese of Los Angeles, who retired to become the pastor of a small parish in the Mojave Desert. T. J. Spellacy seemed to have had the kind of attitude problem with which I could identify, an earlier generation's Maury Ahearne, and I would have liked to have asked him who had ordered him to lay off Blue Tyler and I would equally have liked to have shown him the photograph of the nude Meta Dierdorf that Blue Tyler had kept for fifty years. Like most good detectives I have known, he seemed to sense instinctively when someone was lying to him, and I would have bet that, like the better ones, he thought he was being lied to all the time, not least by the people with whom, and especially for whom, he worked. He was certainly right in his surmise that Blue was less forthcoming than he had claimed in his carefully neutral official report of their meeting ("Subject . . . could add nothing pertinent to the investigation. . . . Subject said she knew of no friend of deceased called Vida. . . ."), but I suspect his hunch was equally the result of an inbred antagonism toward Lilo Kusack and others like him who would have thought he was a not-overly-bright flatfoot, and who would have made little effort to conceal it, given their access to echelons in the department to which he was not privy. Had he known, as I did, that Meta Dierdorf was or had been the mistress of J. F. French, he would have taken enormous pleasure, I expect, in bringing the boom boom into the open and watching the squirming of the principals and their attendants, even if it brought him no closer to solving the murder itself.

◄○►

Lieutenant Spellacy was nothing if not thorough. He questioned every tenant in the seventeen apartments at the El Coronado as to their whereabouts the night of the murder and what they might conceivably have seen or overheard that could add a piece to the puzzle, and all he discovered was that Dr. Otto Ress in B-2 was so addicted to morphine that the state of California had lifted his license to practice medicine, and that Mrs. Hedda Flintoff in E-1 had suffered a broken nose and two black eyes earlier that week at the hand of her estranged husband, Samuel, but was unwilling to press charges; upon further investigation, it was found that Samuel Flintoff was in Cedars of Lebanon Hospital the day of the murder, having undergone an operation for testicular cancer. Mrs. Sarah Gabler in F-2 told Lieutenant Spellacy that Hendrik Nixon, the fourteen-year-old son of Mr. and Mrs. Maurice Nixon in F-1, exhibited unnatural sexual tendencies—Mrs. Gabler said she had to keep telling the boy not to finger her female Airedale; Mr. Nixon in turn replied that Mrs. Gabler had for three years been a patient under psychiatric care for delusionary tendencies at a private hospital in Pacific Palisades, a charge that was in fact true. Lieutenant Spellacy also learned that the option of Mr. Archie Sullivan in H-2, a director of second-feature Westerns, had not been picked up by Republic Pictures, and to make ends meet he was working for an escort service and as an adagio dance instructor at the Biltmore Hotel downtown until he could get back into directing.

◄○►

A Mrs. Fredella Humble of Altadena, California, wrote to "Detective in Dierdorf Case, Los Angeles, California," and in due course the typewritten letter found its way to Lieutenant Spellacy: "I am not a crank," Mrs. Humble wrote. "I am a simple housewife who has a God-given gift of clairvoyance and I am duty-bound to tell you that the murderer in this case is a Negro, perhaps a chauffeur of someone living in the same building, or a handyman or someone like that. I am a woman of sixty-five years and during my long life I have had many such clairvoyant experiences." Another letter, from a Mrs. Grace Prosper of Los Angeles: "May I call your attention to the fact that we dames lead the field in detective fiction, and I sometimes think that police departments could do with more women operatives, and I am *not* referring to female flatfoots, political appointees, or tough matron types (if you get my meaning)." Mrs. Jack Mills, of West Hartford, Connecticut, wrote: "Upon reading of the death of Meta Dierdorf in the *Hartford Courant*, I feel it is my duty to tell you what I know about her past. Meta and I were classmates (I was Georgette Duffy then) at the Saybrook School in Holmby Hills (Los Angeles) before she transferred to that school at the movie studio, which I think was a mistake and a bad thing, because it put her in contact with many people not of the Christian religion, with all their different customs, et cetera. This crime would not have happened if Meta had stayed at Saybrook with her co-religionists. I can truthfully say I charge and blame her father Matthew Dierdorf with the death of his daughter. Indirectly he is the murderer because of the lack of parental guidance and attention he gave her, giving her a big allowance instead of a father's love. I think it was his idea that Meta mix with those people, even though she was not pretty enough to be a star, and bit her fingernails, because he thought people of the Hebrew persuasion might invest in his business and it is well known that they have a gift for making money." Dorothy Estrella of 3218 Hollywood Boulevard wrote: "My boyfriend Harold Eustis is a sex maniac and his organ is so big it tears me some times, especially if he is

drunk, and if that girl was torn, you should question Harold
Eustis, because he was drunk and didn't come home that night.
Please do not use my name as my husband is in the service of his
country." Harold Eustis had in fact been drunk the evening of
July 26, 1945. He was arrested in Cahuenga Pass at 9:30 P.M.
by Officer D. D. Hilliard of the California Highway Patrol,
charged with violation of PC Section 367D, driving under the
influence, and placed in the lockup at the Glendale police station. The following morning, he pleaded guilty in Glendale
Municipal Court to violation of PC Section 367D, was given a
thirty-day sentence in the county jail, sentence suspended, and
fined twenty-five dollars. There was no mention in either the
arrest record or charge sheet of the dimensions of his member.

◄◊►

The cloth found stuffed down Meta Dierdorf's throat and into
her esophagus was finally identified as a crepe tetra nonelastic
bandage, ten inches in width, made in France and not sold in
this country since the start of the war. A canvass of local medical
and surgical supply houses, as well as both civilian and military
hospitals, was unable to find any remaining stock of this bandage, or records of sales in the past to pharmacies, hospitals, or
doctors. A medical wholesaler in Chicago said he had fifteen
rolls of the bandage in question still in stock, but that the company's last sale of the ten-inch nonelastic tetra was in November
1942, when purchasing agents for England's Royal Navy had
bought one hundred thousand rolls. Acting on this information, Lieutenant Spellacy checked with the harbormaster of the
Port of Los Angeles, and learned that HMS *Resolve*, a Royal
Navy aircraft carrier, had put to sea at 2045 hours the night of
July 26, 1945, along with six escort vessels. During the squadron's two-day layover in port, all officers and men had been
confined to their ships; after the squadron sailed, the force commander informed the U.S. Navy shore patrol that one British
officer, two petty officers, and eight seamen were absent and
unaccounted for. Ten of these eleven were quickly rounded up
and remanded to the Long Beach brig, while the body of the

eleventh, Lieutenant Commander Alastair Drummond, RN, washed up naked on the beach at San Pedro three days later, he apparently having drowned while trying to swim from the *Resolve* to Terminal Island. The two petty officers and eight seamen were eliminated as suspects as it could be proven that none had ventured far from Long Beach the night of the murder; Lieutenant Commander Drummond was listed as a suspect until Royal Navy authorities informed the Shore Patrol that he had been about to be accused of oral and anal copulation by an able seaman on the *Resolve,* and it was determined that he had committed suicide rather than face the indignity of a court-martial that would have led to his being sentenced to a naval prison and cashiered from the service.

◄◦►

Using Meta Dierdorf's address book, her photo albums, and her considerable correspondence, and with the assistance of provost marshals at military facilities both in this country and abroad, Lieutenant Spellacy and his investigators interrogated, fingerprinted, and eliminated one hundred and nine officers and enlisted men from all the services as possible suspects in her murder. The crime-against-person reports of all sex crimes in the months preceding and following her death, whether resulting in homicide or not, were examined for any similarities in M.O. to the Dierdorf case. Nameless suspects were identified only as being "left-handed" or having "tattoo of naked woman with pubic hair on right arm" or as "dope fiend." Two nights after Meta Dierdorf was killed, and only three blocks away from her apartment at 8497 Fountain Avenue, there was an attack against a young woman living alone that also involved a bandage. Miss Evangeline McGuinn, a twenty-year-old cashier at the Fox Wiltern Theater, reported that after counting the box office receipts for the 9:00 P.M. showing of *The Story of G.I. Joe,* she had returned to her apartment at 1016 Hancock Avenue, listened to Jimmy Dorsey on the radio, and then had gone to bed. At 11:30, she was awakened by a male Caucasian, age twenty to thirty years, approximately five feet ten inches tall, with a medium build. The attacker had apparently entered the apartment via a rear door with a broken latch. According to the crime-against-person report filed with the LAPD:

Victim stated she was awakened by a man who had his hands around her neck. Susp said, "I don't want to rape you, all I want to do is kiss you all over. If you scream, I'll fix it so you can't scream." Susp then took victim's hands, and tied them behind her back with an Ace bandage. Victim said she had purchased said bandage when she had sprained her wrist when she fell from a step ladder while painting her apt in the spring. Ace bandage was in her bathroom medicine cabinet. After tying vict's hands, susp raised vict's nightgown and began to caress her body with his lips, finally placing his mouth on her private parts. Susp then said. "I think I'll change my mind and rape you after all." Vict stated, "Under other circumstances, I might enjoy this, but as you see, I am very upset." At this, susp apologized and told vict not to scream. Vict said, "He then proceeded to play with himself until he came." Vict pointed out several apparent semen stains on carpet where susp had been kneeling. A few seconds after susp left the house, vict McGuinn heard a car start and drive away down rear alley. Vict was able to remove Ace bandage, and after waiting to make sure susp would not return she dialed operator and asked her to call police. Susp did not remove anything from vict's apt, even though she was wearing amethyst ring and had $57 in her purse.

F. Y. Masaryk
Robbery-Homicide
Investigator (Primary)

CC: Lieutenant Spellacy for Dierdorf File

‹○›

From Lieutenant Spellacy's notes:

1) how'd he know Ace bandage was in medicine cabinet? ck it out first? she tell him?

2) bet she knew him? likes getting tied up? there's them that do.

3) "Under other circumstances I might enjoy this." Under any circumstances, I bet.

4) "Until he came," she says. Since when do nice girls say "came." "Climax" is what they say, or "You know," something like that. This is a live wire, this one. Re-interrogate HOLlywood 3685.

I wondered if Lieutenant Spellacy had something other than interrogation in mind for the live wire at 1016 Hancock Avenue, Hollywood 3685, and if the circumstances were right for Evangeline McGuinn to enjoy it.

◄○►

Other leads vanished, other trails led only to dead ends. As if by rote, Lieutenant Spellacy sent letters:

With reference to above subject, Wallace Morris, who was executed at Walla Walla January 15, 1948, I would appreciate some information respecting the subject which might connect him to a similar unsolved murder I have open in my files. Specifically if subject Morris was known to be in the Los Angeles or southern California area o/a July 26, 1945.

And again:

I would greatly appreciate if you would question Jack Tunney Kiefer, who as I understand it is to be executed at Utah State Penitentiary for a similar crime, and ascertain if he was in the vicinity of Hollywood, California, o/a July 26, 1945.

The last official entry in the case file was the reply to a letter Lieutenant Spellacy had sent, in 1952, seven years after the murder of Meta Dierdorf, to the police chief in Fort Smith,

Arkansas, about a murder suspect, Emory Lyon, who had come to Lieutenant Spellacy's attention via a report distributed by the Federal Bureau of Investigation. Emory Lyon had crammed a towel down the throat of his latest victim before he had raped and killed her. There was no reason to believe that Emory Lyon had strangled Meta Dierdorf, as his area of criminal activity centered on the Southwest, but in the absence of any other evidence, the M.O. of the crime seemed at least to warrant an inquiry. The reply from the chief of police in Fort Smith, Arkansas, to Lieutenant Spellacy read:

This man is a professional hitchhiker and murderer. He claims he has been hitchhiking since he was 14 years of age. The states he has been hitchhiking mostly in are Arkansas, Texas, Oklahoma, Kansas, Colorado, New Mexico, Arizona and Utah.

We have him definitely connected with five murders in Arkansas and one in Kansas. When we start questioning him about murders outside the state of Arkansas, we will definitely question him about your murder in Los Angeles.

There was no further communication in the Dierdorf murder book from the Fort Smith, Arkansas, police department. Yet in this single cryptic communiqué (available, I suppose, only to me, and perhaps to Lieutenant Spellacy during the lonely hours during which he was trying to tie any threads together), there was the clearest possible sense of life's improbabilities, of the way the path of Emory Lyon, a professional hitchhiker and murderer from Arkansas, the Land of Opportunity, could happen to cross, however indirectly, the equally haphazard path of Blue Tyler, child star and box office champion. As had the paths of Harold Eustis, Evangeline McGuinn, Lieutenant Commander Alastair Drummond, RN, and the red gelding named Oscar. I would argue that consideration of these improbabilities is a recipe for madness.

◄◦►

After thirty years in the LAPD, Lieutenant T. J. Spellacy finally retired in October 1963. Clipped to the last page of the Dierdorf murder book was a handwritten note, dated the day of his retirement:

"V, Vida—who?"

◄◦►

It is compelling to read the minutiae of a homicide investigation, and to see the number of lives touched by that investigation, and how often, in the course of the digging and detecting, a mosaic of petty treasons, moral misdemeanors, quiet desperation, and even evil as an abstraction is uncovered having nothing to do with the crime in question, only with the permutations of life itself. I wish I could tell you that my own examination of the evidence, when I was armed with information unavailable to Lieutenant Spellacy, helped solve the murder of Meta Dierdorf, as it would in a tidier narrative, and that her killer was one of my principals, or in some way connected to them, but in fact she will probably rest in eternity with her murderer undiscovered. In one of his private notes, remember, Lieutenant Spellacy had wondered if she was "just unlucky," and just unlucky seems a perfect description of this beautiful, spoiled, unloved, wanton, larcenous, and not-overly-bright child. Meta Dierdorf is, however, not simply a digression, the kind English departments tell you occur so often in what they call the "baggy monster" novels of the great Victorians—*Vanity Fair,* say, or *Bleak House,* or *Middlemarch.* As you may have intuited, I did ultimately learn the identity of "V," "Vida," or "Vide," and while the knowledge was eminently helpful in driving my narrative toward its conclusion, it was just another salacious sidebar to the unseemly and unlucky life of Meta Dierdorf.

Beautiful, spoiled, unloved, wanton, larcenous, and not overly bright—words that might also have described Blue Tyler.

Who was lucky.

Or perhaps just unlucky in other ways.

III

I T WAS CHUCKIE who cleared up the identity of "V." I had let him see the forensic photographs and some of the more lewd and lubricious passages of the crime book—the confession of Captain Benedict that he was responsible for two but not three of the used rubbers in Meta Dierdorf's bedroom, and that the semen in her mouth was not his, particularly titillated him, as did Dorothy Estrella's comment on the size of Harold Eustis's organ—and it was after he had read it that I happened to mention to him the mysterious Vida.

He shook his head.

Sometimes referred to as "V," other times as "Vida," and still other times as "Vide."

Vide? he said suddenly.

You know?

It was Blue. That was her nickname at that stupid studio school. I haven't heard it in fifty years.

Why Vide?

French. For her initials.

B.T., I said incredulously.

No, Jack. M.T. For Melba Toolate.

I don't get it, Chuckie, I said with some irritation.

Just listen. She hated being called Melba. But for some bu-
reaucratic reason, her name was never legally changed until she
was in her teens. So she was registered as Melba Toolate with
the Los Angeles County department of whatever it was that had
oversight at the school. Anyway, all the students took a begin-
ners' French course. Her initials were M.T. M.T. as in "empty
glass." *Empty* in French is—

Vide, I said.

And that's what they called her at the school. Vide. She didn't
mind that. As long as no one called her Melba. She was always
spouting her ludicrous French on the set.

It has a certain je ne sais quoi, she had said that first day at the
Autumn Breeze trailer park, and *I bet you never thought you'd
hear any of that French shit in some RV camp in Hamtramck,
Michigan, the reason is I took French at the studio school and I
always had a French governess all those years I was at Cosmo, the
number-one box office star in the country, that was Mr. French's
idea, Mr. French's French idea, that's cute.*

And her schoolmate Meta:

*V demain—$$$$$ . . . Vide—ici avec Monsieur Pepe La
Moko, ooo la la, peut-être cinquante dollars . . . beaucoup
l'argent pour ma silence . . .*

—◇—

If I had to make an educated guess, Chuckie O'Hara said, I
would bet that apartment was where Walker Franklin was boning her. I mean, he couldn't just check into a hotel with her, it
was simply not done, even if she was of age, and she couldn't do
it at home, because the staff was all on Moe's payroll, and she
certainly wasn't going to go down to Central Avenue, that was
for a cruiser with a taste for danger.

Like you, I said.

Like me, Chuckie said, smiling as if remembering days of
youth and thunder and a perpetual bone. They had to have a
place to meet, a place they could get in and out of without
anyone seeing them, and I think Miss Dierdorf might have provided it, and if anyone asked questions, they were just two little
girls doing their homework together. The father was never

around much, he was always one step ahead of the law, from what you tell me, and this kid was essentially on her own. For Blue, a dream setup.

When did she begin sleeping with Walker Franklin?

Right after Carole Lombard died. I was supposed to direct her in *Cotton Candy*, but the Marines called me up, and Alan Shay was assigned to the picture. The night before I reported to Camp Pendleton, this was in February 1942, maybe March, there was a party for me. That's when she hinted about it. A few years before, it was at the wrap party for *Lily of the Valley*, I think, she'd caught me in the kitchen doing something naughty with the butler, and after that she told Aunty Charlton everything.

Her way of paying back Moe, I said.

Can you blame her?

Then she gets knocked up and goes to Lou Lerner, the studio doctor, and he takes care of it.

He was a sleaze, Lou, Chuckie said. He was going to get arrested for selling morphine one time, then Lilo made some calls, and after that he was in Lilo's pocket. You went to get a blood test, and Lilo knew the results before you did.

What about Blue and the girl then?

A little teenage muff-diving, I'd assume, Jack. Nothing serious.

Chuckie, she's kept her photograph ever since. Had dozens of postcards made. She still carries them around with her.

First love and other sorrows, Chuckie said.

But she was blackmailing her.

No, not really. It gave Blue a place she could go fuck without anyone really knowing about it. She had the money, and the other girl was broke. Teenagers don't think in terms of blackmail. She was helping her friend out.

You think Lilo knew?

Lilo knew everything, Chuckie said. I used to think it was Lilo who counted out the thirty pieces of silver for Judas Iscariot. Or at least negotiated the price.

And then Moe picked up on the girl, I said.

Kismet, Chuckie said.

Did Lilo fill Moe in?

I wouldn't think so. It was Lilo's card to play. Why fill in Moe until he had to?

The way he kept what he knew about Blue and Walker Franklin for a rainy day, I said.

Exactly.

One thing bothers me, Chuckie.

You want to know why Arthur just volunteered it to you about Meta and his father?

Right.

Because Arthur didn't know what and how much you knew, Chuckie O'Hara said. You were being just as cagey as he was, Jack, Arthur knew that, and he was just trying to buy time.

─◇─

Bad dreams.

Too many questions. Where had Arthur been the night Meta Dierdorf was killed?

In San Francisco, it turned out, with Blue and Lilo Kusack, showing a propaganda film he had made about women war workers to President Truman, there with Mrs. Truman, who was christening the aircraft carrier *Manila Bay* at the Mare Island shipyard.

As alibis go, not bad.

And where was Melba Mae Toolate?

No sightings, Maury Ahearne reported in his nocturnal check-ins. But the word was out. He had friends. The friends owed him.

Maury was suffused with a sense of self-importance.

And Meta Dierdorf had just been unlucky.

IV

"YOU GOT A FAX MACHINE?" It was nearly four in the morning, and it took a moment to shake myself awake and recognize Maury Ahearne's voice. I muttered yes, and gave him the number. I knew enough not to ask him what it was. It would be on the fax, which began coming through almost immediately. It appeared to be a letter. The childish script was unmistakably that of Melba Mae Toolate. "Happy birthday, baby, wherever you are now," the letter began. "You'd be 42 this year, twice as old as I was when I had you, and if you've learned one thing by now you've learned that all men are snakes . . ."

The letter went no further.

The telephone was ringing. "Where'd you get this?" I said as soon as I picked up, wide awake now.

"The guy who runs the trailer park where she was," Maury Ahearne said. "August Johnson. There's a new couple in that RV she was in, and the wife found a whole bunch of these in a folder wedged behind the medicine cabinet. All dated the same day back through the years, twenty years or more, none more than a page or two long, some just a few lines, all beginning the same way. The one you got was the last one."

"The date was the day before she skipped."

"That's it," Maury Ahearne said. "This lady, the one that rents Slot 123 now, she gives the folder to August Johnson, and he gets in touch with me. Like I told him to . . ."

". . . when you busted into her RV, and told him it was police business and scared the shit out of him."

"Oh," Maury Ahearne said. "And I just thought he was a citizen doing his duty."

I had no tolerance for his jokes anymore. "Can you send them to me?"

"I'll have copies made." Meaning he would keep the originals. The originals might have monetary value. "You know she had a kid?"

"No."

"The kid is where the money is," Maury Ahearne said.

—◇—

Even after reading the letter Maury Ahearne faxed, I was still not entirely convinced Blue Tyler actually had a daughter. I had of course read about one in the clips, and about its putative fathers, but I thought it more than likely she had concocted a daughter the way a child invents an imaginary friend. It seemed to me a cri de coeur from a lonely, aging, perhaps periodically mad woman in Slot 123, Forsythia Lane, at the Autumn Breeze trailer park and recreational vehicle encampment, a woman whose only real family life after she was abandoned by Cosmopolitan Pictures was with the shut-ins she visited in her position as chairperson of the Shut-in Committee at St. Anton the Magyar's Church, in Hamtramck, Michigan 48212.

But after reading the entire packet of letters, I was not so sure.

The letters were all handwritten, on lined notebook paper (from the kind of spiral notebook I had seen her buy at Farmer Dell's what now seemed a century ago), every one dated, but without the year included. I rechecked the date Jacob King was assassinated; the anniversary of his death was eight months less nine days before the date on each of these letters, meaning that if indeed the child did exist, Blue was pregnant the night Jacob was murdered. Jacob King was sleeping with her in the appropriate time frame, and Arthur French would not deny that he was also. Not that they were the only candidates. She had a history of sport- and grudge-fucking, and her capacity for holding a grudge for some slight, real or imagined, from one of her equals or betters, was bottomless; her method of payback was to favor social inferiors with her favors—gofers and chauffeurs, grips and gaffers. It was a pointless promiscuity, the kind of revenge a child indulges in, but of course a child was what she was, even unto her exile at the Autumn Breeze in Hamtramck, Michigan.

There was a chatty quality about the letters, as if she had just finished talking to her correspondent on the telephone and wanted to add a few things she had forgotten to say, so there was no need for any sort of preamble or identification of the players. I tried to sort them chronologically, but since the year was not included in the date, it was often difficult. If the order seems haphazard, so too was her life.

Happy birthday, baby, wherever you are now,

You're 21 today, the same age as I was when you were born, and you might be wondering why I never got in touch with you before this, but that was because it was part of the deal, I couldn't try to contact you, or write you or anything. But now you're 21, the age of consent (and is that a laugh, my age of consent was 13), and you can come looking for me if you want. You'll have to get it out of Arthur, but he won't tell you, and the guy called Max won't either. So let me give you a little background. I was a big movie star one time, the biggest in the Industry, and then I got pregnant and wanted to have you. It wasn't done in those days, look at what happened to Ingrid when she got knocked up by that wop, a word I'm not supposed to say today, but that's what he was, an Italian guy. I got pregnant the first time when I was 14 (I hope that doesn't make you think I'm some kind of slut or something, I was just mad at some guy, I don't want to say who or why, and it was by this other guy, the first guy would've killed me if he found out), and the second time when I was 17, that was an accident. I was doing tea with an actor who was a pretty big star at the studio (not as BIG as me), I was in a couple of pictures with him, and he was always billed after me, below the title, I was always above, it was in my contract, and I wasn't careful, and, well, you know. Lou Lerner took care of me both times. Lilo fixed it, he had something on Lou, now he had something on me. With you it was different, I just knew I wasn't going to let Lou Lerner near me. It caused a real big stink, this was after Chuckie and all that stuff in Washington. I mean, I had to agree to give you up, I was a star, and like I said, look what happened to Ingrid. I never even saw you, it was done by what they call a C-section, and I was out with the anesthesia, and when I woke up, you were gone, I never knew who you went to, Arthur said Jimmy took care of that, he said he didn't even know who you went to, but you never know when Arthur is telling the truth or not. I'll finish this tomorrow.

She did not finish the next day.

Happy birthday, baby, wherever you are now,

It's no big deal, not having a mother, I never did either, you get right down to it. I had a bunch of governesses and shit, and Irma, who bought me for a bus ticket (get Arthur to tell you that story, it's a doozie), she was OK, Irma, Mr. French just didn't like to have her around, she made him nervous, and then there was Chloe who was a dyke. What I'm trying to say is this, I didn't have a mother either, and

I turned out OK, Clark Gable gave me an Oscar one year, I never liked Clark, I told him once you could bunk in his ears, they were so big, and he didn't like it much. It was Carole Lombard I liked.

The letter ended there.

Happy birthday, baby, wherever you are now,

The thing about being a movie star is that you never really had any friends, because people my own age weren't as famous as I was or as rich, and so I couldn't hang around with them, Mr. French didn't like it. So there I was like seven years old, pretending Bob Hope was my best friend. Meta at the studio school was different. She was like me, not as famous, but alone a lot of the time, living by herself with maids and stuff, and by her wits, Arthur said, the state should step in and take care of her, put her up for adoption like you were. He was such a pill sometimes. Arthur said her father was a confidence man, I didn't know what that was at the time, but I do now. Arthur wanted to get rid of her at the studio school, he said her father was the type who would cause trouble one day, but by that time Moe had latched on to her, and Moe liked her to come up to his office, and Arthur was in the service (big war hero making movies, and living at home at Willingham, it wasn't like Chuckie in the USMC getting shot at), so he wasn't around to make that much of a stink. That was how me and Meta became such friends, we had this secret about Moe we shared together. She was funny about Moe. He had this secret entrance to his office so no one'd know he was seeing someone, and he'd be dressed up in boots and riding breeches when she went up there. Me and Meta tried it a couple of times, but she wasn't that way, and I guess I wasn't either, we just liked each other. She let me use her place to meet people, that was another secret we had together. I took a picture of her nude when she was 15 or 16 yrs old, real arty, and she was going to take one of me, but she never got around to it, and then she got bumped off. Moe wouldn't let me go to her funeral, I had to go to some Catholic church instead. To tell the truth, I thought Moe might have done it, but he was at a preview of *January, February* in Santa Barbara that night, and everyone stayed over at the Biltmore. The picture was a real piece of shit, Alan Shay directed it, and Moe said that was when he knew Alan was a Commie. I think of Meta a lot. She used to call me Vide, and I'd call her Plein (figure that out, you're my daughter, so you can't be some dumbbell) or Doc, after her initials. When I left L.A., I found the picture of her, and I had a lot of copies made, I didn't want to lose any, because she was my best friend, after Arthur.

Happy birthday, baby, wherever you are now,

I had better years than this last one. I got married again, to Teddy someone, I can't remember his last name, because we were only married one day when he died, my seventh husband, I think. The way he died was after we got married we went to this baseball game at Tiger Stadium, front row in the second deck, and we got a pretty good buzz on with beer and some joints Teddy had. Then someone named Jason something hits a home run, and Teddy gets to cheering so hard he fell out of the stands into what they call the bullpen. The fall killed him. I just got out of there. I'd only known him a day or two, I don't know why we got married, we just did, so it wasn't like I was all broken up, we never even did it married. I landed in Ypsilanti, with the rest of Teddy's stash, and I got busted. In all those years I never called Arthur, not once, that was the deal, but that time I did, I thought it was all over, I was at the end of my rope, what with my husband dying one day and me getting busted the next, and Arthur said he'd take care of it. He got hold of the guy called Max, Max was a lawyer, he said, and Max must've done something, because I was let go without bond, and then the charges were dropped, and that's when I moved to Pontiac. So what do you think of your old mother now?

From Maury Ahearne:

On September 14, 1979, during a game between the Tigers and the Cleveland Indians at Tiger Stadium in Detroit, a fan fell out of the upper deck into the visitors' bullpen after a grand slam home run by Tiger first baseman Jason Thompson. The fan, subsequently identified as Eduardo Burke, address unknown, suffered massive internal injuries and was pronounced dead on arrival at Immaculate Conception Hospital. Toxicological tests administered during Eduardo Burke's autopsy indicated that the levels of alcohol in his system exceeded the legal definition of drunkenness, and there were also indications of extensive use of cannabis. The body of Eduardo Burke went unclaimed, even though there was a wedding license in his pocket, listing his intended wife as Melba Mae Tyler. A check of the Wayne County Hall of Records showed that Eduardo Burke and Melba Mae Tyler were married by a city magistrate on the day of his fatal accident. It was the seventh marriage recorded for Mrs. Burke. The Detroit Police Department had an outstanding bench warrant calling for the arrest of Eduardo Burke because of his failure to appear in superior court on the charge of selling illegal controlled substances.

Happy birthday, baby, wherever you are now,

Arthur told me once that Jacob's death was a kind of peace offering. A ritual sacrifice, he said. I don't know what that means either. It was Jimmy's way of telling Lilo, Arthur said, it's over, let's get on with the peace. I never told Jacob about me and Meta. I would have, I suppose, but then he was this ritual sacrifice thing.

Happy birthday, baby, wherever you are now,

To think I have a daughter 30 yrs old today. It makes me feel a hundred. I've been clean for two weeks now. Not bad for a 50 yr old broad. Or an old 50 yr broad. I think your father was Jacob, but it could've been Arthur. I never saw you, if I saw you I could say which one you favored, Jacob was so beautiful. I hope it was Jacob. Of all the men I knew at that time of my life, he was the only one didn't treat me like some kind of prize puppy, I was real to him. I mean, I know he liked me because I was a movie star, everyone did except Meta, but he really liked me because I was me. Lilo said I would've dumped him sooner or later, it was the way of the world. Lilo was such a shit. You know something Jacob did? This was when we first began going out. He seemed to know he wasn't going to live long, even then before the bad shit happened, and he bought himself a plot at the Westwood mortuary. That was where he wanted to be buried, with all the movie stars and stuff. I thought it was creepy, buying a plot in a graveyard, that and the way he said he wanted a big marble gravestone, from Italy, he said. Arthur said the trouble with Jake was he wanted to be one of the goyim, and I said Arthur, there's no goyim in the Industry, and Arthur said, the Industry invented the goyim. I think about that a lot.

Happy birthday, baby, wherever you are now,

It may be your birthday, but I got a nice present today. I went to the bank this morning, and the ass't manager, he said my semimonthly deposit check had been upped from $500 to $750, and what was I going to do with all that money, put it in a T-bill, he called it, and I said it was none of his fucking business. I wanted to call my benefactor, but I am not supposed to know who he is, but if you are interested, his father's real name is Moses.

Happy birthday, baby, wherever you are now,

 This year's been kind of a blank.

Happy birthday, wherever you are now,

 God, I hate being 60. It's ten years worse than being 50.

Happy birthday, baby, wherever you are now,

 I didn't even know that Rita'd died until I read Lilo's obituary. "Once the consort of Rita Lewis, Mob bag lady," is what the obit said. I wish Lilo'd been alive to read that. It would've given him a heart attack. The thing is, I got to like Rita in the end. Her and Chuckie. Outcasts of the islands is what Chuckie called us. What islands, I said. I watched her testify on TV. Some old fart senator was giving her a hard time, and she was just laughing at him. I was with this guy, he was an A.D. for Henry Hathaway, and we were watching Rita and doing it, and watching and doing it, and he called me Miss Tyler all the way through it, a first for me. The guys I have known. There was this movie star, I can't say his name, he's still alive, he got the AFI Lifetime Achievement Award a couple of years ago, and when he was with me, all he could do was jerk off. He had this little bitty thing, about the size of a lipstick, he didn't have much to play with. Your old mom shouldn't be telling you this stuff, but all I do about sex these days is think about it. You ever think about me? I think about you all the time. I wonder if you're famous, like I was. I look at magazines all the time, looking for someone looks like me or Jacob, or maybe me and Arthur, although the thing about Arthur was, he was so careful, he always wore something, even when I said it was all right, I was wearing my diaphragm. If I got knocked up, it wasn't that he was worried about marrying me, it was that I would miss a start date, and the whole Cosmo schedule would be postponed, it was always the studio first with Arthur. I knew I was taking a chance with Jacob, but it was a chance I wanted to take. I used to think if I had to tell you who your father was, I would say it was Arthur, even if he wasn't, because not everyone would want Jacob King as a father. I said to him once have you ever killed anyone, and he nodded, and I said more than one, and he nodded, and I said more than thirty, and he shook his head, and I said more than twenty, and he shook his head, and I said more than ten, and he didn't move, so I guess it was somewhere between ten and twenty people, if you can believe him. Arthur said Jacob once put out someone's eye with a blowtorch, but Jacob said he had never done that. The truth is, I think Arthur liked to hear about all those people Jacob did, because I think Arthur might have liked to do it once, just to see what it was like, and I think the one he wanted to do it to was Moe.

Happy birthday, baby, wherever you are now,

You'd be 42 this year, twice as old as I was when I had you, and if you've learned one thing by now you've learned that all men are snakes . . .

I wondered why she had not taken the letters with her. I can only think now it was because she left her trailer in such a hurry after Maury Ahearne broke into it, and had forgotten that she had hidden them behind the medicine cabinet.

I never found out the answer.

V

"I THINK WE SHOULD all think this through and try to see where it's taking us," Sydney Allen said.

"What Sydney means is he's not sold on Blue having a kid," Marty Magnin said.

"I'm not convinced a child's a viable asset," Sydney Allen said. Set up on easels around his office at Columbia in Culver City were production sketches of a picture he seemed to be preparing, and the sketches did not look as if they belonged to my as-yet-untitled script of the Blue Tyler story, the one he had assured me would be his next film. "Every film has its own ecology, and for Blue to have a child would destroy the ecological balance of the love story, as it were. It would put us in two different time frames, and that's always difficult, cinematically speaking."

"Its ecosystem would be upset," I said. "The symmetry of its food chain."

"Exactly," Sydney Allen said. I think he thought I was agreeing with him.

"Sydney thinks she's an unnecessary complication," Marty Magnin said.

I had never seen Marty deferential, especially to a director, but then his last four pictures had been flops, the blame for which he had artfully deposited in other laps, but not so artfully that he could afford to be the bully he so naturally was, especially with success. I peered at the sketches, trying to guess the story line from them. There was what seemed to be a grain elevator, with wheat pouring into it, and there seemed to be a railroad-engine switching yard. No. Jacob King did not fit as Casey Jones.

"She destroys the arc," Sydney Allen said. The arc is what directors talk about when they are stalling. "I see a picture as a suspension bridge with two spans . . ."

"A suspension bridge doesn't have an arc," I said. "An arc is a precise geometrical configuration."

"You know what Sydney means," Marty Magnin said irritably. He had been reduced to interpreting Sydney Allen to a recalcitrant me, and it did not make him content.

"No, I don't."

"Jack, you don't like me much, do you?" Sydney Allen said.

"That's a reasonable assumption, Sydney. But actually I rarely give you a thought. It's the arc, the ecological balance of film, the suspension bridge and all that horseshit I mind. All you have to say is that you have another picture, you have a start date, and you want to put this one back, and you want me to be happy about it."

"Actually I don't care if you're happy or not."

"Then we understand each other."

Marty Magnin tried to soothe. "We just think it's time we went in another direction." He paused. "With another writer."

"On what?"

"The script," Marty Magnin said.

"Marty, you're forgetting something," I said. "I told you I'd work up a script. On spec. I never released the rights."

"Not that it matters," Sydney Allen said. "Her story is public domain."

"But my notes aren't." I rose and pointed to the grain-elevator sketch. "What's this picture called?"

No one spoke for a moment.

"*Empire*," Marty Magnin finally said. He and I had been through too much together for him to ignore the question. "The Kansas wheat wars. Action. Night riders. Cruise and Kidman. They met Sydney over the weekend at Mike Ovitz's in Aspen, and signed on this morning."

The actors were of no interest to me. "And this is a grain elevator?"

"Nice to see you, Jack," Sydney Allen said. He seemed taller, and as he tried to steer me out of his office, I saw he was wearing cowboy boots. "As always."

"And somebody is going to fall into the grain elevator, and a load of wheat's going to fall on him, and he's going to suffocate and die, right?"

"Sydney's idea," Marty Magnin said. "When we were all schmoozing with Michael." Marty considered the sketch. "How'd you know that anyway?"

"I read *The Octopus*," I said. "Sydney only steals from the better sources."

Marty looked from Sydney Allen to me. He had obviously never heard of either *The Octopus* or Frank Norris. Not that stealing anything from a classic would ever cause him to lose any sleep.

"Bottom line, Hollywood pictures don't make it," Marty Magnin said. "You're rich, finance it yourself, you and the *fageleh* snitch."

VI

WHY DID YOU HAVE TO FIND HER, Jack? Arthur French said.

—◇—

Arthur was recuperating at Willingham. With all the riding he had done, and all the spills he had taken, his knees finally wore out and had to be replaced, and so he had come to Los Angeles to get the operations done by the chief of orthopedic surgery at Cedars. I had talked to him in Arizona a number of times on the telephone but had never mentioned the letters. I wanted to show them to him in person, to see how he reacted, and his immobility after the two knee surgeries made him a captive audience, one in a certain amount of pain, unable to ride off into the sunset as he had so often done in Nogales, unable to deflect a question with an evasion as easily as when he was in his prime. I always tended to forget that Arthur was twenty-odd years older than I, because he had so vigorously taken to the outdoor life, but as I watched him reading the letters in his wheelchair at Willingham, wearing pajamas and a bathrobe, his legs resting on an ottoman, I realized that he was old, as were both Blue and Chuckie, the only other survivors of this random chain of events forty years earlier.

Why did you have to find her, Jack?

—◆—

So there was a daughter?

She wouldn't abort, Arthur said. There were screaming fights with J.F. and Lilo and me, but she still insisted on having it. That was the real reason *Broadway Babe* was postponed, not because of the score. She went to this place in Connecticut. It was like a safe house. She could have the child there, and not in a hospital, and nobody would talk, because silence was truly golden. It cost an arm and a leg.

How'd you explain her absence?

We just said she was making a career change, she was a grown woman now, she'd bought a ranch in Colorado, she loved the solitude and the fresh air, and then she was going to Europe before she started shooting *Broadway Babe*. Her first real vacation in ten years. The usual crap, but people believed studios those days.

If she was only going to give it up for adoption, then why have the kid?

She wanted to make a point, Jack. And she thought she could put it someplace where she could watch it grow up, without having any real responsibility for it. With a little weep when it went off to kindergarten. Standing outside the schoolyard, like a rich Stella Dallas. Life was always a movie to Blue, movies were her only frame of reference. It was Lilo who was finally able to talk some sense to her. Or maybe it was just that she was sick every morning and she was getting fat and the romance of having a baby and being a mother was wearing off. Like a rough cut that went on too long.

Jimmy Riordan took care of the adoption?

He had it placed even before Blue arrived at the place in Connecticut.

Why?

He felt guilty, I guess. About Jake. A kind of . . . what do you Catholics call it?

Penance, I said. Do the penance and you're granted absolution. (I had never thought I would be discussing the fine points

of confession with Arthur French.) Whatever happened to
Jimmy Riordan anyway?

He bought himself a good name, Arthur said.

How?

Morris died less than a year after Jake was killed. Natural
causes, in his own bed. As he always wanted. He went to sleep
one night and didn't wake up. His death was Jimmy's ticket to
respectability, and he'd been preparing for it, needless to say,
since long before Morris died. He knew where all the bodies
were buried—literally and figuratively—all the deals and all the
payoffs, and a lot of people wanted to make sure that information never got out. So Jimmy negotiated a lawyer's deal. Anything happened to him—food poisoning, an automobile
accident, a fall in the shower, anything—then everything he
had, and he had everything, was shipped to the feds. It was his
insurance policy, and the premium he paid was his silence. So he
spent the rest of his life doing good works. He died in 1970,
1971, around there, a stroke.

Any family?

There was a wife, but she left him early on. J.F. used to say
Morris was more than she was willing to handle. Then she died,
of cancer, I think.

Children?

None.

Where is Blue's daughter now? I asked.

I don't know.

You don't know or you won't tell?

I don't know.

I don't believe you, Arthur.

A flash of the old Arthur: I'd be surprised if you did.

And disappointed . . .

A weary smile. Yes.

And all those years, you were sending Blue money?

I guess there's no point in denying it now.

No, I said.

He sighed. It began after she came back to New York from

Italy. I'd been keeping tabs on her over there, and sometimes if I knew she was short, I'd see that a little something got sent her way. Jimmy did, too. It was Jimmy who suggested we give her a regular . . . stipend, I guess you'd call it. I said I'd take care of it, she was my responsibility, not his, I just wanted him to work out the details. Jimmy's people, I mean his legitimate people, got in touch with her, and they gave her an ID number and a telephone number she could call collect, and they told her she should get a bank account, and there would be something deposited twice a month.

She knew it was from you?

I was the logical candidate, wasn't I?

And you never saw her?

Not after she went to Mexico, no. That was in 1950, 1951.

All those years she never got in touch with you?

Directly just that once, when she got arrested in Michigan. But then she'd send me those things in the mail I mentioned, the tapes and the clippings and things. It was a way of keeping in touch.

Arthur closed his eyes. I thought he might be weeping, but perhaps he was just trying to preserve the memories. I changed direction. You knew the girl in that picture I showed you was Meta Dierdorf, didn't you?

He opened his eyes and waited a beat. Yes.

Why did you lie to me then?

A pained expression crossed his face. She was somebody I simply hadn't expected to come up. And I didn't want to give anything away I didn't have to. So I lied. I'd never seen the picture before. And I never knew they had this . . . episode together. Arthur stared at me sadly. I've always liked you, Jack. I just never thought of you as the hound of heaven.

I wasn't sure that was intended as a compliment. Who is Max, Arthur?

A lawyer. Like Blue said.

He fixed the Ypsilanti beef?

He made it go away, yes.

458 · JOHN GREGORY DUNNE

So he knows what strings to pull?

Arthur was getting back into form: When you hire lawyers, you expect them to know what strings to pull.

Even in pain and as old as he was, Arthur was not entirely leveling with me. I think he was incapable of it. I did not know exactly what he was omitting, or why, but I knew I was not getting the whole story.

Does Max have a last name?

Yes.

I was trying to be patient: Then what is Max's last name, Arthur?

Arthur hesitated, as if running over the possibilities.

Look, Arthur, I said. If a drug charge was settled in Ypsilanti in 1979, then the charge sheet and the name of counsel are a matter of public record. And by now you know that sooner or later I am going to track down that counsel's name, and if counsel was a local Ypsilanti lawyer appearing for an out-of-state attorney, then I, or an intermediary, in this case a cop I know in Detroit named Maury Ahearne, an eight-hundred-pound gorilla, believe me, one of us, count on it, is going to drag the name of that out-of-state attorney from the local attorney. I have not come this far, Arthur, to let you jerk my chain.

Riordan, Arthur said. His name is Max Riordan.

◄◦►

Denis Maxwell ("Max") Riordan, Jimmy Riordan's nephew and the junior United States senator from Florida, a Republican from Orlando, listened to what I had to say and then threatened suit if I implied that anything illicit had transpired between his uncle and Morris Lefkowitz. Uncle Jimmy was Mr. Lefkowitz's attorney, no more, Max Riordan said, a right guaranteed under the Constitution of the United States of America, any citizen is entitled to representation, whatever public attitudes of revulsion may exist toward that citizen, the defense of Jimmy Hoffa by Edward Bennett Williams being in this great tradition. In any event, Max Riordan continued, my uncle and Morris Lefkowitz were never social friends or business partners, their relationship was protected by the attorney-client privilege, Morris Lefkowitz was never arrested in seventy-seven years of robust good health, the James Francis Riordan Chair in Jurisprudence at the University of Florida Law School is one of the nation's most prestigious endowed professorships, and the annual James Francis Riordan Lecture in Miami was eagerly anticipated in the legal community, F. Lee Bailey has been a Riordan Lecturer, and Edwin Meese as well, and to imply, as you seem to be implying, Mr. Broderick, that my uncle Jimmy was just trying retroactively, and out of a guilty conscience, to buy himself a good name, is criminal slander, et cetera and so forth, and to be frank, I expected more from the son of Hugh Broderick, who served this nation and so many of its presidents so well.

Max Riordan was an idiot, but then I have always had a low tolerance for politics and politicians. He was up for reelection, a difficult race, and the idea that he would sue me for unspecified allegations about Jimmy Riordan and Morris Lefkowitz was a bluff, not the sort of thing he would wish played out in the tabloids during a political campaign. He had his uncle's name, but not the smarts I had come to appreciate so as I dug into the history of James Francis Riordan. In any event, I was more interested in something else.

Where is Blue Tyler's daughter now?

I don't know.

Of course you do, Senator. Jimmy Riordan never let anything go. He would have had her name and the name of her adopted parents in his papers.

That information would be privileged, Mr. Broderick.

Senator, Jimmy Riordan's will was probated in New York. According to the terms of that will—and I had my lawyers look it up in Manhattan Surrogate Court before I came here—you were his sole noninstitutional beneficiary. There was also a single trust, set up in 1949, and the will stipulated that upon your uncle's death, or if he were to become physically or mentally impaired, you would succeed him as its trustee. As you did in 1969, when James Francis Riordan suffered the cerebral incident that ultimately caused his death. A portion of the income from that trust went to a couple named Moira and Brendan Kean for the care and upbringing of their adopted daughter, and of that daughter only, not of subsequent issue should there be any. The balance of the income went to increase the value of the trust. When the adoptive daughter came of age, or upon the death of her adoptive parents, whichever came first, she would become the beneficiary of the trust. If her adoptive parents were still alive, they would receive an allowance from the trust, unless the trustee, with cause, decided otherwise. Am I on the money so far?

Max Riordan, R-Fla., stared at me without replying.

Brendan Kean was a former assistant D.A. in Queens, I continued. Chief prosecutor in all the rougher homicide cases. A city kid. Grew up in Inwood, went to St. John's and St. John's Law School. Right?

Still no reply.

He went into private practice. Specializing in criminal law. He was one of the lawyers your uncle Jimmy hired to defend Jacob King in the Philly Wexler case.

Max Riordan stirred uncomfortably in his chair.

Brendan Kean and his wife had no kids. And if your uncle was going to place Jacob King's child, he wasn't going to place it with someone he didn't know. Someone he wasn't sure of. That was never Jimmy Riordan's way.

What do you hope to gain from this, Mr. Broderick?

Nothing, Senator. I just want to close a book that never should have been opened in the first place.

—◇—

I thought it would end after I saw Max Riordan. Brendan and Moira Twomey Kean were never told the name of their daughter's natural parents, nor of Jimmy Riordan's role in the adoption. Lack of evidence notwithstanding, however, I would have been surprised if Brendan Kean, given his background, had not made a few discreet inquiries, and perhaps even some discoveries. The Keans named the girl Teresa, and never had any other children of their own. Teresa was by all accounts a loving child given only to the usual rebellions of adolescence—youthful experimentations with sex and controlled substances—a bright student as well, who earned a scholarship to Smith and married soon after graduation. The marriage did not last. A second marriage also ended in divorce. Having no children, she applied to Yale Law School and was accepted; on admission to the bar three years later, she reclaimed her maiden name and worked in her father's Manhattan law office until his death in a small plane crash in 1977, on a flight to his summer house at Cape May, on the Jersey shore. After his death, she moved to Washington as an advocate for an organization lobbying on behalf of victims' rights, a not-insubstantial irony, considering her natural father's propensity for making victims. In time, she became the organization's president and spokesperson. As it happened, I was aware of Teresa Kean's name and had seen her briefly several times, arguing her case on the Sunday talk shows and the *Mac-Neil/Lehrer NewsHour*. She seemed bright, articulate, and attractive, but otherwise she had made little impression on me, advocacy politics not being an area in which I had much interest. Her mother was still living, in a retirement community in California, and Teresa Kean visited her regularly. She knew she was adopted, had known since she was a little girl, but had never shown any inclination to discover the names or whereabouts of her natural parents.

<o>

I told Max Riordan I would not attempt to contact Teresa Kean, and that if in the natural course of events I did happen upon her, the secret of her birth was safe with me. I also told him that if my path did cross Melba Mae Toolate's again, as was not unlikely if she were still alive, I would not reveal to her anything I had learned about her daughter.

There it should have ended.

But life is rarely so simple.

PART FOUR

RETROSPECTIVE

I

M Y FATHER WAS invariably referred to as "Billionaire Hugh
Broderick" in the press, to the point that a few years ago,
when I was doing publicity on a picture I wrote (and the
fact that the screenwriter was doing publicity is a comment in
itself on the quality of the film, which the stars and the director
were now pretending they had nothing to do with), the interviewer asked if it was not true, as he had heard, that once when
I was a child I had asked my father why he was not called Bill
instead of Hugh if his first name was Billionaire. If memory
serves, I laughed heartily at this absurdity; the exchange occurred on a live morning television show, and however much
one might like to call the host an asshole, it is the rare guest
who, at 7:00 A.M., can summon the kidney to do so. The laugh
was taken to mean assent, and as so often happens, this assumed
assent found its way into the texts about my father, with the
result that the story has turned up in two books about him, and
a television documentary as well, the story having achieved the
status of holy writ, a means of humanizing a man who in truth
was only rarely capable of being human.

My father favored me with the same indifference he showed
toward the rest of mankind, the blood kinship between us offer-

ing me no special discount. I actually rather liked the old bastard, especially the way he never backed down. He fucked my first wife—after we had divorced, it is true, but I do not think it would have made much difference if we had still been married; she was there for the taking, and he was a taker—and he made no apologies for it when some years later I confronted him with the fact. I could not emulate him in many ways—he was sui generis, an ignoble savage for whom convention was just another piece of china that deserved to be smashed, and I had been civilized, Lord Greystoke to his Tarzan, but we did share an arrogance, in my case watered down, although less so as I grow older, and perhaps more a product of his money, and my share of it, than of his genetic pool. Unlike most of my compatriots in the picture business, I had a listed telephone number, and my father was the reason. Until the day he died, his name was always in the directory, "BRODERICK, Hugh," with both his office and home numbers listed. Often he would pick up the telephone himself, when it rang, beating secretary or butler to it, always answering without the amenity of "Hello," just a simple "Yes," or occasionally a disconcerting "What is it?" More often than not, "What is it?" would elicit a surprised, "Who's this?" To which my father would reply, "Who you were calling," and then hang up, advantage Hugh Broderick. It was this constant search for any edge, however small, that led him to list his telephone numbers in the first place; many of the people who called were those he had bested in some business venture or whose abilities he had publicly denigrated, and who in turn wanted satisfaction. A mistake. My father had the manners of a billy club and the tact of a fart; abuse was his natural dialect, his way of keeping trim. So I also listed my number, less to imitate him—a pale way, at best—than because I could imagine the waves of his contempt coming at me from beyond the grave if it were unlisted. You're just like all those other Hollywood Hebrews, he would have said, a phrasing he often used when trying to get a rise out of me—he seldom failed to do so—because not to respond was to run the risk of being told that my backbone had the tensile strength of a strand of linguini. Listing my phone number was really just a painless affect—who would call a screenwriter anyway?—leading to only a few unwanted calls, most of which could be brushed off.

Although occasionally there were those that couldn't.

—◦—

"Yes." With age, I answered the telephone the same way my father had, and for much the same reason.

"Mr. Broderick?"

"Yes."

"Will you hold for Barbados Brown?"

I was once more reading Melba Mae Toolate's birthday letters to her unknown daughter, now known to me, and saw no reason to hold for anyone with a name as ridiculous as Barbados Brown. "No."

A moment later, the telephone rang again. A rich, velvety voice. "Mr. Broderick, this is Barbados Brown."

"Yes." She seemed to think I would know who she was, or perhaps would say something about her name.

"From Oprah." A pause. "Winfrey." When I still did not respond, "*The Oprah Winfrey Show.*"

"Yes."

"I'm Oprah's executive producer and head talent coordinator."

"Yes."

"And we—that is to say Oprah and I—would really love to have you on a show we're planning."

"No."

A laugh meant to be engaging. "You are the most monosyllabic man."

I did not answer.

"Or the rudest.

"Thank you for calling, Ms. Brown."

"A full sentence. We're actually getting somewhere. You know, I didn't think you people listed their telephone numbers out there . . ."

"Out where?"

"Hollywood."

"I don't live in Hollywood."

"Well, it's all the same thing."

"No, it's not. Hollywood has a different area code."

"See, we're having a conversation."

"Ms. Brown . . ."

"Call me Barbados . . ."

Not as long as I can draw breath, sweetheart. I thought of hanging up, but she would just call back again. I waited.

"My mother actually named me Barbra. After Streisand. Because I'm from Brooklyn too. Then as I got in touch with my ethnicity, I changed it."

She sounded like a guest on her own show. In spite of my resolve, I said, "Because your family came from Barbados?"

"See, my name is such an icebreaker . . ."

I knew I should have kept my mouth shut. This time I did. Too late.

"Actually my roots are in the Antilles."

"Not specifically Barbados, though . . ."

"The world of negritude."

I took a deep, unfortunately audible, breath.

"Do you have difficulty relating to people of color, Mr. Broderick?"

I wondered how often she had pulled that one on recalcitrant guests. "No, I don't, Ms. Brown. But I am not going on your show, you are wasting your time and mine . . ."

"But I saw you once on GMA, and you were wonderful. I remember that hilarious anecdote about your father. Bill." The bitch must have ordered up the tape. "You've worked for Sydney Allen, haven't you?"

I did not reply. I had a bad vibration about where this was going, and Sydney Allen's name only confirmed it.

"I'm sure you know Sydney wants Oprah to star in his new film." In other words, Sydney must have told Oprah she was perfect for the part as a way of getting on the show to start some preproduction heat on *Empire*. Or perhaps Oprah was hustling Sydney for a part. "*Triplets*. Did you do the screenplay?"

I had never even heard of *Triplets*. But then Sydney's plate was always full.

"It's such a delicious idea. About an African-American woman—Oprah, of course—whose sister and her European-American husband—Sydney said he was looking for a young Bob Redford—are killed in a plane crash, and he'd been raising his three children from his first marriage—they're Anglo-Saxon, of course . . ."

". . . and triplets." Shame was foreign to Sydney Allen.

"That's right. You're not the grouch you pretend to be, Mr. Broderick."

I think she expected me to say Call me Jack. "It's been nice talking to you, Ms. . . ."

"I haven't even told you what your show is about, Jack."

"It doesn't matter, Ms. Brown, I'm not going to be on it. So thank you for—"

"Jack, I am told—or rather Oprah was told—that you had rediscovered Blue Tyler . . ."

That fucking Sydney Allen.

". . . and she was a bag lady or something in Minnesota, is that right?"

"No." Minnesota was not Michigan. And bag ladies did not have small annuities from Arthur French.

"Then you didn't find her?"

"Ms. Brown, I have nothing to say on this subject."

"Then you did find her?"

"Good-bye, Ms. Brown."

"And isn't it true she has a child, a little girl, who must be almost thirty or something now?"

"I have no idea."

"No idea if she has a daughter, or no idea if . . ."

"Please, Ms. Brown."

". . . if Jacob King was its father."

"Good-bye, Ms. Brown."

"Oprah's going to do this show, Jack, whether you're on it or not, but you're the only one who can protect her memory, her dignity. That's why you'd be such an addition to the show. A necessity. It'll all be done in such good taste, not like Geraldo, all he'd want to know is who she balled. We'll have clips from *Red River Rosie* and *Carioca Carnival* and *Little Sister Susan,* we've gone through boxes of Kleenex looking at those films, they're not even on tape, did you know that? Oprah had to get prints from Cosmopolitan Pictures, and then we had to rent a screening room. Sydney and his producer, a Mr. Martin . . ."

Marty Magnin. I should have known.

". . . were so helpful. If we can get the mother and the daughter together, and you, well, if you are thinking of doing a book on this, Jack, I don't need to tell you, because you are a very bright man, what the ratings of *The Oprah Winfrey Show* are, and what that means in terms of copies sold, you can become a very rich man—"

"I have to hang up now, Ms. Brown." This time I did.

Marty Magnin was in meetings all day. Sydney Allen was on his way back to New York on the Cosmo jet.

I drove out to Trancas to be alone. I walked on the beach and watched the sun set, and when I got home, my answering service said that Barbados Brown had called three times, Oprah Winfrey twice, and a Mrs. White in Anaheim, who had not left a number.

—◦—

The telephone rang at nine the next morning.

"Yes."

"Jack?"

"Yes."

A note of uncertainty. "Jack Broderick?"

"Yes."

"This is Lily White."

The Mrs. White from Anaheim. I did not know any Mrs. White in Anaheim. I did not know anyone in Anaheim. I thought of hanging up, but there was something about the voice.

"You don't remember me, do you?"

It was coming back to me now. *Lubricated or unlubricated.* The Socially Responsible Single. A one-night stand in a terrace condominium in a less Grosse Pointe with a divorced mother of two. *Things to dislike about sex. The bad breath in the morning. The curly strand of pubic hair on the tongue. The acrid smell of postcoital micturition.* The tenured professor of fucking's downside. *Would you please go? Just call a cab and go. Go. Please go.* And go I had. To meet Melba Mae Toolate in a cab heading in the wrong direction. "Of course I remember you." Better than you could possibly ever know. From your bed to Blue Tyler's latest disappearance and Meta Dierdorf's murder. To Arthur French and Chuckie O'Hara and U.S. Senator Denis Maxwell ("Max") Riordan, R-Fla. "What are you doing in Anaheim?" My bright voice. "Visiting Disneyland?"

"Yes."

"Are the children with you?" The Mensa child. *Were you hurting the man, Mama, when you were biting him.* What was her name? Fern. And the boy. *His peepee sometimes sticks up like the man's.* Terence. "Terence and Fern."

"No."

"So you're visiting Disneyland?" Emphasis on the "you're." I was sounding inane.

"I'm here for a convention of travel agents. At the Disneyland Hotel."

Of course. She was a travel agent. *In the travel business, you tend to meet people with return tickets.* "A perfect place for it." Another inanity. "Disneyland."

"I was wondering if perhaps . . ." Her voice trailed off. ". . . we could have a drink." She hesitated. "Or something." The "or something" carried a hint of sexual invitation, and she immediately tried to haul it back. "I mean . . ."

"I'd like that." Considering all that had happened since I left her apartment that night a few short months before, I probably

474 · JOHN GREGORY DUNNE

at least owed her a drink. On the other hand, perhaps my life would be neater had she not thrown me out with my open-return ticket. Certainly it would be less complicated. And would have affected fewer people. "What's good for you?"

"I don't have a car. All the convention meetings are here at the hotel, so I didn't . . ."

"No problem. I'll come to you." I'll come to you was Hollywood talk. I was sounding like an agent. At least I didn't say Let's do lunch.

"It's in Anaheim, it must be far, I mean, I've never been here before, everything seems so far, there's no need to put yourself out, I can get a cab . . ."

I wondered why she was so nervous. "Don't be silly. It's not that far." Only a hundred miles round-trip. "Say noon. Twelve-thirty. At the hotel. I'll call up from the desk. We can have lunch with Mickey and Minny."

"With who . . ."

"Mickey and Minny. Mouse. Disneyland."

"I'm sorry. I should've got that. That'd be nice, Jack."

◄o►

The traffic was lighter than I anticipated and I was early arriving at the hotel. There was no answer in her room. I looked in the coffee shop and the dining room. She was not in either place. The lobby was full of travel agents and their families wearing Mickey Mouse headgear and carrying Disneyland paraphernalia. I checked out the newsstand. She was not there either. I called her room again. No answer. I went to the reception desk.

"Welcome to the Disneyland Hotel, sir, how may we help you?"

"Do you have a Mrs. White registered?"

The room clerk pressed some keys on his computer. "A Mrs. B-for-Barbara White, Miss G-for-Georgia White, Ms. L-for-Lily White, or Mrs. P for—?"

"L-for-Lily," I said.

"She checked out, sir."

"Checked out? When? I just talked to her a couple of hours ago, I was supposed to meet her here . . ."

"About fifteen minutes ago. Let's see." The room clerk bent over his computer again. "Her room was prepaid, four days, she's leaving a day early, I had to tell her she couldn't get a refund on the last day, prepaid is nonrefundable."

"Do you know where she was going?"

"LAX. She was taking the airport bus."

"When did it leave?"

The clerk checked his watch. "It actually won't leave for another five minutes, at twelve forty-five."

"Where?"

"In front of the hotel, sir. Ask the doorman. You can't miss it."

―◦―

She was sitting on the bench at the LAX bus stop, wedged between two elderly women travelers, a Valpack and two small suitcases at her feet. A pair of enormous white-rimmed sunglasses nearly covered her face, which was propped in her left hand, two fingers drumming against her lips, and she seemed oblivious to the conversation the two women were loudly carrying on over her, the rides they had taken, the food they had eaten, the presents they had bought for their grandchildren. For a moment I thought of not intruding on her. If she had suddenly decided after we talked to return to Detroit without seeing me, then who was I not to respect her change of heart, and the reason behind it. Ours was an interlude with consequences unforeseen by me, and at the moment I did not need further consequences. Then she removed her sunglasses, and when she looked around she saw me.

"Hello, Lily."

She stood and smoothed the wrinkles from her lavender linen dress. "Hello."

She appeared to be several months pregnant.

―◦―

"I shouldn't have called you," Lily White said, avoiding my eyes, stirring the spoon around in her iced tea. "But I suppose the only reason I came to this damn convention was to call you. You see, after we . . . well, after that, I figured out who you were. I mean, even in Detroit, the Brodericks aren't exactly unknown. It's not a family that's spent a lot of time incognito, is that the right word?"

On the money.

"Then when I got pregnant, I was going to say you were the father, even though I knew you weren't, I was very careful, if you remember, and I'm a lot of things, but I don't think I'd make a very good extortionist. I want you to believe that."

I did. She had after all cut and run.

"I was just desperate. Panicked. But I couldn't go through with it." A rueful smile. "Even if I could've got away with it. Which I doubt."

It was not a confession I had ever expected to hear at a coffee shop in Disneyland. "Do you know the father?"

"I seem to gravitate to men with Hertz rent-a-car agreements." I remembered the self-deprecating tone. "And they to me."

"Couldn't you have got it fixed?"

"Yes. Sure." She took a deep breath. "But I wanted the kid." She seemed to be searching for words. "You see, when I found out, Harry . . ."

I tried to remember Harry. "Your ex-husband?"

A quick nod. ". . . he wasn't exactly understanding. He said I was an"—she paused and swallowed hard—"an unfit mother. And he was going to try and get custody of—"

"Listen, you don't have to tell me this."

"Who else can I tell it to? Donald fucking Duck? Some shrink? I don't like shrinks. It's like confession, except you've got to pay for it." She took off her sunglasses. Her eyes were red. "You probably don't remember that babysitter I had."

The fat one with the zits I had given a ride home to. *You can feel me up if you want,* she had said. "I think I gave her a ride home."

"She told Harry I was . . ." She couldn't finish the sentence. "You know," she said finally. I could imagine what the babysitter had said. *She fucks everybody, you know.* Her parting shot when I declined the invitation to feel her up. "I don't think he really wants the kids. I know Patty doesn't, she doesn't even like them." Patty. The second wife. "It's only . . . some men are just shits, you know that? And it's like they've got to prove it every now and then."

It was not a proposition I was prepared to argue. It takes something of a shit to cruise a Socially Responsible Singles session, the object to milk his gland.

Some men are shits. All men are snakes. Two sentient women reflecting on my gender.

"I'm sorry, I shouldn't drop this on you." She smiled. "Especially as you were meant to be part of my game plan." She put her sunglasses back on. "Look, I missed the bus, can you give me a ride to the airport? And that's all I want from you, I promise."

◄o►

I waited until Lily's plane to Detroit pulled away from the gate. Her amniocentesis had indicated the child was a boy, her travel business was on the upswing, finally, cross your fingers, and she thought Harry would back off his threats, he was too cheap to go through a custody hearing anyway, I just needed someone to talk to, you're like a priest, you know that, all you do is listen, like in confession, and boy, do the priests love me, I'm better than Court TV.

"You can call me, you know."

"I'll try not to, Jack. But thanks." She gave me a quick kiss, then, as she started down the ramp, turned and said, "I'll be okay."

I thought she would be. I had met her only twice, but Lily was a woman who expected to be bruised, and she also expected to prevail.

Not a bad combination.

◄o►

I got stuck in traffic on my way home from LAX. As I turned up Chadbourne Avenue, I saw the television truck outside my house, and kept on driving past it.

II

I T WAS A CIRCUS.
Oprah broke the story. Blue Tyler had been discovered
after all these years, only to disappear once again. She had a
daughter, and Jacob King was the father. As I had refused to
appear, I then easily became the villain of the Oprah scenario: I
had seen and interviewed Blue Tyler and was trying to copyright her life, in hopes of getting a large book contract and
multimillion-dollar movie deal; that I was scarcely broke and
had no need for such a hustle went unmentioned. It was a slow
news period, and after Oprah aired, finding Blue Tyler became a
national scavenger hunt, with *Rolling Stone, People,* the *National Enquirer,* and the other sleazier supermarket tabloids
holding out the prospect of tens of thousands, perhaps hundreds of thousands, of dollars for whoever found her. WHERE IS
BLUE TYLER? ran a headline in the *Los Angeles Times,* and variants
followed in newspapers across the country. The police department in Ypsilanti, Michigan, released the mug shots taken when
Melba Mae Tyler was arrested there in 1979 for possession of
controlled substances, and Herb Pallance, the manager of
Farmer Dell's in Hamtramck, scoured the surveillance videos at
Location 27 and came up with a sequence showing Melba shopping; with computer enhancement, it was shown on *Hard Copy,*

with Herb providing commentary on Melba Mae Toolate's clever use of rebate coupons, especially on double-coupon day at Farmer Dell's. Herb also mentioned that he remembered me, and that he suspected from the start that I was taking advantage of Melba, because he was the only one who had believed her when she said she was an old-time movie star, a friend of Clark Gable and Humphrey Bogart, and people like that, it was something she did not want to talk about and he respected that, unlike me. *People* ran a cover story, under the slash, WHO WAS BLUE? WHERE IS MELBA?, with the cover photo a shot of Melba Mae Toolate pushing a loaded shopping cart at Farmer Dell's; that same week, both *Time* and *Newsweek* put Blue on the cover, the *Time* cover showing Blue receiving her baby Oscar from Clark Gable, while *Newsweek*'s cover was a photo of Blue and Jacob King at the premiere of *Red River Rosie*. Every day, there were Blue sightings. In Colorado, Connecticut, Oregon, and New Mexico; in Louisiana, Montana, Pennsylvania, and Arizona. Camera crews nested outside Chuckie O'Hara's house in the Hollywood Hills, and telecopters flew over Arthur French's ranch in Nogales, not realizing that he and his knee replacements were still in residence at Willingham; the nightly news shows ran clips from *Little Sister Susan* and *Carioca Carnival* and *Lily of the Valley* and *Red River Rosie*. As Blue's favorite director, Chuckie was interviewed on all the major networks and cable systems, and the grainy newsreel footage of his appearance before the House Un-American Activities Committee was replayed from coast to coast. Arthur kept out of sight, not even contacting me, his silence a reprimand. Once more my picture was in the news, and the photographs no newspaper or magazine or TV channel could resist were the mug shots taken after I was arrested for killing Shaamel Boudreau, front and side views, with the booking number NYPD-45-23-9387. "The Curse of the Brodericks" was another story line, with all the old and salacious stories of sex and money and intrigue in high places. On *Prime Time*, Sam Donaldson and Diane Sawyer agreed that the public's right to know mandated that I share any information I might have about Blue Tyler, and that I answer questions about whether I had a sexual relationship with her, the first time this came up. My alleged attempts to copyright Blue's life became a *Nightline* show about journalistic ethics, with R. W. Apple of *The New York Times* pondering the responsibility of the press, as usual ponderously (how that responsibility applied to me I was not sure, although it was a subject I had seen him cogitate on frequently on TV, usually after the press had overlooked a savings-and-loan or atomic-waste scandal); Ted Koppel said I had declined an opportunity to appear on the show "for whatever reasons of his own, reasons he must think valid" ("Or profitable," R. W. Apple interrupted), and Pauline Kael talked about the dark and perverted sexuality of Blue Tyler's film presence; she was the only one on the show who made any sense. Then *Geraldo*. With three women who claimed to be Blue Tyler's daughter, one even saying she had been in touch with her at a homeless community in Alaska, via a Ouija board. *Inside Edition* was contacted by Maury Ahearne, and, after a deal paying him $7,500 for one-time use was negotiated, he went on the air with the photos of Meta Dierdorf, her bush and her breasts distorted on camera by squiggly lines, and with the letters identifying the mystery woman of Blue's youth. Maury neglected to say how he had come upon these finds, nor was he asked; he also hired my agent to represent him, both for television appearances and for future sales of the Meta Dierdorf photograph, the Blue Tyler letters, and what my agent called "other evidentiary material in his possession," meaning, I suspected, those tapes of Blue's that he had duped. *Unsolved Murders* reran its old segment "Who Killed Meta Dierdorf?" with a coda added about Meta's liaison with J. F. French; the coda also subjected J.F.'s alibi—his attendance at the preview screening of *January, February* in Santa Barbara the night of the murder—to a scrutiny so filled with innuendo that it would have been actionable had he still been alive. Both Raul Flaherty's *Messenger of Death: The Life and Times of Jacob King* and Waldo Kline's *Jake: A Gangster's Story* were scheduled for reissue by their publishers. August Johnson, the manager of the Autumn Breeze trailer park and RV encampment, was interviewed by Bryant Gumbel on the *Today* show, and on *Good Morning America*, eyewitnesses in Detroit described to Charles Gibson how Eduardo ("Teddy") Burke fell to his death from the upper deck at Tiger Stadium on the day he became Blue Tyler's seventh husband. On the *MacNeil/Lehrer NewsHour*, Norman Podhoretz argued that the country's morbid fascination with a woman who was both promiscuous and a sexual deviate and who had given birth out of wedlock to a killer's child showed the deleterious effect of liberalism on the nation's moral core. That Blue might have had a lesbian affair with Meta Dierdorf made her a cover girl on *The Advocate,* and the New York Film Festival announced that it would open its fall festival with a retrospective of Blue Tyler's films, with Blue as the event's special guest of honor.

There was only one problem.

No one could find Blue Tyler.

◄○►

In the end, she called Arthur.

She had been on the road ever since she left Hamtramck, always heading west, however haphazardly, traveling by bus and Amtrak, sometimes hitchhiking, a week here, three weeks there, traveling light, with just the one old suitcase still held together by a piece of rope. Twice a month she would go to the Western Union office in whatever town or city she had stopped, call the number Jimmy Riordan's legitimate people had given her years before, and wait for her semimonthly check to be telegraphed to her. She stayed in motels and RV camps, always paid cash in advance, and discouraged overtures of friendship. When the stories about her began to break and her photograph seemed to appear simultaneously on all the nation's newsstands and television channels, she knew it was only a matter of time before she was discovered, and not in the studio-controlled way she would have chosen if she still had script approval of her own life.

It was when this realization finally struck home that she telephoned Arthur in Nogales, only the second time she had called him in forty-two years, and the first since her arrest in Ypsilanti in 1979. The Mexican maid said Arthur was still in Los Angeles recuperating from knee surgery, she could not give out the number, but if there was a message it would be relayed to him.

You tell him Wanda Nash called, Melba Mae Toolate said, you tell him it's important, and she gave the maid the number of a pay phone in Cortez, Colorado, where she could be reached at six o'clock that afternoon, local time.

◄○►

I'm at the end of my rope, Arthur, Blue Tyler said when she picked up the pay telephone on the first ring. Everyplace I go, people look at me. It's like when I was a star. People say you look just like . . . and I just say my name is Wanda Nash, a lot of people say I look like her. I need a place to hide, Arthur, it's like my life's been taken away from me, maybe I've been alone too long, I didn't think it'd be like this . . .

Here's what I want you to do, Arthur French said.

◄○►

I was surprised when Arthur called me, since I knew that he blamed me for all that had happened since the story broke. My error was finding Blue; in Arthur's scheme this was a willful act, one that negated the possibility of Blue living out her days, more or less contentedly, as Melba Mae Toolate, with Arthur as her faraway provider and guardian angel, a role that was, of course, his *me absolvo*. To find her, in this interpretation, was to take advantage of her. Needless to say, it was self-serving for him to think this, as everyone, not excluding Arthur or myself, had in some way been taking advantage of Blue Tyler from the time she was four years old. But if Arthur was to help Blue, I was the one person he could call, because he was a sick, reclusive old man and I was his only friend, however strained that friendship had become, as well as his only contact with Melba Mae Toolate. He had also requested that I bring Chuckie along with me to Willingham, a considerable concession, because he knew Chuckie detested him, but Chuckie had known Blue Tyler as well as anyone ever had, he had been the keeper of her secrets, and there was no one else still alive who shared that kind of intimacy with her.

Arthur told us about the call.

"Where the hell is Cortez?" Chuckie said.

"Colorado," Arthur said. He was still confined to his wheel-chair and seemed to be in some pain. "On the way to Monument Valley."

"Monument Valley?" Chuckie said incredulously, and when Arthur nodded, Chuckie turned to me and said, "Jack Ford country, Jack must've shot half dozen pictures there."

"That's why she wanted to see it," Arthur said. "Remember *Fort Apache*? Well, she's convinced herself Jack wanted her to play Philadelphia . . ."

". . . the part Shirley Temple played," Chuckie explained to me. I had never seen him so in his element. It was as if he was in preproduction, attending to casting. "Blue could never stand Shirley. She called her Lollipop, and she used to swear Shirley was a midget."

Arthur smiled. "In drag." He tried to readjust his legs on the ottoman, and the effort made him suddenly wince. "Now she says that after she got into her trouble, it was the studio that forced Jack to give the part to Shirley. She thinks if she had played Philadelphia, things would've turned out better for her."

"And that's what brought her to Cortez?" Chuckie said, shaking his head. "Jack Ford never would've let her play that part." It had been years since he had been on a set, but he still understood the chemistry of film. "She's living in a dream world." He hesitated. "Is she . . ." He could not finish the sentence, but we knew that he meant was she crazy.

"She occasionally"—I sought the most mitigating phrase—"wanders from reality."

Arthur nodded. The weeks of recuperation had cost him his range tan, and his skin looked gray and slack.

"I'd like you to go get her, Jack," Arthur said.

"All right," I said, surprised. "But how does she feel about it?"

"Okay. You made an impression. Mainly by not saying any-thing to anybody." Speaking was an effort for Arthur, and he paused to catch his breath every few sentences. "You fly to Denver. I've chartered a plane that'll take you from there to Cortez, it's a tiny little airport, no jet traffic. Pick her up and bring her to Nogales."

"I'll go with you," Chuckie said.

"No," Arthur said. "You and I'll go down to Nogales together, Chuckie. We knew her in the old days. Jack's the only one who knows her as Melba. I think we should keep the two lives separate for a while.

"I booked her into a Days Inn as Wanda Nash," Arthur said to me after a moment. "Prepaid. I told her not to move until you get there. Get her down to the ranch quick. It's only an hour's flight. They're expecting Mr. Broderick and a guest."

I rose and shook Arthur's hand. It was strange seeing him and Chuckie together, each well over seventy-five, embarking on a new adventure, the director and the head of the studio, Arthur being commanding, Chuckie being subversive, as it was in the old days.

"Jack," Arthur said, a smile crinkling the corners of his mouth. "When we get this behind us, we should get back to work on our transplant picture. What were we going to call it?"

"*To an Athlete Dying Young*, Arthur," I said.

◄○►

There was no answer in Wanda Nash's room.

"You know who she looks like?" the woman at the Days Inn desk said. Her plastic nametag identified her as Patia, and there was a rash of tiny, angry pimples on her chin.

"Blue Tyler," I said, cocking a forefinger and pointing it at her. "Everyone says that. Especially since all this stuff started happening. I think she's getting a little sick of it, you want the truth."

"Live your own life, that's what I always say," Patia said, nodding vigorously in agreement.

"Absolutely," I said.

I waited for an hour. The sun was beginning to go down, and the small airfield did not have night lights.

"You know Wanda?" Patia said, picking at her chin sores.

"She was a friend of my dad's." As indeed she might have been in her prior incarnation.

"Is that right?"

"Listen, I just want to make sure she's okay. Is there any way you can let me take a look at her room. She's not as young as she used to be, and I want to make sure she's okay."

"We're not supposed to."

"You can come with me."

"Maybe she went shopping."

"Any place to shop here?"

"Not really." Patia tapped her pencil on the counter. "She into Indians? There's a lot of reservations around here, Utes, Navajos. Maybe she went on a tour."

"No, I don't think so. She knew I was coming . . ."

"Well . . ."

"I'd really appreciate it . . ."

"You the police?"

"If I was a cop, I'd've been in there by now, wouldn't I?"

"You're the media, aren't you?"

"No."

Patia slapped the counter. "I knew she was that Blue Tyler, I just knew it." She took a key from a box and I cursed myself for being so easy to read. "That could be a lot of money coming my way, and I saw her first, I'm not going to split it with you."

We raced down the corridor. I knocked on Number 47. No answer. Patia elbowed me aside and unlocked the door. The room was empty. The bed had not been slept in. There was nothing in the drawers, nothing in the closet, nothing in the medicine cabinet. The paper covering on one of the bathroom glasses had been removed, a toilet seat cover was crumbled in a wastebasket, and the triangular fold in the toilet paper had been removed, but those were the only indications that anyone had ever been in the room.

We went back to the desk. A couple in shorts and backpacks were impatiently banging the bell at the desk. For a moment,

Patia hesitated, unsure whether to register the new guests or to follow me. "We're full up," she said.

"The sign outside said Rooms Available," the woman back-packer said.

"Been so busy, haven't had time to change it," Patia said, following me out the door.

"You got a car?" she said outside.

I had rented one at the airport. The sun was down, there was no way I was going to get out on the plane that night, and I had to shed this virago. "Will you give me a lift?"

I got the answer I expected. "Not in your lifetime, buddy."

I watched Patia as she roared out of the parking lot. I had no idea where she was going. Nor, I expect, did she. Greed with no destination. I went back to the pay phone in the lobby and dialed the general aviation hangar at the airport. My pilot was a short, bowlegged man named Neal whose only answer to anything I asked was "Okay by me." The copilot was his son, Neal, Jr., who was so taciturn he hadn't said a word since I picked up the plane in Denver. "We're not going to get out tonight, Neal, so I'll get us a couple of rooms here in town, we'll have some dinner, a couple of drinks, and I'll figure what I'm going to do next."

"Okay by me, Mr. Broderick, it's your tab."

"I'll come out, pick you up. There's a Ramada we can stay at, and a steak place I noticed on the way in."

"Okay by me," Neal said. "You're going to run into a real traffic jam, though."

"Why?"

"That accident."

"What accident?"

"You didn't hear the sirens?" He pronounced it "sireens."

"What accident?" I repeated.

"Some old lady, out on 160, on the way to Kayenta, over in Arizona. There's a stoplight there at the airport turnoff . . ."

I had seen it coming into town. I could feel a chill in the pit of my stomach.

". . . after that it's bye-bye, baby, nothing but open road all the way to Kayenta."

"What happened?"

"This old lady, waiting there at the light, well, she just ups and puts herself and her suitcase under the rear right wheels of this eighteen-wheeler refrigerator rig stopped at the light, the light goes green, and the driver takes off, he feels this bump, and pulls over to the side, to see what's wrong, and there's this old lady, my boy, Neal, Jr., saw her, she's flatter'n a goddamn pancake . . ."

I felt as if the breath had been sucked out of my lungs. *A good visual*, Melba Mae Toolate had said to me in Hamtramck when I had read her the story about the elderly woman in Chicago who had placed herself under the wheels of a transcontinental moving van on Michigan Avenue. I began to hyperventilate.

"You okay, Mr. Broderick?"

"Fine, Neal, fine." I did not know what else to say. "I have some things I have to do, so why don't you and your boy grab a ride into the Ramada, we'll meet up later, okay?"

"Okay by me, Mr. Broderick, it's your tab."

◄◦►

I identified the body. She was a mess. *A good visual*. Sweet Jesus. Every blood vessel in her head seemed to have ruptured, and it was as if she was wearing a purple fright mask. I tried to comprehend why she had run from the Days Inn when the safe haven Arthur had offered was so close at hand. I could only think it was because she had been running for forty years, and running had become a habit too ingrained to break. Chuckie had once said that Blue Tyler movies always had happy endings, but Blue Tyler could never escape Melba Mae Toolate, and Melba's life was never destined to end with a walk into the sunset, slow fade to black. I console myself that she had finally become totally unbalanced, but I also know that I wanted to abjure responsibility for reading her the item about the woman on Michigan Boulevard. As she considered her options out there at the airport turnoff, I can only suppose that seeing the refrigerator truck stopped at the traffic light caused some flickering brain cell in her memory bank to flash suddenly, and thought was translated into demented action. If it were not that, I wanted to believe, it would have been something else.

We always want so much to believe the unbelievable.

◄◦►

After I left the medical examiner's office, I called Arthur in Los Angeles. He listened without a word, then asked if I could call him back in five minutes. It was Arthur's way; he would not ever let me hear him cry. When I called back, he was perfectly composed. He would charter a jet in Denver, and he wanted me to fly to Los Angeles with Blue's body. *We were the only family she ever knew,* he had told me a short time before, and now the sole surviving member of that family was bringing her home.

The press arrived the next morning. I was no stranger to celebrity death. I could say "No comment" in every possible way, and not take offense at any offensive question. Why had she picked so grotesque a way to die? I was asked; I said I had no idea. As suicide is a criminal offense, Blue's suitcase would have to remain in the property room of the Montezuma County sheriff's office until it was released by the county attorney. I was surprised at how little was in it. A few of the Meta Dierdorf photographs, a framed snapshot of an almost boyish Arthur in black tie, laughing. Clothes. Sensible shoes. An uncashed money order for seven hundred fifty dollars. An annotated copy of Raul Flaherty's *Messenger of Death,* the annotations mainly "B.S." in large block letters. A few pieces of jewelry, one or two of which were perhaps valuable. Three cans of Chicken of the Sea tuna fish. Her tapes. Her tiny special Oscar. And a will leaving all her possessions to Arthur French.

When the paperwork attendant to Blue Tyler's death was completed, a hearse took her casket to the airport, and the two Neals and I flew her to Denver, where we picked up the chartered G-3 to Los Angeles. To avoid the press, the plane landed at Ontario, and the casket was transported to the Heyer & Sobol Funeral Home & Mortuary in Studio City.

There was no service, only a laying to rest of Blue's ashes. It was Arthur's idea to put them in the crypt with Jacob's. Arthur, who always tried, and sometimes failed, to do the right thing. Years before, Jimmy Riordan had seen to it that the name on the crypt was changed from Yakov Kinovsky to Jacob King, and that Jacob's name, his dates, and the inscription were all in brass letters. Arthur, Chuckie, and I were the only mourners. Somewhere in his Cosmopolitan Pictures memorabilia, Arthur had dug out an old Tiffany calling card with the name Blue Tyler printed on it, and under her name he had written "1927–1991." Arthur's instructions were that Blue's name and dates would have the same brass lettering as Jacob's, and as the inscription, "But westward, look, the land is bright."

◄◦►

I read about Arthur's death in the international *Herald Tribune* a year later. I was in Spain scouting locations with that season's new genius director, and saw the headline on the obituary page: MOGUL'S SON, 78. Poor Arthur. Dead of a heart attack at the ranch in Nogales, but at seventy-eight still identified as J.F.'s son. Chuckie flew down for the funeral. It was so butch, he said when I called him from Madrid, everyone was on horseback. He and Arthur had become close that last year as a result of everything that happened. Friends, Chuckie said. Arthur and Aunty Charlton, can you believe it? But when you reach our age, Jack, you take your friends where you find them.

In his will, Arthur left me the unfinished portrait of Jacob King, the one his body came to rest against the night he was killed. The accompanying letter said that Blue had taken the portrait after Jacob died, and that he had bought it from her when she went to Italy to evade her subpoena from the Kefauver Committee. The painting was basically worthless, but it was a way of giving her money.

I'm sorry I had so many secrets, Jack, Arthur wrote in his letter, but thanks for everything. He signed it, An Athlete Dying Old.

The picture was exactly as I had heard, Jacob in jodhpurs,

laced boots, beige shirt, and a polka-dot ascot, a fantasy aristo-
crat in an imaginary land, an America of privilege that in some
odd way could have been imagined only by people like J. F.
French, and desired by people like Jacob King. Reality was the
small dark blotch at the lower right-hand corner of the picture,
where Jacob's blood had leaked against the canvas.

I put the picture in storage. I imagine that someday when my
effects are itemized, someone will find it and wonder who the
subject was.

◄◦►

Chuckie died.

The bugler at his graveside blew the Marine Corps hymn,
slow tempo, then taps.

I cried.

III

I THINK OF BLUE OFTEN. Think of the life she led, and try to understand why she turned out the way she did. Sometimes I comfort myself with the idea that Blue Tyler had a better life, even with all its turmoil, than she would have had if she had remained Melba Mae Toolate, but such speculation is idle, academic, perhaps even dishonest. When she was a newborn infant, her mother, the lady who dropped her the way an animal does, as she said in the tape she had sent Arthur, sold her to a stranger for a bus ticket. Her father she never knew; if there was a stepfather, he never appeared. Her life until the age of four, when she went to the open dance call at Cosmopolitan Pictures, was a blank. She remembered always being on the move with Irma. She remembered Needles, and San Bernardino rang a bell, but she remembered little else. Where she learned to dance she could not recall. How Irma learned about the open dance call at Cosmo she did not know. Why Irma thought she had talent remained a mystery, but she did, and her life was forever changed. Melba Mae Toolate became Blue Tyler, named after the allegedly favorite color of Chloe Quarles, J. F. French's lesbian wife, and after John Tyler, allegedly J.F.'s favorite president, whose birthday he claimed to share, but did not.

We were the only family she ever knew, a mixed blessing, at best. Irma was pensioned off, Chloe was discouraged from being alone with her, her education was entrusted to studio spies and to governesses named Madame. She not only could not name the forty-eight states, she very probably did not even know that there were forty-eight states. By the time she was seven, she was making six thousand dollars a week. When she was fourteen, she should have died in a plane crash, but she did not because she was on her knees fellating her benefactor in a Las Vegas hotel suite. The lesson she absorbed from that encounter was never ever to let anyone take advantage of her again, and if her formal education and her vocabulary seemed inadequate to the demands of the world beyond the one she knew, her cunning was infinite. Her only yearning was to meet someone, anyone, who wanted nothing from her. Jacob King wanted nothing from her, and she fell in love with him; that he had been a murderer, without remorse, many times over was for Blue Tyler only incidental information. Meta Dierdorf also wanted nothing from her, except the secrets they shared, and Blue fell in love with her as well; that Meta was murdered by a person or persons unknown only increased Blue's suspicion of the world at large. Beyond Meta and Jacob, there was never anyone who did not want something from her.

Not even I.

She was a star.

She never really learned to be likable, except on camera.

Considering her life, how could it have been otherwise?

-◦-

Why did you have to find her, Jack?

I have pondered Arthur's question many times while lying awake in the middle of the night, and the best answer is, Why does the sun come up, Arthur? Wherever he is, I am not sure he would understand, or let me off that easily.

It happened.

Finding Blue gave purpose back to a life that had gone off the rails after Lizzie was killed. Finding her brought me back to the land of the living.

Consider the ifs.

If the Fiat Spider had not spun out of control and killed Lizzie. If I had not hit Shaamel Boudreau with $331 worth of Bergdorf-Goodman sheets. If Maury Ahearne had not told me to fuck off. If I had not gone to the Socially Responsible Singles meeting. If Fern had not cried in the night. If Lily White had not told me to go, please go. If. If. If.

A compendium of ifs. Eliminate any one, and Melba Mae Toolate might still be alive, planning the triumphant comeback of Blue Tyler.

Still.

There was a cost.

Blue was never the most reliable witness to her own life, less a real person than the product of her own considerable imagination, constantly reinventing herself as the occasion and her own psychic need dictated. It was her intention, once contact was made (however fortuitously) and identity established, that I be the agent, or perhaps the director, of her latest reinvention, the of course uncredited collaborator in the continuing fabrication of the Blue Tyler myth, in all its many, and to her fascinating, chapters. Via me, she hoped to define a clearer image of the Blue Tyler she never tired of trying to perfect. That I might perhaps not be willing to go along with this collaboration never crossed her mind. In the end she was just another diversion for a public with an insatiable appetite for diversion, and I was the agent of that diversion, a co-conspirator in her death.

Non me absolvo.

◄◊►

Lily named her baby Charles. She is married again and living in Cleveland. He didn't have a return ticket, she scrawled on the wedding announcement.

◄◊►

I also made up with Marty Magnin. Why not? He made me laugh. One night last summer we were having dinner at Morton's when he suddenly began blowing kisses to a party at an adjoining table. It's the people at Cosmo, he said, they've bought the rights to that chick's story, you know, the big wheel in victims' rights.

I turned around, and recognized her immediately. Dark like Jacob King in his portrait, oddly beautiful in the way Blue Tyler was, with the same shock of white hair over her left brow that Melba, in her later years, had. She caught my eye and held it, unwaveringly, to the point where I wondered if she recognized me in turn, and knew that we shared the same secret. I was sure she did.

"Teresa Kean," I said to Marty.

"You know her?"

"Only from seeing her on TV."

"That whole victims' rights area. You should've thought of it, Jack. It's a great story. She's a great story."

"Yes."

"You want to meet her?"

"I don't think so, Marty. Thanks, anyway." I knew how much he wanted to go over and sit down with them. "I'm going to make this an early night."

With almost palpable relief, Marty joined the Cosmo table and I went out into the cool of the evening. As I handed my claim check to the valet parking attendant, I suddenly had a powerful urge to return and introduce myself to Teresa Kean. I knew your mother, I wanted to say. Tell me about her, I was sure she would say.

—◇—

No.

No more ifs added to the compendium.

It had to stop here.

ACKNOWLEDGMENTS

I lived in Los Angeles for twenty-four years, and both knew and worked with a number of people who were active in the motion picture business during the late 1940s, when much of this book takes place (a time when I was still a high school student in New England). Their children were my contemporaries, and many became friends. It is from the memories and photo albums of parents and children that I was able to absorb and retain so much of the atmosphere of that period. My brother Dominick Dunne was instrumental in my meeting so many of the people to whom I listened, and it is safe to say that without his easing my entrée into the community this book probably would not have been written. Of those who have died, I can only say I think of them still as living. In no special order, I would like to thank Constance Wald, Collier Young, Evarts Ziegler, Philip Dunne, Lillian Hellman, Peter Davis, Johanna Mankiewicz Davis, Irving Paul Lazar, Brooke Hayward, Jean Stein, Billy Wilder, Barbara Warner, George Stevens, Jr., Daniel Selznick, George Cukor, Daniel and Lilith James, Ivan Moffat, Jean Howard, Natalie Wood, R. J. Wagner, Christopher Isherwood, Gavin Lambert, Otto Preminger, Rupert Allan, Diana Lynn, Mickey and Paul Ziffren, Richard Roth, Steve Roth, David Brown, Michael Levee, Kenneth Tynan, Richard Zanuck, and so many, many others; the failure to include them is mine.

Philip Dunne's memoir, *Take Two*, is essential to any understanding of the period; Phil (to whom, unfortunately, I was not related) was both a gentleman and a gentle man, more charitable and forgiving toward those who named names than many of his colleagues. A. Scott Berg's *Goldwyn* and Otto Friedrich's *City of Nets* are necessary books, offering a sense of the time, as does Neil Gabler's *An Empire of Their Own*, the best book about Hollywood I have ever read; my Congressman Wilder's address about the Communist menace is a free translation of an actual speech in the *Congressional Record* by Congressman John Rankin of Mississippi, as quoted by Mr. Gabler. Jean Howard's photo memoir, *Hollywood*, absolutely captures the look and the spirit of the place.

My gratitude also to Robert Scheer for his profile of Edgar Magnin in the *Los Angeles Times*, to Paul Dean, also of the *Times*, for his piece on the anatomy of a bullet wound, to Art Harris of *The Washington Post* for his piece on coupon shopping, and to Linda Yglesias for her profile, in the New York *Sunday News*, of Anita O'Day, who fell off the planet; from each of them I drew fact and texture. Sharon Lieberman and José Otavio Raymundo made life infinitely easier. Finally a special mention to Bernie Brillstein, who planted the seed, and as always what I owe to Joan Didion is incalculable. I thank them all, and absolve them of any flaws in *Playland*; those are mine, and mine alone.

For further information about Granta Books
and a full list of titles, please write to us at

Granta Books

2/3 HANOVER YARD

NOEL ROAD

LONDON

N1 8BE

enclosing a stamped, addressed envelope

———————————

You can visit our website at

http://www.granta.com